Pedagogy, Intellectuals, and Dissent in the Later Middle Ages

This book is about the place of pedagogy and the role of intellectuals in medieval dissent. Focusing on the medieval English heresy known as Lollardy, Rita Copeland places heretical and orthodox attitudes to learning in a long historical perspective that reaches back to antiquity. She shows how educational ideologies of ancient lineage left their imprint on the most sharply politicized categories of late-medieval culture, and how radical teachers transformed inherited ideas about classrooms and pedagogy as they brought their teaching to adult learners. The pedagogical imperatives of Lollard dissent were also embodied in the work of certain public figures, intellectuals whose dissident careers transformed the social category of the medieval intellectual. Looking closely at the prison narratives of two Lollard preachers, Copeland shows how their writings could serve as examples for their fellow dissidents and forge a new rapport between academic and non-academic communities.

RITA COPELAND is Professor in Classical Studies and Comparative Literature at the University of Pennsylvania. She is the author of *Rhetoric, Hermeneutics, and Translation in the Middle Ages* (Cambridge, 1991) and the editor of *Criticism and Dissent in the Middle Ages* (Cambridge, 1996). She is also co-editor (with Wendy Scase and David Lawton) of the annual *New Medieval Literatures*.

CAMBRIDGE STUDIES IN MEDIEVAL LITERATURE

General editor
Alastair Minnis, *University of York*

Editorial board
Patrick Boyde, *University of Cambridge*
John Burrow, *University of Bristol*
Rita Copeland, *University of Pennsylvania*
Alan Deyermond, *University of London*
Peter Dronke, *University of Cambridge*
Simon Gaunt, *King's College, London*
Nigel Palmer, *University of Oxford*
Winthrop Wetherbee, *Cornell University*

This series of critical books seeks to cover the whole area of literature written in the major medieval languages – the main European vernaculars, and medieval Latin and Greek – during the period c. 1100–1500. Its chief aim is to publish and stimulate fresh scholarship and criticism on medieval literature, special emphasis being placed on understanding major works of poetry, prose, and drama in relation to the contemporary culture and learning which fostered them.

A complete list of titles in the series can be found at the end of the volume.

Pedagogy, Intellectuals, and Dissent in the Later Middle Ages

Lollardy and Ideas of Learning

RITA COPELAND

CAMBRIDGE
UNIVERSITY PRESS

PUBLISHED BY THE PRESS SYNDICATE OF THE UNIVERSITY OF CAMBRIDGE
The Pitt Building, Trumpington Street, Cambridge, United Kingdom

CAMBRIDGE UNIVERSITY PRESS
The Edinburgh Building, Cambridge CB2 2RU, UK
40 West 20th Street, New York NY 10011-4211, USA
10 Stamford Road, Oakleigh, VIC 3166, Australia
Ruiz de Alarcón 13, 28014 Madrid, Spain
Dock House, The Waterfront, Cape Town 8001, South Africa

http://www.cambridge.org

First published 2001

Printed in the United Kingdom at the University Press, Cambridge

Typeface Garamond 11/13pt   *System* Poltype ® [VN]

A catalogue record for this book is available from the British Library

Library of Congress Cataloguing in Publication data

Copeland, Rita.
Pedagogy, intellectuals, and dissent in the later Middle Ages: Lollardy and ideas of
learning / Rita Copeland.
p.   cm. – (Cambridge studies in medieval literature; 44)
Includes bibliographical references and index.
ISBN 0 521 65238 3 (hardback)
1. Education, Medieval – Great Britain.   2. Great Britain – Intellectual life – 1066–1485.
3. Lollards – Intellectual life.   4. Reformation – Early movements.   I. Title.   II. Series.
LA631.3.C66 2001
370′.942–dc21   00-045544

ISBN 0 521 65238 3 hardback

For my husband, David, and my mother, Evelyn

Contents

Acknowledgments

A book about intellectuals, teaching, and heresy might well intensify its author's own reflections on being part of modern academic culture. While writing this book I have had many opportunities to appreciate the astonishing generosity of those who are committed to teaching and learning. It is a pleasure to record my debts to many individuals whose conversation, advice, and expertise have helped form this book and prompted me to refine its arguments: Alastair Minnis, Paul Strohm, Jody Enders, Martin Camargo, Miri Rubin, Gareth Stedman-Jones, Jonathan Burt, Robin Kirkpatrick, David Aers, Robert Stein, Helen Cooper (and, with Michael Cooper, also a gracious host in Oxford), Derek Pearsall, Anne Hudson, David Lawton, Wendy Scase, Barbara Hanawalt, Nicholas Watson, Ralph Hanna, Anne Middleton, Fiona Somerset, Louise Fradenburg, Larry Scanlon, Aline Fairweather, Christopher Braider, Colleen Page, Daniel Birkholz, Bruce Holsinger, Barbara Harlow, Paula Rabinowitz, Maria Damon, John Mowitt, Andrew Elfenbein, John Watkins, and Ralph Rosen. For the making of this book I am especially grateful for the intellectual friendships of Ian Wei, Nicolette Zeeman, Kantik Ghosh, and David Wallace. I am very much indebted to the labors and collective wisdom of Marjorie Curry Woods, Steven Kruger, and Mary Carruthers, who read and commented astutely on the whole manuscript at various stages of its drafting. All of these people I have mentioned contributed powerfully to the generation of ideas in this project, some of them in ways that might surprise them. I learned a great deal as well from the insights of two anonymous readers for the Press. Shirley Garner, department chair, has been a vigorous defender of scholarly research, and protector of its most precious resource, time. It is also a great pleasure to acknowledge the assistance and interest this project received from two editors at the Press, Katharina Brett and Linda Bree.

Support for this project was provided by a fellowship from the American Council of Learned Societies in 1995–6, by research awards from the

xi

McKnight Foundation and the Graduate School at the University of Minnesota, and by research funds at the University of Pennsylvania.

Parts of this book were given as lectures at Harvard University, University of Notre Dame, University of Groningen, University of Western Ontario, University of Bristol, Oxford University, University of Wales-Cardiff, University of Exeter, Columbia University, University of Minnesota, University of Pennsylvania, University of Colorado, and Indiana University. I am grateful to the colleagues who invited me for those visits, and to the audiences who stimulated and challenged me on those occasions. I also want to thank students in graduate seminars at the University of Minnesota, University of Bristol, and University of Pennsylvania, who disputed ideas as fiercely as any medieval intellectuals.

Parts of chapters 1 and 2 appeared (in condensed form) in *New Medieval Literatures* 1 (1997). An early version of chapter 4 was published in *Bodies and Disciplines: Intersections of Literature and History in Fifteenth-Century England*, ed. Barbara Hanawalt and David Wallace (Minneapolis: University of Minnesota Press, 1996).

General introduction: pedagogy and intellectuals

> For every image of the past that is not recognized by the present as one of its own concerns threatens to disappear irretrievably.
>
> Walter Benjamin, *Theses on the Philosophy of History*, 5

This epigraph, taken from Walter Benjamin, suggests the double responsibility of historiography to the present and the past. The main historical concerns of this book are the role of pedagogy and the role of intellectuals in a medieval dissenting movement. But the politics of teaching and the social functions of intellectuals are also crucial concerns of modern cultural reflection. Modernity hardly recognizes itself in the Middle Ages; on the other hand, medievalists have often argued the explanatory power of the Middle Ages for the conditions of modernity. What this book offers, however, is a study of issues that were of profound importance for the Middle Ages and that will disappear from our historiographical map if we do not recognize them as being important to ourselves. I do not offer this account of pedagogy and intellectuals in a medieval dissenting movement in order to explain modern conditions of teaching and intellectual labor. Rather, my interest here is to make visible certain forms of medieval cultural knowledge which historiography has suppressed because it has imagined that these could not be medieval forms of knowledge, because moderns (including modern medievalists) have not seen their own concerns in these images of the past.

The largest questions that this book asks are: what were the politics of teaching in antiquity and the Middle Ages, and how are these made visible in a dissenting movement; what were the politics of childhood; what was the role of intellectuals in facilitating not only habits of dissenting thought but oppositional pedagogies; what was the relationship of intellectual work to a community; and how does a dissenting community reinvent the function of intellectual labor? Because this book approaches the subject of learning and dissent from two different – but fundamentally connected – inquiries,

1

pedagogical discourse and intellectual labor, I will begin here by placing each in historical and theoretical perspective.

1 PEDAGOGY

In November 1406, the Lollard preacher William Taylor delivered an inflammatory sermon at St. Paul's Cross in London, in which he promulgated Wycliffite ideas about clerical disendowment. The sermon prompted an immediate response from the orthodox establishment. The following day an orthodox master preached a counter-sermon in the same place, and before long Archbishop Arundel had summoned Taylor to account for his beliefs. Taylor failed to answer the summons, and in the early months of 1407 was excommunicated by the archbishop's order.[1]

At the end of his sermon, Taylor puts forth another Wycliffite idea, that it is the duty of preachers to share the bread of Scripture among the people in their own vernacular language, a directive, he notes, that Lollard preachers can implement only under the pressure of prosecution. Taylor observes that a certain kind of literal reading of Scripture is an appropriate pedagogical tool:

> But now is ther a tribulacioun – was ther neuer noon sich – for he that pretendith himsilf moost parfiit cristen man, bothe because of staat and of ordre, pursueth anothir cristen man that to this eende comyneth in the lawe of God for to lerne it and enfourme, as he is holdun, his sogetis and for to be saued bi it. And certeyn to deuely a dede is it for to chace men fro knowyng of the lawe of God. For, though it be not spedy to boistous puple in manye sotiltees to curiously ocupie her wittis, in tokenynge wherof Crist in the gospel of this day comaundide not the puple but his disciplis to gadere the relifs of the feste, yit for to werne the puple the greete and historial mater of the gospel were noon othir but to kille hem.[2]

There is a sense of shock that Taylor registers here, where he speaks of persecution that is unprecedented in its vehemence ("now is ther a tribulacion – was ther neuer noon sich"), and perhaps incomprehensible because Lollard preachers feel that they are just continuing an old way of going about things.

---

[1] The excommunication was probably an indirect response to the sermon: more likely it was issued for Taylor's failure to answer Arundel's summons. For nearly two more decades, Taylor continued his career as a heretical preacher. After years of fitful investigations leading to an abjuration in 1420, he was tried in February 1423 before Archbishop Chichele as a relapsed heretic, and in March handed over to the secular arm and burnt at Smithfield in London. See Wilkins, ed., *Concilia* 3: 404–13, for the proceedings against Taylor, detailing years 1419–22; and see biography in Hudson, ed., *Two Wycliffite Texts*, xiii–xxv, and Emden, *An Oxford Hall in Medieval Times*, 125–33.

[2] Text in Hudson, ed., *Two Wycliffite Texts*, 22–3. Here and in all following Middle English quotations, the Middle English character "thorn" has been modernized to "th," and the character "yogh" has been modernized to "g," "y," or "gh."

What is new is not what they are actually doing, but rather this state-sponsored persecution. What is that "old way" of going about things? That is what I want to explore in this book by investigating the pedagogical paradigms and traditions that lie behind Taylor's directives and the objections of his adversaries.

On the terms of Taylor's argument, what really kills is not the letter, but the clergy's withholding from the people of the authentic matter of gospel, those truths contained in the letter. For the "literal sense" of Scripture is the implied opposite of the exegetical subtleties that would "too curiously occupy the wits" of popular audiences. It is Scripture unclouded by "manye sotiltees" that offers life; and in the passage just quoted there is perhaps an echo of 2 Corinthians 3.6, inverted so that what kills is not the "letter," but rather refusing the people's desire for the letter of Scripture. The question of just what the literal sense, or reading according to the letter, means in Wycliffite hermeneutics is a complex one; but as Taylor's sermon suggests, Lollard arguments for vernacular preaching and study of Scripture can take a practical, pedagogical, view of literalism without explicitly attaching it to theological or hermeneutical questions about divine language. In this reasoning, the hermeneutical appropriation of the letter is identical with a rhetorical sense of the capacity of an audience. Taylor's view recognizes (or concedes) the limitations of non-literate or at least unlearned laity for whose "wits" the subtleties of exegetical scholarship, especially perhaps allegorical exegesis, are a too curious distraction. A Latin Wycliffite sermon makes a more detailed rhetorical case for aiming at the specific capacities of audiences:

> Preachers must preach to their audience such truths as they can readily convey, informing the laity in a way that is appropriate to their condition and judgment, and clerics in a way that is appropriate to their station and capacity . . . Preachers ought to preach to the local people and expound the word of God openly and clearly, and not obscure the truth from them under scholastic subtleties.[3]

But what is the context for such affirmations of a certain literalism, here meaning a clear and open reading of Scripture unclouded by scholastic subtleties, in relation to a practical assessment of audience capacities? In terms of its place within the wider framework of Lollard textual communities, the concession to the capacities of an audience signifies more than simply a common pastoral stance: as I will suggest here, it must be understood in terms of its application to the dynamics of "classroom" as well as pulpit. Moreover,

---

[3] Quoted from Bodleian MS Laud Misc. 200 in Hudson, *The Premature Reformation*, 273. Unless otherwise noted, all translations are my own. On the Latin sermons in this manuscript, see von Nolcken, "An Unremarked Group of Wycliffite Sermons in Latin."

3

this valuation of literal reading is not the same as the hermeneutical model of the literal sense that Wyclif articulates in the *De veritate sacrae scripturae*, nor that adumbrated by Nicholas of Lyre before him, nor that amplified or contested by such figures as Jean Gerson and Thomas Netter in the early fifteenth century. Yet in Lollard polemic, as well as in anti-Lollard (and in general anti-heretical) polemic, this practical model of the literal sense comes to be tangled up with ancient and contemporary hermeneutics of the literal sense.

In other words, the literal sense is not one thing, and to approach it as if it were is both to occlude the cultural complexity of its history and to reproduce some of the very confusions under which some of the actors in this historical drama labored. Among modern historians the literal sense has been seen primarily as a hermeneutical issue, especially in studies of heresy polemic. But as I will show here, it must also be seen as a pedagogical issue, specifically a problem associated with elementary pedagogy. The identification of the literal sense with childhood has an ancient lineage in discourses of elementary pedagogy. This long-established association between childhood and the literal sense informs the role that the literal sense plays in later heresy polemics; but this role is often confused with, and beclouded by, the simultaneous presence of academic hermeneutical attitudes to the literal sense. It is important, therefore, to tease out the particular force of pedagogical traditions in late-medieval conflicts over heresy and heretical reading communities.

In outline, the problem explored in the first part of this book is what it meant for non-clerical adults to be willingly identified with reading according to the literal sense. To be seen to be reading for the letter, or for the mere surface (including the "story" or fable), was to risk being identified with the cognitive conditions of childhood. What might this mean for a new class of adult, non-academic readers, that is, lay Lollards, who claimed that the literal sense is adequate to a complete understanding of Scripture? Through what ingrained assumptions about childhood and the literal sense did their orthodox adversaries receive Lollard claims about the adequacy of the literal sense? And why could academic readers enjoy the pleasures of a literalist hermeneutic when they pronounced the literalism of lay readers a scandal?

There are three interlinked themes that I will trace here in order to recover what lies behind the convictions, expressed in the sermons by Taylor and the anonymous Lollard quoted above, as well as in other Lollard writings, about lay access to Scripture through its literal sense: pedagogy, childhood, and the bearing that these two categories have on inherited ideas of the literal sense. The picture that I present here of lay textuality in the Lollard movement is not framed primarily in terms of Latin and vernacular, but in terms of a structure of dissenting pedagogy. What was Lollard pedagogy dissenting from? I suggest here that it was responding to a tradition much older than the conflict between the authority of Latin and the *arriviste* claims of vernacular textuality, a conflict that could not be said to have come into existence before the twelfth century.[4] Lollard pedagogy was dissenting from ancient traditions of intellectual hierarchy, and especially representations of elementary teaching, traditions that carried with them deeply engrained assumptions about the borders between childhood and adulthood, as these conditions stand for states of political disenfranchisement and political agency.

To explore Lollard pedagogy and the traditions against which it dissents requires a long view of intellectual and institutional history, a perspective that must begin with antiquity and its production of discourses about learning. Since much of the tradition that I explore here as the historical precondition of Lollard attitudes to teaching is in fact classical, my approach may certainly raise the question: what has Quintilian or Plutarch, Macrobius or Proclus, to do with a heretical religious movement of late-medieval England? The ideologies and practices associated with Wycliffism and Lollardy have been mainly the possession, historiographically speaking, of synchronic regimes of social and literary historicisms. For the most part, and for reasons that are obvious, the textual effects of the Lollard movement have been read as products of, or factors in, historically localized intersections of the fourteenth and fifteenth centuries: theology and ecclesiology; English sacramental and devotional practices; social and political ruptures of Ricardian and Lancastrian England; and literary and intellectual relations in late-medieval English culture. The very topicality and self-conscious political urgency of Lollard writing invites such materialist analysis. In many respects such horizontal cultural historicism has been the dominant model in English medieval literary studies in general, both in more traditional forms of literary history which work within standard terms of periodization, and in the more recent historiographical moves in the direction of Foucauldian archaeologies (however broadly construed) which explicitly resist the explanatory teleologies of "grands récits" in favor of closely synchronic focuses.[5]

The most general critique that can be made of the dominance of the synchronic model, whether in its broadly historicist or more technically materialist focus, is that it exerts a certain pressure to forget or simply to

---

[4] On vernacular bibles in twelfth-century France, for example, see Hamilton, "Wisdom of the East: the Reception by the Cathars of Eastern Dualist Texts," 40–1 (and on Occitan in the thirteenth century, 58); Biller, "The Cathars of Languedoc and Written Materials," 66; Robson, "Vernacular Scriptures in France."

[5] See, for example, the discussion in Scanlon, "Unmanned Men and Eunuchs of God: Peter Damian's *Liber Gomorrhianus* and the Sexual Politics of Papal Reform," 41–3. See also the important critique of periodization and synchronic historicization in Wallace, *Chaucerian Polity*, xiii–xvii, 54–64.

ignore the force of long-established orders of discourse, especially those that have been naturalized in local cultural relations. Synchronic analysis of culture cannot, by itself, account for points of intersection, on the horizontal field, with discourses of ancient intellectual and political lineage that leave their imprint on the most sharply politicized categories of late-medieval culture. In recent years the study of sexuality has most prominently exemplified a turn from a synchronic focus or from conventional norms of periodization towards a vigorous reinstatement of the other "half" of the Foucauldian analytical paradigm, diachronic genealogies, a kind of analysis "which can account for the constitution of the subject within a historical framework . . . that is, a form of history which can account for the constitution of knowledges, discourses, domains of object . . . without having to make reference to a subject which is either transcendent in relation to the field of events or runs its empty sameness throughout the course of history."[6]

A diachronic approach to the Lollard movement does change our perspective on the issues that inform and shape its own polemics and those of its adversaries. Within the immediate temporal terms of fourteenth-century history, the analysis of the fundamental notions of orthodoxy and heterodoxy proceeds along a strictly religious axis that brings the Lollard movement into necessary historical relations with earlier and later controversies over theological and ecclesiological precepts. But Lollardy is also radical, or indeed heterodox, in its educational ideologies. The constitution of a discourse about pedagogy from antiquity onwards represents a kind of institutional orthodoxy that is distinct from theological rules, although it can at times complement and support, at other times intersect with, religious orthodoxies. Pedagogical orthodoxies, whose filiations need to be traced through their own long history, were thoroughly naturalized in the environment of late-medieval culture and politics, so much so that they were virtually homologous with religious orthodoxies. In other words, I am suggesting that there are several axes of orthodoxy and heterodoxy that meet in the Lollard movement. A diachronic perspective requires that we sometimes shift attention from those issues that have occupied center stage in synchronic analyses of late-medieval dissent, notably ecclesiology and sacramentality and their literary effects, for some of Lollardy's most radical moves cannot be assimilated to its contemporary literary or devotional environment. The Lollards and their opponents

---

6 Foucault, "Truth and Power," 117. On the diachronic in the history of sexuality, see Scanlon, "Unmanned Men and Eunuchs of God"; and for a view on the relation between the modern and the premodern in the history of sexuality, see Fradenburg and Freccero, "Caxton, Foucault, and the Pleasures of History," xiii–xxiv. Foucault's own *History of Sexuality* is his finest exemplification of the principle of diachronic history as genealogy; and volume 3, *The Care of the Self*, is the most concentrated illustration of writing the history of a "field of discourse."

are also playing out the logic of educational discourses that were already in circulation in the late-classical period.

Synchronic analysis of the Lollard movement has also placed tremendous emphasis upon the opposition between Latin and vernacular as the principal theme devolving from the governing social categories of *clerici* and *laici*. This certainly takes its cue from polemic within Lollardy and against Lollardy, since vernacular translation of Scripture, and arguments for and against translation culminating in Arundel's statute against translation, were perhaps Lollardy's most defining (and self-defining) historical expressions. But such an emphasis in modern scholarship also reproduces the very terms of Lollard and anti-Lollard polemic. I would offer here that there are other strong currents, of much older lineage than Latin–vernacular, also at work in the opposition between *clerici* and *laici*. The difference between clergy and laity may have expressed itself in the terms that were of the greatest contemporary urgency. But what also informs the binarism clergy–laity is a long tradition within pedagogical and philosophical discourse about the uses of the literal sense for certain audiences, and allegorical or spiritual senses for other audiences. Significantly, neither the English sermon by Taylor nor the anonymous Wycliffite sermon, both quoted at the beginning of this introduction, mention the vernacular as the defining issue in presenting Scripture to lay people. Rather, they focus on presenting what Taylor calls the "historial mater" of Scripture, that is, the matter of Scripture on its own terms, unclouded by subtleties. These two examples can remind us that there are issues beyond the binarism of Latin–vernacular that inform Lollard polemic about access to Scripture. The injunction to teach laity through the literal sense can take us back to the earliest pastoral directives, such as the three-fold structure of Scripture found in Origen's *De principiis* which, says Origen, exists "ut simpliciores quique aedificentur ab ipso, ut ita dixerim, corpore scripturarum (sic enim appelamus communem istum et historialem intellectum)" ("that the simple may be edified by what I might have called the 'body' of Scripture, for so do we call the common and literal narrative meaning").[7] But behind this association of laity with the literal sense lies another domain of discourse, the identification of literal reading with the cognitive limitations of childhood. In antiquity, the identification is cast in pejorative terms; and in Christian ecclesiastical discourse, the association of laity with unlearned simplicity could be conflated with the intellectual limitations of childhood.[8] In order to understand what kind of valuation the Lollard writers place on the association of laity with the literal sense ("historial mater") it is necessary to

---

[7] Origen, *De principiis*, book 4, ch. 2. 4 (p. 312).
[8] Cf. Clanchy, *From Memory to Written Record*, 226–7, on the *laici–clerici* binarism.

trace the lineages of both pastoral and pedagogical discourses. Thus the antithesis between Latin and vernacular was one manifestation of the primary social distinction between clergy and laity. These political categories also bear the impress of long traditions of pedagogical discourse. In an important sense, therefore, this book uses Lollardy and its textual and social effects to explain certain powerful currents in the history of European thought about teaching and learning.

I turn now to the historical and theoretical problems of pedagogy and childhood, which lie behind the questions about the literal sense to be studied in part 1 of this book.

Pedagogy, in Emile Durkheim's terms, is a "practical theory" of education.[9] In considering pedagogy here, we are tracing out both a set of historical practices and the ideological systems in which those practices take place, or to put it with a slightly different emphasis, the "domains of discourse" to which the processes of education belong and through which these processes are represented. As much as there are sciences of teaching, there are also "imaginaries" of teaching, the ways in which teaching, like other political relations, is figured in cultural imaginations and reproduced as an explanatory mechanism for other political relations. Chapter 1 of this book traces a particular field of application, the pedagogical principle of using the literal sense to teach younger students, so that we see how the literal sense not only was a hermeneutical question, but also was fixed as a category of pedagogical thought. Chapter 2 then considers how the conflict between domains of discourse about the literal sense – as a hermeneutical category and as an elementary pedagogical category – informed and structured polemic against heresy in late-medieval England, and how Lollardy negotiated between these fields.

My assumption here is that Lollardy had a pedagogy: a systematic approach to learning and an understanding of the conditions of learning. Behind Lollardy stretches a domain of discourse about pedagogy that goes back to antiquity. That discourse was deployed in debates about heresy; and the Lollards, in turn, practiced a pedagogy that dissented from, that opposed, prevailing pedagogical discourses which were naturalized in and distributed throughout its contemporary cultural environment. But the assumption that Lollardy had a pedagogy, in the sense both of practice and theory, brings with it certain problems of evidence and of definition.

The problem of evidence largely concerns what we know of pedagogical practices among the Lollards. We have considerable evidence about the

---

[9] Durkheim, *The Evolution of Educational Thought*, xix. See also Lukes, *Emile Durkheim: His Life and Work*, 111.

existence of teaching in Lollard communities. Anne Hudson's account of Lollard education uses the evidence of Lollard books and attitudes to books, as well as the evidence of adversarial polemics and records, legal injunctions, depositions at heresy trials, and abjurations of those condemned of heresy, to build a powerful case for an extensive and systematic, not simply occasional, practice of teaching.[10] The basic devices of Lollard teaching were in some ways consonant with orthodox methods, but also, it seems, highly evolved in terms of their particular and defining roles within Lollard culture. Vernacular reading was the central component of Lollard learning, with and also without teachers.[11] The borderline between teachers and missionary preachers was often blurred, as in the cases of prominent Lollard pastoral figures like William Swinderby of Leicester, active in the 1380s and early 1390s, and William White and Hugh Pye who, along with a number of missionaries and teachers, were the leaders of the Norwich Lollard community of the 1420s.[12] But there are also examples, among the later Lollards, of "reading communities" without a prominent teacher from outside the group, in which local people carry on or possibly imitate the reading sessions: these range from small collaborations, as in the case of two London Lollards who, in 1511, were said to spend many hours together reading the Apocalypse, to the extensive networks of readers and reading groups among the Lollards of Coventry prosecuted in 1486 and again in 1511–12.[13]

Memorizing also constituted an important component of Lollard learning, either for its own sake or perhaps to compensate for non-literacy among sect members.[14] While memorization is a learning technique that closely corresponds with orthodox educational traditions, it was particularly suitable to the non-traditional students of Lollard communities, especially as some scholars have noted, to female participants who were less likely to have acquired the skills of literacy.[15] Among these, there is the often-cited case of Alice Colins of the Lincoln diocese in the early sixteenth century, whom John Foxe describes as being able to recite much of the Scriptures, and whose husband was an owner of many books.[16] Reginald Pecock's report on Lollard memorization castigates them for evangelical arrogance: those "whiche nevere

[10] Hudson, *Premature Reformation*, 174–227. [11] Ibid., 187–90.

[12] On Swinderby, see McFarlane, *John Wycliffe and the Beginnings of English Nonconformity*, 91–111, 113–21; on White and Pye and other teachers of the Norwich Lollards, see Aston, "William White's Lollard Followers," and see the comments in Hudson, *Premature Reformation*, 182.

[13] Hudson, *Premature Reformation*, 187 and n. 77, and see also 183 for other examples; McSheffrey, *Gender and Heresy*, 25–46; for other "self-led" communities see also Fines, "Heresy Trials in the Diocese of Coventry and Lichfield, 1511–1512."

[14] I take this category from Hudson, *Premature Reformation*, 190.

[15] McSheffrey, *Gender and Heresy*, 60–1; Cross, "'Great Reasoners in Scripture,'" 370–1.

[16] Foxe, *Acts and Monuments* 4: 222, 234–6. See McSheffrey, *Gender and Heresy*, 60; Hudson, *Premature Reformation*, 191; Cross, "'Great Reasoners in Scripture,'" 371; Aston, "Lollardy and Literacy," 201.

leerned ferther in scolis than her grammer, kunnen suche textis bi herte and bi mouth," and reciting the texts before their audiences, "semen therfore and therbi ful wise."[17] But even Pecock's attack notes the effectiveness of memorization in the absence of formal education beyond the most elementary level.

Discussion also seems to have played an important role in Lollard education.[18] Of all the Lollard teaching devices, discussion is the one perhaps least consonant with methods used in traditional schools, at lower as well as advanced levels. Discussion (in the sense of the relatively unstructured give and take of the modern North American seminar) is not one of the methods of teaching that is pictured in most accounts of the lower schools or even advanced grammar schools of the Middle Ages, which stress instead recitation and question-and-answer techniques. Even in the medieval university, what we would think of as "discussion" between teachers and students seems to have been regulated through the highly formalized structures of question and answer, disputational exercises, or structured public events like the theological *quodlibetales* (in which a master would answer questions "on any topic whatsoever"). Thus established schools seem to offer little precedent for Lollard teaching through discussion. Evidence in depositions points to casual (unstructured) conversations among friends, neighbors, and families outside the sphere of the conventicles. We have, for example, the accounts of conversations in the Norwich community in the 1420s among Lollards or between Lollards and their neighbors, best known through the deposition of Joan Cliffland recounting how her neighbor Margery Baxter evangelized to her on a range of subjects, such as household economy and fastdays, the eucharist, and worshipping images.[19] Among the many suspects proscuted in East Anglia in 1428–31, for which the trial records are quite detailed, the variation of views on subjects like keeping the Sabbath can suggest the results of discussion within (and beyond) conventicles based on the books possessed (and read) by the community and on the tenets proffered by teacher–missionary figures.[20] There is also the example of the Coventry Lollards prosecuted in 1486, about whose beliefs and practices the trial records provide enough information for us to see that the suspects had been holding discussions not simply about texts that they had been reading but about the general theological questions of purgatory and the efficacy of prayers for the dead.[21] Certainly the orthodox authorities believed that part of the threat of

---

[17] Pecock, *The Repressor of over much blaming of the Clergy*, 89.
[18] On this third category of teaching technique, see Hudson, *Premature Reformation*, 192–5; McSheffrey, *Gender and Heresy*, 66–9. [19] Tanner, ed., *Heresy Trials in the Diocese of Norwich, 1428–31*, 43–51.
[20] Aston, "William White's Lollard Followers," 93–7.
[21] Cited in Hudson, *Premature Reformation*, 193–4, from the Lichfield register of Bishop John Hales (1459–1490).

Lollard schools lay in the opening they provided for unregulated discussion, if the seriousness with which Archbishop Arundel's *Constitutiones* (1409) tackled the problem is any indication. The fifth Constitution is directed at schoolmasters; one of its prohibitions is against pupils publicly or privately debating matters of faith or the sacraments of the church.[22] The pedagogically unorthodox device of discussion was clearly seen as the first step towards planting theologically unorthodox ideas. Here, in the repressive measures of the fifth Constitution, is an intersection of the theological and the pedagogical axes of orthodoxy and heterodoxy.

If we know generally how lay Lollards learned, we also know where they learned and what they read. The holding of "conventicles" or schools in private houses where local people met with each other or where a teacher or clerical member of the sect provided instruction, is best documented for the later Lollard period, in the eleven communities prosecuted between the late 1420s and 1530. For the earlier period, the last decades of the fourteenth century and the early fifteenth century, there is less direct documentation of formal conventicles (that is, from the accounts of Lollards actually involved in them), although from 1382 Henry Knighton records that the early Leicester Lollard William Smith, a self-educated layman, held a conventicle or a school ("gingnasium [sic] malignorum dogmatum et opinionum et errorum hereticorum communicacionem" ["a kind of academy of evil beliefs and opinions, in which heretical error was taught"]) at the chapel of John the Baptist outside Leicester, where he was aided by Richard Waytestathe, a chaplain, and then joined by the unbeneficed priest William Swinderby.[23] For this earlier period there are many legislative references to "schools" or "conventicles," or both. "Conventicle" was a term known from the Decretals (in a section from Innocent III, dated 1199) proscribing gatherings of heretics ("occulta conventicula") where talking about Scripture can lead to arrogant usurpation of the office of preaching. Here also the idea of secrecy is stressed, but not necessarily the idea of study.[24] Similar uses of the word are found in English records of the fourteenth century, as in the register of John Trefnant, bishop of Hereford, where it seems to mean any kind of nefarious gathering.[25] But Trefnant's register also describes reading and teaching in "public and private places (*publice vel occulte*) where books in English drawn from the naked text

---

[22] Wilkins, ed., *Concilia* 3: 317. For further discussion see below, chapter 2, pp. 119–22.

[23] Henry Knighton, *Chronicle 1337–1396*, 296–7, 308–9. See also McFarlane, *John Wycliffe and the Beginnings of English Nonconformity*, 90; Aston, "Lollardy and Literacy," 201–2.

[24] Friedberg, ed., *Corpus iuris canonici* 2, cols. 784–5. On secrecy see especially col. 785 ("Deus enim lux vera . . . tantum odit opera tenebrarum" ["for God is true light . . . so much the more does he hate business that takes place in shadows"]). See also Hudson, *Premature Reformation*, 175–6.

[25] *Registrum Johannis Trefnant*, 235 and 411 (on William Swinderby and Walter Brut, respectively).

of Scripture" are heard.[26] The collocation "schools and conventicles" only comes into general use, however, after the statute *De heretico comburendo* of 1401, where the terms appear several times.[27] From the evidence of the fifteenth century, it is clear that some Lollard schools had enough of a formal structure to meet regularly and to have, at times, a fair number of people attending. The Coventry group in 1511 may have had seven people convening; the Norwich Lollards also had a network of private "scoles of heresie."[28]

But just as important as the formal schools were the many informal sites of learning, the conversations about faith or the reading sessions conducted among families and neighbors, which returns us to that least traceable but most powerful educational technique, discussion. This may represent an induction into, or reinforcement of, a habit of thought, rather than "formal training" in exegetical responses, which, perhaps, would be likely to take place under more structured conditions. This takes us also to the heart of an "underground" educational project: learning as an art of resistance that takes place "secrete in aulis, cameris, ortis et gardinis" ("secretly in halls, chambers, gardens, and orchards").[29] All Lollard learning was by nature clandestine; under such conditions the informal site acquires as much power of continuity as the structured "official" conventicle. The Norwich Lollard Margery Baxter invited her neighbor Joan Cliffland and Joan's maidservant to come "secrete in cameram dicte Margerie noctantum et ibidem ipsa audiret maritum suum legere legem Christi eisdem, que lex fuit scripta in uno libro quem dictus maritus solebat legere eidem Margerie noctantum" ("secretly and by night into the chamber of the said Margery, and there she would hear Margery's husband read the law of Christ to them, which law was written in a book which the said husband used to read to Margery at night").[30] In the Norwich prosecutions and others, notably of the Coventry Lollards, clandestine conversations that emerged from household readings are reported: in the inquisitorial records they become traceable events with their own formal powers of pedagogical cause and effect, representing, in legal terms, not simply the powers of sedition ("words as deeds"), but a distinct technique of educating for sedition, a highly effective form of "training up."[31]

---

[26] *Registrum Trefnant*, 145, 147–8. For further examples of the term in fourteenth-century usage, see Hudson, *Premature Reformation*, 176–7 and notes.

[27] Wilkins, ed., *Concilia* 3: 252–4; for example, "tales vel consimiles conventiculas facienti, seu scholas tenenti vel exercenti" (253). On the terminological impact of the 1401 statute, see Hudson, *Premature Reformation*, 175, 179–80.

[28] Thomson, *The Later Lollards*, 114; on the Coventry group see McSheffrey, *Gender and Heresy*, 25–37; Tanner, *Heresy Trials in the Diocese of Norwich*, 28.

[29] Quoted in Hudson, *Premature Reformation*, 177, from the register of Henry Wakefield, Bishop of Worcester (1375–1395).   [30] Tanner, *Heresy Trials in the Diocese of Norwich*, 47–8.

[31] On "words as deeds" see the discussion of sedition in Aers and Staley, *The Powers of the Holy*, 1–2.

Finally, we have elaborate evidence of what Lollards read, of the texts central to their teaching. Since Lollard books have been studied extensively by Anne Hudson, Pamela Gradon, Margaret Aston, and others, and since this also forms much of the subject of chapter 2, it is not necessary to attempt a survey here.[32] More particular questions of reading matter will also figure in the discussion below. The sum of evidence about what texts Lollards read is that it consisted of both heterodox and orthodox materials: the Bible in the English Wycliffite translations, especially the Gospels (sometimes equipped with English gloss apparatus), and English sermons, tracts, and polemics; but also orthodox devotional texts and matter from the pastoral repertoire of basic doctrinal instruction, as well as the Psalter in Rolle's translation and commentary, which underwent some Wycliffite revisions.

In the preceding pages I have summarized some of the most important and well-studied points about Lollard education. These general questions of evidence can now bring us to a more particular concern. There is good evidence that Lollard pedagogical work, its teaching devices, sites of learning, and textual materials, were used for elementary instruction, "elementary" here in the sense of what we can provisionally call "adult literacy acquisition." I will return below to this provisional category to refine the definition of "elementary." But we can look first at some of the evidence. At least one-fifth of the Lollard men in fifteenth- and sixteenth-century trial records were literate, and a very tiny percentage of the women.[33] Many of the records that describe family groups assembling for readings certainly suggest initiation into literacy through such informal but repeated encounters with texts, but it is hard to distinguish one individual's aural encounter from another individual's potentially literate engagement with texts.[34] From the early decades of the movement there is the often-cited example of William Smith, the blacksmith from Leicester, whom Knighton reports as having taught himself to read and write out of zeal for new beliefs.[35] In the early sixteenth century, the servant Roger Dod, a Lollard of Burford, was, according to Foxe, taught the alphabet by his employer, the vicar John Drury (also a Lollard), so that he could understand (and read?) the Apocalypse.[36] It is also possible that the

---

[32] Hudson, *Premature Reformation*, 200–17 and the articles collected in *Lollards and Their Books*; the articles collected in Aston, *Lollards and Reformers*; Hudson and Gradon, eds., *English Wycliffite Sermons*; see also Deanesly, *The Lollard Bible*; and von Nolcken, *The Middle English Translation of the Rosarium Theologiae*.   [33] McSheffrey, *Gender and Heresy*, 165–6.

[34] Examples are numerous. See McSheffrey, *Gender and Heresy*, 103, and Foxe, *Acts and Monuments* 4: 226. For a general comment, see Hudson, *Premature Reformation*, 186.

[35] Knighton, *Chronicle*, 292; see Aston, "Lollardy and Literacy," 201–2; Orme, "Schools and Society from the Twelfth Century to the Reformation," 7.

[36] *Acts and Monuments* 4: 237.

literate women from the well-organized Coventry communities acquired their literacy through contacts with the movement.[37]

Before turning to the kinds of internal evidence among Lollard books that might suggest their use or suitability for literacy instruction, it can be helpful to look to some continental analogues for the acquisition of elementary literacy among lay members of other heretical sects. We have several very good descriptions of literacy acquisition by new members of the Waldensian sect. In a report by the Anonymous of Passau, a Dominican inquisitor of the mid thirteenth century, one of the causes given for the spread of heresy is elementary education. The lay followers of the Waldensians:

> Men and women, big and small, learn and teach incessantly, day and night. An artisan who works during the day learns and teaches at night. Such is their eagerness to learn that they scarcely have time to pray. They also teach and learn without books. They also teach in the leper houses . . . Even a disciple who has been with them for only seven days searches for someone he can teach, like one fold of the curtain pulling the next. If one of them makes excuses, saying he cannot learn, they say to him "Learn just one word each day and after a year you will know three hundred; in this way you will make progress."[38]

This is a remarkable description of a medieval "night school," literacy training for adults that promises progress even by one word at a time. Another account of literacy acquisition comes from one of the preachers (*barbes*) of the later Waldensian movement, who describes the recruitment and initiatory education of new preachers:

> Our people come almost always from herding animals or agriculture, aged twenty or, in most cases, thirty, and utterly unlettered. During just two or three winter months they are put to the test amongst us over three or at most four years, to see if they show suitable character. During these months they are also taught to read and write, and to commit to memory all of Matthew and John, chapters from all the epistles which are called canonical, and a good part of Paul.[39]

---

[37] McSheffrey, *Gender and Heresy*, 59.

[38] "viri et femine, parvi et magni, nocte et die non cessant discere et docere; operarius in die laborans, nocte discit vel docet. Ideo parum orant propter studium. Docent eciam et discunt sine libris. Docent eciam in domibus leprosorum . . . Item discipulus septem dierum alium querit quem doceat, *ut cortina cortinam trahat.* Qui excusat se, quod non possit discere, dicunt ei: 'Disce cotidie unum verbum, et post annum scies trecenta, et sic proficies!'" Anonymous of Passau, *De causis heresum,* 70. Translation by Patschovsky, "The Literacy of Waldensianism from Valdes to c. 1400," 131.

[39] "omnes nostri recipiendi emanant fere a bestiarum custodia aut ab agricultura aetatisque viginti quinque et plerunque triginta annorum et prorsus literarum expertes. Et inter nos trium aut ad summum quatuor tantum duobus aut tribus mensibus hybernis probantur, si congruis praesent moribus. Et etiam his mensibus docentur literas coniungere et legere et memoriae mandare omnia Matthaei et Joannis omniumque epistolarum, quae dicuntur canonicae, capitula et bonam partem Pauli." Text in Vinay, *Le confessioni di fede dei Valdesi Riformati,* 36. Translation by Paravy, "Waldensianism in the

Strictly speaking, Waldensian learning is not comparable with Lollard learning, because the two movements differ widely in terms of their social and demographic conditions and their internal structures.[40] Significantly, in the practices described here, the Waldensians are educating a cadre of preachers with a kind of formality that does not resemble anything known about Lollard society. But what is valuable about these descriptions is that they provide a somewhat detailed picture of what adult education, especially literacy acquisition, might have looked like in a dissenting community. And this is really what we do not know with much clarity about Lollard learning. While we have a good picture of the general devices of learning (reading, memorizing, discussion), the sites (formal and informal) where learning took place, and the kinds of texts likely to be used, we do not have a good picture of what basic literacy education or other kinds of elementary instruction among the Lollards would have looked like on the ground.

How would it actually have proceeded? Would it, like the teaching of the Waldensians, have proceeded one word per day over the course of a year? In the case, apparently, of Roger Dod of Burford, it began with the teaching of the alphabet. If we take the example of Roger Dod, can we assume that induction into literacy in Lollard "schools" looked like literacy training in ordinary schools, in a fashion that had barely changed from Roman antiquity, beginning with learning the letters of the alphabet, and then syllables, words, and pronunciation?[41] Obviously since Lollard literacy was mainly a vernacular one, the teaching would not require initiation into a strange language through hearing and repeated reciting of what was heard. But given that there is a certain formality to Lollard learning, it is reasonable to ask what kind of evidence there is for their most basic pedagogical practice. What we do not possess is evidence for the actual procedures of their "classroom" practice, the kind of evidence that we have in multiple forms for orthodox education: horn books containing the ABC ("abeces"), and school primers also containing the ABC and catechetical texts, as well as the many kinds of texts that indicate quite clearly how grammar itself was taught, including word lists, mnemonic verses, model sentences, student notebooks, and compilations with school-masters' glosses.[42]

Dauphiné (1400–1530)," 160. See also Audisio, "Were the Waldensians More Literate than Their Contemporaries (1460–1560)?" 180.

[40] See Patchovsky, "The Literacy of Waldensianism," 130; more generally on Waldensian society, see Gonnet and Molnar, *Les Vaudois au moyen âge*, 75–83.

[41] For good details on this method, see Riché, *Ecoles et enseignement dans le haut moyen âge*, 222–4; and see also Orme, *Education in the West of England 1066–1548*, 2–3.

[42] See especially Alexandre-Bidon, "La Lettre volée: apprendre à lire à l'enfant au moyen âge"; Orme, "Early School Note-Books," "A Grammatical Miscellany from Bristol and Wiltshire," and "A School Note-Book from Barlinch Priory."

What we can assume is that literacy began in the ways that it did for many lay people, in their homes. Lollard texts do not indicate, with any consistent clarity or detail, how they would have been used for literacy teaching. Of course, many Lollards did not become literate. And on the other hand, many of those who could read would have acquired basic skills before coming into contact with Lollardy, in the ways that many children of the merchant, artisan, and even laboring classes came into literacy: as "petty" scholars in local schools or under the more informal guidance of occasional teachers, where, by the fifteenth century, they may have encountered more English letters than Latin.[43] Others would have acquired their literacy as a kind of "occupational skill," where reading is picked up casually in family or work environments, from relatives, neighbors, and employers.[44]

One possible indication of an environment of literacy instruction in Lollard circles is the presence of orthodox materials associated with elementary learning, especially primers. Primers were liturgical or catechetical books. The catechetical versions, most closely associated with classroom instruction, might contain the ABC along with the Lord's Prayer, the Hail Mary, the Creed, the Ten Commandments, the seven deadly sins, and so forth. The liturgical primers, or Books of Hours, contained the gradual and penitential psalms and other liturgical and devotional materials.[45] While most primers were in Latin, English versions of both types circulated in the fourteenth and early fifteenth centuries. There are a number of examples of Lollards owning primers, including Alice Rowley of Coventry, some of the Lollards of Winchester, and possibly John Baker/Ussher of Tunstable near Norwich.[46] However these primers were used in Lollard circles, the ecclesiastical authorities viewed them with suspicion, and indeed English primers disappear after the middle of the fifteenth century, because ownership of them was linked with heresy.[47]

It is clear, however, that some texts were used to introduce readers, not to

---

[43] Moran, *The Growth of English Schooling 1340–1548*, 41–2; Orme, *English Schools in the Middle Ages*, 66–8.

[44] Literacy as an "occupational skill" is documented for the early sixteenth century in Laquer, "The Cultural Origins of Popular Literacy in England, 1500–1800," especially 257; and see Cressy, *Literacy and the Social Order*, 36–41.

[45] See the English and French primers for elementary education reproduced by Plimpton, *The Education of Chaucer*, 19–33, 41–79; for the Book of Hours in English, see Littlehales, ed., *The Prymer or Lay Folk's Prayer Book*, and Littlehales, ed., *The Prymer, or Prayer-Book of the Lay People in the Middle Ages*. See the extensive discussion on Books of Hours by Duffy, *The Stripping of the Altars*, 209–98; and Moran, *The Growth of English Schooling*, 42–6.

[46] For Coventry see Thomson, *The Later Lollards*, 113, and McSheffrey, *Gender and Heresy*, 70; for Salisbury and Winchester, see Foxe, *Acts and Monuments* 4: 230, 236; for Norwich, see Tanner, *Heresy Trials in the Diocese of Norwich*, 69.

[47] Duffy, *Stripping of the Altars*, 213; Moran, *The Growth of English Schooling*, 44–5.

letters, but to relatively advanced exegetical practices, the *mise en page* of scriptural commentary, the difference between text and gloss, authentic text and exegetical authorities. This kind of initiatory lesson, introducing the *ordinatio* of text and commentative apparatus, is most notable in the *Glossed Gospels*, discussed in chapter 2. What this suggests is that "elementary" instruction may have many meanings, or that we must understand "elementary" in reference to more than one level of instruction.

The question of the level of learning leads us into problems of definition. "Elementary" is a modern term, a tool of the historiography of education. Historians of medieval education sometimes use it to designate instruction before grammatical training, that is, the stage before the formation of literacy in its proper sense of understanding and construing the written Latin language; but it can also be used to designate the early stages of the grammar curriculum itself. Medieval evidence does not always indicate that there was a clearly recognized distinction between the "elementary" level of pregrammatical pupils ("petty" scholars learning song and the alphabet) and the beginning levels of reading.[48] I will use the word "elementary" here as a term that describes the association, in medieval discourses, of certain levels of learning with childhood. In this sense my use of the term designates another kind of social imaginary, the way in which the notion of "elementary" functioned in the medieval pedagogical and political imagination as a sign of childhood, regardless of the biological age of the learners.

With the evidence that we have for the existence of a Lollard pedagogy, how do we define the character of that practice? On the one hand, Lollard pedagogy could be described as the most elementary kind of literacy teaching, in the sense of its cultural identification with childhood beginnings. But on the other hand, it could equally be described as an advanced program of exegetics: here it could be seen as literacy acquisition for the purpose of attaining exegetical competence, an education in letters that bypasses the trivium education of the higher grammar schools and the university arts course to proceed directly to the disciplinary territory claimed by theological science, the study of Scripture and theological authority. Given that we do not know with certainty what Lollard education – whether described as elementary or advanced – looked like on the ground, in its ordinary, material routine, where do we look for parallels? Can we indeed translate what we know about education in orthodox grammar schools to Lollard adult schools? I have explored some aspects of this question in the preceding discussion of evidence, where I considered how the practices of reading and memorization,

---

[48] Moran, *The Growth of English Schooling*, p. 42.

but not discussion, can be seen in some ways to correspond with standard educational techniques of the lower schools. But if looking to orthodox education of children in petty schools and grammar schools does not provide a satisfactory parallel, would we then turn to available models of adult learning in the Middle Ages? The most obvious model of adult learning is the very conventionalized program of the universities, where pupils studying for the lowest degree, the baccalaureat, can range in age from late adolescence to mature adulthood. But it is precisely the highly programmatic character of university learning that makes it an even more distant choice as a model for the adult pedagogy of Lollard communities. There are firmly traceable connections between the *content* of university studies and teaching within Lollard communities, a subject which will be explored here in chapter 3. And it will be a central argument of this book that Lollard intellectuals bring a teaching mission from the university milieu to their heterodox communities. But however much university subject matter or intellectual teaching mission find a place in local Lollard communities, we cannot look to university instruction for a practical model of lay adult education among the Lollards.

Lollard teaching and learning redefined pedagogy: this is why orthodox teaching traditions afford few satisfying parallels to Lollard practice. This is the most fundamental question of definition. I have summarized the broad evidence of Lollard teaching, but that leaves us with the problem of defining the theoretical parameters of the teaching. Here I want to open a more broadly theoretical perspective on pedagogy, within which the concerns of this study can be located. Pedagogy is the most political and politicized of discourses. The classroom, whether of children or adults, is the theater of political discipline; in organized, and even non-organized, forms of resistance, the classroom is also the theater of counter-discipline. Medieval legend gives us an emblem of classroom rebellion in the story told by Prudentius (culled from classical historiography) of the martyrdom of Cassian of Imola, the *magister litterarum* pierced to death by the styluses of his own pupils who in this way vented their rage and resentment against the grammar teacher's punitive discipline, his floggings and other chastisements.[49] That the pupils were actually the instruments of the pagan civic authority who found in them willing hands to carry out the persecution of Cassian for his Christian beliefs (so that the legend of their quintessential classroom rebellion also conveys Cassian into the annals of Christian martyrology) renders their pedagogical resistance part of the larger theater of political discipline.

Certainly the relationship between the classroom and the state has been an

---

[49] Prudentius, *Peristephanon* 9. For further discussion of this legend and its sources and later versions, see Copeland, "Introduction: Dissenting Critical Practices," 1–23.

overriding theme of radical and postmodern pedagogical theory. This is well exemplified in the sociological work of Stanley Aronowitz and Henry A. Giroux, who show how school curricula, as traditional sites of struggle, and as discourses and organized structures of social relations, at once express and enforce particular relations of power.[50] For Aronowitz and Giroux, postmodernism, with its anti-foundational emphases on diversity and contingency, and its constructivist critiques of knowledge, disciplines, and social texts, is a promising theoretical avenue "for radicalizing the emancipatory possibilities of teaching and learning as part of a wider struggle for democratic public life and critical citizenship."[51] In their largest terms, the relations of power expressed by school curricula are constructions of statehood, as in certain forms of nationalist mythologies that constitute an order of pedagogical authority – both within and beyond the schools – in which "the people" are invoked and signified as the objects of instructive narratives about the emergence of the nation.[52]

On this model, pedagogical discourse, whether instantiated at large in nationalist mythologies or at the individual level of school experience, is rigidified, static, top-down. This rigidity might be seen, of course, as endemic to Western pedagogical canons, a tradition whose constitutive project might always be, as Barbara Johnson has put it, the teaching of ignorance: "Are our ways of teaching students to ask *some* questions always correlative with our ways of teaching them *not to ask* – indeed, to be unconscious of – others? Does the educational system exist in order to promulgate knowledge, or is its main function rather to universalize a society's tacit agreement about what it has decided it does not and cannot know?"[53] The notion that the Western teaching enterprise is as much about suspending insight as delivering it, creating conditions that prohibit inquiry outside certain epistemological frameworks, bears comparison with what Durkheim has considered to be the insulating conditions of the premodern and modern school. For Durkheim, it was the early Christian monastic school that embarked on a new educative model, that of taking over the child in his entirety, imbuing the child with a certain "attitude of the soul," in a certain moral *habitus*, accomplished by placing him in a singular environment which satisfies every need. "This is, indeed, the distinguishing feature of the *convict*, the earliest type of boarding

---

[50] Aronowitz and Giroux, *Postmodern Education*, 89.   [51] Ibid., 82.

[52] See Bhabha, "DissemiNation: Time, Narrative, and the Margins of the Modern Nation," 297.

[53] Johnson, "Teaching Ignorance: *L'Ecole des Femmes*," 173. The collusions of ignorance with knowledge in relation to diverse regimes of truth are theoretical questions that much critical discourse has extended beyond pedagogical canons, notably in the context of gender and sexuality studies which use pedagogical language as a trope towards exploration of gender and knowledge, as in Johnson's essay, and much more broadly in Sedgewick, *Epistemology of the Closet*, 4–8, 77–80.

school." Nurturing this attitude in children rests on the idea of conversion, the changing of stance and position, directing a whole community towards one goal within a self-enclosed moral environment. In this kind of nurture, Durkheim sees the origins of the modern model of educational environment which delivers not pieces of knowledge, but rather a complete and interiorized *habitus*.[54] In Durkheim we have a double recognition, both of the innovatory success and resilience of the early-medieval school as an organized moral environment, and of its likeness to the environmental self-sufficiency of the prison, which also inculcates its knowledges in relation to a single regime of truth.

Yet of course pedagogical labor is not limited to the rigid, narrative order that expresses and enforces relations of power, as we can see from recent as well as, it is to be hoped, premodern history. For example, a recurrent theme in current scholarship on national liberation movements is the pedagogical work represented by literatures of resistance: many organized Third World political resistance movements have used poetry and narrative as part of popular literacy campaigns for children and adults. Such educational campaigns can be acutely self-reflexive in their method, making traditional pedagogical hierarchies an object of their critique along with the political regimes that they are challenging.[55] And here, in a gesture of disciplinary reflection, I would suggest that the materiality of pedagogical labor may represent the most powerful theoretical and historical link between contemporary postcolonial studies and medieval studies, because the genre of pedagogy is a mechanism that resistance movements across history, from medieval to modern, have most in common. Pedagogy is a category that maintains continuous and real historical value from the premodern to modernity. In this way the present study of pedagogy and dissent in medieval England looks to premodern resistance pedagogies not only to acknowledge the differences between past and present, but to understand what most insistently links past with present.

The most radical contemporary pedagogical thought, exemplified prominently by Paolo Freire, bell hooks, J. Elsbeth Stuckey, and Henry A. Giroux, takes recent histories of class and national resistance struggles into the domain of theory in what might be called the "liberationist" school of pedagogical critique.[56] The "liberationist" model of thought is most explicit about the

---

[54] Durkheim, *The Evolution of Educational Thought*, 28–30.

[55] See Harlow, *Resistance Literature*, 13, 43–50, 55–72.

[56] Freire, *Pedagogy of the Oppressed*; hooks, *Teaching to Transgress*; Stuckey, *The Violence of Literacy*; among Henry Giroux's many books, see *Schooling and the Struggle for Public Life* and *Theory and Resistance in Education*. The literature in this field is extensive, and I have cited here only a few of many prominent names. For further discussion and references, see Aronowitz and Giroux, *Postmodern Education*.

replication of large political orders – the nation state, domestic and international economic and industrial policies, and political disenfranchisement based on racial or class identity – in local classroom orders and teaching methods. To a large extent, this school of thought is also concerned with adult literacy and the teaching of adults in university and non-university settings: Freire and Stuckey in particular focus on teaching adults outside the academy.[57] The focus on educating adults gives this "liberationist" school its particular activist edge, because it sees the classroom not as insulation from political experience, but as a material link with the learners' political and economic struggles.

This radical school of pedagogical thought still draws much of its inspiration from the work of Paolo Freire, the Brazilian educator, political activist, and literacy campaigner, whose most famous book, *Pedagogy of the Oppressed*, was first published in English in 1970. Among Freire's most important themes are, first, the undoing of teacher–student hierarchies as a way of undoing larger, more invidious subject–object structures of society that underwrite class inequities; and, second, what he calls the "drive towards reconciliation," which must begin by solving the teacher–student contradiction, striving towards a structure in which both parties can be teacher and student. Freire speaks of what he calls the "banking" model of teaching, in which education becomes an act of "depositing" where the teacher, as narrator, fills students up.[58] The "banking" model might be seen to correspond with Barbara Johnson's analysis of teaching as the exegetical genre *par excellence*, where teaching seeks to fill in all the possible gaps and refuses acknowledgment of its own lacunae. In Freire's hands, liberationist pedagogy is a revolutionary program involving the education of traditional objects of oppression: the poor, the disenfranchised. In the hands of later generations of more academic educators and theorists such as bell hooks and Henry Giroux, liberationist pedagogy is presented more as a form of critique than as a program of revolutionary action. But for Freire and for his theoretical legacy, a critical pedagogy makes oppression and its causes the objects of reflection by the oppressed: it makes the learners' own political and pedagogical situation the object of their inquiry.[59]

Such radical theoretical approaches to the study of pedagogy need not be confined to the immediacy of modernity. The concerns of postmodern educational theory should be of no less relevance or value to our investigations of medieval culture than the concerns of other arenas of postmodernist debate, such as literary theory, gender studies, philosophy, psychoanalysis,

---

[57] See further, Freire, "The Adult Literacy Process as Cultural Action for Freedom."
[58] *Pedagogy of the Oppressed*, 52–7. [59] Ibid., 30.

and materialisms. Yet scholarship on the politics of education in early (premodern) periods has taken little account of the potentialities of postmodern educational theory for reading the history of pedagogical cultures. Among a very few scholars of early education who have made explicit links between postmodern pedagogical thought and their own projects in the premodern, Rebecca Bushnell most notably brings contemporary radical pedagogies to bear upon her readings of humanist educational policy.[60] Anthony Grafton and Lisa Jardine's book *From Humanism to the Humanities* is sometimes cited in this regard, but their study is concerned more with modern revaluations of humanist education than with modern pedagogies as links with the premodern past.[61]

The relevance of modern radical pedagogies to thinking about Lollard models of learning is in fact striking. One might look at Freire's writing and almost see a blueprint for the Lollards' dissenting pedagogy. Certainly Freire's major theme of undoing teaching hierarchies in favor of distributing pedagogical agency between teachers and students resonates with Lollard themes, as we will consider more closely in chapter 2. The Lollards' "Cato-book" – the basic and most common reading matter, their equivalent of the *Distichs of Cato* compilations that were the ubiquitous readers of medieval classrooms – is the Gospels (in various forms), a text which stimulates the teacher as much as the student, and over whose literal sense the teacher in theory would claim no greater possession or control than any reader in the community. What is most remarkable about Lollard education is that it repossesses the technology of teaching, taking structures borrowed from elementary pedagogy – the literal sense, introductory glosses, the "Cato-text" of the Gospels, the basic elements of literacy acquisition – and divorces them from the ideology that traditionally governs elementary education. And just as contemporary "liberationist" pedagogy focuses on the political self-realization of adults, Lollard pedagogy was a response to the political experience and aspirations of adult learners. Lollard education makes the learners' own political and material situation, as they constitute a new class of students, the object of their own reflection and inquiry.

Finally, the radical themes of Lollard pedagogy throw into relief how childhood was traditionally used as a symbolic category in medieval educational and social thought. For one poignant articulation of this symbolic discourse, we can look to an example provided in Richard de Bury's *Philobiblon* (1345), which is a defense of the "paternal care of books" written by a

60 Bushnell, *A Culture of Teaching: Early Modern Humanism in Theory and Practice*, 185–202.
61 Grafton and Jardine, *From Humanism to the Humanities: Education and the Liberal Arts in Fifteenth- and Sixteenth-Century Europe*.

self-described bibliophile and book collector. In a passage in the chapter on the proper physical care of books, Richard writes:

> Nor let a crying child admire the pictures in the capital letters, lest he soil the parchment with wet fingers: for a child instantly touches whatever he sees. Moreover, the laity, who look at a book turned upside down just as if it were open in the right way, are utterly unworthy of any communion with books.[62]

Children and laity are yoked together in one thought, in one conceptual collocation, so that the impulsive dirty fingers of the child and the rude ignorance of the layperson are almost exchangeable attributes. Richard's exclusion of crying, teary-fingered children from communion with books need not, on its own, signify beyond itself in terms of the social symbolic.[63] But in its immediate collocation with laity and their form of unfit "dirtiness" – their rude illiteracy – we can see the ideological investment of preserving a discourse of childhood as a debased category. Childhood as a category of abjection works as an instrument of political exclusion when it can be transferred, applied metaphorically, to other social groups.

Philippe Ariès' argument that there was no separate "sentiment de l'enfance" in the *ancien régime* has come under considerable and sustained critique by recent scholars, notably among them Danielle Alexandre-Bidon, Shulamith Shahar, and Barbara Hanawalt.[64] My own study furthers this critique, although not on the terms of social historians' material evidence. My evidence, rather, is based on the ways in which a category of childhood was deployed as something separable from children. In discourses of education, childhood constituted not just a cognitive category (describing the parameters of what children can be expected to know or learn), but a political category which could be articulated with such vehemence and at times precision that it was exportable, detachable from the actual concerns of childrearing and applied to other social conditions of dependency: laity, non-literates, non-clerics.

---

[62] "Puerulus lacrimosus capitalium litterarum non admiretur imagines, ne manu fluida polluat pergamenum; tangit enim illico quicquid videt. Porro laici, qui librum aeque respiciunt resupine transversum sicut serie naturali expansum, omni librorum communione penitus sunt indigni." Richard de Bury, *Philobiblon*, 158–60.

[63] Indeed, Richard's galaxy of unfit readers also includes lazy scholars with poor hygiene, anyone (clergy, scholar, scullion) with dirty hands, "iuvenes impudentes" who fill the margins of books with practice alphabets, and the "latinista" and the "sophista" who each tries out his penmanship on the page (156–60).

[64] Ariès, *L'Enfant et la vie familiale sous l'Ancien Régime* 134 ff; Alexandre-Bidon, "La Lettre volée"; Shahar, *Childhood in the Middle Ages*, 1–4, 95, 143–5; Hanawalt, *Growing Up in Medieval London*, 5–9. See also Swanson, "Childhood and Childrearing in *Ad Status* Sermons by Later Thirteenth-Century Friars."

One of Ariès' positions is that age mattered little in the educational culture of the Middle Ages because of the mixing of ages in the schools, because subjects were studied in simultaneous fashion rather than by hierarchical progression from one subject to the next, and because of the recursiveness of the curricular system as a whole.[65] Taking account of the fact that he is speaking primarily about elementary training in medieval France, and that English grammar schools (as he acknowledges) maintained a greater degree of curricular hierarchy than their French counterparts, we might accept his evidence and yet question the conclusions that he draws. I would suggest that age matters all the more in such a context, not necessarily or specifically as a biological condition, but as an ideological condition. The boundary between intellectual childhood and adulthood would be effected through notions of the "rudiment," through pedagogical processes associated with rudimentary levels of learning rather than with particular age groups. Childhood can become portable – and discursively very powerful – as a category because it can signify a kind of social dependency equivalent to a rudimentary intellectual level. Like categories of gender, femininity or masculinity, childhood signifies in ways far beyond biological essentialism. Childhood is a construction which is maintained as "natural" through historical and cultural meanings attached to it.

The most important legacy of ancient and medieval pedagogical discourses is their separation of childhood from adulthood, and their successful detachment of the category of childhood from biological age. The association with childhood of certain educational mechanisms, especially reading according to the literal sense, makes childhood a political category which can be used to define and repress any social group whose pedagogical engagement is deemed to be restricted to the rudiments, that is, to childish levels of apprehension. But it is the work of a dissenting community to challenge the common sense of a naturalized order. The success of Lollardy's radical pedagogy is that it refused to reproduce the fundamental distinction between childhood and adulthood which had been served, traditionally, by identifying childish reading with the literal sense.

2 INTELLECTUALS

"Intellectual" and "intellectuals" as nouns are essentially modern words. The plural "intellectuals" commonly designates, in both positive and negative senses, a particular group or social entity, even a class (whether professional or

---

[65] Ariès, *L'Enfant et la vie familiale*, 149–62.

more loosely collectivized), defined by the kind of work or activity it performs, or more broadly, by the kind of power that it claims or with which it is invested. These are necessarily general definitions, because both the term "intellectuals" and the social entity it designates are so historically contested that they can only take on precise outlines when viewed as particular historical effects. In the following remarks I offer a synthetic survey of recent discourses about intellectual functions and roles.

The modern notion of intellectuals as a specific social entity – the term as sociological label – is best traced to its use in France during the Dreyfus Affair. Zola's *Manifeste des intellectuels*, published in *L'Aurore* on 14 January 1898 (one day after the publication of his *J'Accuse* in the same venue), presented a vehement protest against the outcome of the trial of Dreyfus. It was signed by writers, scientists, industrialists, physicians, lawyers, academics, and members of the Académie Française, including, along with Zola himself, Marcel Proust, Anatole France, Gustave Lanson, Mario Roques, Léon Blum, Lucien Herr, and many other figures, some of considerable fame and some of lesser notability.[66] The signatories, otherwise quite disparate figures in terms of their professional affiliations and the social and political spheres in which they moved, produced themselves as a collective entity through their public identification with a critical, oppositional stance. The contradictions of this collective identification that almost implausibly traversed professional, social, and political affiliations – for example, the Académie Française and the Sorbonne, conservative and avant-garde authors, the "intelligentsia" and the popular press, or a writer like Zola himself who had never attained membership in the Académie but who managed to enlist some of its most celebrated members as signatories to this letter of protest – have been lucidly analyzed by Régis Debray and others.[67] Such a new identification along critical lines, but across established social and professional lines, could be seen to represent a certain "aristocracy of thought" whose self-expression seemed to observe no traditional principle of social organization, but rather a spontaneously self-proclaimed elitism, as described, for example, in the conservative Maurice Barrès' response to the *Manifeste des intellectuels*: "Ces aristocrates de la pensée tiennent à affirmer qu'ils ne pensent pas comme la vile foule" (*Le Journal*, 1 February 1898).

---

[66] See Pagès, *Emile Zola, un intellectuel dans l'Affaire Dreyfus*, 325–31, for extracts of the first and second "protestations" (*L'Aurore* 14 and 16 January 1898). There were twenty lists of signatories for the first letter (published between 14 January and 4 February), and eighteen lists for the second "protestation" (published between 16 January and 4 February). Hundreds of names were collected. The full text is in [Zola], *Livre d'hommage des lettres françaises à Emile Zola*.

[67] Debray, *Teachers, Writers, Celebrities: the Intellectuals of Modern France*, 50–5; Charle, "Champ littéraire et champ du pouvoir: les écrivains et l'Affaire Dreyfus."

The suspicion of such an "aristocracy of thought" that passes judgment through the rule of intellect certainly attends the use of the term "intellectuals" in English from the eighteenth century onwards, accompanied here by suspicions of post-Revolutionary French republicanisms which also declare themselves independent of monarchy and church. In this respect the legacy of English political thought from Edmund Burke through the later nineteenth century is that a nation organized around a double adherence to the institutions of state and church needs no separate class of thinkers who do not represent the interests of established national institutions.[68] Indeed the English coinage "intelligentsia," from Russian, could provide a coherent focus for such suspicions, designating as it does a group with distinct and self-conscious intellectual interests which set it apart, as an elite or oppositional constituency, from other groups, even from academics and scholars.[69] And as Francis Mulhern argues, the emergence of an intellectual meritocracy in Britain between the world wars occurred as a struggle within the universities, pitting a new class of young professionals who claimed literary studies as a force for broad cultural direction against older traditions of the non-"professionalized" gentleman-scholar.[70]

Marxist thought has given the most continuous theoretical momentum to the problem of intellectuals: whether they exist, or ought to exist, as a social entity of their own whose critical function is to formulate theory and policy, or whether they represent articulate and theoretically directive strata of existing social classes. In other words, one great problem has been to consider *where* intellectuals, if they do form a distinct group, are socially located.[71] Such arguments within Marxist social theory culminated in the work of Antonio Gramsci, whose brief but concentrated remarks on traditional and organic intellectuals have formed the point of departure for much later-twentieth-century consideration of these issues. On Gramsci's argument,

[68] For example, from Burke, *Reflections on the Revolution in France* (1790): "I hear on all hands that a cabal, calling itself philosophic, receives the glory of many of the late proceedings, and that their opinions and systems are the true actuating spirit of the whole of them. I have heard of no party in England, literary or political, at any time, known by such a description . . . We know, and what is better we feel inwardly, that religion is the basis of civil society, and the source of all good and of all comfort . . . The consecration of the state, by a state religious establishment, is necessary also to operate with an wholesome awe upon free citizens . . ." Text from *The Writings and Speeches of Edmund Burke* vol. 8, *The French Revolution, 1790–94*, 140–3.   [69] See Williams, *Keywords*, v. Intellectuals.

[70] Mulhern, Introduction to Debray, *Teachers, Writers, Celebrities*, xx.

[71] One *locus classicus* is the formulation of Marx and Engels in *The Communist Manifesto*: "Finally, in times when the class struggle nears the decisive hour, the process of dissolution going on within the ruling class . . . assumes such a violent, glaring character, that a small section of the ruling class cuts itself adrift, and joins the revolutionary class, the class that holds the future in its hands . . . now a portion of the bourgeoisie goes over to the proletariat, and in particular, a portion of the bourgeois ideologists, who have raised themselves to the level of comprehending theoretically the historical movement as a whole" (91).

intellectuals do not constitute a separate class, but rather every class has its own intellectuals. Nevertheless, in a move that will have a considerable theoretical legacy, he distinguishes between organic intellectuals who are created by and alongside every new class in the course of its development, functioning as the technical, directive, organizational "specialists" of that class, and traditional intellectuals, who have carried out intellectual functions in service of established ecclesiastical institutions and their later secular academic and civic formations (a group often termed a "clerisy"), and who previously represented the "organic intellectuals" of those institutions in their emergent state. A professionalized "clerisy," without visible class ties, supersedes the body of new organic intellectuals.[72]

Once it is established or agreed *de facto* that intellectuals do constitute a distinct constituency – for example, with the series of post-Dreyfus "intellectual committees" issuing manifestos on the major political subjects of their historical moments, from fascism to Algerian independence,[73] or with the attention of sociologists to intellectual work and intellectual function as concrete categories of descriptive and historical analysis[74] – the question then becomes not where are intellectuals socially located, but rather, what will they and should they actually do? The question of what intellectuals should do is still rooted, of course, in where they are, from what social or professional constituency they draw their identities. But the new question shifts emphasis to their political positioning and rhetorical function: should intellectuals speak from a position of autonomy or of social specificity? Does their authority to speak derive from their willed detachment from particular social or institutional interests and affiliations, a detachment that has been variously construed as magisterial or marginal; or do they fulfill their "vocation" only through their grounding in social specificities, whether institutional (notably the university) or particular class or local political interests? This is a much-discussed opposition which has been summarized as the "call

---

[72] "The Formation of the Intellectuals," in Gramsci, *Selections from the Prison Notebooks*, 5–9; see also Sassoon, *Gramsci's Politics*, 122. It is interesting to note that Walter Benjamin (writing in exile in Paris in the early 1930s, approximately during the same period that Gramsci was writing from various prisons in Italy) sounded a variation on the theme of the invisible class ties of intellectuals. Benjamin argues that the intellectuals have come adrift from earlier ties to the humanistic concerns of the bourgeoisie, but are also unassimilable to the proletariat. Their status gives the illusion of new emancipation, as they seem to constitute a free-floating entity between classes, which Benjamin likens ironically to "the freedom of the Lumpenproletariat" (those whose economic condition is so degraded that they have no apparent class ties). Thus the condition of intellectuals has become that of a "mimicry" of proletarian existence without ties to the proletariat. See Benjamin, "Zum gegenwärtigen gesellschaftlichen Standort des französischen Schriftstellers," 789.

[73] See Debray, *Teachers, Writers, Celebrities*, 55 for the "watershed" manifestoes of 1919, 1935, and 1978, as well as for examples of other "intellectual committees."

[74] See, for example, Rieff, ed., *On Intellectuals*, a collection of essays by American and British sociologists; see especially the essay by Parsons, "The Intellectual: a Social Role Category."

for micropolitical actions in place of the grand tradition of autonomous dissent."[75] These questions, of course, might beg the much larger and contested question of what is the intellectual vocation itself (a question adjacent to, but different from, the earlier problem of the very existence of intellectuals as a distinct entity). "Definitions of the intellectual are many and diverse," as Zygmunt Bauman has written, but they have "one trait in common, which makes them different from all other definitions: they are all self-definitions. Indeed, their authors are the members of the same rare species they attempt to define. Hence every definition they propose is an attempt to draw a boundary of their own identity."[76] Pronouncements about intellectual vocation issue from the sectors that already define themselves as "the intellectuals," whether from within the academy (literary critics, philosophers, social scientists, and others) or from outside the academy (notably writers as well as political and social commentators).[77]

Thus it is also within and among those interested sectors that debates about the autonomy or groundedness of intellectuals are conducted. Julien Benda's *La Trahison des clercs* (1927) provides one of the now-classic arguments for a kind of pure and unconstrained autonomy of intellectuals, a detached, disinterested form of humanistic service, transcendent or universal rather than yielding autonomy to partisan political interests. It is an argument embracing an unworldly "clerisy": Benda's use of the word "clerc" over a word like "intellectual" is significant, for it is meant to evoke a notion of particularly academic unworldliness, a kind of magisterial or clerical withdrawal into a non-partisan sanctuary governed by speculative rather than temporal or practical concerns where intellectuals may become "the officiants of abstract justice."[78] In other words, the arena of speculation, the academic "priesthood," is not in itself understood here as a sphere of practice. Benda is not explicit about the university itself as the locale of such withdrawal, but the (romanticized) notion of a university clerisy, whose speculative concerns remove them from interest in what Bruce Robbins calls the "social embodiment" that their thought may assume, certainly informs Benda's vision.[79]

75 Ross, "Defenders of the Faith and the New Class," 126, describing some of Foucault's celebrated arguments on this subject. Cf. Ross' discussion of the "autonomy" question, 107–8.

76 Bauman, *Legislators and Interpreters: on Modernity, Post-Modernity, and Intellectuals*, 8. See also the typology of intellectuals in the Western tradition in Sadri, *Max Weber's Sociology of Intellectuals*, 74–81.

77 Debray remarks, "when an intellectual decides to take the intellientsia as an object of reflection, it is usually as a subject for a confession, curse or a sermon and not as an object of study." The "intelligentsia" is, in Debray's words, a "sociological aporia" to itself (*Teachers, Writers, Celebrities*, 18). This is well and concisely illustrated in the subject of Pierre Bourdieu's excursus, "The Hit Parade of French Intellectuals, or Who Is to Judge the Legitimacy of the Judges," in *Homo Academicus*, 256–70.

78 Benda, *The Treason of the Intellectuals*, 51. On Benda, see Mulhern's introduction to Debray, *Teachers, Writers, Celebrities*, viii–ix, and Debray's own discussions, 18–19, 139.

79 Robbins, Introduction to *Intellectuals: Aesthetics, Politics, Academics*, xv.

Benda's condemnation of intellectuals who have forsaken disinterested detachment is echoed in more recent denunciations from the right, notably Norman Podhoretz's *Breaking Rank: a Political Memoir*, which castigates American intellectuals in the 1960s for having repudiated their proper scholarly, artistic, or thinking vocation by stepping into political activism. But in other recent lamentations over intellectuals who have lapsed from their traditional vocation, it is the university itself that is seen as the corporatizing structure that has co-opted intellectuals and deprived them of their proper marginality as free voices of opposition speaking from and for a public sphere. Some of the most interesting of these condemnations have issued from the left, as in Russell Jacoby's *The Last Intellectuals: American Culture in the Age of Academe*, which decries the loss of "independent intellectuals"; and here one could also cite Barbara and John Ehrenreich's influential essay "The Professional-Managerial Class," which is less condemnatory in tone, but which explores the contradictions of university-based intellectual opposition in America during the 1960s.[80] Finally, we might take Bruce Robbins' work as a significant example of a strong mediating position, one that "accept[s] that the university is itself a 'ground' in both senses [restriction and foundation], enabling as well as restricting the activity of intellectuals."[81] This is a theoretical position which will warrant further elaboration here for its value as a tool of historical analysis.

These debates about the autonomy of intellectuals as a class also subtend another category of discourse which concerns the representation of the individual intellectual. The model that continues to exert perhaps the most attractive power, despite the often rigorous critiques to which it has been subjected, is that synthesis of humanism and romanticism in what Paul Bové has described as the Nietzschean image of "the isolated, struggling, heroic, oppositional figure rising above and against the treacheries of the past and present." Nietzsche constructs such a voice in the *Genealogy of Morals*, in terms borrowed from Byron: marginal, ascetic, sublime, adversarial, but also self-ironizing, the critical intellectual as genealogist whose materialist and scientific demystifications of the structures of power and knowledge are never sufficiently turned to account for his own mysteriously "self-generated origin."[82] This influential and powerful, but also mythologizing, model can lead

---

[80] See also Ehrenreich's interview, "The Professional-Managerial Class Revisited," which asserts some almost impassable boundaries between academic and non-academic feminisms. See the survey and analysis of these various positions in Jennings and Kemp-Welch, "The Century of the Intellectual: From the Dreyfus Affair to Salmon Rushdie."

[81] Robbins, Introduction, *Intellectuals: Aesthetics, Politics, Academics*, xviii; and see Robbins, *Secular Vocations: Intellectuals, Professionalism, Culture*, 180–8.

[82] Bové, *Intellectuals in Power: a Genealogy of Critical Humanism*, 11, 12–15.

in various directions, whether to the notion of the magisterial or "leading" intellectual (disciplinary specialist or sublime cultural interpreter), or to the skeptic who refuses the privilege of such essentializing difference (Bové's reading of Foucault against the Nietzschean model[83]), or even, as in some of this model's most recent avatars, to the elevation of the literary critic, whose social marginality is almost always assured, to the role of exemplary critical intellectual.[84]

The events in Paris of May 1968 constituted a watershed for poststructuralist re-evaluations of the role of intellectuals. An important trend that can be traced here is the turning of theoretical discussion from the general question of intellectual vocation to the more particular issue of intellectual effectiveness. These discussions have maintained and renewed their urgency long after the immediate effects of May 1968 and have carried far beyond the interests of the intellectual circles concerned immediately with interpreting those events.[85] From what position can intellectuals most effectively speak? Here discussions regularly return to Michel Foucault's distinction between the universal and the specific intellectual.[86] What Foucault describes as the "universal" intellectual is derived from long-standing models of intellectuals as an autonomous group, although the figure is now individualized, as the speaker of "truth to those who had yet to see it, in the name of those who were forbidden to speak the truth: (the intellectual) was conscience, consciousness, and eloquence."[87] But this model of the intellectual on the left, who "spoke and was acknowledged the right of speaking in the capacity of master of truth and justice," and who "was heard, or purported to make himself heard, as the spokesman of the universal," has been made obsolete by the events of May 1968, with its reconfigurations of alliances between professional intellectuals and labor organizations.[88] "The intellectual's role is no longer to place himself 'somewhat ahead and to the side' in order to express the stifled truth of the collectivity"; it is rather to work "within specific sectors, at the precise points where (intellectuals') own conditions of life or work situate them (housing, the hospital, the asylum, the laboratory, the university, family and

---

83 Bové, *Intellectuals in Power*, pp. 209–37.
84 See, for example, Bové, *Mastering Discourse: the Politics of Intellectual Culture*, and Robbins, *Secular Vocations*, 57–83.
85 The best example of the continued and renewable urgency of the questions of intellectual effectiveness raised after May 1968 is the monumental collection *Marxism and the Interpretation of Culture*, edited by Grossberg and Nelson. See also the reflections in Readings, *The University in Ruins*, chapter 9, "The Time of Study: 1968" (135–49), on the Paris uprising's repositioning of university students in relation to the public sphere.
86 The most cited reference for this is Foucault and Deleuze, "Intellectuals and Power." Foucault reprises and elaborates the distinction in the interview "Truth and Power," 110–11, 125–33.
87 Foucault and Deleuze, "Intellectuals and Power," 207.   88 Foucault, "Truth and Power," 126.

sexual relations)."[89] This returns us, of course, to the question of "grounding": it is the "local, specific struggle" carried on in relation to the conditions of his life and work as an intellectual ("his field of research, his place in a laboratory, the political and economic demands to which he submits or against which he rebels, in the university, the hospital, etc.") that can "take on a general significance and . . . have effects and implications which are not simply professional or sectoral."[90]

Foucault's model of the specific intellectual has been compared, sometimes by way of severe critique, with Gramsci's celebrated model of the organic intellectual. They have certain elements in common, but whereas Gramsci's examination of the role of the organic intellectual proceeds through a careful demystification of intellectual work in itself, Foucault is seen to fall back into a certain abstract idealism about the contributions of intellectual work even in its specific and localized form.[91] Indeed, the heuristic value of Foucault's distinction between universal and specific intellectuals seems to reside in the harsh criticisms it has produced, for the privilege it seems to confer on the intellectual's own agency in struggles against dynastic regimes of truth and for its continued emphasis on the privilege of the intellectual to perform a diagnostic function. Foucault is thus seen simply to localize in the specific intellectual the truth-proclaiming powers of the universal intellectual.[92]

Is there a transhistorical concept of the "intellectual"? More precisely, is there a category of thought, practice, identity, self-knowledge, corporate or group sensibility that is traceable, transhistorically, according to what is often denoted by the modern concept or term "intellectual"? Certainly within modern applications of the term to contemporary conditions, there is an assumption that the Middle Ages offers a self-consistent, unified standard of the intellectual function which survives into the modern era to represent a narrow but powerful model of the disinterested pursuit of the ideal, the sacred. Here, for example, is how Andrew Ross invokes the "medieval clerisy" as if it can stand in for a clearly defined norm of "autonomy from socially determined criteria":

> Edward Shils, Talcott Parsons, and Régis Debray have all described, albeit
> with different aims and emphases, how the social functions of the medieval

---

[89] Foucault and Deleuze, "Intellectuals and Power," 207–8; Foucault, "Truth and Power," 126.

[90] 'Truth and Power," 129.

[91] Radhakrishnan, "Toward an Effective Intellectual: Foucault or Gramsci?", 80–7.

[92] Radhakrishnan, "Toward an Effective Intellectual", 68–70, 74–5; Spivak, "Can the Subaltern Speak?" 275. See also Said, "American Intellectuals and Middle East Politics," 144. For a valuable summary of the major theoretical strands in discussions of the intellectual's relation to the state, especially with a view to the way that gender is inscribed in these positions, see Rabinowitz, *Labor and Desire: Women's Revolutionary Fiction in Depression America*, 42–5.

clerisy are still vestigially present in the modern idea of the intellectual. As a relatively unattached, classless stratum (to cite Karl Mannheim's enduring but ever contested definition), confined to the "pure," as distinct from the "applied," branches of the humanist and technical intelligentsia, the quasi-religious function of defenders of the faith is to eschew all partisan involvement in the name of a devotional commitment to higher principles – God, Art, Science, and other "institutions of truth." If their work and thought happens to have concrete political effects, this is because it is genuinely prophetic, and not because it bends under pragmatic pressure from a secular, institutional patron. This is not to say that intellectuals ought never to voice political sentiments or opinions, but that they should only do so in their capacity as citizens and not as ex officio intellectuals.[93]

Ross is describing a tradition of discourse, not necessarily a historical fact: there is a modern discourse of intellectual disinterestedness which in turn is ascribed to the Middle Ages where, Ross implies, the discourse began. But while Ross is not trying to posit a fact of medieval practice, he assumes the historical facticity of such a unified discourse in the Middle Ages. The Middle Ages serves as a point of origin for a notion of devotional commitment to higher principles and of prophetic, rather than pragmatic intervention in worldly affairs. Medievalists can, of course, dismiss such an assertion with the inevitable lamentations about the historical brutishness of modernists, whose exquisite powers of discrimination among cultural nuances seem to leave them as soon as they reach a date before, say, 1789. But rather than simply lament this (and similar) assertions about a monolithic medieval intellectual ideology, it can be useful to tease out what is wrong with the assertion of this transhistorical category, a "medieval clerisy" that is still vestigially present with us.

Was it the case that a singular discourse about intellectual detachment from "socially determined criteria" actually obtained in the Middle Ages? Does not the statement by Ross (and the assumptions of the well-regarded sociologists he cites) reflect a tendency to universalize for all medieval intellectual discourses one discrete model of intellectual work, that of monasticism? Among medievalists, in turn, monasticism itself has been too readily mythologized in terms of a general principle of the "love of learning and desire for God." Certainly a generalized notion of a medieval clerisy engaged in devotional service to "institutions of truth" bears little resemblance to the multiple and complex systems of pragmatic interests and investments, from individual career advancement to broader pressures of institutional self-governance, and to enmeshment in civic, state, and ecclesiastical politics, that shaped the

---

[93] Ross, "Defenders of the Faith," 108.

academic cultures of medieval universities.[94] Moreover, what is the evidence that medieval schoolmen always or typically spoke of their work in terms of a "devotional commitment to higher principles," that is, that they generated a unified discourse of disinterestedness, however much at variance that discourse was with their practices? Similar questions might be posed more particularly of monastic discourses and practices of learning, which the passage quoted above from Ross treats, synecdochally, as a part for the whole (that is, medieval monasticism is the most celebrated and familiar model of medieval intellectual labor, and therefore it can stand for the whole Middle Ages): indeed, throughout the later Middle Ages, monastic orders found themselves in conflict with their rival institution for academic dominance, the friars, and adapted their practices to engage locally and at large with state affairs.[95]

What we can say of such generalizations about a politically disinterested "medieval clerisy" is that they are either exported back to the Middle Ages by commentators on modernity seeking historical explanation for a principle that seems irrationally out of keeping with modern secularism, or generated and accepted by medievalists invested in (or seeking identity with) a nostalgic image of less secular times. The notion of a "medieval clerisy," an unattached, classless stratum unified around devotional commitment to higher principles, may be a convenient apparatus for explaining present historical conditions; but it is not a good tool of historiography, because it elides medieval intellectual culture rather than seeking to explain it.

But as we have seen, the term "intellectual" itself, as a substantive denoting a certain kind of person, a member of a special class (or in Mannheim's definition, a "classless stratum"), is also a modern term. How do we historicize this modern category, with its network of associations, and extend it to medieval conditions of intellectual work and professional status? This is a key historiographical question for modern study of medieval learning. The term "intellectual/s" had no meaning during the Middle Ages, as various scholars applying the term to the history of medieval schools and universities have acknowledged.[96] The Middle Ages would have recognized terms such as

---

94 Finely exemplified in Shank, *Unless You Believe, You shall not Understand: Logic, University, and Society in Late Medieval Vienna*, a sociocultural account of intellectual history, which examines shifts in debates over the compatibility of Trinitarian doctrine and Aristotelian logic at the University of Vienna in the contexts of the Great Schism, the Council of Konstanz, and the destruction of the Viennese Jewish community in 1421. The formation of the Paris schools gives similar evidence: see Ferruolo, "The Paris Statutes Reconsidered." 95 See Cannon, "Monastic Productions," 331–2.

96 See Verger, "Condition de l'intellectuel aux xiiie et xive siècles"; Boureau, "Intellectuals in the Middle Ages, 1957–95"; Dahan, *Les Intellectuels chrétiens et les juifs au Moyen Âge*; Brocchieri, "L'intellectuel"; and notably, Le Goff, *Intellectuels au Moyen Âge* (translated as *Intellectuals in the Middle Ages*), preface to the 1985 French edition, xiii–xiv, and Introduction to the 1957 edition, 1. I cite the English translation here (references in the text) because it conveniently brings together materials from both of the French editions.

scolares (either for students in particular or schoolmen in general), *magister, clericus, philosophus, litteratus* (a large and imprecise term extending beyond the schools), *eruditus, doctor,* and even *professor* (in a limited sense, designating one who professes a subject, rather than a professional title).[97] There is no medieval term that would comprehend the social and ideological implications contained in the modern use of "intellectual."

On the other hand, the pedigree of applying the terms "intellectual/ intellectuals" to the Middle Ages has been well established since the appearance, in 1957, of Jacques Le Goff's *Intellectuels au moyen âge.* Le Goff used the term at the time with conscious anachronism, and even with a nod in the direction of Gramscian analysis. But he made the term stick not as a transhistorical concept, but rather as a term that could be given a value for a specific historical moment. For Le Goff, intellectuals acquired cohesion as a group by the practice of a particular activity, the profession of thinking and sharing their thoughts: the "alliance between personal reflection and its dissemination through instruction characterized the intellectual."[98] Yet, despite the success of Le Goff's historical re-evaluation of the concept, the terms "intellectual/s" are still not accepted or used comfortably by medievalists in all quarters. The terms have found a more secure usage among French and other continental historians of the Middle Ages than among Anglo-American historians of medieval English universities. If we look through continental bibliographies on the medieval university, we will see that the terms, as substantives, appear quite commonly; such would not be the case in bibliographies of British scholarship on medieval Oxford and Cambridge (and here American scholarship tends to resemble its British counterpart). We will not find the terms, as nouns, used with any confidence or freedom in, for example, the *History of the University of Oxford* to characterize university schoolmen and their professional associates in the environs of the universities as a cohesive class, or to designate them as a group of people possessed of a special outlook. Obviously this is a question of national, cultural factors that shape particular historiographical traditions. As noted earlier, the concept of an intellectual "class" that would cross academic, political, and professional lines has had a mixed reception in English history and social thought from the late eighteenth century. Such ideological suspicion of this broad concept may be reflected in traditions of scholarship on the history of the university that resist such a large conceptual category, especially one that would displace a strong and positivist model of academic professionalism with one that has less well-defined (if also more far-reaching) sociocultural implications. This resis-

---

97 See especially Verger, "Condition de l'intellectuel," 39–40, and Brocchieri, "L'intellectuel," 201–4.
98 Le Goff, *Intellectuals in the Middle Ages,* 1.

tance to the term "intellectuals" as anachronistic when applied to premodern academic culture may also speak to the specialist role that British and American historical scholars see themselves occupying as academic professionals.

Whatever their success in penetrating various national historiographical conventions, are the terms "intellectual" and "intellectuals" applied to the later Middle Ages necessarily anachronistic? I would like to turn here to two different historiographical arguments that address this issue: the sociocultural approach of Jacques Le Goff's *Intellectuels au moyen âge*, and the epistemological perspective of Alain de Libera's *Penser au moyen âge*. Neither Le Goff nor de Libera assumes that the meaning of "intellectual" for the Middle Ages is self-evident; yet each uses the term with the conviction that no other term, and certainly no term derived from medieval usage, will serve to comprehend the complex of social functions and corporate relations, or the elaborations and refinements of mentalities, that constitute this new social type that emerges with the university in the later Middle Ages. For both, the category "intellectual/s" marks the historical location of a set of concepts rather than a transhistorical sameness.

Le Goff's well-known argument is that the appearance of the intellectual as a distinct social type in the twelfth century was bound up with the appearance of the towns: "A man whose profession it was to write or to teach – and usually both at the same time – a man who, professionally, acted as professor and scholar, in short an intellectual – that man appeared only with the towns" (6). Le Goff's picture of the intellectual as urban artisan whose labor depends upon, and is organized by, the social economy of the town, has been received with enthusiasm as well as with some doubt. Is it truly applicable beyond Paris? Were there not also internal ecclesiastical renovations and traditions that served to structure the institutional mentality of the university?[99] My concern here, however, is not with the absolute sustainability of Le Goff's thesis, but rather with the historiographical orientation that enables him to achieve a definition of the intellectual that is specific to medieval social formations. On Le Goff's account, using the term "intellectual" allows for shifting attention "away from the institution to individuals, from ideas to social structures, customs, mentalities" (Preface to 1985 French edition, xiii). Le Goff's retrospective articulation here of his historiographical motivation is an unmistakeably Gramscian one (indeed, as he notes, Italian medievalists have since taken up and developed the Gramscian inspiration of his own study). It looks to characterize intellectual activities not through their

[99] See Dunbabin, "Jacques Le Goff and the Intellectuals"; Verger, "Condition de l'intellectuel," 40–1.

intrinsic nature (as in a history of ideas), but through the "ensemble of the system of relations" in which they achieve their particular social role; and it replaces the intellectual "institution," which can be too easily abstracted in terms of sets of rules, curricular programs, and a self-generating bureaucracy, with what Gramsci would call the groups and individuals who "personify" that ensemble of relations.[100] In the simplest sense, Le Goff places his inquiry outside the parameters of traditional intellectual history; but neither does it fit neatly within the conventions of socioeconomic history. What is particular to the formation of this social type in the twelfth and thirteenth centuries is the professionalization of intellectual work through its identification with other kinds of urban artisanal labor. On this urban professionalized model, the activities of research and teaching are joined together for the first time towards an economically productive end: ideas as products which can be reinserted into the intellectual "economy" as sources of profit and power (1985 Preface, xvii). The artisanal metaphor can be extended to virtually all features of university life: for example, there are tools of the trade (the paraphernalia of writing, books as instruments) and a systematic technology which is teachable as method (82–92).

Again, whether or not one agrees with the particulars of these arguments (and there have been many efforts to refine and reconfigure Le Goff's historical picture), what emerges crucially from Le Goff's analysis is a way of understanding how a category of activity could define itself so successfully and distinctively that it could, in turn, be exported beyond the university. It is within the social economy of the town that Le Goff sees exchange and rapport between university and non-university intellectuals. It is also because of the socioeconomic infrastructure of the town that he seeks to avoid categorical distinctions between intellectual contributions of university members and those of other lettered people – lawyers, judges, notaries, grammar teachers – who were the "artisans of the power of towns," the "intellectuals of urban growth." Similarly, he would resist drawing lines between academics and *littérateurs* who may have tenuous university connections (for example, Rutebeuf or Villon), or intramurally, between the ranks of eminent scholar-interpreters (the celebrated *magistri* or *doctores*) and the lesser disseminators who compiled, popularized, and preached (1985 Preface, xvii–xix). Here too Le Goff is deploying the Gramscian strategy of considering function over intrinsic content to describe intellectual work.[101] And it is around the

---

100 Gramsci, "The Formation of the Intellectuals," 8.
101 In another Gramscian gesture, Le Goff suggests that the intellectuals, as urban artisans, came into being as functionaries, as good servants of church and state bureaucracies (xvi). His reading of Gramsci here is somewhat elliptical: Le Goff classes their performance as church and state functionaries with that of the "organic intellectuals," whereas on Gramsci's terms the activities of such functionaries,

question of function – a constellation of practices – that intellectual identity itself could become a kind of product to be exported. Alain Boureau speaks of the "constitution of a group of medieval 'intellectuals'" around "the ethical and religious obligation to decipher" which actualizes itself in the urban environment of the twelfth and thirteenth centuries.[102] That obligation itself must be defined and justified as a legitimate and productive form of labor (104): differentiated from manual work, possessed of a technological system that distinguished its work from other labor and yet brought it closer by analogy with artisanal production, it is the very consciousness of itself as engaging in a distinct enterprise that could be said to be its most exportable product.

Indeed, while academic labor differentiated itself from manual work, the very sense of "making a product" was also what distinguished it completely from conceptions of learning in earlier monastic institutions. Le Goff's paradigm of an artisanal self-consciousness is readily exemplified in the language in which the new social formation of intellectuals represented its interests. An early thirteenth-century *summa* by Robert de Courçon explicitly makes the identification between artisanal and intellectual work, to justify the fees paid to masters in the Arts Faculty. Robert notes that the teaching of language and of other liberal arts, such as geometry and arithmetic, is a trade, equivalent to the exercise of mechanical skills such as those of the artisan, the carpenter, and the farmer and, like such labor, ought to be paid.[103] More generally, on explicit analogy with the artisanal, urban guilds, students were seen as apprentices of their masters, and masters in turn formed themselves into horizontal guild structures that both showcased and protected their professional expertise.

If Le Goff's social history sees intellectual labor exported outside the university by virtue of its rapport with urban artisans, Alain de Libera's intellectual history sees the figure of the intellectual created in the overflowing of university culture into lay society, in the passage of philosophy *extra muros*.

especially in relation to the church, comprise the stratum of the "traditional intellectuals," those who serve established class and state powers, occupying long-standing functionary roles that seem to operate apart from class ties. Contrary to Le Goff's suggestion here, it would seem that the "new" intellectual class is "organic" precisely in its relationship with urban artisanal structures, not in its more traditional service of church and state powers. We may, however, refine the Gramscian scheme in the light of a more precisely historicized picture such as that which Le Goff's book gives: this new stratum of intellectuals serves at once new functions, in relation to the emergent urban artisanal classes, and traditional functions, in relation to established church and state mechanisms.

102 Boureau, "Intellectuals in the Middle Ages, 1957–95," 146.

103 Cited in Baldwin, *Masters, Princes, and Merchants: the Social Views of Peter the Chanter and his Circle* 1: 126; 2: 86, n. 68. Later scholastic thought also made the analogy between artisanal expertise and the intellectual *habitus*: see Minnis, "The *Accessus* Extended: Henry of Ghent on the Transmission and Reception of Theology."

It is an epistemology and an ideology of the intellectual that de Libera wants to trace, the creation, not just of a social function (as in Le Goff), but of a "human type." De Libera sees his enterprise as compatible with Le Goff's, but he moves it in a new direction. The object of his inquiry is the way in which intellectuals lived and thought the "intellectual project" itself, a history of intellectual consciousness in the thirteenth and fourteenth centuries (358, n. 5); the aim of the book, in the largest sense, is to reinstate the Middle Ages as a "thought" era in contemporary philosophy studies, especially in France. It is not a history of ideas per se, but a history of how the thought process itself might have been conceptualized to produce the intellectual *habitus* – a mentality, a posture, a discourse of self-representation and self-evaluation: in short, how medieval academics and their lay counterparts would recognize and articulate the intrinsic characteristics of intellectual identity. It is the process of the "deprofessionalizing" of philosophy in the later Middle Ages that de Libera seeks to trace: the university exports an attitude about thinking itself, one that met the aspirations of non-professional social groups, an attitude that passes out of urban universities to be claimed by vernacular cultures.

De Libera's thesis is that while the universities projected a particular *habitus* of the intellectual, they were only an episode in its formation. The discourse of the intellectual was not born of itself within the universities nor even of their rapport with towns. It was a discourse learned, internalized, and adapted from specific sources, that is, the conception of the philosophical life formulated by Arab philosophers, the first medieval inheritors of ancient Greek philosophy. The importation from Arab thinkers of a philosophical ideal allowed its diffusion beyond the university because that ideal was itself the product of a non-university, lay environment: Arab philosophical discourse was produced out of a non-academic (in the Western, institutional sense) intellectual environment. University Aristotelianism in the thirteenth century is a stage of mediation, a processing of a model of philosophical life: it sees the development of an attitude capable of being exported beyond the university because that attitude is itself an import. What comprises that attitude? According to de Libera, it has three facets: a notion of philosophical asceticism; intellectual felicity or happiness (*la félicité mentale, l'idéal de noblesse*); and a form of intellectual detachment or serenity (*liberté de l'esprit*) that took on some resemblance to so-called mysticisms (although the one should not be confused with the other). These notions constitute an ideal of philosophical contemplation, of intellectual ascesis, something that university academics could discover as a kind of benefice ("la bénéfice de plaisir") that the university–church apparatus could not distribute as a career reward (147).

The paradox that de Libera explores is how an ideal unrealizable within academic structures could, by discourse alone, turn itself into a model to be projected out into lay, vernacular cultures. In Dante's *felicità mentale*, de Libera sees one form of the integration of the lessons of intellectual identity; with Meister Eckhart's preaching to lay audiences, that ideal crosses the threshold of heresy, radically overstepping the boundaries of academic institutions and magisterial function. Thus on de Libera's argument, one cannot search only within the university for the realization of a human type projected by the university far beyond itself (351).

On Le Goff's and de Libera's arguments, one does not need a university career to be an intellectual in the Middle Ages: but the formation of the intellectual figure or *habitus* needs the dynamic interaction between the university and its non-professional cultural environment. This is the particularly medieval social and epistemological construction that they trace. The category of intellectual emerges out of something that is both produced by the university and thoroughly detachable or portable from it. What distinguishes that identity or formation is precisely (and only) that it was exportable: for Le Goff, it is a practice of thinking and teaching in an urban environment that reconfigures the social and economic meaning of intellectual work, and that indeed could not survive the economic and demographic vicissitudes of the late fourteenth century that, among other effects, turned university intellectuals into a self-proclaimed elite caste; for de Libera, the university is the site that processes and mediates a "discipline of thought and a model of comportment" (351), an "intellectual ascesis" that can be embodied by university academics but that also implies a certain critical distance from the role of academic functionary and from the system of career reward that is the infrastructure of university professionalism. It is not that the medieval academic needed to choose between functioning within the university and being a critical intellectual (an artificial division and choice that, de Libera suggests, has been enforced upon modern academic–intellectual culture), but rather that the role of the critical intellectual, that *habitus*, is detachable from the university environment that first imported and then projected it, even if it remains always connected with university cultures. This insight is not to be confused with the modern question of the "autonomy" of intellectuals: in fact, de Libera warns against imposing notions of intellectual "disinterestedness," so much associated with Julien Benda's denunciations of the "trahison des clercs," onto the Middle Ages. The critical intellectual of the Middle Ages is not autonomous of political or institutional structure and even interest; rather, the role of critical intellectual is transferable, movable among social and political contexts and interests. It is not a "natural" *habitus* of the university academic: it is a role, indeed a discipline, that is learned, and thus available for appropriation across social contexts.

I do not propose to take either of these perspectives, Le Goff's or de Libera's, fully on board here. But they represent possibly the two most significant historiographical attempts by medievalists to trace a historically specific discourse for the category of intellectual/s in the Middle Ages. These perspectives, which seek historically specific grounds in medieval culture for the discursive operation of a category that is so much identified with the historical mechanisms of modernity, will certainly always have their detractors, who will object to the broadness or even the conceptual abstraction of the category "intellectual/s." But to locate a medieval formation of the intellectual is certainly not to claim that there is a transhistorical category of the intellectual, any more than inquiries into medieval constructions of "woman," "sex," "childhood," "friendship," or even "work" would imply that a transhistorical sameness adheres to these discursive categories. To reject a historically localized category of the intellectual and to whittle the term away in favor of individual professions will produce micro-categories of *magistri* and *scolares*, lawyers and grammarians, parish priests and artisans, or notaries and other functionaries, but will deny us any mechanism for explaining how these diverse types could have, at certain times and under certain circumstances, performed similar roles and engaged in a common discourse of self-representation.

How then do we understand the particularities of the category "intellectual" for the Lollard movement? The present book is not about the Lollard movement as a whole, and it is not intended only as a contribution to the history of Wycliffism and Lollardy in themselves. It is meant to contribute to our understanding of the representations of intellectuals and the pedagogical imperative in the later Middle Ages, and it turns to Wycliffite writings and Lollard history because this late-medieval textual–social event foregrounds such representations with particular clarity and power. Lollardy constructed itself conspicuously and self-consciously around programs of pedagogical activity, inflecting traditional pedagogical models with new valences in ways unprecedented among other medieval religious heterodox movements. The Lollards also gave a new visibility and new value to the rapport between academic intellectuals and a non-academic community, to the cognizance of intellectual work as a distinctive order of activity, and to the roles of "intellectuals" as mediators of a certain kind of work and *habitus*. As a dissident discourse that emerged out of a university culture, Lollardy commands attention for the ways in which it organized and transmitted its "intellectual projects."

40

These questions can only be apprehended, I propose, within the framework of "exportation," that is, that a certain intellectual project can be both defined within the university environment and exported by it to be appropriated by communities that have no other professional ties with academic culture. My focus here is directed to the particular character of Wycliffite "exports" from the university. Here the historiography on the medieval category of intellectuals can help us to understand the relationship between the Lollard movement and its academic core. Wycliffite–Lollard discourse foregrounds the intellectual rapport – the commerce, the communalities, sometimes even the boundaries – between universities and lay learning, beween the "profession" of teaching and learning and its non-professionalized counterparts, and (to import Gramscian terms here) even between the stratum of the "traditional intellectuals" (those "classless" functionaries of orthodox and established institutions) and the emergent "organic" intellectual strata of other social groups. The intellectual "export" of Wycliffism–Lollardy is not necessarily of the same genre as the critical intellectual posture that de Libera seeks to trace: the Lollard intellectual project would not recognize itself in the general order of "intellectual ascesis" whose progress through Muslim and Western Christian culture Alain de Libera traces.

Rather, the crucial intellectual project articulated and exported by Lollard academics, the project in which they, and some of their non-academic counterparts, come to recognize themselves as critical intellectuals performing a distinctive kind of work, is pedagogy itself. The Lollard movement could be said to raise pedagogy to the status of an exportable intellectual project; and it is with the structure and mechanics of this exportability that my study is concerned. My focus here is directed to those who export, but also to those who embody the process or the effects of the exportation of the "intellectual project" of pedagogy. Pedagogy is both the vehicle of transmission and the substance of what is transported: the pedagogical imperative is the chief product of Wycliffite intellectual labor, and it is also the discourse through which the Lollard movement continues to reproduce itself and its intellectual stratum beyond the university. The university manufactures a teaching technology which in turn both produces academic intellectuals and is itself capable of export: this process can be seen, notably, in the *Glossed Gospel* prologues (discussed in chapter 2), which exploit the resources of traditional university teaching technologies (page layout, keys to glosses, and authoritative commentaries), but restructure those technologies to fulfill a pedagogical purpose that could be directed to the requirements of literacy acquisition. What Wycliffite intellectuals export, in part by means of their teaching technologies, is a pedagogical project that aims to dissolve the boundaries between academic professionals and laity, between Latin and vernacular – in short, that aims to deprofessionalize intellectual identity. In this way, Wycliffite hermeneutics can be only a sub-category of Wycliffite–Lollard pedagogy, for it could have no agenda for exportation and assume no form for distribution were it not part of a more comprehensive pedagogical enterprise. In its particular configuration of the relationship between pedagogy, academics, and intellectuals, the Lollard movement presents a definitive reshaping of earlier hierarchical relationships between the "inner" (literate) and the "outer" (non-literate) circles of heretical groups, such as described by Brian Stock and others.[104]

To account for the structure of intellectual exportations we must also consider the question of individual careers and the extent to which such careers may or may not be representative. But if the Lollard movement genuinely succeeds in dissolving boundaries between academic and non-academic intellectuals, how do we begin to determine what counts as an "intellectual" career? It is telling that the structures of intellectual work as it operates at a great distance from the university environment are not problems addressed extensively in the work of Le Goff and even de Libera, and still less by other historians of intellectual institutions.[105] For these historians the university remains the chief point of reference for discussions even of heresiarchs such as Wyclif or transitional figures such as Meister Eckhart.

But what is most significant about the Wycliffite–Lollard movement in relation to the history of intellectual mentalities, of intellectual "consciousness" and ideology, is its calling into question and its acute foregrounding of institutional assumptions about the links between intellectual formation and the "intellectual project" of pedagogy beyond the university. How, for example, do we negotiate even a rough distinction between academic and non-academic intellectuals in the face of a document like the Lollard Disendowment Bill of 1410, which (among many other possible social improvements) proposes the establishment of fifteen new universities with the proceeds from disendowment of the clergy's temporal holdings, but which has no clear source in academic propaganda, and which indeed purports to be a document presented by the commons?

---

[104] Stock, *The Implications of Literacy.* Among many studies that have reflected the influence of Stock's model of heresy and its textual communities, see for example the following essays from Biller and Hudson, eds., *Heresy and Literacy:* Biller, "Heresy and Literacy: Earlier History of the Theme"; Moore, "Literacy and the Making of Heresy c. 1000–c. 1150"; and Swanson, "Literacy, Heresy, History and Orthodoxy."

[105] See, for example, Verger, *Les Universités au moyen âge*, and Ferruolo, *The Origins of the University: the Schools of Paris and their Critics, 1100–1215*. On the other hand, see most recently Verger, *Les Gens de savoir dans l'Europe de la fin du Moyen Age*, especially chapter 6, "Le monde de la pratique."

> And thus in alle the rewme may men have xv erles, xv m^l knyhtes and squyers moothenne be now sufficyauntly rentyd, and yitt therto xv vnyuersitees and therto xv m^l preestes and clerkes sufficiantly fondon be temperell almesse, yif yt lyke the Kyngand lordes to spenden hem in that vse, and the Kyng to his tresour xx m^l *libri* by yeer.[106]

Many elements of the Disendowment Bill, including the proposal for fifteen universities, are shared with a list of heretical beliefs attributed by their compiler to John Purvey, suggesting that such a group of proposals for the use of resources freed up by disendowment had circulated among Lollard communities for some years before 1410 (the list of Purvey's heresies may date from the last years of the fourteenth century).[107] But Purvey himself has no clear university connections, even though William Thorpe's "Testimony" cites Purvey among Wyclif's circle at Oxford. The posture of the Disendowment Bill can be taken literally, as seeking to express the interests of a non-clerical lay public (the "commons") in the expansion of academic opportunities; it can also be read as a much more deliberately ventriloquist gesture, concealing its own partisan interests and origins under the voice of a fictively general "commons." It can certainly be read as a combination of both.[108] On either reading, or both, it offers the assumption that the university is a focus of particular interest to a lay and non-academic public (the high number of fifteen new universities that could be established would seem to exceed even what might be recognized as in the interests of the king whose potential benefit from disendowment is reflected in other proposals in the bill).[109] It is not in itself surprising that a lay public would find the expansion of universities of some interest: clerical careers were not the only outcomes of a university education, and while Oxford and Cambridge were profoundly tied to the church, there was a certain laicization that began to develop in the fifteenth century.[110] University education could also lead to bureaucratic, political, and legal careers. But fifteen new universities would exceed the needs of a laicization even most broadly understood; and given that university graduates made up only a small fraction of the entire clerical population in pre-Reformation England, it would also seem to exceed the existing

---

[106] Text in Hudson, ed., *Selections from English Wycliffite Writings*, 135–7; quotation at lines 66–70.

[107] The list of Purvey's errors, compiled by Richard Lavenham, is printed in *Fasciculi zizaniorum*, 393 ff. On earlier forms of the proposals of the Disendowment Bill, see Aston, "Caim's Castles: Poverty, Politics, and Disendowment."

[108] See Aston, "Caim's Castles," on the careful construction of the Disendowment Bill.

[109] A full version of the Disendowment Bill, preserved in the *St. Albans Chronicle*, contains the same proposal, but with the wording of five, rather than fifteen, universities. The same proposal found in the list of Purvey's errors, however, gives the figure of fifteen.

[110] See Swanson, "Learning and Livings: University Study and Clerical Careers in Later Medieval England."

requirements of established secular clergy.[111] On any reading, this proposal in the Disendowment Bill is a symbolic gesture, but what set of symbolic relations does it underwrite? I would suggest that it presents one articulation, indeed, even one theorization, of the exportation of the "intellectual project" out of the university. The symbolic relations articulated here are not the foundations of new universities, but the comprehensive social redistribution of the intellectual project of pedagogy and, paradoxically, the dismantling of official institutional regimes that govern the formation of an intellectual caste (a widening of university doors by a factor of fifteen). The very fantasy of fifteen Oxfords and Cambridges is an assault on the symbolic capital that enables the existing institutions to produce and guarantee a traditional intellectual elite.

It is difficult to trace individual Lollard careers because the surviving evidence is often inadequate. For the particular kinds of questions posed here, we would want to consider how individual career trajectories might help to articulate links between university formation and activity beyond the university. The career of the Lollard Peter Payne is one of the very best documented, and we can take it to exemplify one means of historiographical entry into these issues. Peter Payne is well known for his activities both at Oxford and, for the last four decades of his life, in Bohemia.[112] By the time he left England, sometime in 1413–1414, before the Oldcastle uprising, he had embarked on a substantial academic career at Oxford, and had also gained notoriety within Oxford as a strong adherent of Lollardy. It is possible that he was introduced to Wyclif's writings at about 1400 when still in the early years of his studies at Oxford. By 1406 he may have been a regent master; in 1408 he became principal of White Hall, and was principal of St. Edmund Hall by 1410 or 1411 (principals were required to be graduates, and were typically young men continuing their studies, for which the job of principal would provide some financial support). Historians have linked Payne with the visit to Oxford of two Bohemian Hussite students who copied the works of Wyclif to take back to Prague, and have also connected him with the "hoax" of 1406 when a letter endorsing Wyclif was sent to Prague under the seal of the University of Oxford.[113] Whatever Payne's actions in these events, he was called before an Oxford committee in 1410 to discuss heresies and errors on the eucharist, and was finally cited for heresy in 1413, not long after which he left Oxford and went to Prague, where he taught before being admitted as a

[111] See ibid., 95.
[112] The following summary is based on Cook, "Peter Payne, Theologian and Diplomat of the Hussite Revolution." On Payne's Oxford career, see also Emden, *An Oxford Hall in Medieval Times*, 133–61. See also Betts, "Peter Payne in England." [113] The letter is printed in Wilkins, ed., *Concilia* 3: 302.

master at the University of Prague in 1417. From his years at Oxford through his early years in Prague, he produced numbers of theological treatises on subjects close to Wyclif's writings or as expositions of Wyclif's theology. His heterodox beliefs aside, Payne operated squarely within an academic environment, and as one historian has put it, he gained his reputation in Prague as the "Wyclif expert-in-residence."[114] By the early 1420s he became prominent among Hussite theologians, and until the 1440s took a central role in theological, conciliatory, and diplomatic matters of the Hussite revolution.[115] He was an important member of the Prague Consistory (a kind of center coalition of the Hussite movement), and along with considerable and high-level diplomatic services in Bohemia and Poland, he continued to produce expositions, syntheses, and indices of Wyclif's writings. Payne's writings were the most important conduit for the wide promulgation of Wyclif's theology in Hussite Bohemia. But while his orthodox enemies may have regarded him as a popularizer ("Whenever Wyclif is obscure or incomplete," said one, "Payne explains him"), and while he seems to have directed some of his writings to unlearned audiences,[116] Payne was not primarily a popularizing figure. His political and diplomatic reputation rested upon his traditional credentials in theological disputation.

Obviously it is easy to trace the career of a dissident intellectual like Payne, because it took place in those highly visible and high-level public milieux where careful and continuous records are kept, and also because Payne's major activity was in Hussite Bohemia, where his religious heterodoxy came to form part of a political and cultural movement sponsored by powerful social groups. In a certain way, Payne's career is too easy to diagnose: in its outlines it anticipates models of public intellectual activity that have become familiar in modern political contexts, the academically credentialized theorist of a dissident movement who assumes public responsibilities of diplomatic representation, coalition-building, and relaying of theoretical practice. Payne's career gives us a premodern equivalent of what the left has now come to envision in the (still much contested) role of the "specific intellectual" whose effect as a theorizer lies in engagement in "local, specific struggles." In Payne's devotion to promulgating Wyclif's thought, in the expositions, summaries, and indices of Wyclif's writings that he prepared, it is possible to read the effects of a certain pedagogical imperative, although in a limited sense. Here his service lies in facilitating access to Wyclif's thought: he

[114] The phrase is Cook's, "Peter Payne, Theologian and Diplomat," 98.   [115] See ibid., 120.

[116] Quoted in ibid., 170. Cook also describes one short work by Payne that states "Ut autem persone simplices aliquid . . . valeant in materia de trinitate personarum divinis est notandum." It is possible, according to Cook, that this short work on the Trinity may represent a number of texts that Payne prepared for the benefit of Taborite priests. See Cook, Appendix XI, 389–90.

does not enter into the kind of transformative pedagogy that works to deprofessionalize intellectual identity, that reevaluates the structures of hermeneutical agency or the structural relations of master and student.

But for many other Lollard careers the links between academic and public activity do not readily present themselves. This has been notoriously the case, for example, with John Purvey, whose name was traditionally invoked (both by his contemporaries and by later historians) as a central player in the spread of Lollardy beyond the university, and especially as a key figure in the preparation of the Wycliffite Bible, but of whose actual movements during crucial years the evidence has seemed to dissolve under close scrutiny.[117] Purvey has more recently returned to view through evidence connected with his involvement in the Oldcastle uprising, including evidence of books that he had in his possession at the time. He possessed a sermon cycle, and a number of patristic and later Bible commentaries (pseudo-Chrysostom, Gregory, Bede, and Lyre) much associated with Wycliffite biblical production, especially the *Glossed Gospels*. Such information about his books does add new support to the possibility that he was one of those who were directly and closely involved in the vast textual industry of the Wycliffite Bible and its adjacent productions (sermons, Gospel commentaries, and reference materials). As Maureen Jurkowski suggests, the books in Purvey's possession also point to a link between the intellectual activities of translation and commentary and the large-scale public event of the Oldcastle rebellion, as Purvey clearly seems to have had a considerable role in the latter.[118] Yet none of this evidence allows us to do more than speculate (with more confidence or less) about his actual university connections, which remain strangely obscure.

Such obscurity of university connections is even more the case with Richard Wyche, of whose long career as a dissident preacher we have a good amount of evidence together with the extraordinarily detailed account he has left of his imprisonment and examination for heresy at the hands of Walter Skirlaw, bishop of Durham. But there is virtually no information to connect him with university studies beyond the internal evidence of his letter, in which he shows considerable familiarity with scholastic disputation techniques. For knowledge about careers of those who attended Oxford and Cambridge, historians have generally relied upon records of graduates who obtained benefices (or who had other kinds of traceable careers after taking their degrees). But we do not have the same quality of information for those who left university without taking a degree, among whom could be counted a certain proportion of the secular clergy (remembering also that many more of

---

117 Hudson, "John Purvey: a Reconsideration of the Evidence for his Life and Writings."
118 Jurkowski, "New Light on John Purvey."

the clergy had no university experience at all).[119] If we are to place Wyche at Oxford, it would be on these latter terms, as one of many who entered and left the university environment without completing their studies. Most frustrating in this regard is William Thorpe, for whom external evidence of any career, within or outside the university, scarcely exists at all beyond fragmentary records. Yet the text purporting to be Thorpe's autobiographical testimony provides incomparably rich detail about the processes of intellectual formation, of the self-fashioning of intellectual identity, of the articulation of an intellectual project within an academic circle, and of that project's capacity for exportation beyond the university in the form of a pedagogical imperative (as in Thorpe's verbal motif "all my lore"). Are we to reject the potential for identifying Purvey, Wyche, and Thorpe with an "intellectual project" because we cannot place any one of them with certainty at Oxford? As I have suggested throughout the foregoing discussion, the idea of the "intellectual project" is imbricated with and informed by university culture, but it is not the sole possession of the university, and it is not coterminous with the institutional boundaries of the university.

Does this make the definition of intellectual too wide? We could surely place any well-read, articulate, or theoretically directive person within this definition of intellectual, and a Gramscian perspective would certainly invite us to do so. But this is not a book about all intellectuals. It is about dissenting intellectuals, about those who are formed by – who come into being through – a dissenting movement, who define intellectual identity and the intellectual project in relation to a distinctively articulated project of political and religious dissent, and whose dissent is organized around a pedagogical imperative. It is about those who could be said to initiate that project, about the project itself, and finally about those who could be seen to embody the long-range effects of that initiative. And thus the discussions in this book move from the project of pedagogy itself, as configured around the contested status of the literal sense (chapters 1 and 2), to representations of the pedagogical imperative in the prison narratives of Wyche and Thorpe (chapters 3 and 4), whose individual embodiments of the intellectual project resonate with the collective embodiments recorded in inquisitorial texts.

With respect to the particular formation of dissenting intellectual identities, I wish here to return to a consideration raised earlier: the distinction, so crucial to contemporary debate, between the universal ("autonomous") and the specific ("grounded") intellectual. In a limited sense, this distinction serves as a good heuristic for delineating the concerns of this book. My

---

[119] Swanson, "Learning and Livings," 81, 87, 95.

interest here lies with those who emerge into historical visibility in relation to a specific project, with those who might be called "specific intellectuals," whether in relation to the largest concerns of a social and religious dissenting movement or the more particular effects of a transformative pedagogy. These are not intellectuals whose work is to "diagnose the episteme" while standing "somewhat ahead and to the side" as magisterial spokesmen of the universal. Yet their self-representations, their claims to "specificity," are not without certain profound contradictions, as the questions that can be asked of the William Thorpe narrative, with its nostalgic evocations of a vanished academic community, will suggest.

But in a much more important respect, this distinction imposes an unfortunate caricature on medieval intellectual activity. The very structures of medieval intellectual activity obviate this distinction, as any discerning historical work will reveal: here it is worth remembering that Gramsci's remarks on the Middle Ages are among the most historically sensitive, and that Gramsci is never guilty of imposing such a distinction upon intellectual medieval cultures. The distinction between universal and specific intellectuals, or between "autonomous" and "grounded" intellectuals, is a modern one. As I suggested earlier, the notion of an intellectual "caste" or "aristocracy" or even constituency which exists independent of class and institutional ties, and which is seen to exemplify a "pure pursuit of truth," is one of those inventions (and sometimes myths) of modernity which cannot be imported back to the Middle Ages, and which is imported back only when modernity needs to conceal from itself, needs to explain away, the most troubling ruptures within its own episteme. This becomes obvious, for example, in the historical hollowness of Andrew Ross' invocation of a "medieval clerisy," vestigially present in the modern idea of the intellectual, devoted to the pursuit of truth. This represents – however risible the paradox – the postmodern imaginings of a historical genealogy for something that modernity cannot recognize as its own invention, that there can be an intellectual elite that claims to have no ties to anything other than devotion to truth. Indeed as Le Goff shows so elegantly, this model of the solitary, non-partisan intellectual is entirely a humanist invention, humanism's fiction about itself. In Le Goff's view the emergence of this model signalled the passing of the medieval intellectual, who was tied inextricably and self-consciously to towns, and to the public institutions of church, state, and university, and who wanted to conceive intellectual labor in terms of producing a commodity as concrete as anything produced by hand. No importing of the term "intellectual" to the Middle Ages can work effectively, can serve any useful purpose, if it retains this baggage of modernity. If the notion of intellectual autonomy – such as that envisioned by Julien Benda – is an invention of modernity, the notion of a "medieval clerisy" is also a modern invention. If the modern notion of intellectual political engagement across class and professional interests was born with Zola's *Manifeste des intellectuels*, it was born precisely to contest that lingering humanist (and thus modern) notion of the magisterial, "autonomous" intellectual.

So this book does not seek to draw distinctions between universal and specific intellectuals: that is modernity's problem. Rather, it seeks to distinguish, to bring to the foreground as a historically visible group, those intellectuals who were formed by dissenting movements and who exported or embodied a certain intellectual project, pedagogy. Here we might pause over Jacques Verger's characterization of the medieval university intellectual: "an urban worker," yet also attached to clerical privileges and latinity,

> the intellectual founded his activity on a narrow social base, which in certain cases reduced itself down to the dimensions of a caste, restricting his vision of the world as much as his aptitude for intervening effectively in its affairs . . . Fiercely jealous of his autonomy won after hard-fought struggle, often rootless . . . he did not, however, have an acute enough consciousness of his specific condition to play, in his contemporary society, that critical role that for us moderns represents the quintessence of the intellectual.[120]

This suggests that the university is a "ground" for intellectuals in the sense of restricting their activity and narrowing their scope. It suggests that hard-won academic and institutional autonomies could produce a kind of disengaged, inward-turned caste: not autonomous in the sense of a magisterial or politically disinterested "classless stratum," but rather in the sense of institutionally confined. But as the textual–social event of Lollardy, with its academic origins, demonstrates, the university could also serve as an enabling "ground" in the sense of a foundation for critical activity in the form of exporting intellectual capital. It demonstrates how a quintessentially academic program, the pedagogical imperative expressed in the "obligation to decipher," could transform public political culture.

[120] Verger, "Condition de l'intellectuel," 47–8 (my translation).

PART 1

From pedagogies to hermeneutics: childhood, the literal sense, and the heretical classroom

INTRODUCTION

From antiquity onwards, the literal sense was used as more than a mechanism of hermeneutical distinction. It was used to separate children from adults, childish learning from mature textual apprehension. As such, it was also a measure of discrimination enacted on the bodies of children, and a form of symbolic infantilization enacted on the bodies of certain classes of adults. Pursuing a diachronic genealogy, I consider here how pedagogical discourses of ancient intellectual lineage left their imprint on the most sharply politicized categories of late-medieval culture: from Quintilian, Plutarch, and Macrobius through early- and later-medieval discourses of education to late-fourteenth-century debates in England about lay learning, hermeneutical agency, and the political subject.

Clifford Geertz has remarked that common sense, including notions of the literal sense, "remains more an assumed phenomenon than an analyzed one."[1] To be sure, the hermeneutical tradition of the literal sense, that tendentious, thorny, academic and theological tradition of debate about literal and figurative, or literal and spiritual reading of canonical and sacred texts – a tradition that extends from antiquity, from Middle Platonist and Neoplatonist theologizing of Homer and other poets – has been the object of minute analysis for the history of ideas, especially for the history of hermeneutics.[2] But there is another long tradition of the literal sense that, by comparison, has been so taken for granted, has been so much an assumed phenomenon, that its most powerful manifestations are scarcely remarked. This is the pedagogical tradition of reading according to the "letter" of the text.

[1] Geertz, *Local Knowledge*, 77.
[2] See Lamberton, *Homer the Theologian: Neoplatonist Allegorical Reading and the Growth of the Epic Tradition*; Pépin, *Mythe et allégorie*; Gersh, *Middle Platonism and Neoplatonism: the Latin Tradition*; Dawson, *Allegorical Readers and Cultural Revision in Ancient Alexandria*; Whitman, *Allegory: the Dynamics of an Ancient and Medieval Technique*. For a brief overview of ancient and medieval allegory, see Freytag, *Die Theorie der allegorischen Schriftdeutung*, 15–43.

The pedagogical tradition shares with much of the academic and theological hermeneutical tradition the notion that the literal sense has a preparatory function. Yet, of course, late-medieval hermeneutics from the thirteenth century onwards revalues the literal sense to the degree that in some cases, from Wyclif and Wycliffite writings (notably portions of the General Prologue to the Wycliffite Bible) and beyond, to such a pillar of orthodoxy as Jean Gerson, and to figures as diverse as Savonarola in Italy and Bishop Madrigal in Spain, the domain of the literal sense radically expands to assimilate virtually any avenue of access to the divine author's intention.[3] Under this revaluation, with its roots in Thomistic thought, what is now called the literal sense is no longer merely a preparatory stage, or a point of departure for apprehension of higher or deeper spiritual meanings: it is the very horizon of exegetical endeavor, elevated to primary status as the terminus, the goal of hermeneutical inquiry. Do we see a corresponding change in the pedagogical model of literalism, where the literal sense might accrue new value when it is put to use in the charged contexts of Lollard polemic about universal access to Scripture and, more importantly, of dissenting classroom practice? How do these contexts reveal crucial points of intersection between classroom models of the practicality of literal reading and academic theological models of a literalist hermeneutic?

In broad ideological terms, the literal sense comes to be used as a wedge, a sign of difference, between orthodox and heterodox hermeneutics. But literal reading is also a historical practice, nowhere more palpable than in classrooms. Tracing the trajectory of the pedagogical model of the literal sense – a field still largely unexplored – allows us to see the transformative role of this practice in the social and textual relations of a dissenting community. While I do not wish to divorce the pedagogical tradition from its hermeneutical counterpart, I want to recognize its particular history, so as to understand the role that it can assume – in the later Middle Ages – as the contested political property of hermeneutical agency. Thus I am interested here in what people *did* with the literal sense, or what they thought they were doing with it: for whom it was intended, how it should be used, what kinds of pedagogical values were assigned to it; how it worked within traditional and counter-establishment structures of learning. Here I acknowledge that in many of the

---

[3] On Gerson, see Froehlich, "'Always to Keep the Literal Sense in Holy Scripture Means to Kill One's Soul': the State of Biblical Hermeneutics at the Beginning of the Fifteenth Century" (with reference to Gerson's upholding, on political grounds, a strictly literalist interpretation of Scriptural law [condeming the tenet "semper tenere litteralem sensum in sacra scriptura est occidere animam suam"] at the Council of Constance during the year 1415). For more discussion of this tenet and Gerson's response see below, p. 110, n. 24. On Savonarola and Madrigal, see Minnis, "Fifteenth-Century Versions of Thomistic Literalism: Girolamo Savonarola and Alfonso de Madrigal."

readings that follow I concentrate more on how large systems and discourses exerted power than on how individual practices returned and disputed that power. The reasons for this "long-view" critical approach are that certain discourses of education were handed on to become instrumental in other debates about laity, heresy, and popular reading. In other words, it is important to show how the foundational claims of discourse about the literal sense reiterated themselves over time: and in chapter 1 we will see how ordinary school texts (linking us to classroom practices) tended to reproduce these assumptions. When I turn to consider dissenting communities, what I will be looking at is not simply how practice subverted or disputed discourse, but rather how discourse itself changed, how the governing pedagogical paradigms of a millennium underwent profound transformations. Here indeed is the best evidence for the power of practice.

I want to suggest here how very radical the Lollard heretical "classroom" is for the way that it redeploys the literal sense. This radicalism consists in the effective translation of academic and theological debate about the literal sense into a politically coherent pedagogical tool. In chapter 2 I will consider the evidence of a series of texts – sermons and Gospel commentaries – representing Lollard teaching practices, which point to an inversion of traditional pedagogical paradigms of the literal sense as a state of hermeneutical disenfranchisement. In Lollard teaching, the *pedagogical* practice of the literal sense becomes the locus of individual *hermeneutical* agency, and the pedagogical function assumes a new value as the truly political wedge of a dissenting hermeneutical system.

The arguments of Lollard preachers about clear and open exposition of the scriptural text according to the intellectual receptivities of audiences seem to resonate with medieval pedagogical arguments about the uses of the literal sense; this is why it is important to examine the medieval pedagogical traditions, to see how such arguments are deployed and thus also to see how Lollard educational discourse modifies the tenor of the inherited traditions. Ancient and medieval theories of education identify the literal sense with elementary teaching, with the preliminary stage of reading and acquisition of literacy (and for the Middle Ages, latinity), and thus with childhood itself. But these theoretical traditions are multi-dimensional, and as practices reproduce the institutional hierarchies which they also sustain. In general, progression to "higher" forms of reading (whether the "allegorical" senses of poetry or the "higher" or "deeper" senses of Scripture) is associated with advancement to adulthood in biological, spiritual, intellectual, and professional terms. Of course, it is important to remember that the literal sense in ancient and medieval pedagogy is associated with more than *littera*: as all of the examples will show, it does involve many aspects of the apprehension of meaning.

I said above that I do not wish to divorce the pedagogical tradition from its hermeneutical counterpart. I might refine this to say that I do not wish to exacerbate a divorce that is already there in medieval discourses of learning. For the two systems do part ways, at least in the forms by which they represent themselves: this parting can be traced to the intellectual and political environment of late antiquity, as we will see in chapter 1. This epistemological division has important consequences for the crisis of the literal sense in the later Middle Ages, especially in the fourteenth and fifteenth centuries. It explains the seeming illogic, the sometimes hysterical incoherence of late-medieval polemic about the use of the literal sense, where the debating parties do not seem to mean the same thing by what they name as "sensus litteralis" or "naked text," or even "plain sense" or "common reason." It also explains why the literal sense seems to be one thing in the hands of academics, and another thing entirely in the hands of lay people, even though both camps claim that the literal sense is an adequate measure of Scripture's meaning.

Revaluing the literal sense from antiquity to the Middle Ages

It is now a commonplace, certainly a well-grounded one, to speak of the intellectual culture of late antiquity in terms of the devolution from republican political ideology and the constriction, or auto-telism, of many forms of learning that had earlier been integrated in the larger discourses of civic life. There has been much said about the narrowness or fragmentation of grammatical teaching and erudition, and similarly about the narrowed and self-referential scope of rhetorical learning, even as the technical refining of these arts is among the most massive scholarly efforts of the period.[1] We also have the more general picture of philosophy as the retreat into "care of the self," where the private self has become the only stable moral fixture for protection against the vagaries and violence of public political life.[2] Even if some of these observations have been made in the spirit of "humanist" critique of an age of intellectual "decadence" (the term "decadent" appears with some regularity in discussions of late antiquity), they are nonetheless valid as observations about cultures of learning in the Empire, especially after the third century.[3]

Within this large intellectual milieu, the picture that we must trace out is formed around an ideology of "depth" and "surface" in late-antique representations of textual engagement. In the schools and intellectual culture of later antiquity, the grammarian was recognized as the master of textual surface. At Rome during the first century BC through the first century AD, the grammarians established their professional identity as teachers of liberal

---

[1] For the notion of a narrowing of grammatical teaching see, among prominent examples, Marrou, *Saint Augustin et la fin de la culture antique*, 3–157; Kaster, *Guardians of Language*, 11–14, 55–8; Bonner, *Education in Ancient Rome*, 97–111. On rhetoric see also Leff, "The Topics of Argumentative Invention in Latin Rhetorical Theory from Cicero to Boethius."

[2] See notably Foucault, *The History of Sexuality*, vol. 3, *The Care of the Self*, 81–95; and Brown, *Power and Persuasion in Late Antiquity*, 35–70.

[3] See Kaster, *Guardians of Language*, 13: "These grim observations [about late antiquity], the product of a warm humanist ideal or the practical good sense of a technological and democratic society, are all the more piercing because they come from the outside. Their accuracy is rather confirmed than negated by the likelihood that most educated men of late antiquity would have shrugged off such criticisms, if they could have understood them at all . . ."

letters and as authorities on literary language.[4] A fundamental and necessary element of that professional identity was pedantry: an erudition about literary language, linguistic usage, and information gleaned from canonical texts that could be pursued legitimately for its own sake.[5] Pedantry about the surface minutiae of texts might be seen, indeed, as the professional *areté* of the *grammaticus*, the self-assured erudition that distinguished him from the more common schoolmaster who provided functional literacy in the scattered and less prestigious "schools of letters."[6]

Suetonius offers a well-known distinction, predicated upon commonly recognized degrees of pedantry, between men of lesser and greater grammatical expertise: the *litteratus*, or in Greek, *grammatikos*, is to be distinguished from the mere *litterator* (*grammatistes*) by virtue of his consummate knowledge of correct speech and writing and his role as commentator on the poets, while the *litterator* has a much more restricted competence.[7] The inferior category (*litterator* or *grammatistes*) signifies a smaller breadth of expertise, or a lower professional status, *on the same plane of inquiry* as the higher category. The *litteratus* (or, by analogy with Greek, the *grammaticus*) had a broader and not merely functional knowledge of literary culture, but he worked on the same terrain as his inferior counterpart, such that their professional boundaries as teachers were often porous.[8] Even the sniping, satiric portraits of grammarians in Aulus Gellius' *Attic Nights* (middle of the second century AD) do not really question the nature of the grammarian's professional competence. Gellius' contemptuous dismissals of a *semidoctus grammaticus* (15. 9. 6), of *turba grammaticorum novicia* (11. 1. 5), or *isti novicii semidocti* (16. 7. 13) are not condemnations of the scope of grammatical inquiry. Gellius accomplishes two purposes: first, to set the upper intellectual boundary of the grammarian's inquiry, which is to know the rules of language and analyze usages recorded in canonical authors, and to expound the poets with erudite authority, but not to pretend to an intellectual authority beyond the competence of such technical skills; and second, to distinguish between those pedantic professionals who have earned their self-assurance and those who boast of more knowledge than they can demonstrate. It is certainly not the nature of the grammarian's inquiry that Gellius belittles, for he encounters them on their own disciplinary terms, debating them on matters of linguistic usage and grammatical convention. The grammarian might be scorned for

---

[4] Ibid., 51–2.   [5] See in general Marrou, *Saint Augustin et la fin de la culture antique*, 117–24.

[6] Kaster, *Guardians of Language*, 24, 40, 44–7.

[7] Suetonius, *Grammairiens et rhéteurs* (*De grammaticis et rhetoribus*), 4. 2–4. On the problems of historical nomenclature raised by Suetonius, the different values of the terms *litteratus* and *grammaticus* and his analogy with Greek terms, see the editor's explanatory notes, 60–7.

[8] Kaster, *Guardians of Language*, 45. See also Booth, "The Appearance of the *Schola Grammatici*."

his pedantry, but not for the access to linguistic power and cultural prestige that his pedantry bought.[9]

On its own professional terms, then, the grammarian's expertise in the textual surface is a legitimate one. Such affirmation of this aspect of the grammarian's role would have a long history through late antiquity: early Christian theologians, notably Augustine, would proclaim the need in scriptural studies for the grammarian's particular competence in the textual surface, in matters of construing and emending texts.[10] But more telling, however, is the construction of the grammarian's intellectual sphere in contradistinction to that of the philosopher. The grammarian's pedantic engagement with textual surface becomes visible – remarkable – as pedantry and superficiality when it is called upon to mark the intellectual boundary beyond which the philosopher can penetrate. The grammarian is superficial, in pejorative terms, *because* the philosopher is deep. This is a construction that philosophy places upon grammar doubtless on professional grounds, because of certain objects of inquiry common to both disciplines: the study of the same kinds of texts, especially the poets.

There is also another professional opposition involving grammar that is common and highly visible in educational discourse from the Roman Republic and early and high Empire, the rivalry between rhetoricians and grammarians. But this should not be confused with the distinctions between philosophy and grammar, which are of a different order. The construction of rhetoric's superiority over grammar can be correlated with curricular and institutional factors in Roman "secondary" education.[11] The schools of the rhetoricians, which formed the advanced stage of training and occupied the elite position in Roman educational structures, always felt a certain encroachment from the higher levels of the grammatical curriculum. Grammar masters could deliver instruction on certain compositional *technés* which rhetoric masters regarded as their own curricular preserve; Quintilian's complaints on such curricular overlapping are well known. Thus rhetoric teachers continually reaffirmed the special prestige of their instruction by insisting upon a hierarchy of technical competence whereby grammarians would be discouraged from teaching the exercises that rhetoricians claimed as the province of oratorical (advanced) training.

But it is only in the opposition between philosophers and grammarians that we find the crucial theoretical and methodological discourse of depth

---

[9] Kaster, *Guardians of Language*, 55.

[10] See the discussion in Marrou, *Saint Augustin et la fin de la culture antique*, 422–44; more generally, see Irvine, *The Making of Textual Culture*, 118–243.

[11] On the historical and terminological problem of "secondary" schools in Roman antiquity, see Kaster, "Notes on 'Primary' and 'Secondary' Schools in Late Antiquity."

and surface. The professions of philosophy and grammar dealt often with the same materials, producing what were, in effect, different kinds of literary criticism. The schools of the philosophers might fear no encroachment from the *grammatici* in institutional or even curricular terms, for the philosophers, especially in the Greek East, represented the cream of the ancient professoriate, and took advanced students who had been long parted from their grammar masters.[12] But could a grammarian's textual teaching resemble a philosopher's, could a grammarian perform, aspire to, the kind of moral and philosophical "archaeology" of the literary text that could be mistaken for a philosopher's deliberation on the same materials? The surface–depth paradigm served as a powerful methodological (rather than curricular) distinction to enforce professional and intellectual boundaries. Seneca's epistle 108 offers a famous and relatively early (first-century AD) expression of the difference between grammar and philosophy in terms of a methodology, indeed politics, of depth and surface. Seneca compares the outcomes of different professional approaches to the literary text:

> Multum autem ad rem pertinet quo proposito ad quamquam rem accedas . . . in eodem prato bos herbam quaerit, canis leporem, ciconia lacertam. Cum Ciceronis librum de re publica prendit hinc philologus aliquis, hinc grammaticus, hinc philosophiae deditus, alius alio curam suam mittit. Philosophus admiratur contra iustitiam dici tam multa potuisse. Cum ad hanc eandem lectionem philologus accessit, hoc subnotat: duos Romanos reges esse quorum alter patrem non habet, alter matrem. Nam de Servi matre dubitatur; Anci pater nullus, Numae nepos dicitur . . . Eosdem libros cum grammaticus explicuit, primum verba expresse reapse dici a Cicerone, id est re ipsa, in commentarium refert, nec minus sepse, id est se ipse . . . Sed ne et ipse, dum aliud ago, in philologum aut grammaticum delabar, illud admoneo, auditionem philosophorum lectionemque ad propositum beatae vitae trahendam, non ut verba prisca aut ficta captemus et translationes inprobas figurasque dicendi, sed ut profutura praecepta et magnificas voces et animosas quae mox in rem transferantur. Sic ista ediscamus ut quae fuerint verba sint opera. (*Epistulae morales* 108. 24–36)

> (The object which we have in view, after all, makes a great deal of difference to the manner in which we approach any subject . . . In one and the same meadow the ox looks for grass, the dog for a hare and the stork for a lizard. When a [philologist], a [*grammaticus*] and a devotee of philosophy pick up Cicero's book *De republica*, each directs his attention in different directions. The philosopher finds it astonishing that so much could have been said in it

---

12 On professors of philosophy and their students, see Bonner, *Education in Ancient Rome*, 85–7, 157–62; Marrou, *A History of Education in Antiquity*, 206–16 (Hellenistic education) and 253–4 (on Roman study of philosophy).

by way of criticism of justice. The [philologist], coming to the very same reading matter, inserts this sort of footnote: "There are two Roman kings one of whom has no father and another no mother, the mother of Servius being a matter on which there is much uncertainty, and Ancus, the grandson of Numa, having no father on record." . . . When the [*grammaticus*] goes through the same book, the first thing he records in his notebook is Cicero's use of *reapse* for *re ipsa*, and *sepse* likewise for *se ipse* . . . But enough, or before I know where I am I shall be slipping into the scholar's or commentator's shoes myself. My advice is really this: what we hear the philosophers saying and what we find in their writings should be applied in our pursuit of the happy life. We should hunt out the helpful pieces of teaching, and the spirited and noble-minded sayings which are capable of immediate practical applications – not far-fetched or archaic expressions or extravagant metaphors and figures of speech – and learn them so well that words become works.)[13]

Seneca can represent philosophy's depth by acknowledging, in mildly satiric terms, the philologist's and grammarian's proficiency with the textual surface, the matter of historical scholia and linguistic glosses. The superior claims of philosophy rest on a notion of political and moral depth, and therefore on a perceived methodological difference, rather than on judgments of relative professional competence. The grammarian is expert in his own delimited sphere, and in terms of scholarly activity might sometimes, especially in the earlier classical period, see himself as the professional equal of the philosopher.[14]

But several hundred years later the same paradigm of surface and depth can be put to use to express much more than the difference between professional outlooks. Macrobius' *Saturnalia* (early fifth century) brings what is equivalent to the fervor of sacred rite to the philosopher's apprehension of the poetic text, in contrast to what is represented as the grammarian's spiritual obtuseness. Macrobius has one of his speakers in the *Saturnalia*, the orator Symmachus, invoke the surface–depth paradigm as a fixed commonplace by which the man of learning can establish the claims of his own textual acuity by a mere gesture of comparison with the grammarian's self-imposed limitations. In reading Virgil, the grammarians pass over that "wealth of material" with proverbial "dusty feet – as though a grammarian were permitted to understand nothing beyond the meanings of words." The grammarians have set fixed boundaries to their science which they dare not overstep, like religious men who would not transgress into the holy temples of priestesses:

13 Translation from *Seneca: Letters from a Stoic*, trans. Campbell.
14 On this see Booth, "The Appearance of the *Schola Grammatici*," 118, 122; and see also Pfeiffer, *History of Classical Scholarship*, 157.

> sed nos, quos crassa Minerva dedecet, non patiamur abstrusa esse adyta sacripoematis, sed arcanorum sensuum investigato aditu doctorum cultu celebranda praebeamus reclusa penetralia. (*Saturnalia* 1. 24. 13)
>
> (But we, who abjure rude things, shall not allow the inner recesses of this sacred poem to be hidden, but, having searched out the entrance to its arcane meanings, we shall lay open its innermost secrets for the learned to know.)

The vehemence expressed in the *Saturnalia* is a far cry from Seneca's contained satire and almost genial forgiveness of the grammarian's professional biases. In Seneca's text, once the intellectual superiority of philosophy is established, the philosopher and grammarian can co-exist professionally. By contrast, in the late-imperial writings of Macrobius, there is a violent animus against grammarians that seems to carry the weight of more than merely professional distinction. What can be at stake here? Why the almost religious fervor in asserting the philosopher's access to the sacred precincts of textual meaning?

Here we must look to late-antique representations not of the grammarian's art in relation to philosophy, but of philosophy in relation to the grammarian's characteristic milieu, the elementary classroom in the form of the *schola grammatici*, which appeared in Rome by the first century BC.[15] The structure of differentiation according to surface and depth comes to entail philosophy's need to distinguish its own preoccupation with poetic texts from the teaching and reception of the same texts in the *schola grammatici*, where childish apprehension of poetry will be limited to the literal sense, in this context, that is, the textual surface. Indeed, the passage from Macrobius' *Saturnalia* in which Symmachus violently condemns grammarians' specialization has been set up, in a passage immediately preceding, by Symmachus' delivery of a most telling remark, addressed to another character, Evangelus:

> nunc quia cum Marone nobis negotium est, respondeas volo, utrum poetae huius opera instituendis tantum pueris idonea iudices, an alia illis altiora inesse fatearis? videris enim mihi ita adhuc Vergilianos habere versus, qualiter eos magistris praelegentibus canebamus. (*Saturnalia* 1. 24. 5)
>
> (Now that our matter is Virgil, I would like you to tell us whether you think that the works of this poet are fit only for the instruction of boys, or whether

---

15 Booth, "The Appearance of the *Schola Grammatici*," 124. As Booth suggests, the *schola grammatici* did not necessarily represent a more advanced educational level than the *ludus litterarius*, the school conducted by the *litterator* or *magister ludi*, which provided functional literacy to children of lesser social status. Rather it could offer a prestigious "liberal" education to more privileged students who would have begun with private elementary instruction, and in some cases to very young pupils. See also Kaster, "Notes on 'Primary' and 'Secondary' Schools," 329–32, 337–9.

you would allow that they belong to higher purposes? It seems to me that you still regard Virgil's verses just as you did when, as boys, we recited them before our schoolmasters while they lectured on them.)

Can Virgil's poetry be an object of mature, learned, philosophical attention if his poems are also the matter of schoolboys' superficial apprehension? That such a territorial demarcation between childish and mature apprehension of the literary text needs to be made in the philosophical discourse of late antiquity is clear to us from repeated and famous affirmations of it. Here the focus of anxiety about textual surface has been transferred from the grammarian's professional art (a question of methodology) to one of the grammarian's attributes, the ubiquitous institutional sphere of the elementary classroom, where boys apprehend texts through their surface meaning. Thus in late antiquity, the surface–depth paradigm comes into a particular use that was to be long-lived: of fading importance is the distinction between professional approaches (the methods of the grammarian and philosopher), and of a newly magnified importance is the distinction between intellectual childhood and intellectual maturity. As we will see, this newer distinction is expressed through a debasement of the literal sense in its elementary pedagogical role.

In this environment, intellectual maturity represents a precious form of political self-determination. What E. R. Dodds has called late antiquity's "age of anxiety," that period in the Empire from the third century onwards that saw unprecedented political devolution, civil strife, and instability of public life, created the conditions for a new kind of defensiveness within intellectual circles.[16] In the face of invasions and internal political division (much of the latter stemming from unstable imperial successions), and more locally the decline of cities in the western Empire, those prosperous classes which had sustained urban literate cultures also declined.[17] Moreover, the urban curial elites suffered not only new economic pressures, but also certain new political pressures, assaults on the traditional liberties and privileges associated with adult citizenship and with the prestige of curial status, including loss of immunity from public corporal punishment, loss of mobility, the imposition of onerous duties to collect taxes, and even confiscation of their own property should they fail in their assigned duties.[18]

It is not surprising that "the sovereignty that one exercises over oneself"

---

[16] Dodds, *Pagan and Christian in an Age of Anxiety,* especially 3–4. For an overview of the crisis of the third century, see Starr, *The Roman Empire 27 BC–AD 476,* 132–61.

[17] Harris, *Ancient Literacy,* 286–7.

[18] Starr, *The Roman Empire,* 166; Gagé, *Les Classes sociales dans l'empire romain,* 376–83. On judicial flogging as a sign of the diminishment of the privileges of birth and social rank, see Brown, *Power and Persuasion in Late Antiquity,* 30, 50–57, and Ste. Croix, *The Class Struggle in the Ancient Greek World,* 472–3.

becomes one of the most viable responses of the curial classes to the loss of the prerogatives that had been linked with birth and status. These are the social circumstances in which cultural historians trace the intensification of a philosophical and religious "turning inward."[19] But within this very broad current of philosophical response to crisis among the learned of the old elite classes there emerges a more particular theme that is concomitant with the notion of an inward-directed sovereignty: a personal intellectual drive to define the sphere of one's own *political* agency in terms that are independent of birth and class status. In this lies the value placed on achieving a certain kind of political adulthood through the attainment of philosophical insight. In the philosophical literature of this later classical period, we see that a key expression of the drive to assert one's adult intellectual sovereignty is a newly emphatic separation between the elementary learning of children and the mature pursuit of knowledge in adulthood: childhood, and the sphere of elementary pedagogy, comes to stand for political dependency, and intellectual adulthood for political enfranchisement. It should be stressed that this discourse of the philosophers was not about actually educating children: its focus was defining and securing the inalienable properties of adulthood by distinguishing it from childhood. More precisely, philosophical insight, and especially hermeneutical mastery of the deep philosophical truths of texts, must be carefully differentiated from the concerns of the elementary classroom, especially where childish apprehension is associated with the textual surface. This is not so self-evident a point, even though to a modern historian it might seem obvious that elementary learning is distinct from adult philosophical pursuits. Late-antique philosophical discourse used the literal sense to drive a wedge between elementary pedagogical concerns and the hermeneutical interests of intellectual maturity, inserting a division between the two domains that was to be as long-lived in its political consequences as it was actually artificial in its epistemology.

I will be turning to some passages (both well and lesser known) from Neoplatonist writings that exemplify this tendency. But it will be useful to consider first how an earlier period represented the relationship between childish apprehension of textual surface and mature intellectual mastery of textual depth. The outlooks of two early-imperial writers, Quintilian and Plutarch, preserve the remnant norms of republican intellectual ideology. Both writers envision a continuity from elementary pedagogy, including rudimentary appreciation of poetry as story, to the philosophical formation

---

[19] Foucault, *History of Sexuality*, vol. 3, *The Care of the Self*, 85. See also MacMullen, *Roman Social Relations 50 BC to AD 284*, and MacMullen, *Roman Government's Response to Crisis AD 235–337*, 13–24; and Gagé, *Les Classes sociales dans l'empire romain*, 221–47.

of the adult citizen. Both also underscore their conviction in that perceived continuity. Quintilian proposes initiation into the poetic canon as an
intermediate stage in the grammar curriculum, before the pupils can fully
understand the significance of what they are reading:

> Ideoque optime institutum est, ut ab Homero atque Vergilio lectio in-
> ciperet, quanquam ad intelligendas eorum virtutes firmiore iudicio opus est;
> sed huic rei superest tempus, neque enim semel legentur. Interim et sub-
> limitate heroi carminis animus adsurgat et ex magnitudine rerum spiritum
> ducat et optimis imbuatur. Utiles tragoediae, alunt et lyrici; si tamen in his
> non auctores modo sed etiam partes operis elegeris, nam et Graeci licenter
> multa et Horatium nolim in quibusdam interpretari. (*Institutio oratoria* 1.
> 8. 4–6)

> (It is therefore an admirable practice which now prevails, to begin by
> reading Homer and Vergil, although the intelligence needs to be further
> developed for the full appreciation of their merits: but there is plenty of time
> for that since the boy will read them more than once. In the meantime let
> his mind be lifted by the sublimity of heroic verse, inspired by the greatness
> of its theme and imbued with the loftiest sentiments. The reading of tragedy
> also is useful, and lyric poets will provide nourishment for the mind,
> provided not merely the authors be carefully selected, but also the passages
> from their works which are to be read. For the Greek lyric poets are often
> licentious and even in Horace there are passages which I should be unwilling
> to explain to a class.)[20]

The program described here, of elementary literary initiation through partial
comprehension, is probably the most common form that the pedagogy of the
literal sense takes in antiquity and the Middle Ages. But the question of what
the partiality of that understanding should constitute, what the boundaries of
that partiality should be, always remains. For Quintilian, the containment of
understanding at the surface level of poetic fiction presents not just reading
pleasure for the student, but also an opportunity for instruction in points of
grammar and meter, as well as lexemes and tropes (1. 8. 13–16). This model
of elementary instruction through the literal level is most familiar to us
because it continues virtually without interruption into the Middle Ages; we
could cite the example of the twelfth-century Munich glosses on Ovidian
epistles (the *Epistulae ex Ponto* and the *Epistulae heroidum*), associated with
the Benedictine monastery at Tegernsee, which eschew moves towards
allegorization and moralization in favor of syntactical, lexical, and basic

---

[20] Translation from Butler, ed. and trans., *Institutio oratoria*.

mythographic information, unravelling figures of speech and identifying proper names.[21]

Antiquity, however, also polarized this pedagogical model: on the one hand there was the position, familiar from Plato's *Republic* (2. 378), that children should be protected from poetry because they can only grasp the surface meaning, and will fall victim to deceptive fictions because they cannot distinguish the literal from the allegorical;[22] and, on the other hand, the competing notion that children should be introduced to poetry through its story or literal sense, since this is precisely what they *can* grasp. We find the latter position in Quintilian (let the pupils initially take delight in the stories of Homer and Virgil, but also shield them from the licentious matter of the lyric poets). In Plutarch's *De audiendis poetis* (*Moralia* 14–37) we see a certain reconciling of the two positions:

> And so of philosophical discourses it is clear to us that those seemingly not at all philosophical, or even serious, are found more enjoyable by the very young, who present themselves at such lectures as willing and submissive hearers. For in perusing not only Aesop's *Fables*, and *Tales from the Poets*, but even the *Abaris* of Heracleides, the *Lycon* of Ariston, and philosophic doctrines about the soul when these are combined with tales from mythology, they get inspiration as well as pleasure. Wherefore we ought not only to keep the young decorous in the pleasures of eating and drinking, but, even more, in connexion with what they hear and read, by using in moderation, as a relish, that which gives pleasure, we should accustom them to seek what is useful and salutary therein . . . Since, then, it is neither possible, perhaps, nor profitable to debar from poetry a boy as old as my Soclarus and your Cleander now are, let us keep a very close watch over them, in the firm belief that they require oversight in their reading even more than in the streets . . . Similarly also in the art of poetry there is much that is pleasant and nourishing for the mind of a youth, but quite as much that is disturbing and misleading, unless in the hearing of it he have proper oversight . . . For as the mandragora, when it grows beside the vine and imparts its influence to the wine, makes this weigh less heavily on those who drink it, so poetry, by taking up its themes from philosophy and blending them with fable, renders the task of learning light and agreeable for the young. Wherefore poetry should not be avoided by those who are intending to pursue philosophy, but they should use poetry as an introductory exercise in philosophy, by training

---

21 Munich clm 14819 and clm 19480 (*Epistulae ex Ponto*); clm 19475 (*Epistulae heroidum*). See Hexter, *Ovid and Medieval Schooling*, 132–6, 143, and his edition of the *Heroides* glosses, 229–302. These textual glosses are from the same collections in which we find the well-known *accessus ad auctores*: see the collection in Huygens, ed., *Accessus ad auctores*.

22 See, for example, Pépin, *Mythe et allégorie*, 113; Ferrari, "Plato and Poetry," 108–19. Protecting children from lascivious matter was connected also with protecting their sexuality, as Foucault suggests: see *History of Sexuality*, vol. 3, *The Care of the Self*, 190.

themselves habitually to seek the profitable in what gives pleasure, and to find satisfaction therein; and if there be nothing profitable, to combat such poetry and be dissatisfied with it.

In sum, as Plutarch says at the end of his exploration of the uses and dangers of poetic figuration, similitude, and indirection, the young man "may be conveyed by poetry into the realm of philosophy."[23] Whether polarized or reconciled, these views posit a strong relationship between the poetic surface and philosophy, and thus between a pedagogy of the literal sense and a hermeneutics of allegorical reading. As pedagogical faculty, the literal sense is either an obstacle or an avenue to future hermeneutical enfranchisement: but the need to differentiate pedagogies of literal reading from hermeneutical control is also a sign that there is already, in antiquity, a tendency to debase the literal sense in its pedagogical role. In the position exemplified in Plutarch's *Moralia*, where he grants that the faculty of literal understanding can serve an initiatory function, such literalist pleasure in the text will nevertheless yield itself up to the "superior" powers of philosophical understanding and hermeneutical investigation. But even the possibility of reconciling the two opposing pedagogical camps is predicated on a hierarchical valuation of pedagogy and hermeneutics which dictates the eventual supersession of the former function by the latter.

In Quintilian and Plutarch we see how the preparatory function of pedagogies of the literal sense can figure in relation to the desire for hermeneutical enfranchisement. They represent the norms of ancient literary criticism, which could imagine a compatibility of the interests of elementary teaching with those of advanced hermeneutical speculation, and thus could envision a continuity from elementary *pedagogies* of the literal sense to mature hermeneutics and philosophy. The classical model is effectively Aristotelian in its organization, incorporating the idea of learning through physical senses, including pleasure. The self-consciousness of Quintilian and Plutarch in affirming the continuity between the rudimentary pleasure of the literal sense and the philosopher's enlightenment may suggest a certain anxiety for preserving that structure of continuity in a period that is only beginning to see the cultural crisis of philosophy that was to come into its full manifestation in later antiquity. This is only a suggestive undercurrent in first-century writing. In later centuries we see a radical expression of these changes in intellectual ideology.

In late antiquity, the continuities envisioned by Quintilian and Plutarch

[23] Translation from Plutarch, *De audiendis poetis* (or *Quomodo adolescens poetas audire debeat*), in *Moralia*, ed. and trans. Babbitt, 1: 75–81, 197.

seem to give way to representations of a categorical divorce between pedagogical literalism and any kind of hermeneutical inquiry. Let us begin by considering Macrobius' highly influential commentary on the *Dream of Scipio* with its distinctions among kinds of poetic fiction and the attendant distinctions among the kinds of interpretive responses that different forms of fiction require. Chapter 2 of the commentary begins with critics' objections to Cicero's philosophical fictions: "which group it was that, according to Cicero, indulged in superficial criticism, which of them went so far as to put his charges in writing, and finally what reply it is fitting to make to their objections." Citing the Epicurean Colotes' attacks upon Plato's philosophical myths, Macrobius rehearses the familiar argument between poetry and philosophy:

> ait a philosopho fabulam non oportuisse confingi, quoniam nullum figmenti genus veri professoribus conveniret. "cur enim," inquit, "si rerum caelestium notionem, si habitum nos animarum docere voluisti, non simplici et absoluta hoc insinuatione curatum est, sed quaesita persona casusque excogitata novitas, et composita advocati scaena figmenti, ipsam quaerendi veri ianuam mendacio polluerunt?"

> (He [Colotes] insists that philosophers should refrain from using fiction since no kind of fiction has a place with those who profess to tell the truth. "If you wished to impart to us a conception of the heavenly realms and reveal the conditions of souls, why," he asks, "did you not do so in a simple and straightforward manner, instead of defiling the very portals of truth with imaginary character, event, and setting, in a vile imitation of a playwright?")

Macrobius goes on to refute the arguments of such detractors, in a passage that was to become one of the most celebrated pronouncements of late-classical literary theory, a paradigm for later allegorizing of myth:

> nec omnibus fabulis philosophia repugnat, nec omnibus adquiescit; et ut facile secerni possit quae ex his a se abdicet ac velut profana ab ipso vestibulo sacrae disputationis excludat, quae vero etiam saepe ac libenter admittat, divisionum gradibus explicandum est. Fabulae, quarum nomen indicat falsi professionem, aut tantum conciliandae auribus voluptatis, aut adhortationis quoque in bonam frugem gratia repertae sunt. auditum mulcent vel comoediae, quales Menander eiusve imitatores agendas dederunt, vel argumenta fictis casibus amatorum referta, quibus vel multum se Arbiter exercuit vel Apuleium non numquam lusisse miramur. *hoc totum fabularum genus, quod solas aurium delicias profitetur, e sacrario suo in nutricum cunas sapientiae tractatus eliminat.* ex his autem quae ad quandam virtutum speciem intellectum legentis hortantur fit secunda discretio. in quibusdam

enim et argumentum ex ficto locatur et per mendacia ipse relationis ordo contexitur, ut sunt illae Aesopi fabulae elegantia fictionis illustres, at in aliis argumentum quidem fundatur veri soliditate sed haec ipsa veritas per quaedam composita et ficta profertur, et hoc iam vocatur narratio fabulosa, non fabula, ut sunt cerimoniarum sacra, ut Hesiodi et Orphei quae de deorum progenie actuve narrantur, ut mystica Pythagoreorum sensa referuntur. ergo ex hac secunda divisione quam diximus, a philosophiae libris prior species, quae concepta de falso per falsum narratur, aliena est. sequens in aliam rursum discretionem scissa dividitur . . . aut enim contextio narrationis per turpia et indigna numinibus ac monstro similia componitur . . . quod genus totum philosophi nescire malunt – aut sacrarum rerum notio sub pio figmentorum velamine honestis et tecta rebus et vestita nominibus enuntiatur: et hoc est solum figmenti genus quod cautio de divinis rebus philosophantis admittit.

(Philosophy does not discountenance all stories nor does it accept all, and in order to distinguish between what it rejects as unfit to enter its sacred precincts and what it frequently and gladly admits, the points of division must needs be clarified. Fables [*fabulae*] – the very word acknowledges their falsity – serve two purposes: either merely to gratify the ear or to encourage the reader to good works. They delight the ear as do the comedies of Menander and his imitators, or the narratives replete with imaginary doings of lovers in which Petronius Arbiter so freely indulged and with which Apuleius, astonishingly, sometimes amused himself. *This whole category of fables that promise only to gratify the ear a philosophical treatise banishes from its sanctuary to the nurses' cradles.* The other group, those that draw the reader's attention to certain kinds of virtue, are divided into two types. In the first both the setting and plot are fictitious, as in the fables of Aesop, famous for his exquisite imagination. The second rests on a solid foundation of truth, which is treated in a fictitious style. This is called the fabulous narrative [*narratio fabulosa*] to distinguish it from the ordinary fable; examples of it are the performances of sacred rites, the stories of Hesiod and Orpheus that treat of the ancestry and deeds of the gods, and the mystic conceptions of the Pythagoreans. Of the second main group, which we have just mentioned, the first type, with both setting and plot fictitious, is also inappropriate to philosophical treatises. The second type is subdivided . . . Either the presentation of the plot involves matters that are base and unworthy of divinities and are monstrosities of some sort . . . a type which philosophers prefer to disregard altogether;[24] or else a decent and dignified conception of holy truths, with respectable events and characters, is presented beneath a modest veil of allegory. This is the only type of fiction

---

[24] See Whitman, *Allegory*, 95, on Macrobius' contradiction of this in the *Saturnalia*, where he submits such a "monstrous" story (Saturn's castration of Caelus) to philosophical exposition.

approved by the philosopher who is prudent in handling sacred matters.) (Emphasis added)[25]

Here it is not so much the philosopher's *avoidance* of mere literal pleasure in stories that is noteworthy, but the almost violent excision of the *pedagogical* faculty of understanding from any philosophical scheme of inquiry or intellectual progression. "This whole category of fables that promise only to gratify the ear": this is the very model of understanding that classical criticism would deem appropriate to early learning but also envision as continuous with the future philosopher's hermeneutical empowerment. But in Macrobius this category is not only inferior to the philosopher's inquiry, but must be forcibly excluded from the intellectual process. Let it be relegated to "the cradles of nurses." The philosopher's text cannot be contaminated by the surface concerns associated with elementary pedagogy.

This passage from Macrobius is perhaps the best-known expression of late-antique mystification of philosophical lore as that which lies beyond the reach of the uninitiated. But what may be more remarkable about this passage is the way that it implicitly links vulgar misunderstanding of allegory with childish apprehension of the mere textual surface (what promises only to gratify the ear). Macrobius is not alone among late-antique philosophical writers in his use of childhood learning as a thematic subcurrent, a way of marking the difference between hermeneutical discernment and vulgar obtuseness. This is partly a holdover from Plato's discussion, in the *Republic*, of children's incapacity to interpret myth; but whereas Plato's remarks are truly pedagogical in intent (presenting a straightforward consideration of whether young people can handle immoral stories which they might be prone to take literally), Neoplatonist writing seems to put these questions of elementary learning to more complex, ulterior uses, to mark off a sacrosanct territory of philosophical maturity, enlightenment, empowerment.

In his commentary on the *Republic*, Proclus, a Greek Neoplatonist of the fifth century, elaborates Plato's remarks on childhood in ways that – not surprisingly – have more in common with Macrobius than Plato. In effect, Proclus reads Plato allegorically: where Plato (*Republic* 378 a–d) argues that some myths are so dangerous to youths that they must be either heavily restricted or banned outright, Proclus reads this as a justification for the keeping and prizing of such myths because the decoding of the mysteries contained in them is proof of the spiritual elevation of those who can accomplish this:

25 Text in Willis, ed., *Commentarii in somnium Scipionis*, 3, 5–6; translation (slightly modified) from Stahl, *Commentary on the Dream of Scipio*, 83–5. On this passage see Kruger, *Dreaming in the Middle Ages*, 130–2.

Thus if someone among us has shed what was puerile and juvenile in his soul, if he has contained the shapeless energies of the imagination and chosen the intellect as guide for his life, he must then be permitted to enjoy, at every opportunity, the marvels hidden in such myths; if on the other hand he still needs to be educated and refined in his morals, he won't know how to pursue safely the vision of these marvels.[26]

Where Macrobius makes his distinction in terms of the myths that are appropriate to childish as opposed to adult faculties, Proclus is more explicit in focusing on the reader's capacity for discernment of the highest truths concealed in myths. But both drive at the same divorce between childhood and adulthood in terms of an almost unbridgable division between surface and depth.

The implication that learning only the surface meaning is the business of youth is a theme that can also be found outside of strictly philosophical texts. In the *Ethiopica* of Heliodorus, a Greek romance traditionally dated in the fourth century (and sometimes called *Theagenes and Chariclea*), there is an exchange between two characters about how to tell the difference between a true vision of the gods and a mere dream not to be credited as real. The character Kalasiris, who has had such a vision, says that he can know that it was true on the basis of a hint in a passage of Homer's *Iliad* in which Ajax is able to recognize that he had a true vision of the god Poseidon (*Iliad* 13. 71–2): "In the same way that Homer, the wise poet, intimates under an enigma that the vulgar cannot penetrate." When Kalasiris quotes the lines from Homer, the other character, Knemon, responds: "I myself am of that vulgar party, and surely it is to make me feel this that you have recalled those verses to me. It is true that I have been familiar with their surface meaning from the time that I learned to construe the words, but I am ignorant of the theological secrets hidden within the verses."[27] Knemon knows the Homeric verses from his youthful education, but since then he has made no further penetration of the meaning that would allow him to join the ranks of the enlightened, along with his companion Kalasiris. Along similar lines, although with much milder effect, in a spirit that recalls with kindly tolerance the superficial textual gratification of childhood, we can look to a later exposition of the *Ethiopica* known only through a fragment attributed to

---

[26] Translation based on Proclus, *Commentaire sur la République*, notes and French translation by Festugière, 1: 97 (80.25). On this section of Proclus' commentary, see Lamberton, *Homer the Theologian*, 196–7.

[27] Translation based on the French version of Maillon, in Rattenbury and Lumb, eds., *Les Ethiopiques*, 3. 12. 2–3. The explanation of Homer's hint that Kalasiris gives (3. 13. 1–3) is that the wise can recognize the gods by their fixed stares and their gliding movements. See the discussion of this passage of the *Ethiopica* in Lamberton, *Homer the Theologian*, 151.

"Philip the Philosopher." The author has not been identified apart from this fragment, and the text and author are virtually undatable.[28] The narrator "Philip" has been approached by friends to provide a philosophical exposition of "Chariclea's Book" (the *Ethiopica*), to defend it from the charge of being merely youthful trivia. In "Philip's" genial response (prefacing his actual exposition) we see the clear outlines of the late antique division between children's pedagogy and philosophical maturity:

> "That's a strange demand, my friend," I said, "going to winter for spring flowers and to hoary old age for the playthings of childhood. We left these things behind, the milk, as it were, of our infant education, when we reached the philosophic time of life and went on to live in the temples of divine truth. At this point, we have been drawn away from them to the specific forms and language of the philosophy that fits our time of life."[29]

Certainly Neoplatonist hermeneutical inquiry does not exclude consideration of the literal sense: on the contrary, Neoplatonist philosophy and theology infuses the material world with a certain spiritual depth, and its hermeneutics expresses this in an enlarged and enriched treatment of the literal sense.[30] But it remains a very specialized domain of interpretation: in Macrobius and the tradition of non-scriptural poetics, the literal sense is not the "naked text," but is rather associated with the complex operations of the "modest veil of allegory." Nor, of course, does initiation into grammatical study through literal understanding recede or disappear in late-classical pedagogical practice. But that fundamental – if also hierachized – image of continuity between pedagogies of the literal sense and hermeneutics that we saw in Quintilian and Plutarch seems to have faded in later contexts in favor of an image of discontinuity. Indeed, the pedagogical imperative seems to become something of a joke in late-antique Neoplatonist exegesis, its claims upon serious hermeneutical attention represented as comical discordance, as in the ironic self-deprecation of the Fulgentian narrator appealing to his master Virgil:

> Cui ego: Seponas quaeso caperatos optutus, Ausonum uatum clarissime, rancidamque altioris salsuram ingenii iocundioris quolibet mellis sapore dulciscas: nam non illa in tuis operibus quaerimus, in quibus aut Pitagoras modulos aut Eraclitus ignes aut Plato ideas aut Ermes astra aut Crisippus numeros aut endelecias Aristoteles inuersat, nec illa quae aut Dardanus in dinameris aut Battiades in paredris aut Campester in catabolicis infer-

---

[28] Lamberton, *Homer the Theologian*, 148 and note.
[29] Translation by Lamberton, *Homer the Theologian*, 306–7.
[30] See Whitman, *Allegory*, 65, 84–5, 91, 216.

nalibusque cecinerunt, sed tantum illa quaerimus leuia, quae mensualibus stipendiis grammatici distrahunt puerilibus auscultatibus.

(I addressed him thus: "most famed of Italian bards, I beg you cast off your wrinkled frowns and soften the sharp acidity of your lofty mind with a flavor of sweet honey. For I do not seek in your writings what Pythagoras busies himself with in his harmonic numbers, or Heraclitus with his fires, or Plato with his essences, or Hermes with his satyrs, or Chrysippus with his numbers, or Aristotle with his perfect forms; nor am I concerned with what Dardanus sang of powers, or Battiades of demons, or Campester of ghosts and spirits of the lower world. I want only the slight things that schoolmasters expound, for monthly fees, to boyish ears.")[31]

The Neoplatonism of late antiquity, with its particular agenda of dignifying myth and fiction as philosophy and as theology, takes us to the heart of the divorce between pedagogical literalism and hermeneutical inquiry. This is not to suggest that Neoplatonism itself is the point of origin for this epistemological rupture, but rather that it presents an especially vehement expression of late antiquity's sanctification of disciplinary and political boundaries, especially after the third century. In an autocracy where the traditional liberties and privileges of adult citizenship can no longer be guaranteed, the fragile sense of enfranchisement signified by the intellectual adulthood of the philosopher must be carefully differentiated from elementary pursuits and from the quotidian domain of classroom pedantry.

These ancient discourses linking surface and depth with childhood and adulthood as political categories were bequeathed to the Middle Ages and elaborated there under different institutional conditions, both acquiring and confirming new ideological values. Certainly the split, as articulated in late-antique philosophy, between surface and depth, pedagogy and hermeneutics, childhood and adulthood, resonated with scriptural and theological discourses of the literal and allegorical, the exterior and interior senses, and bodily and spiritual understanding.[32] But the pedagogical association with literal reading is a very particular tradition whose history has to be treated, indeed recovered, on its own terms, lest it be overshadowed by and confused with the more familiar theological traditions of giving privilege to spiritual knowledge and textual depth. And this is why, in the foregoing account, I have focused on both educational and philosophical discourses of the literal sense, deliberately viewing them apart from the large and complicated

---

[31] *Expositio Virgilianae continentiae secundum philosophos moralis*, in Fulgentius, *Opera*, ed. Helm, 85–6; translation in Whitbread, trans., *Fulgentius the Mythographer*, 120–1. On reasons for including Fulgentius among Neoplatonist authors, see Gersh, *Middle Platonism and Neoplatonism: the Latin Tradition* 2: 757–65.   [32] On these resonances, see Pépin, *Mythe et allégorie*, part 3, 247–59, 446–74.

tradition of late-antique Christian hermeneutics which so absorbs the educational themes as to make their historical tracks almost invisible. For it bears repeating that the literal sense was not only a hermeneutical tradition, and its "materiality" in the Middle Ages as a practice and as a political issue was not only that of a Christian theology founded on an incarnational mystery: the political materiality of the literal sense lay also in its long-established identification with childhood as both an actual and a symbolic political condition.

But it is useful here to consider briefly – in anticipation of themes that arise in later medieval contexts – how the passage of this ancient paradigm to the Middle Ages was aided by its incorporation into theological imagery about spiritual infancy and adulthood, deriving especially from the scriptural *topos* of milk feeding for new converts to Christ and solid food for the spiritually advanced, for example, in Hebrews 5. 13–14: "Omnes enim, qui lactis est particeps, expers est sermonis iustitiae: parvulus enim est. Perfectorum autem est solidus cibus: eorum, qui pro consuetudine exercitatos habent sensus ad discretionem boni ac mali," which describes spiritual progress in terms of being weaned from milk and taking solid foods (and see 1 Corinthians 3. 2–3, and 1 Peter 2. 2). This scriptural imagery is not specifically about education in a formal sense, or indeed even about how texts are to be understood; and it does not have the sharply hierarchical and polarized cast of late-antique philosophical discourse. But because it traded on traditional imagery of education, it presented certain categories that corresponded with the division between intellectual childhood and adulthood. We find the imagery of milk and meat in many forms and contexts; it might even be seen as the entry point for the Christianization of the idea of literalism as the domain of childhood. Thus, for example, John Scotus Eriugena, in his commentary on the *De caelesti hierarchia* of the Pseudo-Dionysius, can conflate classical and Christian, pedagogical and theological, textual and spiritual in an image that recalls scriptural metaphors of the passage from childhood to adulthood: "Theology, like Poetry, educates us by means of imaginative fictions [*fictis imaginationibus*], adapting sacred Scripture to our intellect, leading our intellect from exterior corporal senses to the perfect knowledge of intelligible realities, as if from imperfect childish understanding [*imperfecta pueritia*] to the maturity of the interior man."[33] Here Eriugena does not use the actual image of milk for infants and solid food for adults, but he draws on that *topos* to link spiritual with educational advancement, and immaturity with surface (exterior) apprehension of texts and realities.

---

[33] Eriugena, *Expositiones super ierarchiam caelestem S. Dionysii, PL* 122: 146. On this passage see Dronke, " 'Theologia veluti quaedam poetria': quelques observations sur la fonction des images poétiques chez Jean Scot."

Antiquity thus produces a number of models of the literal sense as textual surface. First, the professional province of the grammarian is expertise in all aspects of the text's surface, from linguistic construction and verbal meaning to philological and historical information. This was a legitimate professional sphere of literalist engagement which found its medieval afterlife in exegetical calls for close attention to the text of Scripture, from Augustine and Jerome to Roger Bacon in the late Middle Ages. Second, in the Platonic tradition of pedagogical theory, the textual surface poses a risk to children, who cannot properly discern falsehoods and whose cognitive powers cannot take them beyond the surface to achieve more salutary readings of immoral stories; but the opposing view, expressed in the educational thought of Quintilian and Plutarch, is that the appeal of the surface narrative is the very hook to catch children's interest, and that the pleasures of the literal level will convey the child to mature philosophical interest in poetry. Finally, a crucial theme emerges in late antiquity, where philosophers, feeling themselves curiously in competition with grammar school boys for possession of the same kinds of poetic fictions, introduce a qualitative distinction between childish and mature reading, where literal apprehension is debased in its association with childhood, to distinguish it from the hermeneutical depth of the philosopher. This paradigm of surface and depth is not simply a question of giving privilege to the sacred or precious meanings concealed beneath the integument or "veil of allegory," that is, the surface narrative (as Macrobian and other Neoplatonist hermeneutics have usually been read), for it is not only a hermeneutical question. It is also a baldly ideological marker of the difference between political dependency and enfranchisement.

The divorce between pedagogical literalism and hermeneutical mastery of textual depth has a long effect in the Middle Ages, and is traceable among medieval discourses of learning. But the task of finding how it manifests itself is complicated by certain factors. One of these is that medieval pedagogical treatises do not theorize childhood in the overt and extensive way that classical writings on curricular training do: the Middle Ages does not have a Quintilian (or indeed a Plato) who would make explicit links between curricular and cognitive stages of development. For example, the monastic *didascalia* of Hugh of St. Victor and Conrad of Hirsau offer theoretical reflections on curriculum in terms of a hierarchy of authors and the spiritual preparedness of the student, but not in terms of the actual cognitive conditions of childhood; as we will see, these *didascalia* are not concerned with pedagogical order, but with a hermeneutical *ordo legendi*.[34] Conversely, medieval writers who treat

---

[34] For discussion of Hugh of St. Victor and Conrad of Hirsau, see below, pp. 89–97.

extensively of childhood itself, for example, Conrad of Megenberg, are not particularly illuminating about curricular matters: Conrad of Megenberg treats the liberal arts in a highly conventionalized summary fashion.[35] However, what we do find, helpfully, are certain emphatic positionings of literal reading in relation to the elementary curriculum, which gives evidence of the theoretical rationales that underlie pedagogical conventions. Pierre Dubois' plan for education, in his early-fourteenth-century treatise calling for a renewed crusade to Jerusalem, merits particular attention because it is unusual in its linking of curricular progress with a comparatively explicit theory of learning abilities.

We must also remember that in its own elementary pedagogical role the literal sense was by no means devalued: it had a practical application in teaching young students, along the lines laid out by Quintilian, and reflected in virtually all of the evidence we have of medieval elementary instruction in the grammar curriculum. Moreover, children surely benefited from being taught in a way that was perceived as appropriate to their cognitive capacities. Children were not oppressed by instruction through the literal sense, and it is not my intention here to discover medieval traces of the modern *topos* of pedagogy as a form of victimization, in which traditional curricular forms of instruction are regarded (to greater or lesser degrees) as forms of violence perpetrated on children.[36] But when the literal sense is used as a political category, to signify in symbolic terms the province of childhood, it is devalued, especially where it can be used strategically towards another kind of argument. Thus my interest here will be to trace some of the ideological meanings that the literal sense acquired in its association with elementary teaching, associations that, as we will see in chapter 2, could be carried into other social fields.

Another factor that we must keep in mind is the association of surface and depth, childhood and adulthood, with the scriptural *topos* of milk and meat. In these contexts the milk and meat image can be used in ways that appear to be straightforwardly pedagogical, along the lines of Quintilian's advice: "I would urge teachers too, like nurses, to be careful to provide softer food for

---

[35] Conrad of Megenberg, *Yconomica*, book 2/4, chapter 4.

[36] Compare the discussion of this modern *topos* by Enders, "Rhetoric, Coercion, and the Memory of Violence," 37, and the critique of the *topos* by Woods, "Among Men – Not Boys: Histories of Rhetoric and the Exclusion of Pedagogy." In addition to Woods' strong critique of this theme in revisionist approaches to ancient and early modern education, see also the arguments against the modern "horror" at ancient and medieval pedagogy in Carruthers, *The Craft of Thought*, 100–5. The notion of pedagogy as victimization has become commonplace among literary/literacy historians as well as social theorists. Among examples of the former, see Gallop, "The Immoral Teachers," and Jed, "The Scene of Tyranny: Violence and the Humanistic Tradition." Among many examples of the theme among social theorists, where the process of teaching is, inevitably and importantly, connected with processes of ideological indoctrination, see Chomsky, *Language and Politics*, 708.

still undeveloped minds and to suffer them to take their fill of the milk of the more attractive studies" (*Institutio oratoria* 2. 4. 5). But at other times, perhaps more often, the pedagogical associations of the image are intertwined with theological questions of spiritual infancy and maturity, as in St. Anselm's use of the image to describe the degrees of spiritual readiness of oblates to accept a strict monastic discipline.[37] Finally, as we will see, the literal sense comes to be valued as an object of the highest hermeneutical endeavor in study of Scripture, but not in the sense of literal reading in its elementary pedagogical role (nor, by extension, the milk food of spiritual beginners); and here especially the challenge is to understand how exegetical theory established and maintained a distinction between "childish" reading of the letter and reading *ad litteram* as the horizon of mature hermeneutical interest.

What we seek here will not be definitions of the literal sense, but positionings of it. We can begin with examples from the high Middle Ages that suggest how the split between pedagogy and hermeneutics manifests itself in medieval discourses of learning. In the Neoplatonism associated with the twelfth-century cathedral schools we see the persistence of the late-classical divorce between pedagogy and philosophy.[38] Alan of Lille's *Anticlaudianus* is a work of self-conscious elitism representing the high end of teaching the *artes litterarum* and the liberal arts curriculum in the cathedral schools. In the prologue Alan advertises the hermeneutical aspirations and theoretical scope of his book on the perfection of the intellect, offering as much a warning as an invitation to readers:

> Hoc igitur opus fastidire non audeant, qui adhuc vagientes in cunis inferioris disciplinae, nutricum lactantur uberibus. Huic operi derogare non tentent qui altioris scientiae militiam spondent. Huic operi abrogare non praesumant, qui coelum philosophiae vertice pulsant. *In hoc etenim opere, litteralis sensus suavitas puerilem demulcebit auditum;* moralis instructio proficientem imbuet sensum; acutior allegoriae subtilitas perficientem acuet intellectum. *Ab hujus ergo operis arceantur ingressu . . . qui solam sensualitatis assequentes imaginem, rationis non appetunt veritatem, ne sanctum canibus prostitutum sordescat, ne porcorum pedibus conculcata margarita depereat; aut derogatur secretis, si eorum majestas divulgetur indignis.*
>
> Quoniam igitur in hoc opere resultat gratiose syntaxeos regula, dialecticae lepos, maxima oratoriae theseos, communis semita arithmeticae, matheseos paradoxa, musicae melos, axioma geometriae, grammaticae theorema, astronomicae hebdomadis excellentia, theophaniae coelestis

---

[37] Eadmer, *The Life of St. Anselm, Archbishop of Canterbury*, 38–9.

[38] For reconsiderations of Neoplatonism and the cathedral schools, see Häring, "Chartres and Paris Revisited," and Dronke, "New Approaches to the School of Chartres."

emblema, infruniti homines in hoc opus sensus proprios nos impingant, *qui ultra metas sensuum, rationis non extendant curriculum;* qui juxta imaginationis somnia, aut recordantur visa, aut figmentorum artifices commentantur incognita.

(Let those not dare to show disdain for this work who are still wailing in the cradles of the nurses and are being suckled at the breasts of the lower arts [trivium]. Let those not try to detract from this work who are just giving promise of a service in the higher arts [quadrivium]. Let those not presume to undo this work who are beating the doors of heaven with their philosophic heads [Faith/Reason/Prudence, infra 1. 96–107, 6. 14– 28, 7. 150]. *For in this work the sweetness of the literal sense will soothe childish hearing,* the moral instruction will inspire the mind on the road to perfection, the sharper subtlety of the allegory will whet the advanced intellect. *Let those be denied access to this work who pursue only sense-images and do not reach out for the truth that comes from reason, lest what is holy, being set before dogs be soiled, lest the pearl, trampled under the feet of swine be lost, lest the esoteric be impaired if its grandeur is revealed to the unworthy.*

Since there emerge in this work the rules of grammatical syntax, the maxims of dialectical discourse, the accepted ideas of oratorical rhetoric, the wonders of mathematical lore, the melody of music, the principles of geometry, theories about writing, the excellence of the dignity of astronomy, a view of the celestial theophany, let not men without taste thrust their own interpretations on this work, *men who cannot extend the course of reason beyond the bounds of a sense-knowledge,* who, in the wake of dreams of the imagination, either remember what they have seen or, as contrivers of figments, discuss what they have never learned.) (Emphasis added)[39]

This curious invitation both acknowledges and decries the appeal to the senses that lies with the literal sense. The prologue lays out three levels of receptiveness: the literal sense to the ear, the moral sense to the mind or reason, the allegory to the intellect. On the one hand, the recognition of the appeal of the literal sense to boyish ears ("litteralis sensus suavitas puerilem demulcebit auditum"), within a threefold hierarchy of sense and interpretive receptivity (literal, moral, allegorical), might suggest something of a progression from one capacity to the next, on the continuous model of intellectual development that we have seen in Quintilian's pedagogical theory. But on the other hand, as James Simpson shows in his recent exposition of the philosophical questions of form in the *Anticlaudianus,* the very structure of

---

[39] *Anticlaudianus* (prose prologue), text in *PL* 210: 487–8; translation (modified) from Sheridan, trans., *Alan of Lille, Anticlaudianus,* 40–1. Alan's terminology for valuing the sense *behind* the words ("ex quo fiunt verba") over their literal meaning was to achieve notoriety of its own in later centuries, to recur in arguments against heretical appropriation of the literal sense. See discussion below, pp. 109–10.

the poem, its inverted narrative shape, dictates against reading according to its represented action, the literal sense that its words make – in Alan's own terminology from the theological investigations of his *Regulae caelestis iuris,* the "sensum quem faciunt verba." Rather, the poem's "overturning of linguistic procedure" requires that its meaning be discovered through the sense "ex quo fiunt verba," that is, the prior authorial intention or sense from which the words are made.[40] By the internal logic of Alan's poem, the "sweetness of the literal sense" which appeals to the ear leads to no possession of the text's meaning, but rather only of its empty outer form. And indeed in the prologue, the soothing appeal to the ear is quickly equated with the pursuit of sense-images only, with obtuse incapacity for reason, and with the pearls among swine of Matthew 7.6. Does the prologue suggest that the poem assumes the pedagogical function of transforming puerile ears, open only to the limited sensual pleasures of the literal sense, into discriminating intellects? On the contrary, it would seem that the invitation to the "litteralis sensus suavitas" is something of a feint here, for this is precisely what the prologue and the poem eschew as meaningful, the vulgar level of understanding to be excluded from the poem's hermeneutical precincts, as readers are warned away from the deficiencies of this level of reception. It is certainly an understatement when Gervase of Melkley, writing between 1208 and 1216, says that the *Anticlaudianus* "teaches us indirectly more so than directly," even though he does mention it among those texts of the *antiqui* and *moderni* that demonstrate varieties of rhetorical style.[41]

In the *Anticlaudianus*, philosophy conspicuously severs itself from pedagogical literalism. Alan's text may be a rather extreme expression of this among medieval discourses of learning, but this is partly because its artifice lies in its imitation of late-antique Neoplatonist writings. Yet this also suggests the powerful influence of the ancient *topos.* We find a less extreme, but still forceful expression of the ancient paradigm in the work of Alan's older contemporary, William of Conches, who returns to Macrobius' *Commentary on the Dream of Scipio* and tries to recuperate its image of poetry for "children's nurseries," that debased category of puerile "fables that promise only to gratify the ear." William seeks a way to accommodate that category of fables to the precincts of philosophy. On Macrobius' foundational distinction between philosophy's serious concern and merely childish pleasure in superficial stories, William comments:

> *Cunas nutricum* vocat scolas poetarum, quia ut corpora puerorum in cunis lacte nutriuntur, ita animi poetarum edificantur in scolis, vel ita minus

---

[40] Simpson, *Sciences and the Self in Medieval Poetry*, 66–81, especially 67–9; Alan of Lille, *Regulae caelestis iuris*, 136–7 (section XVIII).   [41] Gervais of Melkley, *Ars poetica*, 4, lines 3–4.

77

periti in eis auctoribus, scilicet levioribus sententiis, habent instrui.

(By children's nurseries he means schools of poets: for as the bodies of infants in the cradle are nourished by milk, so minds are nurtured in the schools of poets; or again, so must the less experienced be brought up on the literary authors, that is on matter less heavy [than philosophy].)

Another version of William's commentary on this passage elaborates his reclaiming of Macrobius' "children's nurseries" for high philosophical intentions:

Nutricum cunas vocat auctores, quia ut a nutrice puer in cunis nutritur levioribus cibis, ita discipulus, scilicet in levioribus autoribus sententiis, et causa exercicii, ut levius graviores possit intelligere.

(He [Macrobius] calls the literary authors "children's nurseries": for as the nurse nurtures the infant in the cradle on lighter foods, so is the student nurtured on matter from the lighter authors; this is also for the sake of practice, so that he may more easily understand the heavier ones.) [42]

The surface appeal of mere fables has been so debased by association with the nursery that this whole category has to be reclaimed for legitimate philosophical use. William's justification of fables may at first seem to recall Quintilian's pedagogical program of capturing boys' attention with the superficial pleasures of stories. But William's interpretation of Macrobius' category of fables for the nursery has little to do with children. The children's nurseries have become the "schools of poets" where the intellectual formation of the philosopher takes place; alternatively (in the second version), the children's nurseries are the "literary authors" (the *auctores*) who invite serious consideration and who cannot be consigned to merely surface apprehension of children. The analogy with milk and solid food used in both versions of William's reading serves to distinguish the "lighter foods" of the literary *auctores* from the most advanced matter of philosophy itself; but the entire frame has shifted to the philosopher's training, away from the literalist domain of children.

If these academic texts of the twelfth century suggest how fixed the late-classical model of philosophical "adulthood" has become in the Middle Ages, shaping a discourse of philosophy far beyond the political conditions in which the model first arose, we find this model reinforced at the other end of the educational spectrum, in the way that programs of elementary pedagogy represent engagement with the letter, with meaning at the surface of the text.

[42] Texts and translations of William of Conches' commentary on Macrobius in Dronke, *Fabula*, 68–9 (texts), 17 (translations).

By systematically restricting their purview to a concern with apprehension at the literal level, pedagogical discourses naturalize the identification of the letter or "naked text" with childhood. In terms of practice there is nothing surprising about this identification. But the consistent positioning of literal reading within the domain of elementary pedagogy cemented not only a practical but an ideological equivalence between childhood and the naked text.

From the evidence of elementary grammatical teaching in the twelfth century we have an example of the induction into literacy – *latinitas* – through texts that are deemed to operate *only* at the literal level. The identification of the literal sense with elementary teaching is the rationale for the choice of classical satire, and especially the satires of Horace, as the most effective teaching texts for Latin language acquisition in the high Middle Ages. In elementary Latin instruction in the twelfth century, satire was a preferred genre for teaching Latin – and thus literacy – to young boys because satire was understood to operate at the literal level. Traditional generic classifications of satire, beginning in later antiquity, lay stress upon its etymological association with "naked satyrs," carrying that over – in metaphor – as the hermeneutical "nudity" of satire. As one twelfth-century *accessus* to Horace puts it, satire conveys a simple ethical message of reprehending vice through "naked and open words" ("nudis et apertis verbis").[43] More generally, satire is associated with elementary curricular reading. According to a late-twelfth-century treatise by Alexander Neckham which contains a list of curricular authors, satirists and historians should be introduced to students after they have mastered Donatus, the *Disticha Catonis*, and Theodolus, and before they advance to the *Thebaid* and *Aeneid*: "Deinde satiricos et ystoriographos legat, ut vicia etiam in minori etate addiscat esse fugienda et nobilia gesta [eorum] desideret imitari" ("then he should read the satirists and historians, that at a young age he may learn vices to be avoided and the noble deeds he should want to imitate").[44] Medieval definitions of satire categorize it in opposition to integumental hermeneutics and the corresponding practices of allegorical reading: Conrad of Hirsau says that satire "gets its name from the naked, mocking satyrs, because in this poem depraved morals are stripped of their clothing and mocked"; the commentary on Juvenal attributed to William of Conches explains that satire, like a satyr, is naked, "for there are some writers who cover up [*velant*] their reprehension," but "true

---

[43] Reynolds, *Medieval Reading: Grammar, Rhetoric, and the Classical Text*, 135–49, especially 143–4. For the text of the *accessus* to Horace, which Reynolds quotes and discusses, see Huygens, *Accessus ad auctores*, 52.

[44] From Alexander Neckham, *Sacerdos ad altare accessurus*. The section of the text quoted here is edited by Haskins, "A List of Text-Books fom the Close of the Twelfth Century," 91.

satire consists of naked and open reprehension." This *topos* is still in circulation in the fourteenth century, for example in Guido da Pisa's Dante
commentary, where satire, like the satyr, "is naked and shameless because it
openly criticizes vices."[45] As Suzanne Reynolds shows, satire was thus seen to
be appropriate for beginners because its agreed-upon generic character – the
genre of hermeneutical transparency – obviated elaborate allegorization. The
glosses that teachers would supply on the poem could be directed to those
grammatical questions that arise from the *littera* of the text, or to the moral
lessons of praise and blame that are readily accessible through the naked mode
of satire. Thus twelfth-century glosses on Horace's *Satires* offer little evidence
of allegorizing interest, and overwhelming evidence of the linguistic and basic
rhetorical concerns associated with elementary teaching of the Latin literary
canon.[46] Such a generic choice presents a closed circle. In a sense there can be
no partiality of understanding here because satire is already unclothed: the
practices suggested in the pedagogical discourses of glossing seem to restrict
themselves voluntarily to an order of understanding dictated by theoretical
consensus about the inherent limitations of a genre. Satire's very condition
of nakedness forecloses any manifestation of a reader's hermeneutical
inadequacy.

We find the same marked emphasis on the literal sense of the text in all
other varieties of pedagogical glossing in the high Middle Ages. The works
associated with the two major pedagogical collections of the high and later
Middle Ages, the *Liber catonianis* (known also as the *Sex auctores*) and the
Auctores octo, receive predominantly such literalist glossing (attention to such
matters as the grammatical, narrative, and historical sense of the text, behavioral reinforcement, rhetorical technique, and mythographical information).[47] For example, the various strands of the Aesopic tradition, even the

---

[45] See Minnis, Scott, and Wallace, eds., *Medieval Literary Theory and Criticism*, 116–17, and Reynolds, *Medieval Reading*, 144–6 (from whose citations I have also drawn some of these examples). For Conrad of Hirsau, see Huygens, *Accessus ad auctores*, 76 and Minnis, Scott, and Wallace, eds., *Medieval Literary Theory and Criticism*, 44; for the Juvenal commentary attributed to William of Conches see *Guillume de Conches: Glosae in Iuvenalem*, ed. Wilson, 90–1 and Minnis, Scott, and Wallace, eds., *Medieval Literary Theory and Criticism*, 136–7; and for Guido da Pisa, see Jenaro-MacLennan, *The Trecento Commentaries on the "Divina Commedia" and the "Epistle to Cangrande,"* 26, and Minnis, Scott, and Wallace, eds., *Medieval Literary Theory and Criticism*, 474. Reynolds also cites a Juvenal commentary in Bodleian MS Auct. F. 6. 9 that makes specific reference to the non-integumental character of satire: "et sine integumento Romanorum vicia reprehendit" (*Medieval Reading*, 145).

[46] Reynolds, *Medieval Reading*, 144–8.

[47] On the *Liber catonianis* see Boas, "De Librorum catonianorum atque compositione"; Gillespie, "The Literary Form of Middle English Pastoral Manuals," 66–85. On glosses in the manuscripts of this teaching anthology see Hunt, *Teaching and Learning Latin in 13th-Century England* 1: 59–79, and 2: 3–12 (glosses); Clogan, "Literary Genres in a Medieval Textbook," on the use of these texts as elementary initiation into the study of ethics; and Woods and Copeland, "Classroom and Confession," and references there.

linguistically and formally sophisticated version attributed to Walter of England which would challenge any schoolboy's Latin, are accompanied in codices with this kind of literalist glossing much more consistently than with the elaborate, allegorized apparatuses that were a later, scholarly (although quite influential) imposition on this material.[48] Such literalism is particularly notable in the case of those texts of the *Liber catonianis* that deal with explicit sexual material, Statius' *Achilleid* and Claudian's *De raptu Proserpina.* Marjorie Curry Woods has observed that commentators writing for younger students with the object of making the text intelligible do not censor the sexual content of the poems. Such censorship, usually achieved through allegorized readings of narrative content, is reserved for adult or at least intellectually "mature" audiences.[49] This pattern is even clearer in the teaching of Ovidian texts such as the *Ars amatoria*, where pedagogical glosses betray no squeamishness about sexual material, and indeed walk students through erotic passages with determined attention to lexical and grammatical detail, as in this example from Copenhagen MS 2015 of the twelfth century: at *Ars amatoria* 3. 747, "idest apertis quia nude et aperte. et sine aliqua ambage de coitu loquatur sic," where the gloss underscores its own express literalism through identification with that of Ovid's discourse ("sine aliqua ambage").[50] It is also the attention to the "letter" of the text that serves to distinguish pedagogical glossing from philosophical glossing of texts that are of common interest to both traditions, notably the *Aeneid.*[51]

Pedagogical treatises can also reveal the predilection of teaching practices for using the literal level. As we have seen in the case of satire, the curriculum is organized in such a way that the encounter with texts is segregated according to age. Thus the *Registrum multorum auctorum,* a pedagogical treatise written in 1280 by the German grammar school master Hugh of Trimberg, clearly separates out reading for the youngest pupils from all of the other canonical authors listed.[52] This may seem obvious on the face of it, but

[48] Hervieux, ed., *Les Fabulistes latins depuis le siècle d'Auguste jusqu'à la fin du moyen âge.* See Wheatley, *Mastering Aesop,* 58–96, and appendices 1–5. See also Wright, ed., *The Fables of Walter of England,* an edition of a fifteenth-century Wolfenbüttel codex of the fables accompanied by a full academic apparatus, both literal and allegorical.

[49] Woods and Copeland, "Classroom and Confession," 380–5, and Woods, "Rape and the Pedagogical Rhetoric of Sexual Violence," 64–6.

[50] Quoted from Hexter, *Ovid and Medieval Schooling,* 72; see 72–5 for discussion of this commentary as representative of the erotic explicitness of pedagogical glossing of Ovid. See also Woods, "Rape and the Pedagogical Rhetoric of Sexual Violence," 65. On other examples of literal glossing of Ovid, see Shooner, "Les *Bursarii Ovidianorum* de Guillaume d'Orléans."

[51] See, most recently, Baswell, *Virgil in Medieval England,* 41–83. See also Olson, *The Journey to Wisdom: Self-Education in Patristic and Medieval Literature,* 100–1, on Bernardus Silvestris' commentary on the *Aeneid* and its thematizing of "manhood" as the point when "learning that probes beneath the surface" can begin; in Bernardus' commentary this is represented by books 5 and 6 of the *Aeneid.*

[52] Hugh of Trimberg, *Registrum multorum auctorum,* ed. Langosch.

Hugh of Trimberg's logic has a peculiar force. The treatise is divided into three sections, the first two of which are organized thematically, on the basis of the general fields of knowledge contained in the authors' works listed. First Hugh lists the classical authors who should be read, from histories to poetry and philosophy, along with writings in grammar itself, including works by the "modern" authors Eberhard of Bethune and Alexander of Villa Dei; second, under the study of logic, he lists a panoply of religious writings, ancient and modern, in verse and prose. None of the works in the first two sections are graded according to difficulty or according to the cognitive levels of student readers. But in the third section (lines 648 ff.) he takes up the texts of the *Liber catonianus* and the *Auctores octo*, that is, the *auctores minores* along with other "easy" writings such as the *Lapidarius* of Marbod of Rennes. The rationale for this section is not the kind of science contained in the authors, but the appropriateness of the *minores* to the youngest or least-advanced pupils of the grammar schools: "parvum parva decent" (line 656). Thus where authors are identified with the needs and capacities of the most elementary readers, what matters about them is not their scientific content, the kind of knowledge that they dispense, but rather their positioning as markers of puerile understanding.

Vincent of Beauvais' *De eruditione filiorum nobilium*, written in the 1240s, but so conservative in its orientation and construction that it affords a retrospective view of teaching traditions, revisits ancient conflicts over the pedagogical value of the literal sense: should children be protected from the literal sense (here of pagan fictions), to whose seductions they can only fall victim, or is there utility in learning at the literal level? Vincent's arguments, a tissue of patristic and later Christian as well as classical authorities, fall somewhere between the two poles:

> Sed multum refert, in quibus doctrinis uel in qua doctrine materia erudiantur. At quid enim usque hodie paruulorum sensus et lingue poeticis fabulis ac luxuriosis figmentis imbuuntur? Nam et si doctrina poetica sit utilis quantum ad regulas metricas, inutilis tamen est, immo perniciosa quantum ad fabulas predictas.

> (A matter of some importance is in what doctrines, or through what teaching material, the pupils are to be instructed. For to what ends are the senses and tongues of today's children imbued with poetic stories and sensual fictions? Even if such poetic knowledge is useful in so far as concerns the rules of meter, it is nevertheless useless, indeed pernicious, as far as concerns those poetic fictions.)

Vincent's concerns about the "pernicious" effects of poetic fiction, which echo the concerns of more than a millennium of moralist writings, both classical (Plato and Platonist) and Christian, are of course a good index of the established place of such texts in medieval classrooms.[53] But Vincent locates his concern in the ideological context of grammatical and moral teaching at the literal level. The assumption is that there will be no philosophical allegorizing of the text to come between the aesthetic appeal of the letter and impressionable young minds. Citing Valerius Maximus on immoral fictions, and Isidore of Seville on the vanity of pagan fictions for Christians, Vincent's not unexpected solution (with its precedents, for example, in Bede's study of scriptural tropes) is that Christian writings can provide the requisite poetic materials for literal grammatical and moral study:

> Sunt autem et alii libri metrici eciam antiquissimi, in quibus aeque utiliter, immo multo utilius in arte metrica possent edoceri, verbi gracia libri iuuenci presbiteri de historia quatuor euangeliorum, liber aratoris de actibus apostolorum, liber eciam epygrammatum prosperi, religiosissimi uiri, de dictis beati Augustini . . . In quibus utique possent instrui salubriter et in arte grammatica quantum ad litteram et eciam in fide ac moribus quantum ad ipsam librorum materiam.

> (There are other most ancient poetic books in which the pupils can learn metrical arts just as well or even better, for example, the books of the priest Juvencus on the historical [literal] level of the four evangelists, the book of Arator on the Acts of the Apostles, and of Prosper, a most religious man, the *Epigrammata* from the sayings of the blessed Augustine. In these books, at any rate, the pupils can be instructed in a wholesome way in the art of grammar as pertains to the letter of the text, and moreover in faith and morals as concerns the actual matter of the books.)[54]

The change of material is crucial, not so much because pagan fictions are bad for Christians, but because the matter to be treated in the classroom will only be consumed for its literal sense; it will not be transformed into a different substance through the chemistry of philosophical allegory, and therefore must already be morally nourishing in the raw, *ad litteram*. Conrad of Hirsau, writing a century earlier, makes a nearly identical case in his historical explanation of Sedulius' choice of the Gospels as matter for instructive verse:

> Qui videns suo tempore in disciplinis scolaribus gentilium librorum nenias teri et literas ecclesiasticas prorsus a studentibus negligi, ad communem utilitatem convertens calamum metrice resolvit evangelium, parvulorum primorida sic imbuens, ut infuso veritatis poculo falsitatis amodo non delectarentur absintho.

---

[53] On this point see also Woods, "Rape and the Pedagogical Rhetoric of Sexual Violence," 80, n. 50 (citing Vincent of Beauvais and the reading of this passage by Dagenais, " 'Se usa e se faz': Naturalist Truth in a *Pamphilus* Explicit and the *Libro de buen amor*," 423).

[54] Vincent of Beauvais, *De eruditione filiorum nobilium*, ed. Steiner, 23.

([Sedulius] saw that, in his time, the puerile nonsense of pagan writers was commonly used in teaching in the schools, while ecclesiastical literature was completely neglected by students. So he made his pen serve the common good and turned the Gospels into verse, so instructing the first formative years of children that, having imbibed the draughts of truth, henceforth they would not revel in the poison of falsehood.)[55]

The parameters are set, not by the material itself (for such matter is in other contexts, other environments, infinitely transmutable through the admixture of allegorical exegesis), but by the conditions of practice: the elementary classroom will always be the site of reading *ad litteram*, and that condition determines what should be admitted there.[56]

As all of these historical examples suggest, the literal sense acts as the boundary between a form of enfranchisement and its seeming opposite. It operates within the broad field of what Pierre Bourdieu terms "symbolic power," as a form of action imposing a meaning as legitimate by concealing the (arbitrary) power relationships which are the basis of its force.[57] There is nothing more than the arbitrary, but consensually legitimated, hierarchy of textual depth and surface that really discriminates between hermeneutical adulthood, with its attendant associations of intellectual and political agency, and pedagogical infancy, with its concomitants of dependency and insufficiency. As symbolic power, as sanctioned marker or sign, the hierarchy of allegorical/spiritual and literal senses has the power to act on reality by acting on the representation of reality, the power to produce what it designates, as in the choice of the genre of satire to designate and thereby produce literal readers.[58] It has the power to produce difference by exploiting preexisting differences: biological infancy and adulthood around which the institutional differentiations of learning are organized. By extension it can encompass other premises of difference, to define those who cannot advance beyond intellectual infancy – women, *rustici, vulgari* – and those endowed with reason and hermeneutical perspicacity – men, clergy, *litterati*. Indeed what is fundamental here to the very structure of masculinity is its organization around the difference between childhood and adulthood, which could be said to be more profound in its power to signify dependency and agency – in symbolic and actual terms – than the more visible categories of gender.

That the hierarchy between surface and depth is arbitrary and the more

---

[55] *Dialogus super auctores*, in Huygens, ed., *Accessus ad auctores*, 89–90; trans. from Minnis, Scott, and Wallace, eds., *Medieval Literary Theory and Criticism*, 52.

[56] For a different but related argument about the aesthetic scope of classroom teaching *ad litteram*, see Woods, "In a Nutshell: *Verba* and *Sententia* and Matter and Form in Medieval Composition Theory."

[57] See Bourdieu and Passeron, *Reproduction in Education, Society, and Culture*, 4, 7.

[58] Bourdieu, *Language and Symbolic Power*, 119–21.

successful for occluding the sources of its pedagogical effect is obvious in the fact that it does not matter exactly *what* the literal sense is actually taken to mean: whether it is the sensual, ear-pleasing, nursery-relegated story; or the sensual integumental covering that must be stripped away (but which itself is what we would call the "allegory," as in Fulgentius or Alan of Lille); or even the body of the text itself, an already transparent text or naked meaning (as in the attributes of the genre of satire). What matters is the place that the literal sense designates in the structure of learning. More than a static boundary, however, the literal sense is also associated with what Bourdieu describes as "rites of institution," the passage through progressive levels of discursive mastery linked with ascendance through a hierarchy of institutional power.[59] In academic terms the stages of this passage are always naturalized through the symbolic association with biological "growing up." Thus as all the examples considered above also suggest, philosophical mastery of a text and pedagogy of the literal sense can only matter in relation to each other, a fact which is almost never recognized in scholarly treatments of medieval hermeneutical theory as an autonomous entity. The teaching of reading according to the letter (*litteralis/textualiter*), that is, sounding out the letters themselves, or at the next stage according to its "literal" sense (*sensualiter*), are also inevitably processes of "winnowing out," differentiating between those students who will pass to the "higher" stages of textual mastery associated with hermeneutical control, and those for whom the literal sense is the ceiling of understanding. Paul Gehl has described such a winnowing process in the grammar schools of trecento Florence (which preserve much of the curricular character of earlier monastic schools) in relation to the "transitional function" of Latin readers like the *Distichs of Cato*, which present multi-layered possibilities of reading, where initiation to the text through simultaneous linguistic comprehension and memorization is seen to lay the foundation for more mature, contemplative revisiting of the text's moral dimensions through allegorized commentary.[60] But there is nothing fluid about the "transition" that such readers are intended to facilitate. Initial comprehension through the literal sense is as much a terminus for some as a point of entry for others; and in this context the terminus has a punitive function, enacting a certain kind of symbolic violence on its objects by reinforcing the boundary between pedagogical horizon and hermeneutical ambition.

The literal sense as boundary, however, has much more complex implica-

---

[59] Ibid., 117–26.

[60] Gehl, *A Moral Art: Grammar, Society, and Culture in Trecento Florence*, 31, 116–20. See also Hazelton, "The Christianization of 'Cato': the *Disticha Catonis* in the Light of Late Mediaeval Commentaries," and Black, "The Curriculum of Italian Elementary and Grammar Schools, 1350–1500."

tions for the relations between pedagogy and political power. The boundary does not simply exclude pedagogical knowledges from the circle of political agency: it encloses or contains the objects of pedagogy within the interests of state and other political powers. One extraordinary example of a pedagogy of the literal sense, and one that bears especially on a "politics" of literal reading, is the pamphlet *De recuperatione terre sancte* composed around 1306 by the Norman lawyer and royal advocate Pierre Dubois. In this remarkable political tract Dubois appealed for a new crusade to recover the Holy Land, and offered a program for social and ecclesiastical reform in France to guarantee the success of this enormous military and colonial project. To this end, Dubois devised a scheme for the accelerated education of gifted children (both boys and girls) who would be sent to colonize and convert the East and participate in the recapturing of the Holy Land. From early childhood to early adolescence, for a period of about six years, the boys in particular would undergo a crash course in all the known disciplines, acquiring a smattering of knowledge in everything from grammar and logic to law, medicine, and theology. (Dubois' plan for the girls is somewhat different: he proposes to train them as physicians and marry them off to the Muslim nobility whom they will convert.) For the boys, Dubois' scheme is organized according to a notion of progressive cognitive capacities:

> . . . [instruantur pueri] in Donato, more romano confecto, in accidentibus, declinationibus, et successive in aliis gramaticalibus [sic]. Puer cum audiet librum Cathonis et alios minutos actores, quatuor lectiones habeat in die magnas, prout ingenium poterit sustinere, super quibus non sumpniet . . . declinationes et regimina vocum dicantur eidem primo, postmodum repetat cito super quolibet interrogatus . . . quod cum aliquantulum facere ceperint, semper loquantur latinum, se in hoc omni loco et tempore assuefacientes. Post aliquos minutos actores audiant Bibliam pueriliter ter vel quater in die, de hystoriis ejus et poetriarum tantum per ordinem latinum faciant, quod non scribant nisi rudes . . . Cum totam Bibliam audierint, repetant eam quilibet in die ad minus sexternum unum; similiter de hystoria Sanctorum; et poetarum versus planos tantum modico tempore faciant. Demum cum debebunt audire logicam, in tribus mensibus estatis omnes poetrias audiant; . . . qualibet die per duos doctores sex audiant lectiones, quas fere totas per se possent videre, prestitis hystoriis et figuratis vocabulorum communium. De talibus scripturis ubi non queritur nisi ordinatio et notio figuratorum, potest quilibet juvenis, statim cum incipit proficere tantum, videre et legere sicut de uno romancio.

> (. . . let [the youngest pupils] be instructed in Donatus, to be presented according to the Roman custom, so they will take up the attributes, the

declensions, and the other divisions of grammar in turn. When a boy is hearing the book of Cato and other minor authors he should have four long lessons a day, or as much as his natural capacity can stand; let him not go to sleep over these . . . The declensions and the rules of accent should be read to him first; afterwards let him promptly repeat whatever he is asked for . . .

When the boys have begun to make a little progress in this let them always speak Latin, accustoming themselves to this at all times and places. After some minor authors, let them hear the Bible in elementary form three or four times a day, doing their Latin composition only from its historians and poets in turn since they would write it but rudely . . . When they have heard the whole Bible let them all repeat daily at least one sexternum; likewise with stories of the saints. Of the poets let them make simple verses, but only for a short time. When at length they are about ready to study logic, let them hear all the poetical works during the three summer months . . . Let them hear six lessons every day from two teachers; they should be able to understand these by themselves almost entire, since the stories and illustrations will be set forth in familiar words. Where nothing is sought from such writings except sentence structure and acquaintance with figures of speech, any youth, as soon as he begins to make a little progress, can read and understand them as readily as a romance . . .)

Beginning around the age of eleven, the pupils progress to more specialized study in the art of grammar; while the material is somewhat advanced, we are reminded that these exceptional students are yet small boys:

Inter que premissa, pueri, prout eorum doctores viderint expedire, Doctrinale audiant, quatinus attinet ad declinationes nominum et verborum, et ultimo Grecismum, ita quod sensum litteralem breviter comprehendant, in solempnitatibus aliis nullatenus insistentes.

(While pursuing the prescribed subjects, let the boys at the pleasure of their masters hear the *Doctrinale*, in so far as it pertains to the inflection of nouns and verbs, and finally the *Graecismus*, enough to gain a comprehension of its literal meaning but without any insistence on other interpretive formalities.)[61]

Dubois puts his proposed teaching system to radical rhetorical ends, appealing for the grand imperial design of reconquering and colonizing the Holy Land. But his articulation of this radical purpose exposes its own ordinariness with a stunning clarity. Classrooms are always inscribed in greater structures of political power, whether those relations of power are realized in broad

---

[61] Dubois, *De recuperatione terre sancte*, ed. Langlois, 58–60; English translation from Brandt, trans., *The Recovery of the Holy Land*, 126–8. I have altered Brandt's translation at a few key passages. See also Thorndike, "Education in the Middle Ages," 404–5.

territorial terms – a crusade to the empire of the East – or in terms more locally institutional – monastery, cathedral, guild, city – (although certainly broad territorial and local interests are never mutually exclusive). Here and everywhere, teaching according to the literal sense is wrapped inside the design of political mastery into which the children are gradually credentialized and inducted through the process of chronological and academic growing up: but the actual domain of the literal sense is purposefully voided of any potential in itself to create hermeneutical or political agency. This is not to say – and this needs to be reiterated – that the literal level is inherently a state of ignorance or inadequacy, but rather that it is represented as such; my interest here is in tracing the way it is constructed. Dubois' program exemplifies, in local (and here also limited) pedagogical terms, what can be described more broadly as the "pedagogical narrative" of the state as emergent nation:[62] for the objects or recipients of teaching there is inscription in the pedagogical narrative, their presence authorizing this discourse through their objectification as signifiers of a constituted historical moment (here the cultural conditions that are adduced to rationalize a new crusade). The political effectiveness of this pedagogical discourse relies on a double mode of interpellating its objects: both defining them as teachable (so that they can be conscripted for participation in the colonial adventure) and reinforcing the construction of their necessary ignorance as that which limits what they can be taught (so that teaching at the literal level will guard and conserve a certain ignorance – insofar as the literal sense is perceived as a state of ignorance – and thus limit the expression of any knowing and participatory agency upon the ideological design of instruction). "For instruction to be wholly distinct from education," as Antonio Gramsci remarks, "the pupil would have to be pure passivity, a 'mechanical receiver' of abstract notions."[63] There is a powerful political purpose in the teaching that Dubois recommends, but that purpose cannot be articulated through or within the literal sense. In its strong identification with childhood, and indeed with intellectual infancy, the literal sense is understood as a necessary stage of interpretive and political disenfranchisement, a stage preparatory for, but also necessarily discrete from, future building.

Dubois' pedagogical program incorporates literal reading of the historical and poetic books of the Bible. How is this to be understood in relation to contemporary and earlier hermeneutical perspectives on the literal sense of Scripture? Within the pedagogical discourse exemplified so acutely by Dubois' graduated stages of learning, even reading Scripture for its literal

---

62 As in Bhabha's now well-known coinage: see "DissemiNation," 297–9.
63 Gramsci, "In Search of the Educational Principle," *Selections from the Prison Notebooks*, 35.

meaning is not identifiable with hermeneutical study of the literal sense as defined in exegetical *didascalia*. We can see this clearly when we place Dubois' pedagogical norm of reading the literal sense against the models of reading set forth in twelfth-century didascalic guides to scriptural interpretation. It is perhaps easy to confuse the treatments of the literal sense in monastic and especially Victorine writings with elementary pedagogical concerns. After all, Hugh of St. Victor, who gives some of the richest theoretical pronouncements on learning, casts the scriptural *ordo legendi* in terms that might seem identical with those of a pedagogical order. Hugh describes the order of scriptural study, from the historical or literal sense to allegory and tropology, in the inventional terms of constructing a building, from the foundation to the structure to the "clothing" of the building with paint, and then proceeds by analogy to the order of reading:[64]

> Sic nimirum in doctrina fieri oportet, ut videlicet prius historiam discas et rerum gestarum veritatem, a principio repetens usque ad finem quid gestum sit, quando gestum sit, ubi gestum sit, et a quibus gestum sit, diligenter memoriae commendes . . . neque ego te perfecte subtilem posse fieri puto in allegoria, nisi prius fundatus fueris in historia. noli contemnere minima haec. paulatim defluit qui minima contemnit. si primo alphabetum discere contempsisses, nunc inter grammaticos tantum nomen non haberes. scio quosdam esse qui statim philosophari volunt. fabulas pseudoapostolis relinquendas aiunt. quorum scientia formae asini similis est. noli huiusmodi imitari. "Parvis imbutus tentabis grandia tutus." ego tibi affirmare audeo nihil me umquam quod ad eruditionem pertineret contempsisse, sed multa saepe didicisse quae aliis ioco aut deliramento similia viderentur . . . haec autem non tibi replico, ut meam scientiam . . . sed ut ostendam tibi illum incedere aptissime qui incedit ordinate, neque ut quidam, dum magnum saltum facere volunt, praecipitium incidunt . . . si tamen huius vocabuli significatione largius utimur, nullum est inconveniens, ut scilicet historiam esse dicamus, non tantum rerum gestarum narrationem, sed illam primam significationem cuiuslibet narrationis, quae secundum proprietatem verborum exprimitur. secundum quam acceptionem omnes utriusque testamenti libros eo ordine quo supra enumerati sunt ad hanc lectionem secundum litteralem sensum pertinere puto. (*Didascalicon* 6. 3)

> (So too, in fact, must it be in your instruction. First you learn history and diligently commit to memory the truth of the deeds that have been performed, reviewing from beginning to end what has been done, when it has been done, where it has been done, and by whom it has been done . . . Nor do I think that you will be able to become perfectly sensitive to allegory

---

[64] On the building metaphor and its hermeneutical functions in memory teaching, see Carruthers, "The Poet as Master Builder: Composition and Locational Memory in the Middle Ages."

unless you have first been grounded in history. Do not look down upon these least things. The man who looks down on such smallest things slips little by little. If, in the beginning, you had looked down on learning the alphabet, now you would not even find your names listed with those of the grammar students. I know that there are certain fellows who want to play the philosopher right away. They say that stories should be left to pseudo apostles. The knowledge of these fellows is like that of an ass. Don't imitate persons of this kind. "Once grounded in things small, you may safely strive for all." I dare to affirm before you that I myself never looked down on anything which had to do with education, but that I often learned many things which seemed to others to be a sort of joke or just nonsense . . . But I do not reveal these things to you in order to parade my knowledge . . . but in order to show you that the man who moves along step by step is the one who moves along best, not like some who fall head over heels when they wish to make a great leap ahead . . .

But if we take the meaning of the word more broadly, it is not unfitting that we call by the name "history" not only the recounting of actual deeds but also the first meaning of any narrative which is expressed through the proper signification of words. And in this sense of the word, I think that all the books of either Testament, in the order in which they were listed earlier, belong to this study in their literal meaning.)[65]

The order of reading here is dictated not by the capacities of the reader, but by the order of signification in the text itself. The importance of the literal sense here is not relative to the capacities of readers who will soon outgrow it and pass to other things: its value both within the text and as a principle of hermeneutical inquiry into the text is absolute. Hugh is concerned here with the shape of the text, and with shaping the reader in accord with the demands of the text. The literal sense is not to be recommended because that is "all" that a reader can understand: rather a reader's understanding is to be formed in relation to an absolute structure of the text, with its foundations in historical events or literal narrative, and its elaborate vertical ediface of allegory and tropology. On such interpretive terms, the literal sense will always be a condition of the reader's engagement with the scriptural text; as Mary Carruthers suggests, it will return continually as something like "a mnemonic cue for the reader, a foundation which must then be realized by erecting a mental fabric that uses everything which the 'citadel of faith' tosses up, and then coloring over the whole surface."[66] Thus also Hugh's attention to "small things first" does not represent a pedagogical order, but an *ordo*

---

[65] *Didascalicon*, ed. Buttimer, 113–16; translation from Taylor, *The Didascalicon of Hugh of St. Victor*, 134–7 (I have altered Taylor's translation of the penultimate sentence).
[66] Carruthers, "The Poet as Master Builder," 892.

legendi that is responsible to the intrinsic, meaningful structure of the text.

Indeed, Hugh's pointed interest, in this section of the *Didascalicon* on the literal sense of Scripture, is in restraining over-eager readers from bounding past the literal or historical sense, and in stressing the control that the text must exert over readers when it prepares them to engage its proper order:

> Sicut in virtutibus, ita in scientiis quidam gradus sunt. sed dicis: "multa invenio in historiis, quae nullius videntur esse utilitatis, quare in huiusmodi occupabor?" bene dicis. multa siquidem sunt in scripturis, quae in se considerata nihil expetendum habere videntur, quae tamen si aliis quibus cohaerent comparaveris, et in toto suo trutinare coeperis, necessaria pariter et competentia esse videbis. alia propter se scienda sunt, alia autem, quamvis propter se non videantur nostro labore digna, quia tamen sine ipsis illa enucleate sciri non possunt, nullatenus debent negligenter praeteriri. omnia disce, videbis postea nihil esse superfluum. (*Didascalicon* 6. 3)

> (As in the virtues, so in the sciences, there are certain steps. But, you say, "I find so many things in the histories which seem to be of no utility: why should I be kept busy with this sort of thing?" Well said. There are indeed many things in the Scriptures which, considered in themselves, seem to have nothing worth looking for, but if you look at them in the light of the other things to which they are joined, and if you begin to weigh them in their whole context, you will see that they are as necessary as they are fitting. Some things are to be known for their own sakes, but others, although for their own sakes they do not seem worthy of our labor, nevertheless, because without them the former class of things cannot be known with complete clarity, must by no means be carelessly skipped. Learn everything; you will see afterwards that nothing is superfluous.)[67]

While this is certainly an articulation of pedagogical goals, Hugh's statement seeks to have nothing in common with the pedagogical discourses of the literal sense that I have been considering here. Rather, it was offering itself as a directive for educating twelfth-century readers in a new hermeneutic of the literal sense.[68] Even in a text like his *De tribus maximus circumstantiis gestorum*, which sets forth an elaborate memory pedagogy for learning and retaining the Psalter, the focus of elementary teaching (and this is avowedly intended as an elementary program) is the mnemonic system itself, not the scriptural text. The elementary foundations of memory work are made to be identical with the foundational function of the historical level, a literal sense that is secured in place for ever-more complex hermeneutical exposition:

---

[67] *Didascalicon*, ed. Buttimer, 115; trans. Taylor, 137.
[68] On Victorine use of the commentary, as opposed to the gloss, as a method of educating readers in the literal sense, see Häring, "Commentary and Hermeneutics," 190–4.

Multum ergo valet ad memoriam confirmandam ut, cum libros legimus, non solum numerum et ordinem versuum vel sententiarum, sed etiam ipsum colorem et formam simul et situm positionemque litterarum per imaginationem memoriae imprimere studeamus, ubi illud et ubi illud scriptum vidimus, qua parte, quo loco (suppremo, medio, vel imo) constitutum aspeximus, quo colore tractum litterae vel faciem membranae ornatem intuiti sumus . . . Ista quidem omnia puerilia sunt, talia tamen quae pueris prodesse possunt . . . Ista vero omnia praeludio quodam texuimus, pueris puerilia comparantes, ne forte minima haec rudimenta doctrinae spernentes paulatim diffluere incipiamus . . . Sed sunt quaedam fundamenta scientiae, quae si memoriae firmiter impressa fuerint, facile cetera omnia patescunt. Haec tibi in subiecta pagina eo ordine disposita praescribemus quo ipsa volumus animo tuo per memoriam inseri, ut quicquid postea superedificaverimus solidum esse possit.

Divinarum scripturarum expositio omnis secundum triplicem sensum tractatur: historiam, allegoriam, et tropologiam, id est moralitatem. Hystoria est rerum gestarum narratio per primam litterae significationem expressa. Allegoria est cum per factum hystoriae quod in sensu litterae invenitur aliud sive praeteriti sive praesentis sive futuri temporis factum innuitur. Tropologia est cum in eo quod factum audimus, quid nobis sit faciendum agnoscimus . . . Sed nos hystoriam nunc in manibus habemus, quasi fundamentum omnis doctrinae primum in memoria collocandum. Sed quia, ut diximus, memoria brevitate gaudet, gesta autem temporum infinita pene sunt, oportet nos ex omnibus brevem quandam summam colligere quasi fundamentum fundamenti, hoc est, primum fundamentum, quam facile possit animus comprehendere et memoria retinere.

(Therefore it is a great value for fixing a memory-image that when we read books, we study to impress on our memory through our mental-image-forming power not only the number and order of verses or ideas, but at the same time the color, shape, position, and placement of the letters, where we have seen this or that written, in what part, in what location (at the top, the middle, or the bottom) we saw it positioned, in what color we observed the trace of the letter or the ornamented surface of the parchment . . . All these things indeed are rudimentary [*puerile*] in nature, but of a sort beneficial for boys . . .

All these things truly we weave as a kind of prelude [to our learning], bringing together these elementary foundations, lest we, disdaining the least element of our studies, start little by little to ramble incoherently . . . But these are as it were basics for knowledge, which, if they are firmly impressed in your memory, open up all the rest readily. We have written this [list of names, dates, and places] out for you in the following pages, disposed in the order in which we wish them to be implanted in your soul through memory, so that whatever afterwards we build upon it may be firm.

92

> All exposition of divine scripture is drawn forth according to three senses: story [*historia*], allegory, and "tropology," or, the exemplary sense [*moralitas*]. The story is the narrative of actions expressed in the basic meaning of the letter. Allegory is when by means of this event in the story, which we find out about in the literal meaning, another action is beckoned to, belonging either to past or present or future time. Tropology is when in that action which we hear was done, we recognize what we should be doing . . .
>
> But now we have in hand history, as it were the foundation of all knowledge, the first to be laid-out in memory. But because, as we said, the memory delights in brevity, yet the events of history are nearly infinite, it is necessary for us, from among all of that material, to gather together a kind of brief summary – as it were the foundation of a foundation, that is a first foundation, which the soul can most easily comprehend and the memory retain.)[69]

It has been pointed out that Hugh's writings adhere to the confusing Alexandrian terminology in which history, allegory, and tropology refer both to the levels of scriptural meaning and to the three-fold system of scriptural exposition – both what is in Scripture and how Scripture is to be read. But Hugh's actual treatments of the literal sense also clarify the confusion of the double reference: history is "not only the recounting of actual deeds but also the first meaning of any narrative which uses words according to their proper nature" (*Didascalicon* 6. 3, p. 137). So history is either the historical events or the reading of the text at the level of the *sensus litteralis*.[70] Moreover, the memory system of the events of history that Hugh puts into place in the *De tribus maximus* is the foundation of a literal sense that is actually identified with allegory, where an event found *in sensu litterae* "beckons" to another action in past, present, or future time; the same truth is found in both actions (cf. *Didascalicon* 6. 6, p. 145). The fruits of both history and allegory, he says in the *Didascalicon*, are knowledge, whereas tropology concerns virtue (5. 6, p. 127).[71]

Hugh's identification of history with allegory must be seen as part of the hermeneutical elevation and expansion of the literal sense that is an

[69] Hugh of St. Victor, *De tribus maximus circumstantiis gestorum*, text from Green, ed., "Hugo of St. Victor, *De tribus maximus circumstantiis gestorum*," 490–1. Translation from Carruthers, *The Book of Memory*, 264–5. See also Carruthers, ibid., 168–9; and Zinn, "Hugh of St. Victor and the Art of Memory."

[70] See the explanation by Smalley, *The Study of the Bible in the Middle Ages*, 88, which I have closely paraphrased here. The scholarly literature on this is vast; see notably: Pépin, *Mythe et allégorie*, 234–44, 265–392, 497–500; Häring, "Commentary and Hermeneutics," 195–200 and references; Evans, *The Language and Logic of the Bible: the Earlier Middle Ages*, 67–71; Lamberton, *Homer the Theologian*, 44–82; Dawson, *Allegorical Readers*, 249 and references.

[71] Smalley, *The Study of the Bible in the Middle Ages*, 88–9; see also Carruthers, *The Book of Memory*, 168.

overwhelming trend of twelfth-century academic thought about Scripture and one of its most influential theoretical legacies. This new status of the literal sense has to be understood as quite distinct from the tradition of pedagogies of the literal sense. The divorce between pedagogy and hermeneutics, which earlier had been expressed, and elsewhere continued to be expressed, as a divorce between the *literal sense of pedagogy* and the *allegorical/spiritual senses of hermeneutics*, is now fully played out as a divorce between two paradigms and orbits of the *literal sense*, that of the elementary classroom and that of the exegetical master.

In the course of Beryl Smalley's own elegant exposition of this hermeneutical reevaluation of the literal sense there is a small but acute emblem of the institutionally constructed differentiation of these realms – a difference, as she reveals, that is felt as profoundly in modernity as in the Middle Ages. Discussing Hugh's attempt to chart a visual, literal map of Scripture for the memory in the *De arca Noe mystica*, where he represents himself drawing an architect's plan of Noah's ark so as to inscribe tangibly its very dimensions in the soul, she writes:

> He explains the complicated symbolism of the cubit and its colours and then draws a diagram, carefully explaining how it represents the ark.
>
> *Oh yes! we think of the Kindergarten.* We smile when Hugh, with the gravity of one in the forefront of a scientific movement, rejects Origen's figure of the ark as top-heavy, and when he proposes "little compartments", round the outside, for the amphibious beasts. *Our smile is mistaken: a scientific movement is really afoot.* Hugh is doing, for biblical history, what St. Anselm of Bec and Master Anselm had done for theology in their different ways. He is making the letter a proper subject for study, as they had made the content of the Christian faith. He wants to understand the literal meaning of Scripture exactly, so as to visualize the scene. *He had that curiosity which set explorers in quest of El Dorado and led to the discovery of a continent.* (Emphasis added)[72]

Just so: the casual wit of this aside to the reader reproduces the very extremities of differentiation between the merely pedagogical ("we think of the Kindergarten") and the dignity of the hermeneutical ("the forefront of a scientific movement," "making the letter a proper subject for study," the scientific "curiosity" of continental exploration). Such entrenched literalism, such preoccupation with the event, the letter, is dangerously reminiscent of the kindergarten, and so has to be forcefully distinguished from any contaminating associations with the elementary classroom. It is because they are so

---

[72] Smalley, *The Study of the Bible in the Middle Ages*, 96–7.

much the same – what ultimately is the cognitive difference between appreciating the story that a poem tells and mastering the physical dimensions of Noah's ark as described in Genesis? – that they *have* to be so differentiated. The imperative to enforce this differentiation is not Smalley's: it is the voice of a long tradition that is simply speaking itself through her illustrative observation here, and she reveals that that tradition is as much a part of historiography as it is of history itself.

Victorine hermeneutics certainly represents the high end of twelfth-century didascalic interests. But outside this innovative circle, more traditional monastic didascalic writing also bears witness to the pervasive separation of hermeneutical from pedagogical interests in the literal sense. The *Dialogus super auctores* by the German monk Conrad of Hirsau of the Benedictine abbey of Saints Peter and Paul has become an important marker in the new historiography of medieval literary theory, because it presents a detailed survey of curricular authors in terms of conventions of literary analysis.[73] It is a heterogeneous text, deploying pedagogical *topoi* and observing the genres of elementary pedagogical writing (notably the form of dialogue between master and pupil), even as it embraces the most advanced exegetical concerns. Its heterogeneity can make it seem more of an elementary teaching text than it is: as I noted above, monastic *didascalia* are the exception among pedagogical discourses, for they really are hermeneutical expositions in disguise. Unlike such documents as the collections of glosses in the Munich manuscripts associated with Tegernsee Abbey (see above, p. 63), the didascalic surveys are less reflective of actual monastic classroom practice than they are manifestos of intellectual programs. Thus the *Dialogus super auctores* unfolds as an ethical and philosophical exposition of the liberal arts and their relation to signification (words and things, especially of Scripture), cognition, and spiritual knowledge.

Its treatment of the literal sense is its most heterogeneous feature. The pupil in the dialogue is not the recipient of literalist instruction but rather, as in Hugh's *Didascalicon*, serves as a prompt for a theoretical exposition of the *ordo legendi*. This fictionalized pupil, like Hugh's addressee, is inclined to disdain elementary matters and has reversed his curricular progress, studying the *auctores maiores* without attention to the *auctores minores*, which are the objects of elementary analysis. The master's survey of the curricular *minores* who are appropriate fare for beginners (*tirunculi*) – Donatus, Cato, Aesop, Avianus, Sedulius, Juvencus, Prosper, and Theodolus – reiterates the *topos* of

---

[73] Whitbread, "Conrad of Hirsau as Literary Critic"; Tunberg, "Conrad of Hirsau and his Approach to the *Auctores*"; Curtius, *European Literature and the Latin Middle Ages*, 49, 260, 466; and see the comments by Minnis, Scott, and Wallace, eds., *Medieval Literary Theory and Criticism*, 37–9.

nourishing infants with milk and adults with solid food, where milk feeding is identified with reading *ad litteram* and with those authors for whom the literal sense offers sufficient interpretive leverage.[74] But alongside this pedagogical *topos* of the literal sense Conrad introduces a fourfold hermeneutical system (reproduced from one of his sources, Bernard of Utrecht's *Commentum in Theodolum*): explanation *ad litteram* ("quomodo nuda litera intelligenda sit"), *ad sensum, ad allegoriam*, and *ad moralitatem*. Conrad also makes an uncertain gesture towards synthesis of this secular model with fourfold scriptural interpretation, by adding on the mystical senses of tropology and anagogy.[75] And it becomes clear that in the *Dialogus super auctores* pedagogical discourses of the literal sense simply serve as a point of entry for hermeneutical exposition of levels of signification and the hierarchy of the liberal arts. At the end of the survey of authors, having progressed from the *minores* to the *maiores* (who are not subject to elementary analysis), the text turns to consider the ethics of learning and the nature of the sciences for which reading the curricular *auctores* is preparation. Here Conrad presents an unusual classificatory scheme of the liberal arts:[76]

> sub eo sensu, qui est in significatione vocum ad res, continetur sensus historialis, cui famulantur tres scientiae, grammatica, dialectica, rethorica; porro sub eo sensu, qui est in significatione rerum ad facta mistica, continetur allegoria (aliud enim dicitur et aliud intelligitur), et sub eo sensu, qui est in significatione rerum ad facienda mistica, continetur tropologia, et his duobus, id est allegoricae et tropologicae, famulantur arihtmetica [sic], musica, geometria et astronomia et phisica. In caeteris igitur scripturis solae voces significantur, in scriptura divina non solum voces, sed etiam res significativae sunt, quamvis non in omnibus. Sicut igitur in eo sensu, qui inter voces et res versatur, necessaria est cognitio vocum, sic in illo, qui inter res et facta vel facienda mistica constat, necessaria est cognitio rerum; denique vocum cognitio in duobus consideratur, in pronuntiatione et significatione. Pertinet igitur ad solam pronuntiationem grammatica, ad solam significationem pertinet dialectica, ad utrumque simul, pronuntiationem et significationem, rethorica pertinet. Porro rerum cognitio circa duo versatur, id est formam et naturam: forma est in exteriori dispositione, natura in interiori qualitate, sed forma rerum aut in numero consideratur, ad quem pertinet arihtmetica, aut in proportione, ad quam pertinet musica, aut in dimensione ad quam pertinet geometria, aut in motu, ad quem pertinet astronomia; ad interiorem vero naturam phisica spectat.[77]

[74] Huygens, ed., *Accessus ad auctores*, 72, 73, 79, 86, 89–90, 91.
[75] Ibid., 77–8; for Bernard of Utrecht see Huygens, ibid., 160–2, and his introduction, 16.
[76] On Conrad's classification of the sciences, see the excellent discussion in Tunberg, "Conrad of Hirsau," 92–4 (appendix).   [77] Huygens, ed., *Accessus ad auctores*, 123–4.

96

(Under that sense, which consists in utterances signifying things, is contained the historical sense, which is served by three sciences, grammar, dialectic, and rhetoric. Next, under that sense which consists in things signifying mystical facts, is contained the allegorical sense [whereby something is said and something else understood]. And under that sense which consists in things signifying mystical things to come, is contained the tropological sense. And these two senses, that is the allegorical and the tropological, are served by arithmetic, music, geometry, astronomy, and medicine. While in other writings only utterances signify, in divine scripture not only utterances, but the very things are significative, although not in all things [i.e. not in respect of every sense]. Just as, in that sense which moves between utterances and things, knowledge of utterances is necessary, so in that sense which consists in the relations among things and mystical facts or facts to come, knowledge of things is necessary. Now the knowledge of utterances is considered in two ways, in terms of pronunciation and of signification. Grammar pertains only to pronunciation, dialectic pertains only to signification, and rhetoric pertains to both at once, to pronunciation and to signification. In turn, the knowledge of things engages two aspects, that is, form and nature. Form is in exterior disposition, nature in interior quality. The form of things is either considered in terms of number, to which arithmetic pertains, or in terms of proportion, to which music pertains, or in terms of dimension, to which geometry pertains, or in terms of motion, to which astronomy pertains. Medicine, however, looks to interior [human] nature.)

Here the *topos* of milk for infants and solid food for adults has been transmuted into a broad epistemological structure, a hierarchy of the historical/literal sense (*significatio vocum ad res*) served by the language arts of the *trivium,* and the mystical senses of things signified (allegory and tropology) served by the *quadrivium* and *phisica.* All the language arts pertain to the *sensus historialis,* and thus the whole continuum of curricular authors, from *minores* to *maiores,* are constitutive of that significative order of utterances (*voces*) to things. Scripture is to be differentiated from secular writings with respect to the significative power of both words and things; but the secular *auctores* together with the system of the sciences represent the cognitive path to hermeneutical apprehension of Scripture. So once again, as in Hugh's *Didascalicon,* we have a model of an *ordo legendi* that insulates the literal sense in a philosophical scheme at a distance from merely pedagogical interests.

From its association with the legitimate but narrow inquiry of the grammarian in late antiquity, the literal sense as surface apprehension came to be identified with a certain puerile level of understanding which adult readers were expected to leave behind in favor of philosophical or spiritual depth. This paradigm is of course familiar from scriptural metaphors of milk and solid food, spiritual infancy and spiritual adulthood. What has been traced here is how this paradigm became part of the material, institutional context of elementary classrooms and discussions of curricula, and how effectively the dominant philosophical and hermeneutical inquiries separated their domains from the literalism (superficiality or gratification with surface) associated with childish learning. Even the celebrated *ordo legendi* described by Hugh of St. Victor, which bestows so much renewed value on the literal sense of Scripture, represents an innovative endeavor to bring the literal sense into the orbit of advanced scientific inquiry. It is not a revaluation of pedagogical literalism, but rather the instituting of a new and separate track for the literal sense as the object of magisterial exegetical attention. The old system, the old identification of literalism with childhood, remains firmly implanted in medieval discourses of learning, and it is to the long-range political effects of this tradition, its role in discourses of heresy and in programs of popular theological learning, that we now turn.

2

Lollardy and the politics of the literal sense

In his *Art of Preaching*, Alan of Lille employs a familiar dictum:

> Minoribus autem decet in parabolis loqui, majoribus revelare mysteria
> regni Dei. Parvuli liquido cibo sunt nutriendi, adulti solido corroborandi;
> ne parvulus enecetur per solidum, et adultus abominetur liquidum, ut sic
> singula quaeque locum teneant sortita decenter.[1]

> (It is proper to speak to speak to children in parables, and to show to adults
> the mysteries of the kingdom of God. The very young must be nourished
> on liquid food, adults invigorated with solid food, lest the child be stunted
> by solids, and the adult detest liquids. Thus they should each receive the
> kind of thing befitting their condition.)

However commonplace a pastoral statement this may seem, it contains the
very essence of the institutionalized split between pedagogy and hermeneutics. Speaking in "parables," in this particular context, is simply
another version of the digestibility of the letter as story.[2] And the metaphors
of milk food and solid food have become as much a part of pedagogical
discourse about elementary and advanced reading as of pastoral discourse
about spiritual infancy and adulthood. Behind Alan of Lille's dictum lies a
long tradition, the outlines of which I have traced in the preceding chapter. I
want to turn now to explore the dynamics of pedagogical discourse about the
literal sense in the Lollard controversy, to consider where the institutionalized
split between pedagogy and hermeneutics has led, and what it has become.

In the high Middle Ages, as we have seen with Hugh of St. Victor and his
contemporaries, the literal sense gained favor as a hermeneutical principle for
scriptural study. This interest was expanded and elaborated in elite academic
circles in the thirteenth and fourteenth centuries, and eventually became, as is

---

[1] *PL* 210: 184.

[2] And also, as systematized by Aquinas later on, the "parabolic" sense is part of the (human-produced)
literal sense of Scripture. See Copeland, "Rhetoric and the Politics of the Literal Sense: Aquinas, Wyclif,
and the Lollards."

well known, the signature of Wyclif's scriptural hermeneutics. But it also travelled outside of high academic circles, to become the principle proclaimed by vernacular Lollard exegesis. This is the point at which the literal sense becomes politically controversial. Attacks on lay Lollard reading argue that simple lay people will distort Scripture because their horizons are confined to the literal sense.

Academic study of the literal sense of Scripture is, of course, a different enterprise from consideration of the literal sense of pagan poetic writings or other secular fictions: this is precisely because the literal sense of Scripture is seen not as an entertaining or deceptive fiction (as in Macrobian readings of myths), or as merely human-produced tropological language (as in Thomistic accounts of poetic fiction), but as true. As Aquinas and others put it, the literal sense of Scripture is what the divine author intended. So the study of Scripture's literal sense has a powerful prestige because it represents a crucial and foundational hermeneutical activity. But this, perhaps, is why it is the more surprising that there is so much orthodox academic resistance to the idea of lay people reading Scripture at the literal level, indeed that orthodox writers express such *scorn* for the literal sense in the hands of popular or lay readers. If Scripture's literal sense is true, if its apprehension can represent the highest reach of hermeneutical power, how can it turn so readily into an object of contempt or disparagement as soon as it changes hands from the caste of the academic elite to lay readers?

My exploration here takes its departure from an apparently simple question: what was the difference, in the minds of anti-Lollard polemicists, between the academic fashion, that arose in the twelfth century, for reading according to the literal sense, and lay people bringing a literalist reading to the Bible two centuries later? This question has some obvious answers. The resistance to lay "possession" of Scripture's literal sense is often ascribed to orthodox fears of popular reading without priestly or learned mediation and ultimately to fear of Wyclif's own definition of the literal sense as any sense which is apprehended directly, *immediate*.[3] In the minds of Lollard adversaries, lay people have *only* the literal sense. Yet against this, Wycliffite hermeneutics would claim, on the authority of Wyclif and (more tenuously) on the authority of Wyclif's scholastic predecessors, that the literal sense is all that is necessary for any readers, provided that the reader's means of access to the literal sense is properly anchored.[4]

But behind these explanations there are less obvious answers. Here the

---

[3] On Wyclif's notion of *immediate* apprehension of Scripture see Ghosh, "Eliding the Interpreter: John Wyclif and Scriptural Truth," 210.

[4] See ibid.; and see also some relevant discussions in Simpson, "Desire and the Scriptural Text: Will as Reader in *Piers Plowman*."

problem lies not in the literal sense itself or in arguments over its supposedly inherent limitations, but in who uses it, in the meaning it assumes when it is used by one group of people or another. Why is the literal sense invalid or insufficient when used by lay people? As I want to show here, the issue at stake in the definitional instability of "literal sense" as a polemical term is not a hermeneutical contest between literal and spiritual senses. Rather, the issue in its broadest social and political implications is the territorial difference between the high academic practice of hermeneutics and its long-debased opposite, elementary pedagogy. When Lollard adversaries see lay people reading according to the literal sense, what they see is not the literal sense of scriptural truth, associated in positive terms with learned, academic readers, but instead the literal sense of textual surface, long, and often negatively, associated with pedagogical discourses of childhood and elementary learning. On the adversaries' view, in the hands of lay people it becomes a "different" literal sense.

This study of Lollardy and literalism does not seek primarily to address the history of late medieval hermeneutics or the inner workings of Wycliffite hermeneutics. As in chapter 1, my main concern here is not absolute definitions of the literal sense, but rather how it is positioned among competing social discourses. What I consider here is how the "same" literal sense can be prized in one context and debased in another. The discussion that follows starts with the role of the literal sense in academic (university) hermeneutics of the thirteenth and fourteenth centuries, and moves to its role in polemics about Lollardy, and then to its value in Lollard pedagogical thought and practice.

Scholastic interest in the literal sense is the key intellectual development of the thirteenth and fourteenth centuries linking the discourses of high-level academic establishments with their broadest (and ultimately popular) hetero-dox expressions late in the fourteenth century. Within the schools themselves there is a very clear continuity of hermeneutical program from Aquinas and after him Nicholas of Lyre and Richard Fitzralph, who define the domain of the literal sense by locating it in divine authorial intention. There is also a continuity of theory from the earlier figures to Wyclif's vast elaboration of the theological grounds of these arguments, anchoring apprehension of the literal sense in both logic and in revelation, and from there to the appropriation of those principles in such foundational Lollard texts as the General Prologue to the Wycliffite Bible.[5]

---

[5] See the foundational article by Minnis, "'Authorial Intention' and 'Literal Sense' in the Exegetical Theories of Richard Fitzralph and John Wyclif." On Fitzralph see also Walsh, *A Fourteenth-Century Scholar and Primate: Richard Fitzralph in Oxford, Avignon and Armagh*, 35–6, 171–2. On the shifts in

More specifically, within university contexts there are some local continuities among successive generations of literalist commentators. At Oxford in the second half of the thirteenth century, the Dominican master Simon of Hinton and the Franciscan masters John of Wales and Thomas Docking, following in the wake of Grosseteste's attention to the historical sense of Scripture, produced substantial commentaries (some of encyclopedic breadth) focusing on the literal sense and informed by contemporary learning in natural science and history.[6] The exegetical interests of these historicizing masters stood in contrast to the interests of the (more famous) speculative theologians who were their contemporaries, including Robert Kilwardby.[7] In the first half of the fourteenth century another group of scholars associated with Oxford continued some of the literalist exegetical programs of the earlier period. This later group includes the Dominican Thomas Waleys (ca. 1290– ca. 1349), whose commentaries on the Old Testament, the Psalter, and *De civitate Dei* exemplify the naturalist and historical interests that Smalley associates with the larger circle of "classicizing friars" in the early fourteenth century;[8] the Dominican Nicholas Trevet, whose influential commentaries on Boethius and Livy served to bridge the interests of theological exegesis and historical study of *artes* authors (where his influence also carried far beyond the academy);[9] and Trevet's contemporary, the Franciscan William of Nottingham (d. 1336), whose elaborations of the notion of a *duplex sensus litteralis* (which he divided into both "proper" and "figurative") represents perhaps the clearest theoretical link with Parisian masters of literalist exegesis, from the legacy of Thomistic thought to the more contemporary work of Lyre. Taking further Aquinas' system of reading even parabolic language as part of the literal sense (because it is part of what the author intended), William of Nottingham attempts to clarify the formula "littera gesta docet" by noting that the domain of the literal sense includes more than *gesta*:

emphasis from Thomistic thought to Wyclif's position, see Copeland, "Rhetoric and the Politics of the Literal Sense." For a helpful analysis of the Wycliffite–Lollard position in relation to earlier traditions on the literal sense see Nissé, "Reversing Discipline: the *Tretise of Miraclis Pleyinge*, Lollard Exegesis, and the Failure of Representation."

6 Catto, "Theology and Theologians 1220–1320," 483, 492–6, and references there. On John of Wales see Smalley, *The Gospels in the Schools c. 1100–c. 1280*, 213–26.

7 Catto, "Theology and Theologians 1220–1320," 494.

8 Smalley, "Thomas Waleys O.P.," and Smalley, *English Friars and Antiquity in the Early Fourteenth Century*, 75–108.

9 Catto, "Theology and Theologians 1220–1320," 513–16. William Courtenay notes that for the Dominicans of early-fourteenth-century Oxford, including Trevet and Thomas of Waleys, Thomistic theology and philosophy was not a central influence: see his *Schools and Scholars in Fourteenth-Century England*, 180–2. Courtenay does not, however, consider the more specific issues of techniques of literary analysis and hermeneutical program, in which the Thomistic legacy is much more in evidence. On Trevet see the following articles by Dean: "MS Bodl. 292 and the Canon of Nicholas Trevet's Works"; "Culural Relations in the Middle Ages: Nicholas Trevet and Nicholas of Prato"; "The Dedication of Nicholas Trevet's Commentary on Boethius."

> Loquendo tamen de sensu isto qui precise dividitur contra sensum mis-
> ticum, prout etiam nunc loquimur, secundum communem modum
> loquendi, indifferenter litteralis, historicus seu hystorialis, qui nichil aliud
> est quam rerum gestarum vel figuratarum explicatio, que vel exprima littere
> significatione vel ex prima loquentis intentione consurgit.[10]

(In speaking of that sense – which is distinguished sharply from the mystical
sense – we speak just as we do now, according to common usage, calling it
either literal, historical, or historial. It is nothing more than the exposition
of events or figurations; it is either expressed by literal signification [i.e. by
the letter], or arises from the primary intention of the speaker.)

And late into the fourteenth century, even among those polemicists who
engaged directly with Wyclif's writings, such as the Franciscan William
Woodford, as well as those whose engagement was more indirect, such as
Richard Ullerston, there is no diminution of regard for the literal sense as a
privileged hermeneutical category.[11]

But on the other hand, there is little or no continuity between scholastic
hermeneutical interest in the literal sense and practical considerations of the
literal sense as a tool of preaching and pedagogy, such as we see articulated in
the sermon of the preacher William Taylor (see above, p. 2), who notes that it
is not useful to dwell on "subtleties" when preaching to lay people. Indeed,
we can say that there was an epistemological gap between newly fashionable
scholastic and more traditional (elementary) pedagogical approaches to the
literal sense.

Orthodox schoolmen did have a response, of sorts, to the idea that lay
people would approach Scripture through the *sensus litteralis*. It is clear,
however, that what they saw there was a literal sense of an entirely different
order from what was practiced and expounded in university hermeneutics.
What they saw in the potential of lay encounters with vernacular Scripture
was a version of literal reading in the elementary classroom, the literal sense in
its much older identification with childhood learning. In the Oxford debate
about Bible translation in 1401, the Dominican Thomas Palmer and the
Franciscan William Butler, in determinations against the lawfulness of biblical translation, both invoke the literal sense in relation to the Bible's accessi-
bility to *vulgari*, as if by an established collocation. Both rehearse the
metaphor of milk feeding that is familiar from pedagogical discourse about
teaching the young through the literal sense; and both inevitably conflate that

---

[10] Smalley, "Which William of Nottingham?" 287. See also Minnis, Scott, and Wallace, eds., *Medieval Literary Theory and Criticism*, 205–6; Evans, *The Language and Logic of the Bible: the Road to Reformation*, 43–4.

[11] On Woodford and Ullerston, see Catto, "Wyclif and Wycliffism at Oxford, 1356–1430," 197, 257.

with the pastoral metaphor of the vulgar laity as infants.[12] This triple conflation, the literal sense with milk feeding and and both with the puerility of vulgar laity, has also become one of the hallmarks of anti-heretical polemic.[13] Palmer offers the following judgment:

> *Deut. 22: Si in terra vel in arbore nidum avis inveneris et matrem pullis desuper incubantem, non tenebis eam cum pullis, sed abire patieris, ut bene sit tibi et longo vivas tempore*; quae figura secundum Gregorium significat, quod sensus litteralis, qui est quasi magister aliorum sensuum, dimitti debet, et pulli eius retineri, allegoriae et anagogiae, quia *littera occidit, spiritus autem vivificat.* Quomodo, igitur, simplices illiterati, vel sola grammatica instructi, illos pullos trium sensuum ignorantes, non errarent habentes magistrum, scilicet litteralem sensum, tamen de pullis non curantes?[14]

> (*If you happen upon a bird's nest in a tree or on the ground, and the dam is sitting on her young, you shall not take her along with the young, but you shall let her go, that it may go well with you and you shall live a long life*; which figure, according to Gregory, signifies that the literal sense, which is as it were the master of the other senses, ought to be left behind, and its offspring, that is the allegorical and anagogical senses, retained, because *the letter kills and the spirit gives life.* How then would not simple illiterates, or those of only grammatical instruction, knowing not those offspring of the three senses, be in error because they have only the master, that is the literal sense, yet not troubling about its offspring?)

Here the literal sense, obviously understood in terms of its place in a three- or fourfold hermeneutical system, is rendered insufficient *only* through association with *simplices illiterati*. In the hands of vulgar laity, indeed just in metaphorical association with vulgar laity, the literal sense becomes useless. Or, what may appear even more odd, the literal sense is insufficient for lay reading because it itself is too subtle: so Butler notes, "[cortex] litterae intellectui [difficilis] ad legendum populo" (418). What Butler seems to mean is that the subtlety is a property of what lies within the "cortex litterae," so that the shell is rendered useless to infantile intellects which cannot penetrate

---

12 Butler cites Origen: "Vides ergo, inquit Origenes . . . quomodoaliis utpote perfectis praeparat cibos, sed docens alios inferiores lacte potat ut parvulos, alios oleribus nutrit ut infirmos" ("Therefore you see, as Origen says . . . how he prepares food for some as if for the fully grown, but in teaching others who are of a lower condition he gives them milk to drink, as if they were infants, and others he feeds with vegetables, as if they were infirm") (Deanesly, *The Lollard Bible*, 412); Palmer's references include citation of 1 Corinthians 3. 1–2, "Tanquam parvulis in Christo vobis lac potum dedi, non escam; nondum enim poteratis, sed nec nunc quidem potestis, adhuc enim carnales estis" (Deanesly, *The Lollard Bible*, 423).

13 See the nearly contemporary continental sources cited and quoted in Deanesly, *The Lollard Bible*, for example, 94 (from Flanders) and 107 (from Germany). 14 Deanesly, *The Lollard Bible*, 424.

it. But what else then is the milk food that the infantile *vulgari* are to be fed, if not the literal sense (here we may recall Conrad of Hirsau's association of the literal sense with both actual childhood and spiritual infancy)? Or is it that the literal sense is bad or useless as a hermeneutical principle? Again, not so: significantly Butler calls repeatedly upon the authority of Lyre, whose literal postilla reshaped late medieval exegetical practice.

As these polemics suggest, the long-enduring split between hermeneutics and pedagogy no longer simply signifies the difference between the intellectual advancement of adults and the education of children. Its implications have travelled now to define another field, a political arena of clerical power over a potentially intransigent lay reading public. Jean Gerson, for one, assumed that there could be no hermeneutical framework that might effectively support the promulgation of the literal sense outside regulated academic environments, that is, no respectable hermeneutical system can be expected to accompany the literal sense as it migrates beyond the schools:

> Scriptura Sacra dum per novellos homines inducitur tamquam credenda sit in suis nudis terminis absque alterius interpretis vel expositoris admissione, exponitur gravibus periculis et scandalis nisi solerter provideatur et confestim occuratur. Patet ex praecedentibus. Et quia ad veritatem tales implicant semetipsos in dictis suis prout deductum est in sexta regula, dum aliquando pro se inducunt doctores et inductos contra se non admittunt; dum praeterea vitare volunt glossam omnem, incidunt apertissime in multiplicem contradictionem . . . Et hac praeterea radice pestifera orti sunt et quotidie crescunt errores Begardorum et Pauperum de Lugduno, et omnium similium, quorum multi sunt laici habentes in suo vulgari translationem Bibliae . . .[15]

> (As long as sacred Scripture is treated by modern men as if it should be believed in its naked sense without the aid of any other interpretation or exposition, its exposition is fraught with grave dangers and scandals unless this practice is perceptively foreseen and immediately counteracted. This is plain from precedents. Since such men align themselves with truth in the things that they say, just as if it were something deduced from the seven rules of Tyconius, now at times they invoke men of learning on their own behalf and won't admit opposing arguments; and more than that, they want to shun every gloss, and fall openly into multiple contradiction . . . And from this infected root have sprung, and daily increase, the errors of the Beghards and the Poor Men of Lyon and of the like, of whom many are lay people who have a translation of the Bible in their own vernacular . . .)

As soon as the literal sense of Scripture is associated with lay reading of

[15] Jean Gerson, *De necessaria communione laicorum sub utraque specie*, in Gerson, *Œuvres complètes* 10: 57–8.

vernacular Bibles, the literal sense seems to "jump paradigms": it loses its privileged value as a fashionable hermeneutical principle, and is returned to its debased value as the tool of elementary pedagogy. Certainly this process bears all the marks of what is often recognized in the modern academy as the institutionalization of "high theory," where theoretical discourse within the academy is sharply differentiated from practical pedagogical aims outside the academy, inscribing a certain false dichotomy between theory and practice. The medieval process is recognizable in modern correlatives in which practical critical thought performed outside the academy is delegitimized by the practitioners of theory within the academy.

To cite an extreme example, it is notable that when the Carmelite friar Thomas Netter in the 1420s composes his extensive refutation of Wyclif's hermeneutical program, he collapses the two paradigms together, accusing Wyclif himself, along with his followers, of childish apprehension of the literal sense:

> non pro sententia divinae scripturae, sed pro sua dimicant, ut eam velint esse scripturae sanctae sententiam, quae sua est, tamquam pueri dicentes: Ecce scriptura dicit Christum esse primam literam, et ultimam alphabeti, quia ipsemet dicit: Ego sum [alpha] et [omega]; et tamquam pueri exinde contendant Christum esse illud mutum et sensibile elementum. [16]

> (Their interest is not in the meaning of sacred Scripture, but in their own meaning, because they want the meaning of sacred Scripture to be what is theirs, just like children saying, "Behold, Scripture says that Christ is the first and the last letter of the alphabet, because he himself says 'I am alpha and omega'"; and accordingly like children they contend that Christ is a mutable and sensible element.)

From Netter's historical position, writing a (belated) academic refutation long after the Wycliffite heresy has spread beyond academic confines, and soon after the disaster of the Oldcastle rebellion and at the height of large-scale heresy prosecutions in England and on the continent, it is easy to confuse remote "causes" with present "effects": in this metaleptic historical argument, because Wyclif's scriptural doctrine supposedly *made it possible* for vulgar lay people to appropriate the literal sense of Scripture, Wyclif himself is impugned for the puerility of intellect that was conventionally attributed to his hapless lay followers.[17] A hermeneutical principle that was seen to give rise

---

[16] Netter, *Doctrinale antiquitatem fidei catholicae ecclesiae*, ed. Blanciotti, 2: 236.

[17] Cf. Aston, "Wyclif and the Vernacular," 293: "the contemporaries on whom we must largely depend wrote with a retrospective view that was tinctured by *post hoc, propter hoc* convictions. Theirs was a syllogistic understanding of events: preaching led to revolt; Wycliffites had been preaching; *ergo* Wycliffites caused revolt."

to an unchecked and overweening movement of lay reading according to the literal sense is now identified with the pedagogical paradigm of the literal sense. It is interesting to note here that Wyclif himself employs the language of childish limitation when distinguishing between the surface literal sense of words or verbal images and the true literal sense of divine intention that inheres in the text, even in its mystical senses:

> debemus ergo intelligendo scripturam sacram sensum puerilem abicere ac sensum, quem deus docet, accipere . . . patet ergo, quod antiqui theologi laborarunt ad cognoscendum sensum scripture et dimittendum alios sensus infidelium seu puerorum.[18]

> (Therefore in understanding sacred Scripture we must put aside the childish sense and accept the sense that God teaches . . . Therefore it is shown that the ancient theologians labored to know the sense of Scripture and to repudiate other senses, of infidels and of children.)

It is a nice historical irony that Wyclif was to be impugned for the very kind of literalist puerility that he explicitly shunned; but behind this lies the nicer irony that Wyclif and Netter, while on opposite sides of the ecclesiological coin, both exploited the available cultural discourse that links childhood with superficiality which is dangerous (infidel) when unsupervised.

The orthodox pastoral association of children and laity is not surprising or new. But when we understand how that metaphorical association is also driven by an engrained discourse about pedagogy and the limitations of childhood, we can see why the identification of infancy and laity is so charged, why clerical authorities insist on it so keenly, and why it plays such an important role in arguments about heretical education and its suppression. In the preceding chapter, in the examples that I have given about teaching through the literal sense, it has neither been my intention to rehearse the modern *topos* of "pedagogy as victimization" nor to suggest that classical and medieval systems of language teaching were inherently oppressive of children. Rather, my concern has been to describe the kinds of discourses that such pedagogical theories and practices create, discourses about the delimitations of interpretive and political agency that can be exported to other social fields. Thus I want to argue that the notion of the literal sense as the limited domain of childish comprehension *does* become oppressive when that paradigm is superimposed on the structures of political discourse among adults, when the literal sense as a *pedagogical* category, divorced from the attributes of inter-pretive agency, is used to justify setting limits on what lay adult readers can

---

[18] Wyclif, *De veritate sacrae scripturae*, ed. Buddensieg, 1: 42, 44. On this passage see Ghosh, "Eliding the Interpreter: John Wyclif and Scriptural Truth," 215.

understand. And this is exactly the category that anti-heretical polemic deploys in arguing against lay, vernacular reading of Scripture. It uses categories ready at hand – a conflation of pastoral and pedagogical paradigms – to return adults to the state of intellectual disenfranchisement associated with childhood.

That there were, in effect, two paradigms of the literal sense, as a prestigious hermeneutical principle of late-medieval academic discourse, and as a traditional tool of elementary teaching, leads to a great deal of confusion among parties to polemics. Thus we see how proponents of the orthodox position, on the one hand, and heterodox preachers on the other hand, often retreat to positions of mutual unintelligibility. Orthodox concern about uses of the literal sense can voice itself at near hysterical levels. Something of this "hysteria" can be seen in the spurious meanings that orthodox argument attaches to quite traditional exegetical formulas. In 1389, the Lollard preacher William Swinderby was charged with heresy before John Trefnant, the bishop of Hereford. Recounted in the proceedings among the standard charges laid against Lollards are the following:

> nonnulla heretica, blasphemia, scismatica, ac diffamatoria, sacris canonibus et decretis sanctorum patrum repugnancia, dicere, docere, manutenere, et (quod nephandius est) publice predicare nequiter presumpserunt et presumunt, de die in diem nescientes in semitis iusticie et veritatis dirigere gressus suos, exponendo videlicet sacram scripturam populo *ad litteram more moderno* aliter quam spiritus sanctus flagitat, ubi vocabula a propriis significacionibus peregrinantur et novas divinari videntur, *ubi non sunt iudicanda verba ex sensu quem faciunt sed ex sensu ex quo fiunt*, ubi construccio non subjacet legibus Donati, ubi fides remota a racionis argumento sed suis principiis, doctrinis, et dogmatibus publicis et occultis virus scismatum inter clerum et populum ebullire. (Emphasis added)[19]

(They have wickedly presumed to utter, teach, maintain, and (what is most nefarious) publicly preach certain heresies, blasphemies, schisms, and defamations repugnant to the sacred canons and decretals of the holy fathers; and daily they presume to lead those ignorant in the paths of justice and truth along their ways – namely, by expounding sacred Scripture to the people *according to the letter in the modern fashion* other than as the holy spirit demands, where words stray from their proper signification and seem to be divined anew, *where words are not judged from the sense that they make but from the sense out of which they are made*, where grammatical construction is not subject to the laws of Donatus, where faith is divorced from rational argument – and, through their principles, doctrines, and dogmas,

---

[19] *Registrum Johannis Trefnant*, 232.

to boil up the venom of schism, in public and in secret, between clergy and people.)

Central to these charges is the exegetical distinction between the grammatical meanings of words themselves and the authorial intention behind them, *verba ex sensu quem faciunt sed ex sensu ex quo fiunt*. We have already encountered this distinction, and these very terms, in Alan of Lille's *Regulae caelestis iuris* (above, p. 77). The formulation has an interesting genealogy. Gilbert of Poitiers in the twelfth century had made the distinction one of his own key exegetical principles, and the "faciunt–fiunt" terminology reappears among several different writers.[20] Simon of Tournai (fl. at Paris 1170–1200) uses the formula in his disputations where he wishes to distinguish between intentions and meanings of words or actions, for example:

> Verborum sensus duplex est: sensus quem faciunt verba, et sensus ex quo fiunt verba. Veritas ergo verborum duplex est. Quandoque enim verba sunt vera ex sensus ex quo fiunt, non ex sensu quem faciunt: ut hec, pratum ridet. Qui enim hoc dicit, significare intendit pratum esse causam ridendi. Tamen falsa sunt ex sensu quem faciunt: significant enim risum inesse prato; quod est impossibile.[21]

> (There is a double sense of words: the sense that words make, and the sense from which words are made. Thus there is a double truth of words. Sometimes words are true according to the sense from which they are made, not from the sense that they make: as here, "the meadow smiles." Whoever says this intends to signify that the meadow is a cause of smiling. However, the words are false according to the sense which they make: the words signify that the smile belongs to the meadow, which is impossible.)

The same formula appears in a discussion of heresy in the anonymous *Liber de vera philosophia*: "Heresy is the product of understanding [*intelligentia*], not of Scripture; sense, not words, make the crime. Thus words are to be interpreted according to the sense from which they are made, not from the sense which they make [*ex sensu ex quo fiunt, non ex sensu quem faciunt*]."[22] This exegetical principle clearly gives priority to the intention behind the grammatical surface of the words. Alan of Lille's use of the principle and its terminology in the *Regulae caelestis iuris* derives directly from this twelfth-century tradition.[23] And we have also seen that Alan's *Anticlaudianus* adds

---

[20] Häring, "The Case of Gilbert de la Porrée Bishop of Poitiers (1142–1154)."

[21] *Les Disputationes de Simon de Tournai*, ed. Warichez, *disputatio* 59, *quaestio* 2, p. 167. See also further in the same *quaestio*, p. 168; and *disp.* 5, *qu.* 3, p. 32.

[22] Quoted by Häring, "Commentary and Hermeneutics," 196 n. 211, from MS Grenoble Bibl. publ. 290, fol. 75v. The first sentence, on heresy, is derived from Hilary of Poitiers, *De trinitate* 2. 3.

[23] On Alan of Lille's indebtedness to Gilbert of Poitiers, see Marenbon, "A Note on the Porretani," 355.

another layer of value to this principle by suggesting that reading according to the literal sense of words is not only hermeneutically misleading, but a sign of vulgarity. The *faciunt–fiunt* distinction was a long-lived exegetical directive: it came under extensive discussion as late as the Council of Constance in 1414–18, where it was used to elaborate the theory of a *duplex sensus litteralis* that could distinguish between a "mere grammatical sense" and a "true" inner literal sense.[24]

Bishop Trefnant obviously derived the *faciunt–fiunt* formula from this exegetical tradition in which reading according to the grammatical surface is seen as hermeneutically deficient or at worst even vulgar. But in turning the formula against Lollards he inverts the meaning of the precept: according to Trefnant, the Lollards read in a perverse, willful, *new* way, against the grammatical meaning of words (not subject to the laws of Donatus), preferring not the sense which words make, but the sense out of which they are made. Part of the charge is, in fact, true. Wycliffite hermeneutics does apply the exegetical principle of seeking literal meaning in the author's intention and not just in grammatical surface: the Prologue to the Wycliffite Bible makes direct reference to the notion, derived from Lyre, of the *duplex sensus litteralis*.[25] But as we see, it is hardly a *new* way of reading, and Trefnant's borrowing of the twelfth-century terminology belies his opportunistic characterization of it as new-fangled. Moreover, the pressure to disparage Lollard hermeneutics leads Trefnant into a theoretical muddle: he is in the curious

---

24 The context for the elaboration of this theory at the Council of Constance was not the persecution of heresy (which otherwise played a large role at the Council), but the dispute between the party of Duke John of Burgundy (who in 1407 had ordered the murder of the duke of Orléans) and the Orléanist party under the leadership of Jean Gerson about "licit tyrannicide." The Burgundian party defended tyrannicide on the basis of certain legal and biblical proofs; Gerson and the Orléanist party sought to condemn these proofs, including one that declared the literal sense of Scripture untrustworthy. This proof came to be known as the Eighth Assertion, so called from a list of nine Assertions extracted by Gerson from an earlier speech by Jean Petit, a theology master, defending tyrannicide on behalf of the Burgundian party; these nine Assertions were proposed for condemnation at the Council of Constance in 1415, where they were discussed in detail. Gerson, otherwise a vehement prosecutor of heresy, found himself arguing *on behalf* of scriptural literalism, in a way that was ironically close to certain heretical positions. The opinions recorded at Constance concerning nine Assertions extracted from Petit's speech are printed in Gerson, *Opera omnia*, ed. du Pin, 5: 718–1010. For extensive discussion of the arguments surrounding the Eighth Assertion (the position against the literal sense), see Froehlich, "Always to Keep the Literal Sense in Holy Scripture Means to Kill One's Soul"; on the possible intersection of the Gersonist position with heretical hermeneutics of the literal sense, see 38, n. 33, and see also Gerson's opinion, *Opera*, ed. du Pin, 5: 930 c. Among the statements defining a *duplex sensus litteralis* in terms of the *faciunt–fiunt* formula (adduced in *support* of the Eighth Assertion), is the following: "habent duplicem sensum litteralem, unum quem faciunt, alium in quo fiunt, necessario enim verba litterae generant aliquem sensum superficialem, alium ab illo loquens intendit" ("the words have a duplex literal sense, one which they make, and another in which they are made, that is, the literal words necessarily generate a certain superficial sense which is other than what the speaker intended") (*Opera* 5: 809 c); cf. *Opera* 5: 766 a.

25 "aboute which thing it is to see, that the same lettere hath sum tyme double literal sense . . ." Forshall and Madden, eds. *The Holy Bible . . . made from the Latin Vulgate by John Wycliffe and his Followers* 1: 54.

position of condemning Lollards for not being literal enough, reading words *ex sensu ex quo fiunt*, according to the intention from which the words are made, not according to the rules of grammar.[26] Why does Trefnant seem to get it backwards, apparently controverting the very scholarly authority that he is invoking here? It apparently matters little how scholarly authority defines the best use of the literal sense. What matters to Trefnant is that Lollards "have presumed and presume *to teach* sacred Scripture, expounding it *ad litteram to the people.*" When the literal sense crosses the line from university hermeneutical theory to a practical pedagogy outside the academy (teaching *ad litteram* to the people) it provokes reflex responses. Perhaps Trefnant's view is simply that it is an overstepping of the boundaries of "correct" pedagogical practice to read according to intention and not grammar, which is to deny Lollard pedagogy the kind of hermeneutical authority that enables the reading of intention as part of the literal sense. Heretical appropriation of the literal sense is identical with pedagogical violation of hermeneutical propriety: as the object of reflexive abhorrence they are the same. In this respect we may also recall how the "pearls before swine" image of Matthew 7. 6 can be deployed as a dismissive exclusion of vulgar and deficient readers both in discourses about elementary pedagogy, as we have seen in Alan of Lille's *Anticlaudianus*, and anti-heresy polemic, from Walter Map's records of the Waldensians to Henry Knighton's famous denunciation of the Wycliffite Bible as that which has cast the pearls of holy Scripture before swine, the common *illiterati*.[27] That the image can float between the two contexts, representing what is abjected either from hermeneutical sufficiency or ecclesiological orthodoxy, circumscribing either puerile readers or heretics, is not accidental, for it is the pedagogical exclusion that provides the structure of abhorrence in such discourses of ecclesiological pollution.[28]

Like other orthodox polemicists, Trefnant understands two kinds of literal reading, one scholastic, enshrined in university practice, and one pedagogical. The earlier continuities of hermeneutical purpose in the schools have offered no grounds for resolving the split. It is not to be expected that scholastic thought would provide those grounds, for it was not the job of high academic

---

[26] It is interesting that John Foxe tries to impose some logic on Trefnant's statement, although without much success. Foxe's translation attempts to reverse the terms of the accusation, so that it will sound like a plausible accusation against Lollards: "in that they expound to the people the holy Scripture as the letter soundeth, after a judaical sort, otherwise than the Holy Ghost will needs have it, where the words wander from their proper significations, and appear to bring in, by guessing, new meanings; *whereas the words must not be judged by the sense that they make, but by the sense whereby they be made*; where the construction is not bound to the Donatus rules, where faith is far placed from the capacity of reason" (*Acts and Monuments* 3: 109; emphasis added).

[27] Map, *De nugis curialium*, ed. James, p. 60; Knighton, *Chronicle*, 242–4.

[28] Compare Moore, *The Formation of a Persecuting Society*, 100–39, on clerical fears of pollution by *rustici*.

theorists to set out pedagogical programs for mediating Scripture to unlearned or lay readers (although it is our job as historians to consider how this factor so deeply defined – and in many ways still continues to define – the realm of academic discourse). Thus it is the more surprising that the earliest Lollard preachers, themselves often products of scholastic training, would venture such integration of paradigms. Yet as we see, this bridging only adds to the confusion: because Lollard thought and polemic seems to recognize no important difference between scholastic principles and pedagogical practice of the literal sense, orthodox and heterodox polemicists do not even speak the same language to each other when they speak of the "literal sense." Indeed, the scholastic notion of the "literal sense" remained as firmly fixed within scientific hermeneutical categories as were the earlier Victorine and Parisian models. And so notions of the literal sense as a basic teaching tool for untrained readers were not part of the academic "renaissance" of the literal sense in the high and later Middle Ages. This is how the institutionalized split between pedagogical literalism and hermeneutical systems of the literal sense has come to manifest itself.

Here it is instructive to consider Wyclif's writings. Whatever Wyclif proclaims about delivering Scripture to lay audiences in their vernacular language, his own writings make no clear provisions for mediating hermeneutical structures to create a fully enfranchised *pedagogy* of the literal sense. At the most basic level, despite his aggressive advocacy of vernacular scriptural teaching, Wyclif "seems to have ignored, or been unaware of, the enormous difficulties of the undertaking" of biblical translation; the technical questions of linguistic equivalence in translation only found articulation in the actual process of translating, as recorded in the General Prologue to the Wycliffite Bible.[29] Of course, Wyclif's theological discussions of the unity of truth beyond individual human languages did provide others with a mandate, a theoretical justification, for the actual project of scriptural translation.[30] But there are more complex issues at stake in Wyclif's positions. Let us consider several broad themes that run through Wyclif's writings. The first of these can be seen as an amalgamation of related arguments: all Christians should study

---

[29] Hudson, "Wyclif and the English Language," 91.
[30] For example, *De contrarietate duorum dominorum*, in Buddensieg, ed., *John Wiclif's Polemical Works in Latin* 2: 700: "Lingwa enim, sive hebrea, sive greca, sive latina, sive anglica, est quasi habitus legis domini. Et per quemcunque talem habitum eius sentencia magis vere cognoscitur a fideli, ipse est codex plus racionabiliter acceptandus" ("Language, whether Hebrew, Greek, Latin or English, is like a certain 'habitus' [custom, attire, condition] of the law of God. And by means of whatever 'habitus' the meaning of that law may more truly be known by the faithful, this is the book that is most reasonably to be accepted."). While these are not "practical" considerations, they were to have a practical effect in the long term. On this passage see Hudson, "Wyclif and the English Language," 90, 97–8. The notion that Scripture transcends the contingencies of ordinary language is argued at length in chapters 1–6 of *De veritate sacrae scripturae*. See also Copeland, "Rhetoric and the Politics of the Literal Sense," 17.

the Bible,[31] the preaching of Scripture should be conducted in the language of greatest access,[32] and Scripture itself should be available in the vernacular so that all Christians, clergy and laity, can study it.[33] A second important theme is that there is an element of common sense (including the evidence of the senses) to sacramental understanding and that lay people make legitimate common-sense judgments about matters of sacramental faith.[34] The third theme is that the most profound truth of Scripture, and the truth that is most accessible to and consonant with reason, is found in its literal sense: "quod de racione sensus literalis est, quod sit sensus catholicus inmediate elicitus ex scriptura, et alii tres sensus, si inmediate eliciuntur ex scriptura, tunc sunt literales."[35] The relation between "reason" and common sense in Wyclif's thought is a vexed one.[36] But the efforts to connect this last principle, the profundity and reason of the literal sense, with his evident interest in delivering scriptural teaching to a broad vernacular audience through an appeal to common sense, seem to be articulated mainly in terms of distinguishing between what popular audiences need and what learned audiences want. The *De apostasia* offers an interesting perspective on this:

> Sic igitur instruendus est populus quod sacramentum altaris est secundum suam naturam panis et vinum, sed secundum verbi dei miraculum est corpus Christi et sangwis. Et dicendum est scolasticis quod sacramentum, secundum quod panis aut vinum, subiectat naturaliter omnia illa accidencia que sentimus; sed secundum quod corpus Christi, confert graciam fidelibus ipsa dignis. Istam autem sentenciam propono publicare in populo.

> (The people are to be instructed that, according to its nature, the sacrament of the alter is bread and wine, but that according to the miracle of the word of God, it is the body and blood of Christ. The learned are to be told that the sacrament, as it is bread and wine, puts forth naturally all those accidents that we sense; but as it is the body of Christ, it confers grace on the faithful who are worthy of it. Thus I intend to make this message public to the people.)

---

[31] *De veritate sacrae scripturae* 1: 109, 117; 2: 137, 163 ff.   [32] *De veritate sacrae scripturae* 1: 243.

[33] For example, from *Speculum secularium dominorum*, "Nam scriptura sacra est fides ecclesie, et de quanto est nota planius in sensu orthodoxo, de tanto est melius. Ideo sicut seculares debent fidem cognoscere, sic in quacunque lingua plus nota fuerit, est docenda" ("Now sacred scripture is the faith of the Church, and as much as is set out plainly in orthodox sense, so much the better. Therefore, since laymen ought to know the faith, so in whichever language it will be the clearest it is to be taught"), in *Johannis Wyclif Opera minora*, ed. Loserth, 74. Among other examples of this theme see *De eucharistia*, ed. Loserth, 123–4. For further references among Wyclif's writings on this and related themes of vernacular biblical study, see Deanesly, *The Lollard Bible*, 241–8.

[34] *De eucharistia*, 119, 188, 301–2; *De apostasia*, ed. Dziewicki, 57, 149, 152, 160. On this theme in particular see Aston, "Wyclif and the Vernacular."

[35] *De veritate sacrae scripturae* 1: 123. See also 1: 73, 121–2.

[36] For extensive discussion on "reason" in Wyclif's thought, and on "common sense" in Wycliffite thought, see Ghosh, *The Wycliffite Heresy: Authority and Interpretation*, chapters 1 and 4, respectively.

As Margaret Aston notes, this contains a double address: the people will be given one explanation, the learned another.[37] And it is the double address that is most telling. The hermeneutical principle of the literal sense as a function of reason (here implicit as a factor in interpreting the sacrament of the eucharist) remains fixed in scholastic terms; actual programs for mediating a hermeneutics of the literal sense to vernacular audiences do not emerge from Wyclif's pastoral directives.

We can note a certain parallel here with Taylor's sermon, where he urges preaching to the people without "too curiously" occupying their wits with scholastic subtleties. But Taylor's rejection of "scholastic subtleties" when preaching to the people represents an arena of practice that is vastly removed from the contexts of Wyclif's polemic. What lies behind Taylor's statement in 1406, more than two decades after Wyclif's last writings, is the emergence of a full-scale mediating practice that has effectively closed the gap between the literal sense as hermeneutical principle and the literal sense as pedagogical tool. It is to the evidence of that practice that I now turn.

Lollard pedagogies – the reading practices of the clandestine conventicles witnessed not only by the Bible translations but also by the surviving manuscripts of sermons, Gospel commentaries, and polemical tracts – recognize no real distinction between pedagogical and hermeneutical paradigms. Thus at the same time that it appropriates scholastic redefinitions of the literal sense as the horizon of hermeneutical inquiry, Lollard textual teaching also reclaims pedagogical literalism from its debased value in traditional hierarchies of education. Lollard programs of the literal sense propose to invert the institutional structure of educational development by building horizontally towards an open community of lay, adult readers The theme of "openness" is one of the most important connecting threads of the General Prologue, especially in its invocations of the hermeneutical authority of Nicholas of Lyre as the scholastic mediator of patristic exegesis: "Heere Lire rehersith the sentence of seint Austyn, and of Isidre in these reulis, and declarith hem opinly bi holy scripture and resoun, and countrith not Austin, but declareth him ful mychel to symple mennis witt; and addith more bi scripture and resoun, that Austin touchith not."[38]

I have made some reference here to charged metaphors of the pedagogical tradition – milk feeding, the naked text – that circulate in polemic about heresy and lay reading of Scripture, metaphors that carry traditional discourses about childhood into contested political arenas. But what of explicit references to classroom study or texts? It is useful to consider the kind of

37 Aston, "Wyclif and the Vernacular," 320; *De apostasia*, 253–4.
38 Forshall and Madden, eds., *The Holy Bible . . . by John Wycliffe* 1: 55.

recognition that Lollard and orthodox writers take of the actual pedagogical sources that in so many indirect ways inform their polemic. One of the many Lollard texts in defense of Bible translation, a text that is partially derived from Richard Ullerston's contribution to the Oxford debates about translation, opens by invoking a well-known curricular authority:[39]

> *Agens hem that seyn that hooli wrigt schulde not or may not be drawun in to Engliche: we maken thes resouns.*
>
> Ffirst seith Bois in his boke *De disciplina scolarium*: that children schulde be taugt in the bokis [of] Senek; and Bede expowneth this, seying children schulden be taugt in vertues, ffor the bokis of Senek ben morals: and for thei ben not taugt thus in her yougthe thei conseyuen yuel maners and ben vnabel to conseyue the sotil sciense of trewthe, seyinge the wise man: *wisdom schal not entre in to a wicked soule*. And moche ther of the sentence of Bede; and Algasel in his logik seith the soule of a man is as clene myrour newe polichid in wiche is seen sigt liche the ymage of man. But, for the puple hath not konynge in youthe, the[y] han derke soulis and blyndid so that thei profiten not but in falsenes, malice and other vices; and moche ther of this mater. O, sithen hethen philosofris wolden the puple to profeten in natural science, how myche more schulden cristen men willen the puple to profiten in science of vertues; for so wolde God.[40]

This treatise presents an extensive and sometimes elaborate justification of Bible translation, with appeals to a range of ecclesiastical authorities, from patristic writers to more recent historical figures, the latter including Aquinas, Richard Rolle, and Archbishop Thoresby of York (taking advantage of many of the positive authorities and arguments supplied in Ullerston's treatise).

The authority cited here at the beginning ("Ffirst seith Bois in his boke *De disciplina scolarium*") is especially interesting for its placement in the English text and for what this tells us about the purposes of the Lollard writer. It is one of the many authorities cited in the long Latin text, from which the English writer borrowed it. But in Ullerston's text the reference to "Boecius . . . in libro de disciplina scolarium" (fol. 205r) is buried two-thirds of the way through the treatise, as part of an argument about how established church

---

[39] The text is printed by Deanesly, *The Lollard Bible*, 439–45; it was also edited by Büler, "A Lollard Tract: on Translating the Bible into English." Hudson has examined the complex affiliations of this text, noting that it bears a partial relation to the Latin treatise on translating the Bible whose author she identified as Richard Ullerston from a colophon dated 1401; see "The Debate on Bible Translation, Oxford 1401." Ullerston's treatise gives arguments opposing and supporting translation of the Bible into English. The English tract, as Hudson notes (80) depends on the Latin text for many of the authorities that it lists, but otherwise gives the argument a new and much more controversial framework. The Latin text (unedited) is in Österreichische Nationalbibliothek MS 4133, fols. 195r–207v. Professor Hudson has kindly supplied me with her unpublished transcript of the treatise from the Vienna manuscript, along with a photocopy of the manuscript text itself.

[40] Deanesly, *The Lollard Bible*, 439.

practices will not be undermined if lay people are educated in Scripture in their own language just as children are given moral writings to learn. But the Lollard writer latches onto this citation to give it prominence at the head of his text. The English writer is not interested in assuaging fears about hierarchies coming undone. Here the effect of the citation of the *De disciplinis scolarium* is to resonate with an existing Lollard pedagogical imperative, and to shape a new polemic out of the neutral summary of views presented in Ullerston's treatise.

The anonymous *De disciplina scolarium* is a moral preceptive text of the earlier thirteenth century (ca. 1230–40) that was associated with, and attributed to, Boethius. It had a very wide circulation (over 130 manuscripts), and in more than thirty manuscripts is accompanied by commentaries. It had a particular currency in England, where it was the subject of a commentary in the early fourteenth century (no later than 1309) by the Oxford grammar master William Wheatley. There were also some spurious late-medieval attributions of a commentary to Nicholas Trevet, possibly because Trevet cited the *De disciplina scolarium* in his own commentary on Seneca.[41] *De disciplina scolarium* seems to have been less a classroom text than a guide for teachers about the intellectual and moral formation of young students and the professional formation of prospective teachers (although the distinction between classroom texts and teachers' guides is not always firm; *De disciplina scolarium* is also found in manuscripts that clearly represent Latin readers compiled for elementary and intermediate classroom study).[42] While the text seems to have been aimed for a university milieu, it gained broader influence and authority as a general pedagogical statement.

Thus the English treatise on Bible translation shows us a Lollard writer exploiting a pedagogical tradition (which also has more contemporary affiliations with the Oxford milieu of Wheatley and Trevet, that is, grammar school and university) to legitimize lay hermeneutical aspirations. The program for a "new" vernacular hermeneutics appeals for authority not to recent scholastic practice, but to ancient pedagogical tradition. It invokes an educational practice that is invested with the authority of the ancients, and it

---

[41] See Weijers, ed., *De disciplina scholarium*, 20. On Wheatley see Sebastian, "William Wheteley's Commentary on the Pseudo-Boethius Tractate *De disciplina scholarium* and Medieval Grammar School Education," and Emden, *A Biographical Register of the University of Oxford to A. D. 1500* 3: 2030–31. See also the edition of *De disciplina scholarium* by Ducci, *Un saggio de pedagogia medievale*, and Steiner, "The Authorship of *De disciplina scholarium*." On the manuscripts and commentaries, see Weijers, 36–88; on incunables, see Ducci, 9–12.

[42] See Gehl, *A Moral Art*, 255, describing Florence, Biblioteca Nazionale Centrale, MS Magliabecchi VII, 1064 (s. 14/15), which also contains the *Disticha Catonis*, the *Vita scholastica* by Bonvesin de la Riva (a behavioral manual for students), the *Ilias latina*, and works by Prosper of Aquitaine, Prudentius, and the *Liber de contemptus mulierum* of the Pseudo-Jerome.

situates the present claim for lay reading of Scripture within that educational tradition. Along similar lines, when William Taylor registers shock at the unprecedented persecution directed against Lollard preachers who are just continuing an "old way" of doing things, that "old way" is as much the pedagogical tradition invoked here as the more general apostolic model of preaching.

It is even more significant that the Lollard uses the appeal to the teaching of children ("Ffirst seith Bois in his boke *De disciplina scolarium*: that children schulde be taugt in the bokis [of] Senek; and Bede expowneth this, saying children schulden be taugt in vertues") not to neutralize fears about lay scriptural reading by comparing it with children's learning, but to dignify lay reading by conferring ancient authority on it. The passage in the *De disciplina scolarium* which contains the recommendation of Seneca's works occurs near the beginning of the treatise in a section specifically given over to the fundamentals of early learning, before the treatise moves on to more general and more advanced concerns about institutional and professional matters. There is nothing mysterious about the pedagogical conventions voiced here: moral and intellectual obtuseness will be softened by early ingraining of diligent reading habits and necessary mnemonic exercise, and Seneca heads the list of curricular authors:

> Senece tradicio, Lucani inexplecio, Virgilii prolixitas, Stacii urbanitas, dura Flacci translacio, durior Persii edicio, Marcialis indigna lesio,[43] Nasonis discrecio, sunt indaganda et memoriali cellule commendanda. Ceterorum autem philosophorum prout ingenii suppetit capacitas, nec sub silencio est pretereunda moralitas, ut sic dictaminis sentenciosa vigeat serenitas et metrorum floreat iocunditas.[44]

> (The moral doctrine of Seneca, the unfinished writings of Lucan, the expansiveness of Virgil, the wit of Statius, the writings of Flaccius that resist translation, the even more difficult writings of Persius, the sharp satire of Martial, the discriminating style of Ovid, are to be carefully explored and committed to the treasure-room of memory. In so far as intellectual capacity will permit, the moral works of other philosophers are not to be passed over in silence, for serenity grows out of the sententiousness of prose, and happy delight blossoms from poetry.)

[43] Some readings have "non indigna lesio"; see Ducci's edition, 87 and variants.

[44] Ed. Weijers, 95–6. It is just as likely that the Lollard writer derived the recommendation of Senecan readings as moral foundation from a commentary on the *De disciplina scolarium* rather than directly from the text. Here, for example, is the fifteenth-century gloss on this passage quoted by Bühler, "A Lollard Tract," 179 n.: "Item iuuenes primo instruentur in dictis Senecae, qui multas bonas compilauit epistolas, in quibus iuuenes exemplariter sunt instruendi" ("Likewise youngsters may be instructed in the sayings of Seneca, who compiled many fine letters, in which the young can be instructed by example").

Such notions of a foundational curriculum find echoes later in the English treatise (in a passage whose arguments and authorities are partly abstracted from Ullerston's treatise), where the text links vernacular translation of the Bible with established pedagogies, and where the Lollard writer can raise the issue of the literal sense without following through any of the controversies about its utility that Ullerston's Latin treatise pursues:

> Also seint Thomas seith that barbarus is he that vnderstandith not that he redeth in his modor tunge . . . Sum men thenkyne hem to be barbaros wiche han not propur vnderstandinge of that thei reden to answere therto in her modor tunge. Also he seith that Bede drew in to Englische the liberal artis, leste Engliche men schuldon be holden barbarus . . . Also the grett sutil clerk Lyncolne seith in a sermon that bigynneth *Scriptum est de leuitis*; If (he seith), any prest seie he can not preche, oo remedie is, resyne he vp his benefice; another remedie is, if he wol not thus, record he in the woke [*week*] the nakid tixt of the sonndaie gospel, that he kunne the groos story and telle it to his puple . . . Thus seith Lyncolne, and on this argueth a clerk and seith: If it is leueful to preche the naked text to the pupel, it is also lefful to write it to hem; and consequentliche, be proces of tyme, so al the Bibil.[45]

The Lollard's appropriation of arguments and authorities from the Ullerston treatise is strategic and opportunistic, because the Lollard has converted a neutral summary of views on the efficacy of biblical translation into a strong pedagogical argument that connects English pastoral authorities with recognized school traditions of antique lineage. Thus the (mythologized) "translation" of a liberal arts curriculum is invoked as precedent for Bible translation in English rather than, as is more common in Lollard writings, earlier translations of the Bible into other vernaculars.[46] In this variation on the more common theme, the making of a vernacular biblical hermeneutics is mythologized as a stage in the tradition of *translatio studii*, its origins now linked to the "civilizing" pedagogical program of Bede whose Englishing of the liberal arts is the pedagogical "narrative" of a national formation of Englishness; and this in turn, by the particular logic of the Lollard treatise which adduces the positive example of the "Boethian" classical curriculum, can be seen as a following-through of a Christian–classical civilizing imperative. The making of a vernacular hermeneutics out of weekly preaching of the "naked text" of the Gospels follows in the same historical process as the making of an English nation out of the liberal arts and the curricular authors of the grammar classroom, which are linked by inheritance to a larger classical

---

45 Deanesly, *The Lollard Bible*, 442.
46 In the previous passage (441), the Lollard writer has used the more commonplace argument of precedents for Bible translation in other vernaculars.

imperium. We have seen such "paradigm-jumping" before, among orthodox opponents of Bible translation, where associating vernacular reading of the "naked" scriptural text with elementary pedagogy is a sure strategy of debasing vernacular hermeneutical claims. What has changed in the Lollard text is the valuation of pedagogy itself. We have considered how, in late antiquity, the devolution away from a republican ideology (the remnant norms of which are still evident in Quintilian and Plutarch) is accompanied by the driving apart of pedagogy and hermeneutics, where the political franchise of hermeneutics becomes increasingly mystified as it retreats from earlier discourses of public culture. It is interesting, then, that in the political picture painted by the Lollard text, a pedagogical imperative is linked to a mythology of the nation, and thus also to a hermeneutical agenda that is seen to represent the fulfilment of this historical design.[47] The manufacturing of a notion of political cohesion around the historical processes of a distinctively English pedagogy also situates Lollardy in a peculiar relation with emergent dynastic constructions of English unity in the early fifteenth century. If, as Paul Strohm has shown, the state discourse of early Lancastrian rulers exploited the link between heresy and sedition to demonize Lollardy as the internal threat to Lancastrian claims to legitimacy, Lollard discourses of national cohesion could have yielded the Lancastrians some surprisingly complementary arguments.[48]

There is another text, composed at most a few years after the English treatise on Bible translation, that also makes an explicit identification between pedagogical traditions and new lay hermeneutical aspirations. This is the fifth of Arundel's *Constitutiones* of 1407/9. The fifth Constitution has not evinced quite the interest among modern scholars, nor received so much of the notoriety in its own times, as the sixth and seventh Constitutions, which censor the writings of Wyclif and the circulation of unapproved vernacular translations of Scripture. But the fifth Constitution is, in its own way, a very interesting piece of censorship, and suggests a strategic understanding of the underlying issues of Lollard revisionism. The fifth Constitution concerns grammar masters and how they should conduct their classrooms. It is a brilliant surgical strike at the very heart of radical pedagogy:

---

[47] For similar arguments about Lollard mythologies of fulfilling teleological designs of nationhood, see Nisse, "Prophetic Nations."

[48] Strohm, *England's Empty Throne: Usurpation and the Language of Legitimation, 1399–1422*, chapter 4, "Reburying Richard: Ceremony and Symbolic Relegitimation," 101–27. Strohm's arguments focus mainly on the first fifteen years or so of Lancastrian rule; the English Lollard tract discussed here cannot be dated more precisely than after 1401 and before 1407. My argument here does not suggest that Lollardy is to be historically linked with incipient nationalist movements on the order of Hussitism; on this see Hudson, "Lollardy: the English Heresy?" 143.

Similiter, quia id quod capit nova testa inveterata sapit, statuimus et ordinamus, quod magistri sive quicunque docentes in artibus, aut grammatica, pueros, *seu alios quoscunque in primitivis scientiis instruentes*, de fide catholica, sacramento altaris, seu aliis sacramentis ecclesiae, aut materia aliqua theologica, contra determinata per ecclesiam, se nullatenus intromittant instruendo eosdem; *nec de expositione sacrae scripturae, nisi in exponendo textum prout antiquitus fieri consuevit*; nec permittant scholares suos sive discipulos de fide catholica, seu sacramentis ecclesiae publice disputare etiam vel occulte: contrarium autem faciens, ut fautor errorum, et schismatum, per loci ordinarium graviter puniatur. (Emphasis added)[49]

(In as much as a new vessel, with long use, acquires the taste of what it holds, we decree and ordain that schoolmasters or any others teaching boys in the arts or grammar, *or instructing any other people in elementary studies*, must not introduce in their instruction anything concerning the catholic faith, the sacrament of the altar, or other sacraments of the church, or any theological matter contrary to the determinations of the church; *nor anything concerning the exposition of Scripture, except in expounding the text in the manner customary since ancient times*; nor should they permit scholars or pupils to debate matters of the catholic faith or the sacraments of the church, either publically or privately. Anyone acting in violation of this should be gravely punished by the local ordinary, as a supporter of error and schism.)

Arundel understood the obvious, that schools were important conduits of heretical doctrine. But the careful language and phrasing of this statute also shows how much he understood the more profound, and less obvious, challenges to the very ideological structures of pedagogy. Opening with the phrase "quia id quod capit nova testa inveterata sapit," Arundel's statute also reaches back into ancient pedagogical tradition, using a *topos* inherited from Horace, Quintilian, and Augustine, and found in medieval texts such as Conrad of Hirsau's *Dialogus super auctores*.[50] Citing ancient pedagogical authority, Arundel takes a route much the same as the Lollard treatise's invocation of the Pseudo-Boethius, but towards an entirely different goal. In its classical and medieval occurrences, the *topos* is always used to suggest the impressionability of children's minds, whether for better or worse. Quintilian uses the image in his general remarks on early childhood, in a discussion about selecting well-spoken nurses for very young children so that the latter

---

[49] Wilkins, ed., *Concilia* 3: 317.
[50] Horace, *Epistles* 1. 2. 69–79 ("quo semel est imbuta recens, servabit odorem testa diu"); Quintilian, *Institutio oratoria* 1. 1. 5 ("ut sapor, quo nova imbuas, durat"); Augustine, *De civitate dei* 1. 3 (quoting Horace); Conrad of Hirsau, *Dialogus super auctores*, ed. Huygens, 90, lines 565–7 (also quoting Horace), translation in Minnis, Scott, and Wallace, eds., *Medieval Literary Theory and Criticism*, 52.

will hear and imitate proper speech before they are even ready for formal schooling. Augustine, however, turns the idea towards its most negative implications to complain that the custom of having young boys read vast amounts of Virgil fills their impressionable minds with impious vanities. Arundel's statute relies upon pedagogical tradition to lay the grounds for a project of infantilization. As will become clear, the statute refers not only to school children, but to any group that can be made subject to infantilizing restrictions.

This statute is about keeping heresy out of grammar schools and other elementary teaching. But as the crucial phrase *nec de expositione sacrae scripturae, nisi in exponendo textum prout antiquitus fieri consuevit* suggests, the statute is really also about driving pedagogy and hermeneutics apart, about *reinstating* and enforcing the division between elementary textual learning and hermeneutical control of texts. There is no direct reference here to the literal sense, but these clauses set up a clear distinction between two practices, "exposition of sacred scripture," and "expounding the text in the manner customary since ancient times." The meaning of these two terms, *expositio sacrae scripturae* and *exponens textum prout antiquitus fieri consuevit*, can be determined from the context. What is prohibited is *expositio sacrae scripturae*: presumably this is any kind of commentative activity that would admit controversy. *Expositio* here may be understood as exegesis or "commentary" in the general academic sense of the term, as in a free-standing and continuous commentary on a biblical text.[51] This may be understood as exposition of any level of meaning of the text (and perhaps signficantly, the statute refrains from specifying the kind of commentary meant, whether of literal or mystical senses). What of the second category, the exception from prohibition, *nisi exponendo textum prout antiquitus fieri consuevit*? Here also Arundel appeals to ancient precedents of pedagogical practice. If it is singled out for exception from the general prohibition on scriptural commentary in the classroom, *exponens textum prout antiquitus fieri consuevit* must signify an activity deemed both necessary and uncontroversial. It certainly means elementary grammatical exposition as handed down from traditional pedagogical practice: sounding out syllables, construing *littera* and *sensus*, but not necessarily advancing to *sententia* or deep meaning,[52] learning vocabulary and grammatical forms,

---

[51] The term *expositio* meaning commentary is preserved from classical usage: for example, see Lewis and Short, *A Latin Dictionary*, "expositio" II. The uses of this and other terms (e.g. *glosa, commentum*) have rather complex histories. On the currency of the term as a descriptive title of continuous biblical conmmentaries in the twelfth century (where it was still less common than the term *glosa*), see Häring, "Commentary and Hermeneutics," 176–79.

[52] See Hugh of St. Victor, *Didascalicon* 6. 7–10. Compare the distinction in trecento Florentine education between reading *testualiter* (textually or literally) and *sensualiter* (according to the sense), before reaching the stage of "latinizing" (Gehl, *A Moral Art*, 30–4).

and becoming familiar with the basic tropes and figures of speech. This stage, as we have seen, would also involve grasping the literal sense as *gesta*, or as simple moral content, or as poetic expression (as in the case of the psalms). This is the model of elementary textual exposition handed down from the ancients, from Quintilian, the grammar readers based on Donatus, and the study of Latin language and literature in monastic compilations and school readers such as the *Liber catonianus*; and it is the conservative teaching model assumed in curricular treatises of the later Middle Ages, such as those of Hugh of Trimberg, Vincent of Beauvais, and the Pseudo-Boethius. The fifth Constitution acknowledges that elementary instruction will involve this kind of expository work.

However, the clear distinction between kinds of expository work – traditional grammatical exposition as opposed to *expositio sacrae scripturae* – also signals the recognition that there is a new kind of pedagogy in which the boundaries between elementary elucidation and hermeneutical exposition have become porous. Of course, such a breaking down of boundaries would matter little in the actual teaching of children. If the fifth Constitution were aimed only at the education of children, the distinction between pedagogical and hermeneutical exposition would simply be an ideological one, an intervention at a purely symbolic level to affirm the conventions of thought that regulate the privilege granted to certain spheres of intellectual activity, that delineate scholastic investigations of the literal sense from mere puerile concerns. In actual practice, no one fears that young children will suddenly arrogate to themselves the power to take part in scholastic hermeneutical determinations. But what Arundel seems to have understood is that the breaking down of a difference between two kinds of exposition, and thus eventually between two kinds of apprehension of the literal sense, *really did matter* in a new kind of classroom where non-academic *adults* were being initiated into Bible study at the same time that they were also acquiring the basic tools of literacy. Hence the clause *seu alios quoscunque in primitivis scientiis instruentes*, "or instructing any other people in elementary sciences." The emphasis here is on *elementary* initiation, without specifying who is being initiated, so it can cover adults as well as children. The *De heretico comburendo* in 1401 had already acknowledged the existence of, and prohibited, Lollard conventicles or schools where adult initiation to textual study, by way of the Bible, would have taken place.[53] But as Arundel surely recognized, it would be unrealistic to prohibit lay adults completely from acquiring literacy under any circumstances, or to anticipate all the circumstances, innocent or not,

---

[53] Wilkins, ed., *Concilia* 3: 252–4; on Lollard schooling that would be subject to the prohibitions of the fifth Constitution, see Hudson, *The Premature Reformation*, 82–4, 133, 157–8, 166, 180, 229, 408.

under which such teaching might occur. This clause extends the prohibitions to adult classrooms, and to any unforeseen forms of pedagogical practice in which elementary or "puerile" knowledge might overstep its limits and lay claim to hermeneutical sufficiency.

Taken together, the various prohibitions of the fifth Constitution represent a comprehensive response to the new ideological formations of the Lollard classroom, as well as an acute understanding of the workings and implications of a revisionist pedagogy. Lollard teaching refuses the distinctions between "puerile" and scholastic apprehensions of the literal sense of Scripture, thus also refusing the ideological justifications for limiting interpretive agency in teaching the literal sense. Conversely, the aim of the fifth Constitution is to reaffirm those ideological structures, particularly in that sphere where they really count, in the teaching of adult, lay, vernacular readers who can assert independent hermeneutical agency. Arundel's Constitution turns ancient pedagogical "law" into modern statutory law, legislating that pupils – adults as well as children – remain pedagogical objects, inscribed in a larger design of political mastery in which they can have no direct agency. Arundel's statute is reminiscent of Pierre Dubois' pedagogical regime, where the literal sense defines the limits of what young pupils need to know ("enough to gain a comprehension of its literal meaning but without any insistence on other interpretive formalities," see above, p. 87). Like Dubois describing the place of elementary instruction in a grand political design, Arundel invokes the ancient tradition of grammatical exposition as defense against exploration of deeper meaning. Of course, Arundel takes that paradigm further: his is not simply a pedagogical routine appropriate for young children, but rather a systematized pedagogy of infantilization, an "education" structured around conserving ignorance.[54] It deploys the metaphorical associations of literalist pedagogy with childhood to ensure the "puerility" even of adults.

It might be argued, along such lines, that the directives of such university men as Taylor for preaching a simple and open theme and avoiding scholastic subtleties also infantilize lay vernacular audiences by locking them into an elementary stage of pedagogy. This would be an obvious critique, for it is such a model that informs orthodox clerical programs of popular lay instruction, such as the teaching of basic penitential doctrine, programs that any preacher with standard clerical training would at some point have practiced.[55] But the rationale underlying Lollard directives is more complex. It assumes the adequacy of the literal sense as pedagogical tool for instating an independent

[54] Compare Johnson, "Teaching Ignorance: *L'Ecole des Femmes*."
[55] Such, for example, is the implicit critique in Steven Justice's reading of the class alliances of orthodox and heterodox preachers; see "Inquisition, Speech, and Writing: a Case from Late Medieval Norwich."

and conscientious knowledge of Scripture among the laity. This in turn is the ground and horizon of what, in a kind of Lollard counter-mythology, is represented as a communal hermeneutical praxis. The Lollard priest Richard Wyche had claimed that "it is the obligation of any layman to know the whole gospel, and when he knows it, to preach it."[56] That such hermeneutical communalism may be a mythologizing of actual practice is important, and I will return to this consideration later. But it is also important to consider how such mythologizing represents the imaginative order of a counter-pedagogy upon which a dissenting community constructs and charts its identity and explains its intellectual practices.[57]

In traditional pedagogy, the literal sense marks out the passage from infancy or childhood to intellectual adulthood and to higher forms of understanding. In educational tradition, the literal sense is a signifier of childhood. As we have seen, it corresponds in ideological terms with the age before reason, and as an institutional trope it organizes the child's induction into an eductional system that will become increasingly closed and more selective as the children pass into adolescence and adulthood. Here the biological process of growing up is itself linked symbolically with progress through the educational hierarchy, and with the narrowing, through attrition or exclusion, of the community of credentialized readers. In contrast, the "imaginative order" of the Lollard school, an open or horizontal model of teaching predicated on common pedagogical access to a hermeneutics of the literal sense, offers an educational "system" without the violence of exclusion, attrition, or hierarchy, without the ritualized violence of academic correction and coercion. The Lollard pedagogical order repeatedly represents itself as subverting these "rites of institution." Thus, for example, Lollard polemic locates real power outside the symbolic and temporal order of advancement in the grammar school and university system. The Prologue to the Wycliffite Bible, for example, challenges the symbolic power of what I would call "duration," the idea that real knowledge is produced through prolonged institutional mentoring that coincides with the years of biological development:

> But wite ye, worldly clerkis and feyned relygiouse, that God bothe can and may, if it lykith hym, speede symple men out of the vniuersitee, as myche to kunne hooly writ, as maistris in the vniuersite; and therfore no gret charge, though neuer man of good wille be poisend with hethen mennis errouris ix.

---

[56] *Fasciculi zizaniorum*, 502.

[57] See Strohm's fine discussions of facticity and "social imagination" in relation to codified legal and political systems in *Hochon's Arrow: the Social Imagination of Fourteenth-Century Texts*, 133–4, 143–4.

yeer either ten, but euere lyue wel and stodie hooly writ, bi elde doctouris and newe, and preche treuly and freely agens opin synnes, to his deth.[58]

Here ten years of university schooling are ten years of poisoning: in contradistinction to this the imaginative order of the Lollard "school" dispenses with the rule of teachers as policers or keepers of the official language, and proposes a system without examination except that of "living well and studying holy Scripture."

The same theme is sounded, at more urgent extreme, in the English version of *De officio pastorali*. This tract takes the argument that the elimination of clerical appropriations will not harm learning, even if this cuts the flow of rents to the colleges in Oxford and Cambridge, which produce the masters who go forth and preach to the people: for while studying has long produced much good, it has produced "neuere so myche sithen collegies weren dowid [*endowed*] as dide bifore ther rentis weren proprid [*appropriated*]."[59] Apostolic precedent is the ground for dismantling the academic "rites of institution":

> but sith that apostlis token no siche degre & crist forfendide hem to be clepid maystris, it semeth that this hethen maner brought in in studies discordith fro the gospel; & as preching of apostlis was betere than is preching of thes maystris, so prestis with-oute degre of scole may profite more than don thes maystris . . . & thus yif dyuynite were lernd on that maner that apostlis diden, it shulde profite myche more than it doith nou bi staat of scole . . . & thus men of scole trauelen veynly for to gete newe sutiltees, & to magnefie ther name for ther worchip & ther wynnyng, & the profit of hooly chirche bi this weye is put abac. (427–8)

The occasion of this objection to universities and masters is the corruption of the system of clerical appropriations; but the argument moves sideways into a critique of the system of academic hierarchy and its privileges, where the uncredentialized apostles (who took "no siche degre") are contrasted with the careerist, self-magnifying university masters who teach for vainglory. This last criticism is hardly a new subject: even as it expresses disaffection from academic convention, the Lollard polemic echoes questions about professional self-magnification that had been a regular subject of university quodlibetal disputations in theology since the thirteenth century in Paris.[60] But the

---

[58] Forshall and Madden, eds., *The Holy Bible . . . by John Wycliffe* 1: 52.

[59] Matthew, ed., *The English Works of John Wyclif*, 426.

[60] On this subject and more generally on the structure and content of quodlibetal disputations, see the informative articles by Wei, "The Self-Image of the Masters of Theology at the University of Paris in the Late Thirteenth and Early Fourteenth Centuries," and "The Masters of Theology at the University of Paris in the Late Thirteenth and Early Fourteenth Centuries: an Authority beyond the Schools."

call for reversing institutional privilege in favor of those "prestis with-oute degre of scole" leads further, in the following arguments, to the theme of a communal hermeneutics without any masters at all. Here the tract rehearses some of the Lollard arguments in support of translation of the Bible into English (it serves the people best in their own language; it already exists in other vernaculars; Jerome translated it; the truth of God's meaning transcends the contingencies of human languages; and if parts of the Gospels, such as the Paternoster, are known in English, why not the whole Bible?), and then launches this communitarian proposal:

> Wel y woot defaute may be in vntrewe translating, as myghten haue be many defautis in turnyng fro ebreu in-to greu [*Hebrew into Greek*], & fro greu in-to lateyn, & from o langage in-to another. but lyue men good lif & studie many persones goddis lawe; & whanne chaungyng of wit is foundun amende they it as resoun wole. (430)

The credentials required for overseeing and emending errors of translation are the same as those for any reading of Scripture: as the General Prologue has put it, living well and studying holy writ.

Lollard thought elevates the pedagogy of the literal sense to a new hermeneutical adequacy. As one of the Lollard sermons for the Proper of Saints puts it with forceful explicitness:

> Bysyde lettre of this gospel may men moue doutus of scole; but me thinkuth now it is betture to touche lore of vertewys. We schal byleue that al the gospel, be it neuere so literal, techeth what thing schal befalle, and how that men schal lyue . . . Eche word of this gospel may be toold to this entent; but it suffisuth to haue the roote, and goo lightly to othre wyttis.[61]

The corollaries of the new role of the literal sense are the notion of a communal hermeneutical praxis and a leveling of academic institutional hierarchy. But how are these principles translated into an ethos and performance of the classroom where they might constitute lived social relations? In its very existence the dissident "academy" of the Lollards poses a challenge to official academic structures, such that Lollard schools were repeatedly declared illegal from the 1380s onward, and so driven underground. In this environment there can be no hermeneutical undertaking that is not primarily defined and constituted through the representation of its real political effects and consequences, especially the danger of discovery and violent prosecution. Here the possibility of the hermeneutically "open" text is predicated on its work as the hidden transcript of a dissenting community.[62] Thus by both

---

[61] No. 96, lines 38–41, 62–3, in Hudson and Gradon, eds., *English Wycliffite Sermons* 2: 234–5.
[62] The term "hidden transcript" was coined by Scott, *Domination and the Art of Resistance: Hidden Transcripts*.

adherents and adversaries, Lollard hermeneutical practice can only be understood as a forum for political action. It is under such pressure, and indeed because of it, that pedagogies of the literal sense achieve the power of hermeneutical and political agency.

The marked effects of the policy of openness are not to be found in the content of Lollard biblical exposition, for that is no more "literalist" in a fundamentalist sense than its counterpart orthodox productions. In practice Lollard exegesis is just as receptive to allegorical readings as orthodox exegesis. Thus the passage from the sermon quoted above is less a practical description of expositional technique than an ideological declaration. Lollard hermeneutics could be said to divide itself between the theoretical attempt to fix meaning at the *sensus litteralis* and a practice that actually retains the interpretive flexibilities of traditional multi-layered exegesis.[63] Thus the social effects of the open or literal text are to be found in other aspects of Lollard production, and especially in pedagogical and codicological rhetorics. These in turn point to the level of practice where the transformation of pedagogical tradition actually occurs.

One way to get a purchase on the social function of the open text is to consider how texts used for instruction invite dialogic participation in the activity of teaching. A Lollard sermon on mendicancy from about 1410 (based on Matthew 15.13, "Omnis plantacio quam non plantavit Pater meus"), surviving in four manuscripts, concludes with the following injunction to the audience:

> Now siris the dai is al ydo, and I mai tarie you no lenger, and I haue no tyme to make now a recapitulacioun of my sermon. Netheles I purpose to leue it writun among you, and whoso likith mai ouerse [*peruse*] it . . . And certis, if I haue seid ony thing amys, and I mai now haue redi knouleche therof, I shal amende it er I go. And if I haue such knouleche herafter, I shal with beter will come and amende my defautis than I seie this at this tyme.[64]

It has been suggested that this is the work of an itinerant preacher who left copies of his work with the various Lollard gatherings he visited (probably the small communal reading groups held in private houses), with the expectation of resuming the discussion on his return.[65] Three of the manuscripts containing this sermon are in a tiny pocket-sized format, and two are in the same hand: these latter two, BL Egerton 2820 and CUL Dd.14.30 (2) are heavily worn.[66] From external evidence about circulation of the text we can move to

---

[63] On this problem, see the important discussions in Ghosh, *The Wycliffite Heresy*, Introduction, and chapters 1 and 4.   [64] Text quoted from Hudson, ed., *Selections from English Wycliffite Writings*, 96.

[65] Hudson, *The Premature Reformation*, 184–5.

[66] The third small manuscript is Huntington Library HM 503.

internal evidence for the contexts of circulation. In this passage the teacher opens the exegetical process to the community in two ways: he offers to take corrections on the spot ("and I mai now haue redi knouleche therof, I shal amende it er I go"), and he invites the assembly to look over the text in his absence with a view to his next visit, when he will incorporate necessary emendations. If this is close to a transcript of instructional dialogue and activity, it suggests anything but infantilization of the audience. Indeed, this seems to promise the terms of that politically liberatory educational praxis described by Paolo Freire, in which "the act of helping become[s] free from the distortion in which the helper dominates the helped."[67] The teacher submits his work to a collective project of revision, which, in concrete terms, assumes not only a literate but an exegetically competent engagement on the part of his auditors (in other words, this is not just an authorial humility topos begging indulgence and correction from a hypothetical legacy of future readers). Moreover, the author is no ordinary preacher, but a learned exegete, perhaps a product of the Oxford theology course, who wears and offers his learning in his sermon tract without embarrassment or reservation, in a way not uncommon in Lollard sermonizing.[68]

A later sermon by the same preacher, entitled in the explicit *Tractatus de oblacione iugis sacrificii,* also shows the building of a local textual community. This later sermon, preserved in BL Cotton Titus D. v, contains a reference to the *Omnis plantacio* sermon on mendicancy:

> as I declarid onys in a sermon that beginneth thus: *Omnis plantacio quam non plantavit pater meus celestis eradicabitur.* And for that I seide and wrot in that sermon I write the lasse of thise two poyntis last rehersid . . .[69]

This reveals the kind of ongoing intertextual conversation that can only be predicated on the audience's active knowledge of the earlier sermon. This manuscript also contains a coda in which the preacher proposes to leave the present sermon with his "readers," once again appealing for the intervention of any members of his audience who may be able to emend his text:

> Now I have no lenger leiser to labor in this matir and therfor I make here an end, preying mekeli almighti god that this werke turne to his wirschip and stabling of cristen feith that anticrist now soore enpugneth. And if any man

---

67 Freire, *Pedagogy in Process: the Letters to Guinea-Bissau,* 8, cited in hooks, *Teaching to Transgress,* 54; on related themes, e.g. non-elitist intellectual work, the full participation of adult learners in defining what needs to be known, see letter 11, 99–120.

68 On this author and the two sermons that are his work, see Hudson, "A Wycliffite Scholar of the Early Fifteenth Century," and especially 314, on his Oxford affiliations.

69 BL Cotton Titus D. v, fol. 8v. In citing from manuscripts here and later, I have introduced modern orthography for "thorn" and "yogh," modern punctuation, and modern capitalization of proper names.

finde any error in this writing I wold fayn be warned ther of in purpos to
amende it mekeli. And I put it in the dome of tho that reden this whethur
this be olde lore or newe, or whethur I speke of myn own heed or ellis of the
autorite of goddis lawe and the olde feith of holi chirche.[70]

This local illustration can suggest the kind of agency that Lollard teaching of
the "open" text asks of its lay reading community. Such hermeneutical
dialogue cannot operate without a profound and immediate consciousness of
its own political import; and such activity thus also creates political identification through the making of textual community. The sermon *Omnis plantacio*
reflects upon its own illegal status – thereby defining the status of the reading
community it creates and its own role as "hidden transcript" – by referring to
Arundel's *Constitutiones* and their injunctions against vernacular Scripture
and Wycliffite exegesis:

> that thei maken alle these newe constituciouns and statutis agens these newe
> prechours and her fautors [*supporters*] to exclude heresies and errours and
> al maner fals doctrine. But God woot this is not sothe, ffor knewe I never
> prist that goith aboute and freli prechith the gospel as doen many of these
> that ben callid lollardis . . .[71]

As both the sermons tell us, there is no "leisure" in the world of the
underground school. Indeed, the theme of persecution is echoed in other texts
as an injunction to expect danger: "studye wel Godus lawe, and the trewthe
that suweth of it, and defende it booldely, bothe to prestus and to the world,
and thou schalt haue enemyes to pursuwe the to the deth."[72] Nor is there
room for complacent magisterial authority. Included in the envoi of the
Omnis plantacio sermon is an appeal to the congregation to be on the lookout
for adversaries who would challenge the speaker's conclusions on the "eu-
ydence or colour of hoolie scripture," before whom the speaker will then try
to "declare" himself so that the adversary shall consider himself answered –
although for this the preacher will presume, not upon his own "kunnyng" but
on the truth of God.[73] Just who such adversaries might be, whether other
preachers or members of the sect, or hostile witnesses who would challenge
his teaching on theological as well as perhaps legal grounds, is never made
clear: what is clear rather is a pervasive sense of dangerous insecurity. Here is a
pedagogical community that – by its very existence – turns the act of reading
into individual political agency, the very agency that Arundel's fifth Constitution seeks to eliminate as a condition of elementary teaching no matter what

---

[70] Cotton Titus D. v, fol. 100r.   [71] BL Egerton 2820, fol. 48v; cf. fol. 49r.
[72] No. 96, lines 51–4, in Hudson and Gradon, eds., *English Wycliffite Sermons* 2: 235.
[73] Hudson, *Selections*, 96. See Hudson, "A Wycliffite Scholar," 313.

audience. In opposition to Arundel's crusading mandate for a return to compliant pupils, and unlike the classroom imagined by that earlier master of crusading technology, Pierre Dubois, this is a classroom that insistently inscribes pupils into the political system in which they play a central role.

We know that the small communal readings conducted in clandestine Lollard "schools" such as those suggested by these sermons, or smaller reading groups such as that of the Londoner John Claydon in 1415, likely provided the occasion for the acquisition of elementary literacy for some lay adherents of the sect. The evidence of Claydon offers just such a scene of initiation into literacy. The illiterate skinner of London gathered in his house with John Grime and his servant John Fuller: "ab hora octava ante meridiem illius diei dominicae usque ad et in crepusculum sedebant in domo praefati Johannis Claydon antedicti, circa correctionem et lecturam dictorum quaternorum praenominatorum [i.e. the *Lanterne of Light*], Johanne Claydon, una cum eis pro majori parte dictae diei dominicae ibidem praesente, audiente, et auscultante lecturam et correctionem antedictam" ("from the eighth hour before midday on that Sunday all the way until dusk they were sitting in the aforesaid house of the aforesaid John Claydon, around the correction and reading of the contents of the aforenamed quires, and John Claydon, together with them in the same place for the better part of the aforesaid Sunday, present and listening and paying attention to the aforesaid reading and correction"). Claydon, who commissioned the writing of the book for possession of which he was prosecuted and executed (as a relapsed heretic), had his servant read the book to him and "pronounced it after the words of John Fuller."[74]

Under such conditions of initiation into literacy, the literal sense as a teaching tool can operate as nothing less than an "adult hermeneutics," without the opprobrium of the limitations of childhood and recognized as a site of political agency, with all of the consequences that incurs.[75] This is the pedagogical ethos embodied in a group of texts known as the *Glossed Gospels* which represent a massive Lollard undertaking to make available in English authoritative commentaries that elucidate the "literal sense" of Scripture.

[74] Wilkins, ed., *Concilia* 3: 373.
[75] In a text such as the *Lantern of Light*, we can see how the Lollard use of satire brings together these two textual models, the literal sense as an instrument of elementary teaching and the text as vehicle of political critique. Lollard use of the genre of satire is certainly an immediate product of Middle English traditions of satire and complaint. But it also claims a certain continuity with older pedagogical traditions by lending itself to the purpose of literacy teaching (as in the example of Claydon's copy of the *Lantern*) as well as other forms of instruction, so that its uses recall the older generic attributes of satire as *textus nudus* and appropriate vehicle of teaching. But as the genre of naked critique, satire also carries with it powers of resistance and inversion; in Lollard hands, satire is invested with the potential for immediate political identification.

These are commentaries on the individual Gospels, certainly composed before the statutes against Bible translation of 1407. The various glosses, which survive in nine manuscripts, follow the same format: they quote a passage from the Gospel in English (up to several verses at one time), using a form of the Early Version of the Wycliffite Bible and, breaking the text into *lemmata*, follow it with English commentary derived from impeccably orthodox sources, largely from the *Catena aurea* of Aquinas: the Fathers, Bede, Pseudo-Chrysostom, Bernard, and others. In their physical layouts the manuscripts of the *Glossed Gospels* point to the ways in which Lollard schools conducted group instruction and possibly enabled literacy acquisition: the differences between text and gloss are clearly marked (usually by underlining of text); the sources of the glosses are clearly indicated with the names of the authorities given at the end of the gloss (and sometimes also given in the margins); and the scribes make scrupulous corrections of errors (showing a typical Lollard concern for accuracy rivalling that of Latin academic texts). Some of these features, notably rubrication and underlining to distinguish the scriptural text, are shared with the manuscript layouts of the sermon cycles. In the case of the sermons it has been suggested that the brevity of the texts might indicate their usefulness for reading and discussion in groups.[76] While the *Glossed Gospels* are not brief textual units, the fact that they share with the sermons a form of presentation that would enable a reader's understanding of exegetical form can suggest that the *Glossed Gospels* participate, along with the sermons, in a program of communal instruction with its own distinctive techniques, including discussion of readings.

But the *Glossed Gospels* offer a much more precise account of their own pedagogical uses than the sermons. Six manuscripts of the *Glossed Gospels* contain prologues (and a seventh manuscript a long epilogue) addressed to communities of readers.[77] The address is the interpellative gesture that creates and sustains the mythologizing of communal learning. The prologues explain the layout of the text in the form of a "user's guide," providing what is

---

[76] Gradon and Hudson, eds., *English Wycliffite Sermons* 4: 35–6.

[77] The manuscripts are Bodley 243, containing a short commentary on Luke (no prologue) and a short commentary on John (with prologue); Bodley 143, containing a short commentary on Luke (with prologue); Bodleian Laud Misc. 235 and Cambridge Fitzwilliam Museum McClean 133, both containing the long exposition of Matthew (both with prologue); BL Add. 41175 (the companion volume to Bodley 243), containing short commentaries on Matthew (with prologue) and Mark; Cambridge Trinity College B. 1. 38, containing the short commentary on Matthew with prologue (as in BL Add. 41175), and the short commentary on John as in Bodley 243 (no prologue); BL Add. 28026, short commentary on Matthew (no prologue, but a long epilogue, printed in Deanesly, *The Lollard Bible*, 457–61); Cambridge University Library Kk. 2. 9, long commentary on Luke (no prologue); and York Minster xvi. D. 2 (no prologue), commentaries on the dominical Gospels compiled from BL Add. 28026 (Matthew) and CUL Kk. 2. 9 (Luke), and from commentaries on Mark and John that are no longer extant.

virtually a technical manual to the method of exposition prescribed by the visual organization of the text. In some cases the prologues set forth the pedagogical intentions of the compiler by describing the hermeneutical assumptions that underwrite the formal presentation of the material. The prologue to the "short" exposition of John in Bodley 243 illustrates the range of these functions:

> Oure lord Iesu Crist very God and very man, cam to serve those meke men, and to teche hem the gospel. And for this cause Seynt Poul seith, that he and other apostlis of Crist ben servantis of cristen men bi oure lord Iesu Crist. And eft he seith: y am dettour to wise men and unwise. And eft bere ye the chargis [*responsibilities*] an other of an other. And so ye schulen fille the lawe of Crist, that is of charite as Seynt Austyn expowneth. Herfor a symple creature of God, willinge to bere in party [*in part*] the chargis of symple pore men, wel willinge to Goddis cause, writith a schort glos in Englisch on the gospel of Ioon, and settith *onely the text of holy writ and the opyn and schorte sentencis of holy doctours*, bothe Grekis and Latyns, and allegith hem in general for to ese the symple wit and cost of pore symple men; remyttinge [*deferring/referring*] to the grettir gloos writun on Ioon where and in what bokis thes doctours seyen thes sentences. And sumtyme he takith the cleer sentence of lawis of the churche maad of seyntis, wel groundid in holy writ and pleyn resoun, to dispise synnes and comende vertues. First the text is set and thanne the sentence of a doctour is set aftir, and the doctour is aleggid in the ende of the same sentence. (Emphasis added)[78]

While the text appeals to inherited authority, it does not occlude its own origins by taking refuge in some vast legacy: it announces the conditions of its own making in terms of a responsibility to a particular audience (however conventionally this may be understood or applied) of non-Latinate, un-learned ("symple") people. The integrity of the open text with the "opening" of its message through the "sentence" of holy doctors is represented here as a non-violating approach to the text, the clarification of its proper or literal meaning according to the principle of *intentio auctoris*. Exposition points the way to the meaning that the author of Scripture "intended," which is the essence, in Wycliffite thought and its scholastic antecedents, of the literal sense. This is a theme sounded, with minor variations, throughout the extant prologues, as in the appeal to reason and law in a prologue to the short gloss on Matthew: "in this schort exposicioun is set oneli the text of holy writ with opyn sentensis of elde holi doctours and appreuyd of holi chirche, and summe lawis of the chirche groundid in goddis lawe and

---

[78] Bodley 243, fol. 115v. A portion of this text is printed by Hargreaves, "Popularizing Biblical Scholarship: the Role of the Wycliffite *Glossed Gospels*," 180.

resoun."[79] Hermeneutical and political openness is also expressed codicologically, in the layouts as well as in the kinds of apparatus that the texts supply. The author of the "short John" gloss describes how he has economized on the present apparatus (because this is a "short exposition") by only providing the names of the holy doctors who are the sources of the glosses, in this way both simplifying the technical information and cutting expenses on producing the volume ("and *allegith hem in general* for to ese the symple wit and cost of pore symple men"); he points the readers to the fuller apparatus (containing titles of works and *loci* of citations) contained in the "long exposition" of John (no surviving manuscript of which is known): "remyttinge to the grettir gloos writun on Ioon where and in what bokis thes doctours seyen thes sentences."

Other prologues to the *Glossed Gospels* provide even more technical information about using the text, interweaving layout information with introductory "lectures" about the relationship between text and exegetical authority. The prologue to a longer exposition of Matthew in Laud Misc. 235 exemplifies the complexity of this pedagogical enterprise. Here in effect the adult reader is given a condensed course on textuality and exegetical method, from how to decipher visual cues to a history of patristic exegesis, and from assurances about the doctrinal reliability of the authorities cited to the reliability of the system of citation in the present text, and to contextualization of the exegetical program within Lollard ideologies of social reform:

> For this cause a synful caytif [*caitiff*], hauynge compassioun on lewed men, declarith the gospel of Mathew to lewid men in Englische, with exposicioun of syntis and holy writ, and alleggith onely holy writ and olde doctours in his exposicioun, as Seynt Austyn, Seynt Ierom, Seynt Gregor, Seynt Ambrose, Seynt Crisostom, Seynt Bernard, Grosted [*Grosseteste*] and olde lawes of seyntis and of holy chirche wel groundid in holy writ and resoun; and alleggith also the Maister of Sentence [*Peter Lombard*] rehersynge olde seyntis and doctours, and also Rabanes on Mathew an olde monk and doctour [*i.e. Rabanus Maurus*], rehersynge copiously olde holy doctouris for hym, as Austyn, Gregor, Ambrose, Bede, Illarie, Crisostom, Ierom and many mo. This coward synful caitif alleggith Ierom on Mathew on the same text whiche he declarith; and therfore he alleggith thus "Ierom here," that is, on the same text. First in glos a word of text is vnderdrawen [*underlined*]; thanne cometh glos and the doctour seyinge that is alleggid in the ende of the glos. And aftir that doctour, al the glose suyinge is of the next doctour alleggid, so that the glos is set before, and the doctour alleggid after, who it is and where [*i.e. the name of each authority is given after the gloss derived from him*]; and the same weye of Crisostom in his werk vncomplete on Mathew,

---

[79] BL. Add. 41175, fol. 1v.

euene on the text expowned: and the same maner of Rabanes, for he goth thourout on Mathew. Also in the sarmoun of the lord on the hil, that is on v, vj, and vij chapitris of Mathew, he alleggith Austyn on this maner "Austyn here," that is, on the same text expowned. Whanne he alleggith Gregor, Bernard or Austyn or Ierom in other bokis or other doctour or lawis, he tellith in what bok and what chapitre, *for men schulden not be in doute of treuthe.* And this synful caitif, seeld vnder synne as the postle seith, takith pleinly and schortly the sentence of this doctours with groundis of holy scripturis withouten any settyng to of other men. For the sekenesse of oure peple is so gret that the nylen suffir pore men lyvynge now to reprove her synnes and open here vycis, though thei tellen never so pleynly holy writ ensaumple of cristis lif and his postlis with pleyn resoun. Therfore men [laye] to oure seke peple the plastre of holy writ with thes doctours biforseid withoute more addynge, if god wol in any maner of his grete mercy make hem to knowe and amende her yvel lyvynge and acorde with holy writ byfore that thei of this lyf gon. (Emphasis added)[80]

Under such a regime, the texts use a conceptual framework of the literal sense ("the open and plain sense of Holy Writ") to put an entire exegetical system at the command of a lay audience. The fictionalizing of the teacher's voice under the epithet "pore caitif" serves to elide the sense of magisterial academic hierarchy: it is not the teacher teaching, but the letter of the text (a move that is interestingly reminiscent of the metaphysics of Augustine's *De magistro*). The resonance of this teaching persona with the orthodox *Pore Caitif* texts of the late fourteenth century (which were sometimes inserted in manuscripts with Lollard materials) locates the voice of the teacher in a recognizable penitential rhetoric, so that the text can refer itself strategically to an available mythology of pedagogical humility.[81]

Such a mythology is reinforced in other Lollard writings, notably, for example, the late-fourteenth-century *Piers the Plowman's Creed*.[82] In this text the humility of the speaker is marked by his identification with the most elementary level of learning, the primer with its ABC and catechetical texts:

> Cros, and Curteis Crist this begynnynge spede
> For the faderes frendchipe that fourmede Heuene . . .
> A. and all myn A.b.c. after haue y lerned,
> And [patred] in my *pater-noster* iche poynt after other,

---

80 Laud Misc. 235, fol. 2r; Cambridge Fitzwilliam Museum McClean 133, fol. 2r–v. Much of this is also quoted in Hargreaves, "Popularizing Biblical Scholarship," 180–1.
81 On the tradition and texts of the *Pore Caitif* see Brady, "The *Pore Caitif*: an Introductory Study," and Brady, "Lollard Interpolations and Omissions in Manuscripts of the *Pore Caitif*."
82 On the literary-historical environment of this text, see the survey by Lawton, "Lollardy and the *Piers Plowman* Tradition"; von Nolcken, "*Piers Plowman*, the Wycliffites, and *Pierce the Ploughman's Crede*"; and Scattergood, "*Pierce the Ploughman's Crede*: Lollardy and Texts."

And after all, myn *Aue-marie* almost to the ende;
But all my kare is to comen for y can nohght my Crede. (1–6)[83]

The primer is invoked here as the material form of the text: the first word, "Cros," is the figure of a cross typically found at the opening of a primer.[84] The speaker declares that he has passed from the alphabet ("A.b.c.") to master two basic prayers, and that he desires to move on next to master the Creed, for which he is seeking instruction. The Creed assumes here a double value: it retains its traditional role as an elementary pedagogical–doctrinal text, a signpost along the stages of the primer; but it also becomes a touchstone for a Lollard program of spiritual and ecclesiological reform, a nexus for the most profound signification of faith, as the speaker seeks unsuccessfully among the four orders of friars for someone morally and spiritually equipped to teach him the principles of true belief. As the text moves into stringent anti-fraternal satire, the lowly primer itself becomes a mechanism for the highest aspirations of reformism. In the tradition of *Piers Plowman*, the voice of the only competent teacher who can properly instruct the speaker in his Creed is that of the humble Plowman. Like the voice of the teacher in the *Glossed Gospels*, the Plowman speaks under correction, refusing any magisterial authority:

> But, for y am a lewed man paraunter y mighte
> Passen par auenture and in some poynt erren,
> Y will nought this matere maistrely auowen;
> But yif ich haue myssaid mercy ich aske,
> And praie all maner men this matere amende,
> Iche a word by himself and all, yif it nedeth. (840–5)

Piers the Plowman's Creed adopts a literalism much more radical than that of the *Glossed Gospels*, identifying glossing with the suspect learned traditions of the friars:[85]

> Swiche a gome godes wordes grysliche gloseth;
> Y trowe, he toucheth nought the text but taketh it for a tale. (585–6)

But the rejection of glossing here is not a rejection of teaching: it can be seen, rather, as an expression – albeit extreme or uncompromising – of the pedagogical principle of humility, a rejection of magisterial hierarchy which it

---

[83] Text from Barr, ed., *The Piers Plowman Tradition: a Critical Edition of "Pierce the Ploughman's Crede", "Richard the Redeless", "Mum and the Sothsegger", and "The Crowned King."*

[84] On primers as reading matter in elementary teaching, see above, Introduction, pp. 15–16.

[85] See Scattergood, "*Pierce the Ploughman's Crede*: Lollardy and Texts," who argues from this and similar passages that the position defined in this poem "is essentially an anti-intellectual and anti-academic one . . . the fundamentalist, *sola scriptura*, anti-intellectual wing [of the Lollard movement], which sought truth in radical simplification and a deliberate narrowing of focus" (90–2).

shares with the more overtly academic *Glossed Gospels*. In *Piers the Plowman's Creed* the mutuality of teacher–student locates itself in a communal adherence to a truth found in the text of Scripture without any gloss:

> In loue and in lownesse and lettinge of pride,
> Grounded on the godspell as God bad him-selue. (513–14)

The iterative reinforcement of a "fictive" communitarian voice throughout a network of Lollard and Lollard-associated texts of the turn of the century also underwrites the material presentation of texts and pedagogical apparatuses such as the *Glossed Gospels* and *Piers the Plowman's Creed* by helping to produce the very communities (however "fictively" self-identified) that such instructive presentation supposes.

But the *Glossed Gospels* also move beyond the celebrated fiction of humble communitarian teaching by actually providing the technical materials of exegetical "user's guides." The literal sense is the package of a complete program of instruction, from elementary to advanced concerns, from visual discrimination between text and gloss to epistemologies of truth ("for men schulden not be in doute of treuthe"). Hermeneutical inquiry and basic pedagogical concerns meet – in a way that has no precedent in medieval educational discourses – in this induction into the *letter* of the text. The prologue provides, without embarrassment, the kind of basic codicological training that would be the daily stuff of the grammar school – how to identify *lemmata*, how to identify the name of an authority, how to know where the text ends and the gloss begins. The presentation of such basics is reminiscent of the instruction requested by the pupil in Conrad of Hirsau's *Dialogus super auctores*, who asks to know how to "enter" a text, to be taught the difference "inter titulum et prefacionem et proemium et prologum . . . inter explanationem et expositionem" ("between title and preface and proem and prologue . . . between explanation and exposition").[86] Conrad has the figure of the pupil articulate the need for pedagogical beginnings, creating a space where it is appropriate, indeed safe, for the learner to declare ignorance of the material construction of a text so that he can be informed. But the prologues to the *Glossed Gospels* take the safety of pedagogical beginnings a step further by grafting it onto a hermeneutical project of professedly the highest and most advanced order.

The prologue to the short exposition of Matthew in BL Add. 41175 makes this process of textual discrimination even clearer by explaining the reasons for the text's layout:

> The text of the gospel is set first bi itsilf, an hool sentence to gidere; and

---

[86] *Dialogus super auctores*, ed. Huygens, 72.

136

> thane sueth the exposicioun in this maner. First a sentence of a doctour
> declarynge the text is set aftir the text, and in the ende of that sentence the
> name of the doctour seiynge it is set, *that men wite certeynli hou fer that
> doctour goith.* (Emphasis added)[87]

These prologues hold in suspension a grand contradiction: they assume an audience that is at once textually untrained and textually hyperconscious, whose hermeneutical aptitude and astuteness must be acknowledged as the very condition of initiation into codicological literacy. This is a crucial contradiction, and it is more than a record of the textually "knowing" illiteracy of insurgents laying claim to a culturally familiar domain of textuality.[88] We must remember that a technical user's guide *at this level* is unprecedented in academic commentary. In university texts we do see explanations of layout techniques to assist readers in distinguishing between kinds of text or parts of the text; but such technical explanations normally accompany and advertise innovations in the *ordinatio* of commentary texts, such as Peter Lombard's prologue to the *Sentences* in which he draws attention to the new finding devices he has supplied (here chapter lists to facilitate searching), or later compilers' prologues that introduce further innovations in the ways that commentary sources are cited and distinguished.[89] In other words, in university texts the language of technical apparatus serves a narrowly self-referential purpose. By contrast, in the *Glossed Gospels* this technical language is the meeting place of elementary instruction and individual hermeneutical mastery so that, as another of the texts puts it, any "reader or hearer hath there fre devinynge by which either he approveth that that plesith or reprove that that offendith."[90] Nowhere do these prologues speak of progressing to "higher" levels of exegetical or doctrinal competence: there is no stage beyond this one. Indeed, the only discussions of "figurative" reading recapitulate arguments elaborated in the General Prologue to the Wycliffite Bible (and elsewhere), setting forth the Augustinian distinction between what must be read "properly," according to the letter, and what must be taken as allegory, "spiritual understanding pertaining to faith," so that all interpretation can be brought

---

[87] BL Add. 41175, fol. 1v.

[88] The line of argument of a "knowing" insurgent illiteracy is exemplified by Justice, *Writing and Rebellion: England in 1381*, 51–66. But for different pespectives on textual hyperconsciousness, see Crane, "The Writing Lesson of 1381"; Green, "John Ball's Letters: Literary History and Historical Literature"; and Scase, " 'Strange and Wonderful Bills': Bill-Casting and Political Discourse in Late Medieval England."

[89] See Rouse and Rouse, "*Statim invenire*: Schools, Preachers, and New Attitudes to the Page," 206–7, on Peter Lombard, and 208–9 on the new finding devices introduced by Herbert of Bosham in his edition of the Lombard's *Magna glosatura* (ca. 1170–76).

[90] BL Add. 28026, fol. 186v, epilogue to short exposition of Matthew. Note that this specifies both readers and hearers, suggesting a range of educational effects that the Gospel project might produce among its users.

into accordance with the rule of charity (and in Wycliffite and scholastic thought, this kind of figurative speech is part of the literal sense, because it is what the author intended).[91]

The prologues also define a new pedagogical community by performing the very moral and institutional critique that the "open" text is supposed to enable, including critique of the legal censorship of the very project now before the audience, the *Glossed Gospels*. The prologue of Laud Misc. 235 contains a long polemic on the "enemies of holy church," beginning, in the passage cited above, with a denunciation of those who would not suffer "poor men" to use the "plain reason" of Scripture to recognize and reprove sin, and continuing in its most categorically pedagogical vein, "sotil enmyes and weiward eretikis *letten cristen peple*[92] to knowe, here, rede, write and speke holy writ in englisch bi feyned colours seyynge that thei shul not preche neithir gedre cumpanyes to here goddis word spoken and red of lewed cristen peuple, though charite stire the men so myche therto."[93] The "feyned colours" of adversarial arguments are of course implicitly contrasted with the "plain," "open" text of Scripture itself which is delivered to dissenting "cumpanyes" of "lewed cristen peuple" in its unoccluded literal sense. The literal sense is both the site for critique of, and the remedy against, the "hypocrisy and tyranny" of enemies, as in the apocalyptic imagery of the prologue to Luke in Bodley 143: "And the beste armees of cristen men agens this cursid cheueuteyn [*chieftan* (*of the forces of antichrist*)] is the text of holy writ and namely the gospel and *very and open ensaumple* of Cristis lyf and his apostlis."[94]

Given the kind of technical apparatus that texts like this supply, we can see how Lollard instruction sets out to reproduce, in condensed and intensified form, the institutional apprenticeship of the schools. It is not surprising, therefore, that such a system might also reproduce the symbolic power of "duration," the legitimizing and naturalizing effect of prolonged institutional mentoring: for example, we have the assertion by the Lollard John Smith of Coventry in 1486 that it was necessary to attend Lollard schools for one year before one might know the right faith.[95] But it is more than apprenticeship that contributes to the naturalizing power of reproduction. The model of a communal hermeneutical praxis is the counter-institutional mythology that is also key to this process of reproducing academic induction. The very notion of a horizontal classroom, expressed in the *Glossed Gospels* (and elsewhere)

[91] Laud Misc. 235, fol. 1r; this material is printed in Forshall and Madden, eds., *The Holy Bible . . . by John Wycliffe* 1: 45–9 foot, with corresponding passages in the General Prologue, 45–9 main text.
[92] Underlined in red.   [93] Laud Misc. 235, fol. 2v.
[94] Bodley 143, fol. iv v. Emphasis added.
[95] Quoted in Hudson, *The Premature Reformation*, 180, from the Litchfield episcopal register.

through the theme of sending the text out to readers for correction, is the mythology that works against the order of an academic hierarchy, even though comparable forms of hierarchy are necessarily present (for example, within the reading group, the differentiated status of those who possess literacy and those who do not yet possess it).[96] The very nature of heretical discourse is to sever adherence to ordinary orders by producing a new, and inevitably self-naturalizing, system of common sense: and this is the kind of symbolic action by which institutions, whether established or heterodox, can act on reality by acting on the representation of reality.[97] Thus in the *Glossed Gospel* prologues, the rhetorical appeal to the specific capacity of an audience works towards constructing the lay "pupil" as political subject rather than pedagogical object of a political design. The subject of instruction and interpretation is the audiences themselves: their economic role in the production and distribution of the texts; their control of a historical tradition of exegesis and its mechanical apparatus; and the application of scriptural interpretation to their own identities as dissenters. And however imagined this order of community is, it becomes its own program of institutional induction, and the reality upon which individuals can act. It is no wonder, then, that the Lollard "school" can produce affirmations of loyalty to its particular form of mentoring, such as that of the Coventry Lollard John Smith. And of course, the harsher the process of induction, the more profound the adherence to the institution itself. Here the existential conditions of initiation into the dissenting "academy," the real dangers associated with reading "underground," dangers that the Lollard texts themselves recognize and comment upon, are certainly the largest terms upon which the heretical community organizes the coherence of its pedagogical practices.

This study of the literal sense and pedagogy has emphasized a long historical perspective, moving from antiquity to fifteenth-century England. From this long perspective, we can see late-medieval controversies about learning and the literal sense in relation to much earlier institutional histories that set the stage for later terms of debate. We have seen that in the fourteenth century, the literal sense was not only a hermeneutical tool, but was also an acutely determined political category of long historical lineage. The literal sense had

---

[96] The epilogue to the Matthew commentary in BL Add. 28026 asks "If ony lernd man in holy writ fynde ony defaute in this glose, sette he in the treuwe and cler sentence of holy doctouris; for this is the greet desire of this pore scribeler" (fol. 186r; also printed in Deanesly, *The Lollard Bible*, 457). The same theme is expressed in the prologue to the short commentary on Matthew (BL Add. 41175, fol. 1v; Trinity College Cambridge B. 1. 38, fol. 1r). On differentiated status of the literate and non-literate in Lollard conventicles, see McSheffrey, *Gender and Heresy*, 58–61.

[97] See Bourdieu, *Language and Symbolic Power*, 119, 127–36.

thus acquired various meanings – as interpretive system, as pedagogical method, and as a symbol of the difference between adulthood and childhood – when it entered the charged environment of late-medieval heresy. On its entrance into this scene, it was already a powerful mechanism for organizing competing discourses of knowledge and political agency.

The central theme of the Lollard classroom was the notion that the literal sense as a pedagogical tool can be reclaimed as an instrument of hermeneutical control. This radical theme presents an ideological reversal that could not have been produced and articulated solely out of contemporary confluences of ecclesiology and spiritual non-conformism. In its revalution of the literal sense as an "adult hermeneutics," the teaching of the Lollard heretical classroom does not look like other contemporary forms of vernacular devotional practice and instruction. For it is not simply that Lollardy opens the Bible and biblical exegesis to vernacular audiences: rather, the Lollard classroom unmakes long-standing distinctions between the symbolic domains of childhood and adulthood. Lollard teaching insists that elementary learning does not have to be "childish" learning, with all of the political restrictions attendant upon notions of childhood. At this most profound level it challenges the foundations of academic professionalism. Lollardy redefines the fundamental conditions of scriptural knowledge by asserting that what non-clerical adult audiences can know is the very horizon of an adequate and politically enabling hermeneutics. It refuses pastoral formulas that equate laity with puerility; and it does so by rejecting the historical baggage of pastoral condescension, the association of pedagogical literalism with presumptions of childish limitation.

Thus far we have considered how traditional and heterodox discourses represent those who are taught. Now we will turn to the other side of the pedagogical equation, to consider how those who teach are recognized and represented. In the following part we will examine how dissenting intellectuals come to be known – to their communities and to their adversaries – through the distinctive work that they perform as embodiments of the project of pedagogy.

PART 2

Violent representations: intellectuals and prison writing

INTRODUCTION

The heretical classroom envisions the leveling of traditional magisterial hierarchies. How, accordingly, does the dissenting community reimagine the work and reconfigure the social relations of intellectuals? R. I. Moore notes that heresy differed from other objects of persecution in the Middle Ages "in being identifiable with personal leaders and possessing its own structures of personal authority."[1] Intellectuals assume the roles of teachers, advocates, and representatives, and also of mobilizers and witnesses. They embody a political position which they articulate to and on behalf of a certain public, a community that can define itself through its public advocates and expositors. The intellectual leaders of medieval heretical groups are the most visible participants of their resistance movements. And it is with that particular visibility that they must occupy the already problematic space that official legal structures make for self-representation among dissidents.

One of those spaces – in no way an abstract one – from which dissenting intellectuals speak is prison. Two Lollard writers come forward to us through "personal" narratives of interrogation under imprisonment: the Lollard priests Richard Wyche and William Thorpe. While these heretical intellectuals are hardly unique for having suffered imprisonment, or for having produced important writings while under some kind of detention, the configurations of history and narrative form that condition the accounts of Wyche and Thorpe give us texts that cannot fit general categories. On the other hand, these two texts do speak directly to general, even paradigmatic questions about intellectuals, dissenting communities, and the possibilities of "representation." The very singularity of these texts is also what allows them to speak paradigmatically: by turning the focus onto the personal and even the autobiographical, they speak through, rather than suppress, the problems of visible identity and personal authority; and they foreground the question of

---

[1] *The Formation of a Persecuting Society*, 133.

how intellectuals might know themselves in relation to their communities, a knowledge played out through textured images of their own lives placed at risk.[2]

It is important to distinguish these texts from other examples of medieval and early-modern writing by political prisoners. Unlike prisoners of war, factional fighting, or political intrigue, for example, the prison writers Albertanus of Brescia, Charles d'Orléans, or James I of Scotland, Wyche and Thorpe are under internal political detention.[3] But unlike others imprisoned by their own state, from Boethius to Thomas Usk and George Ashby, Wyche and Thorpe are representatives of a recognized dissident group, rather than the hapless, tragic victims of political disfavor, factionalism, or even state paranoia. Moreover, unlike the writings of better-known political prisoners, such as Boethius and, later, Usk, as well as other heretics under detention, the narrative accounts of Wyche and Thorpe testify specifically to their interrogation and to the mechanics of inquisition under detention.

In this way their texts do not simply teach (in the manner of doctrinal expositions), but also make the legal–pedagogical process of interrogation the subject of rhetorical *manifestatio*. Thus while these writers share some historical circumstances with the Lollards Walter Brut and William Swinderby, who wrote in self-defense while awaiting trial, the texts of Wyche and Thorpe do not belong with these others in a single larger generic category. For similar reasons we can differentiate between the narrative accounts of interrogation by Wyche and Thorpe and actual trial records which contain suspects' responses to interrogation, including those of the best-known Lollard intellectuals, Hereford and Purvey. The anonymous *Opus arduum*, a commentary on the Apocalypse written in 1390 while its author was incarcerated, shares some compositional circumstances with the texts of Wyche and Thorpe, although it is not, like theirs, a personal narrative. But while it is not of one generic piece with the Wyche and Thorpe accounts, the *Opus arduum* offers itself as a teaching text, thus linking it with certain features of their narratives and inviting comparison with them, as we will see in chapter 3.

The accounts of Wyche and Thorpe could be likened to the personal and often polemical letters of Jan Hus written during his imprisonment in Constance while he was on trial and awaiting execution in 1415. But despite their emotional directness and their situational drama, Hus' letters do not present the same kind of sustained narrative of the mechanics of interrogation

---

[2] Edward Said, *Representations of the Intellectual*, 11–14.
[3] On prison themes in Charles d'Orléans, James I, Thomas Usk, and George Ashby, see Boffey, "Chaucerian Prisoners: the Context of the *Kingis Quair*." On Usk's "Appeal," see Strohm, "The Textual Vicissitudes of Usk's Appeal," in *Hochon's Arrow*, 145–60. On Albertanus (*De amore*), see Powell, *Albertanus of Brescia*, and Wallace, *Chaucerian Polity*, 213–21.

and counter-strategy as the accounts of Wyche and Thorpe. Individual letters are notable for their treatment of highlights of confrontation and maneuvering between Hus and his examiners at Constance, but the narrative effect is one of selectiveness rather than continuity.[4] Perhaps this is because Hus was so public a figure, his trial so much an event carried out in the full view of the historical record, including the eyewitness account of the proceedings prepared by his friend Peter of Mladoňovice, that the burden of narrating his opposition did not fall solely on Hus' shoulders.[5] Hus' story was told by many people; Wyche and Thorpe must tell their own stories.

Of course the common ancestors of the witnessings of Wyche and Thorpe as well as of other prison or interrogation narratives by Christian dissenters are the Acts of the Apostles and Paul's prison epistles. All such texts, up through the Protestant Reformation, participate quite consciously in the literary-spiritual tradition of Acts and the Pauline epistles: empathy with the radicalism of the early church is central to the self-definition of later Christian radicalism, which by its nature (and by the very etymology of "radical") looks backward to the purist beginnings of the apostolic church and of Christian community. Boethius' *De consolatione philosophiae* may be the literary precedent of choice for writers whose religious orthodoxy is never in question, who invoke Boethius' themes of fortitude in the face of unjust suffering, notably, for example, Thomas Usk in his *Testament of Love*. But for religious dissenters, Acts, with its scenes of the apostles' imprisonment and interrogation by the religious establishment, and the Pauline epistles, with their personal witnessing of faith, are much the more resonant generic references. Like the apostles, Wyche, Thorpe, and other religious dissenters represent a new sect within an existing church, speaking as members of that church even as they are persecuted by its orthodox establishment. Here Acts may be more particularly relevant to the later dissenters. Beyond the scenes of imprisonment, punishment, and physical suffering, the parallels between Acts and the narratives of Wyche and Thorpe that would have been most resonant for English Lollard audiences would be the work of teaching, proselytizing, and forming faithful communities.

But noting the parallels with scriptural genres is not sufficient to explain the power of the Lollard narratives within their contemporary late-medieval settings. Thus what I propose to explore here are the particular contemporary

---

[4] For such highlights see, for example, letters 9 and 34 in the sources collected in Spinka, ed. and trans., *John Hus at the Council of Constance*, 252–4, 293–4. Hus' complete correspondence is edited by Palacký, *Documenta Magister Johannis Hus.*

[5] The English translation of the *Relatio de Magistro Johanne Hus* by Peter of Mladoňovice is in Spinka, *Jan Hus at the Council of Constance*, 87–234. It is edited by Novotný, "Historické spisy Petra z Mladoňovic a jiné zprávy a paměti o M. Janovi Husovi a M. Jeronymovi z Prahy."

conditions of dissident culture which would make such resonances meaning-ful to early-fifteenth-century audiences. The work performed by the narra-tives of Wyche and Thorpe, including the work of recalling the earliest Christian witnesses, is achieved through the urgency of the contemporary social environment which produces the dissenters and their writings. Wyche and Thorpe are late-medieval intellectuals, and it is in this social role that they can realize and embody the ancient apostolic model of radical religious dissent and teaching. This is one of the most important ways in which our understanding of scriptural parallels must be nuanced: Wyche and Thorpe are objects of unusual attention from orthodox authorities not just because they are proselytizers, but because they represent a particular social category in contemporary culture, that of the intellectual who has taken his project of producing knowledge *extra muros*. They are recognizable members of an intellectual caste, and in this they differ from charismatic figures of authority in other, earlier contexts of religious dissidence.[6]

As Gramsci argued, it is inadequate to essentialize intellectuals apart from the kinds of work that they perform in a particular social organization. This is also the principle that lies behind modern readings of the sociology of medieval intellectuals, most importantly in Le Goff's historiography. In his essay "The Formation of the Intellectuals," Gramsci, himself writing from prison, attempts to redraw the definition of intellectual "work"; however well known his arguments have become, it is worth quoting here from a crucial passage of the essay:

> What are the "maximum" limits of acceptance of the term "intellectual"? Can one find a unitary criterion to characterise equally all the diverse and disparate activities of intellectuals and to distinguish these at the same time, and in an essential way from the activities of other social groupings? The most widespread error of method seems to me that of having looked for this criterion of distinction in the intrinsic nature of intellectual activities, rather than in the ensemble of the system of relations in which these activities (and therefore the intellectual groups who personify them) have their place within the general complex of social relations . . . All men are intellectuals, one could therefore say: but not all men have in society the function of intellectual.[7]

In this analysis it is social function in "the ensemble of [a] system of relations" that takes precedence over ordained professional status and over the privileges but also marginality that attend on traditional intellectual claims to auton-

---

[6] Compare these Lollard figures with the charismatic dissidents of the earlier years of the millennium; see Stock, *Implications of Literacy*, 101–6.
[7] "The Formation of the Intellectuals," *Prison Notebooks*, 8–9.

omy. The intellectual function, in whatever group or social context it is elaborated, is "to bring into being new modes of thought" (9). Gramsci's analysis shifts attention from the intrinsic features of intellectual work (however those would be determined) to the possibility of intellectual agency within political structures, especially as such models of agency would challenge traditional categories of intellectual work as necessarily self-marginalizing.

How might we begin to describe the "ensemble of the system of relations" in which the activities of Lollard intellectuals have their place? The prison writers considered here are members of the traditional professional class of intellectuals (academics, clergy). Their professional status affords them certain privileges in their treatment by legal authorities, both in discursive spheres where their views are accorded unusual (and commensurately more hostile) attention, and in the material and legal conditions of their detainment, because systems of imprisonment tended to distinguish between clerics and lay persons.[8] Yet these intellectuals do not serve the interests of their professional class. Indeed, the landmark theme of Lollard educational beliefs, as articulated paradoxically by the movement's own intellectual core, is disdain for the division of labor between intellectuals and "followers." That this passionately held tenet cannot be sustained in practice in this (or any) heretical movement dominated by charismatic schoolmen or other intellectual leaders is precisely the complex of social relations out of which intellectual labor must redefine its function. While these writers cannot speak from outside their real professional and class affiliations, in speaking against the interests of that class they elaborate another role for their work. That role is elaborated out of the scene of prison, a space that they turn into the scene of school. Thus, for these writers, the product of intellectual labor, as well as the social function of that labor, is pedagogy itself.

In order for their work to be effective, intellectuals must, of course, become known, beyond their immediate circles, to history and to public memory. Making themselves known to their larger communities and to history is also part of the "ensemble of the system of relations" in which these medieval figures assume the function of intellectuals. How are they to be known? Necessarily through their narratives; but their texts also raise many problems of representation, questions of the kind of self that can emerge into literary and historical "knowability" in the face of violent legal opposition. Indeed, their narratives etch them sharply out of the opposition that confronts them.

---

[8] On imprisonment of clerics, especially in bishops' prisons, see Pugh, *Imprisonment in Medieval England*, 18, 48, 51, 102, 134–9, 352, 360–1; see also Peters, "Prison before the Prison: the Ancient and Medieval Worlds."

A brief illustration from the Thorpe narrative can suggest here the scope of the questions of representation to be explored further in the following chapters. William Thorpe's account of his examination by Archbishop Thomas Arundel at Saltwood Castle on 7 August 1407 climaxes with a scene that could be called paradigmatic of the dissenting intellectual's claim on "representation," meaning both self-construction and public advocacy on behalf of a constituency. After what seems an endless day of interrogation and cross-interrogation between Arundel and Thorpe, Arundel breaks into violent exasperation with Thorpe's passive–aggressive resistance and refusals to submit to ecclesiastical authority:

> And the Archebischop seide to me, "Submitte thee than now here wilfulli and mekeli to the ordenaunce of holi chirche whiche I shal schewe to thee."
> And I seide "Sere, acordingli as I haue rehersid to you I wole be now redy to obeie ful gladli to Crist the heed of al holi chirche, and to the lore and to the heestis and to the counseilis of euery plesyng membre of him."
> And than the Archebischop, smytyng with his fist fersli vpon a copbord , spake to me with a grete spirit, seiynge, "Bi Iesu, but if thou leeue suche addiciouns, obeiynge thee now here withouten ony accepcioun to myn ordinaunce, or that I go out of this place I schal make thee as sikir as ony theef that is in Kent. And avise thee now what thou wolt do."
> And than as if he hadde been angrid, the Archebischop wente from the copbord where he stood to a wyndowe. And than Maluerne and another clerk camen nerhond to me, and thei spaken to me manye wordis ful plesyngeli, and also other wise, manassynge me and counseilynge me ful bisili to submytte me, either ellis, thei seiden, I schulde not ascape ponyschinge ouer mesure. For I schulde, thei seiden, be degratid, cursid and brent and so thanne dampned.[9]

This scene presents itself as a kind of interrogational spectacle, with all the gesture of dramatized inquisition. The angry Arundel pounds the cupboard with his fist and strides impatiently to a window, while his clerks, presented here as mere lackeys, continue the subordinate work of harrying the prisoner, by turns cajoling and threatening him. As this brief passage can suggest, the intellectual's emergence into "knowability" as a public representative relies on the process of self-representation, with all the tension and personal risk of an adversarial encounter. Thorpe as subject becomes knowable through what can only be called a "violence of representation." At their most basic, the mechanics of interrogation are violent: Arundel rages, the clerks harrass, and Thorpe is threatened with everything from imprisonment as a common criminal ("I schal make thee as sikir as ony theef that is in Kent" – erasing the

---

[9] Text in Hudson, ed., *Two Wycliffite Texts*, 87–8 (hereafter page numbers noted in the text).

privilege of clergy to be distinguished from other prisoners) to degradation from his priestly office, malediction, burning, and damnation. It is through such acts of suppression that legal powers make the dissenter knowable as someone outside the law; through such terms that the law "represents" – and in this way essentializes – dissent and the dissenter. And these are the terms that must be engaged in Thorpe's own self-narrative, that inform his self-representation through the discursive mechanics of opposition, where he can come into being as a historical identity only through positing a negative relationship between self and others, in a way that reproduces the law's essentializing procedure.[10] The means by which Thorpe can be known as a dissenter are laid out by the external mechanics of legal and inquisitorial representation, and these become inseparable from the process of representing his own subjectivity.

These terms of violent oppositionality also frame the representation of his public function as advocate for and example to a community. The scene of the impatient Arundel and the menacing clerks continues with the clerks making one last attempt to persuade Thorpe of the wisdom of submitting to ecclesiastical authority by invoking the examples of Thorpe's former confederates who have since recanted and made "good" of their choice:

> "But now," thei seiden, "thou maist exchewe alle these myscheues, if thou wolt submitte thee mekeli and wilfully to this worthi prelate that hath cure of thi soule. And for the pitee of Crist," thei seiden, "bethinke thee how greet clerkis the bischop of Lyncoln, Herforde and Purueie weren and yit ben, and also Bowland, that is a wel vndirstondynge man, which alle foure haue forsaken and reuokiden al the lore and opynyouns that thou and sich other holden! Wherfore, sith ech of hem is myche wiser than art thou, [for as thou confessidist er this, these men weren thin infourmeris and techeris,] we counseile thee for the beste that bi ensaumple of these foure clerkis sue thou hem [now in the weie of truthe as thou didest bifore in the weie of errour], submittinge thee as thei diden . . ."
>
> And I seide to these clerkis that thus bisili counseileden me to sue these forseide men, "Seres, if Philip of Repingtoun, Nicol Herforde, Ion Purueye and Robert Bowland, of whom ye counseilen me to take ensaumple, hadden thei forsaken beneficis of temperal profit and of worldly worschip, so that thei hadden exchewid and alyened hem from alle occasiouns of couetise, and of fleischly lustis, and hadden taken hem to symple lyuynge and wilful pouerte, thei hadden hereinne gouun good ensaumple to me and to manye other for to haue sued hem. But now, sith alle these foure men haue schamefulli and sclaundrousli don contrarie, consentynge to resceyuen and

<hr />

[10] Compare Armstrong and Tennenhouse, eds., *The Violence of Representation: Literature and the History of Violence,* "Introduction: Representing Violence," 6–9.

to haue and holden temperal beneficis, lyuynge now more worldli and fleischly than thei diden biforehonde, confourmynge hem to the maneres of this world, I forsake hem hereinne and all her sclaundrouse doynge . . .

And thanne the Archebischop seide to his clerkis, "Bisie you no lengir aboute him, for he and other such as he is ben confedrid so togidre that thei wolen not swere to ben obedient and to submitte hem to prelatis of holi chirche." (88–90)

Here the condition of his "knowability" as an intellectual representing a public (in the double sense of advocacy and exemplification) is to be "known" through radical opposition to his natural intellectual confreres, Repington, Purvey, Hereford, and Bowland, who stand both for the forsaken terms of scandalous example and for the legal authority that can "know" Thorpe by pronouncing him outside its terms of conformity.

To put this in its broadest context, beyond the self-narratives of individual intellectuals, we should consider how dissent itself only comes into being through oppositional recognition. It is "summoned" or "hailed" through a certain violence of representation which, like the juridical reprimand in Althusser's exemplification of the social formation of the subject, compels dissent into its subjected and thus knowable status.[11] Dissent as attitude, action, or habit is ushered into formation through the interpellative gestures of representation, whether that gesture is rumor or outright denunciation, or the social control of propaganda, or even the more complex gestures of recognition from within, the welcome "hailing" among participants that invites self-identification with a community that has been defined as outside the law. The recognition of dissent thus also relies on the rhetorical design of narratives, plots with beginnings, crises, resolutions: trial records that end in abjurations or sentences; or as we are exploring here, testimonials and quasi-hagiographical accounts; or related articulations of compulsion under the reprimanding "summons."

However, it is not simply that representation – the reprimand or welcome – ushers dissent into being. For it is even more the struggles within and among narratives, the resistances within the project of representing resistance, and often most significantly, what escapes recognition, that produce the oppositionalities of dissent as habit or practice. I intend here to trace out such points of resistance in the prison narratives of Wyche and Thorpe, those elements of the texts that most sharply engage with (or are engaged by) violent representation, by forms of misrecognition and the suppression of other competing identities. These points of resistance within their narratives are

---

[11] Althusser, "Ideology and Ideological State Apparatuses (Notes Towards an Investigation)", in *Lenin and Philosophy and Other Essays*, 170–7.

also, as I want to show, the mechanisms through which their functions as critical intellectuals, "bringing into being new modes of thought," take shape.

In the chapters that follow I will consider how these intellectuals leave records of their teaching projects, their identities, and their historical moments. In his prison narrative, Richard Wyche engages a Lollard schooling in the disputational techniques of evasion, so that he leaves to the public record a method of defiant self-representation in the face of inquisition. His text exemplifies how to match interrogational pressure with argumentative finesse; the legacy he leaves is not an image of himself, but rather an image of what can be taught. Thorpe's text is also a didactic exemplification of intellectual method, but it isolates the figure of the intellectual, who is seen grasping at the claims of historicity while struggling against the historical forces that would negate the power of academic intellectuals to bring their project to a broader community.

3

Richard Wyche and the public record

The most important struggle faced by the Lollard intellectuals writing from prison is one that is common to what is often the autobiographical mode of prison writing. One modern prison writer, Ngugi wa Thiong'o, has expressed this struggle well in the preface to his detention memoir: "I have, therefore, tried to discuss detention not as a personal affair between me and a few individuals, but as a social, political, and historical phenomenon."[1] Moving beyond personal narrative, converting self-formation into a "social, political, and historical phenomenon," is the claim that the Lollard texts also make explicitly, as both their envoys indicate, even while their strategies for accomplishing this end may not resemble those of celebrated twentieth-century prison writers like Ngugi, or, more recently, Ken Saro Wiwa and Nelson Mandela, who have spoken directly to the political and historical implications of modern imprisonment.[2] It is worth noting that the testimonies of Wyche and Thorpe are virtually the only narratives of the Lollard movement, outside of official trial records (including such heterogeneous matter as John Oldcastle's examination), that offer fully realized personal, and in that respect "biographical," accounts. That the only personal testimonies of the Lollard movement should be accounts of interrogation under detention is not in itself surprising, since there is no situation that more sharply defines the dissenter.[3] Where other personal "testimonies" exist, such as the curious pair of letters that Wyche and Oldcastle wrote in 1410 respectively to Jan Hus and Woksa von Waldstein in Bohemia, the accounts tend to retreat into the conventional salutations of apostolic epistles.[4]

What are the historical conditions that call for these prison narratives with

---

[1] Ngugi, *Detained: a Writer's Prison Diary*, xi.

[2] Ken Saro Wiwa, *A Month and a Day: a Detention Diary*; compare Mandela's account of his years on Robben Island in his autobiography *Long Walk to Freedom*, 379–510.

[3] Compare Franklin, *Prison Literature in America*, 249–50: "People who have become literary artists because of their imprisonment tend to write in an autobiographical mode. The reason is obvious: it is their own personal experience that has given them both their main message and the motive to communicate it."   [4] For discussion of these letters and references, see below, pp. 185–7.

all of their personal and situational specificity? Wyche's letter, the earlier of the two prison narratives, provides the more obvious point of entry into the historical record. Wyche was a priest of the Hereford diocese. His letter shows him displaying the disputational confidence of one with academic training, but actual links that he may likely have had with Oxford are shadowy and cannot be pinned down.[5] He was active in Northumberland in 1401–2, and while preaching there (probably in Newcastle) in 1402, he was summoned to appear before Bishop Walter Skirlaw of Durham.[6] On 7 December 1402, he was interviewed by Skirlaw at Bishop Auckland, near Chester-le-Street, and, failing to make a satisfactory answer at this meeting, was excommunicated and sent to the bishop's prison in the castle at Bishop Auckland, where he awaited further examination. From this date in December 1402 to sometime in March 1403, he was incarcerated and periodically brought before the bishop or the bishop's chancellor for further examination. In March he was pronounced a heretic, laid under major excommunication, and was detained in prison awaiting degradation from his orders. At this late point in the process, just after he was returned to prison for the last time, Wyche composed his long letter to a lay friend living in Newcastle, in which he described in great detail the fitful proceedings against him, the attempts by the bishop and other authorities to make him recant and affirm his faith in orthodox teaching.[7] The immediate consequences of these proceedings are

---

[5] Hudson suggests, as a "remote possibility," that the colleague "Jacobus" mentioned in the letter (535; for citation of the letter, see note 7 below), with whom Wyche was accused of collaborating in spreading heresy in Northumberland, may be William James, fellow of Merton College (*Premature Reformation*, 90); cf. Workman, *John Wyclif* 2: 339. On the basis of the appearance in a single Prague manuscript of Wyche's letter and a Latin version of William Taylor's 1406 sermon (see note 7 below), Hudson has also made the tentative suggestion that the connection between Taylor and Wyche may be closer than previously thought; that the transmission of Wyche's letter to Bohemia might also have involved other figures with definite Oxford connections, William Thorpe or Peter Payne, is put forward with even more caution; see Hudson, "William Taylor's 1406 Sermon: a Postscript." For another hypothesis about Wyche's links with Oxford, interpreting evidence in the manuscript containing Wyche's letter (a medieval scribe's mistaken attribution to Wyche of a treatise on the eucharist in the same manuscript), see von Nolcken, "Richard Wyche, a Certain Knight, and the Beginning of the End," 149, n. 60.

[6] On Wyche's activities in the north, and the context for his appearance before Skirlawe, see Snape, "Some Evidence of Lollard Activity in the Diocese of Durham in the Early Fifteenth Century."

[7] Wyche's letter is edited by Matthew, "The Trial of Richard Wyche" (hereafter cited in the text by page number). The sole copy of the letter is found in Prague, National (formerly University) Library MS III. G. 11, fols. 89v–99v. That it is found only in a Latin version does not preclude the possibility that it was originally composed in English (since it was addressed to a layman); preserved in the same manuscript (directly following on the text of Wyche's letter) is a Latin text of William Taylor's 1406 sermon, of which there is also an English version (Oxford, Bodleian MS Douce 53, fols. 1r–30r), edited by Hudson, *Two Wycliffite Texts*. On the Latin version of Taylor's sermon in the Prague manuscript, see Hudson, "William Taylor's 1406 Sermon." The manuscript contains, in addition to the Taylor sermon and the letter by Wyche, a number of writings by Wyclif as well as by Jan Hus. The Wyclif texts in the manuscript are listed by Thomson, *The Latin Writings of John Wyclyf*, 314. The contents of the whole manuscript are described by Truhlář, *Catalogus codicum manu scriptorum latinorum qui in C. R. Bibliotheca Publica atque Universitatis Pragensis asservantur* 1: 536–8.

well known: he was brought to recant at some date between late 1404 and early 1406, recorded in the *Fasciculi zizaniorum*.[8] But the evidence of Wyche's heretical activity also continues for the next three decades: in 1410 he wrote a letter to Jan Hus, dated the same day and from the same place as a letter that John Oldcastle wrote to the Bohemian noble Woksa von Wald-stein; he was imprisoned again in 1419–20; and in 1440 he was convicted as a relapsed heretic and burned at Smithfield in London.[9]

During the period that Wyche was in Skirlaw's prison, Skirlaw and his chancellor were also hunting other heretics in Durham. Between February and April 1403 Skirlaw examined three priests who were possibly Wyche's associates in Northumberland: James Nottingham, John de Roxburgh, and John Whitby.[10] Wyche also recounts that it was reported to him, while he was in prison, that Skirlaw's chancellor had found a Lollard "master" at Newcastle, one Robert, whom Wyche identifies as Robert Herl ("Et con-salutetis me fratri meo Roberto Herl qui in causa Dei et quodammodo pro me suscipit obprobria" [Matthew, 542] ["And send greetings to my brother Robert Herl who in God's cause and in a way on my account received abuse"]).[11] From May 1403 there is also a mandate against a Robert York of Newcastle, whose Lollard connections (at least to judge from the nature of the accusations against him) are very obscure; but this Robert, who was master of the Trinitarian hospital of Wallknoll, may perhaps be identified with the "magister" of "Balknolle" whom Wyche mentions as one who should secretly read his letter ("ut secrete legatur magistro meo de Balknolle" [Matthew, 541]).[12]

Skirlaw's busyness in hunting out Lollards in Durham diocese is perhaps a sign of intensified interest in prosecuting heretics in the years immediately following the heresy statute of 1401, *De heretico comburendo*, imposing a death sentence on obdurate heretics.[13] Skirlaw's activity at this important juncture certainly accords with earlier patterns of newly energized adminis-trative and investigative measures against heresy in other dioceses following on events of large consequence, as after the Uprising of 1381, and after the

---

[8] *Fasciculi zizaniorum*, 501–5; for dating see Snape, "Some Evidence of Lollard Activity," 359.

[9] See the summary of Wyche's later career in Thomson, *The Later Lollards*, 148–51; and see the discussion below, pp. 183–90. On Wyche's career see also Emden, *A Biographical Register of the University of Oxford* 3: 2101.

[10] Snape, "Some Evidence of Lollard Activity," 356–7, 359; Matthew, "The Trial of Richard Wyche," 535, citing a possible reference to James Nottingham ("Jacobus et ego subvertimus populum in North-umbria"), and 541, where Wyche entrusts his letter to one Bhytebi i.e. Whitby.

[11] And see Snape, "Some Evidence of Lollard Activity," 358.   [12] Ibid., 359.

[13] On the context and immediate effect of this legislation, see McHardy, "*De Heretico Comburendo*, 1401."

"Merciless Parliament" of 1388.[14] Beyond Skirlaw's investigations, there is no evidence of significant Lollard activity in Durham or in the north in general in the fifteenth century; the early sixteenth century saw a small number of cases.[15] Martin Snape, who has done the fullest research on the Lollards of the diocese of Durham, believes that the five men investigated during and just after Wyche's confinement, along with the various sympathetic clergy and lay people of Newcastle mentioned in Wyche's letter (another thirteen persons), represent a small, established Lollard community of that town and its environs.[16] But either that Lollard activity did not survive Skirlaw's prosecutions of the group's leaders, or, as is equally possible, the community's further activities went unrecorded by later bishops who had less enthusiasm for "heresy-hunting."[17] Skirlaw died in 1406, and the records of his successor Thomas Langley, bishop from 1406 to 1437, make no specific reference to Lollard activity in the diocese.[18] Of course Wyche's own career as a Lollard outlasted Skirlaw and Langley both, but his activities after 1405 until his burning in London in 1440 leave no trace in the Durham diocese.

One more intriguing fragment of evidence for Lollard activity in the diocese is contained in Wyche's letter. In the envoy he indicates that certain books he has requested will reach him if sent to a priest named Henry of Topcliff, who lives next to the church of Auckland St. Andrew (near Bishop Auckland, where Wyche was imprisoned). This priest, Wyche says, "habet fratrem in Topcliff qui desponsatur sorori domini Wilhelmi Corpp" (Matthew, 543) ("has a brother in Topcliff who is betrothed to a sister of William ?Corpp"). As Anne Hudson has pointed out, once we account for the curious spellings of English names in this Bohemian manuscript (as in other Bohemian copies of English texts), and for the easy confusion of *c* and *t*, it is possible to identify this last-mentioned name as that of William Thorpe. This would accord with the claim leveled against Thorpe, recounted in his testimony (internally dated 1407), that he had preached throughout the north country for the past twenty years. Beyond the possibility that Thorpe was himself active in the diocese of Durham, this evidence also offers the provocative suggestion that Wyche and Thorpe knew each other as confederates in their heterodox preaching.[19]

The same reasons for the Newcastle community coming to light, that is,

[14] Richardson, "Heresy and the Lay Power under Richard II," 10. For interesting parallels with heresy-hunting in Lincoln diocese in the 1380s and early 1390s, see McHardy, "Bishop Buckingham and the Lollards of Lincoln Diocese." [15] Thomson, *The Later Lollards*, 192–201.

[16] Snape, "Some Evidence of Lollard Activity," 361.

[17] Thomson, *The Later Lollards*, 192; McFarlane, *John Wycliffe and the Beginnings of English Nonconformity*, 111. [18] Thomson, *The Later Lollards*, 192–3.

[19] Hudson, *Two Wycliffite Texts*, lviii, 29.

the proximity to the *De heretico comburendo* statute of 1401, the burning of the Lollard priest William Sawtry, and the heightened apprehension of heresy as a state interest, doubtless also account for Wyche's promptings to write of his experience. While *De heretico comburendo* was really the culmination of two decades of the involvement of secular powers in the prosecution of heresy, the burning of Sawtry (directly after the statute's passage) certainly had a singular psychic impact on members of the heretical community, as John Purvey's hasty recantation within a week of Sawtry's execution shows.[20] At a sensitive moment for the new dynasty, the burning of Sawtry was certainly calculated to make an even broader impression; but the impact of the message that it was intended to deliver (the union of dynastic power with ecclesiastical authority) would have been felt not only directly, but in combination with many other disturbances at the turn of the century: rebellions and the prosecution of various perceived enemies of the new regime.[21] That Wyche's account, not just his actual trial, but his undertaking of a dramatic self-representation from prison, comes so soon after 1401, does suggest how the sense of personal danger, and, more important, the sense of personal stake in public discourse, had risen to the surface.

Wyche's is the first known account by a Lollard under examination to elaborate a personal relationship with a community and with that community's interest in the public record. Wyche's autobiographical narrative follows on over a decade of vigorous supression, punctuated by the notable, highly personalized examples of the recantations of Hereford in 1391 and Purvey in 1401, the latter during the same week that Sawtry was led to the flames. Wyche records that Purvey's recantation was read to him (either as news or, more likely, as example) while he was in prison ("ductus sum assummacione ante episcopum et legerunt coram me revocacionem Purvey et voluissent me credere sicut ipse revocasset" [Matthew, 537] ["I was led by summons before the bishop and they read before me the recantation of Purvey and wanted me to believe he had recanted in this manner"]). Certainly the threat of burning is a theme, explicit as well as implied, throughout his account. An Augustinian master who visits him in prison after one of his earlier interviews with the bishop warns him: "Nisi egeris secundum

---

[20] Richardson, "Heresy and the Lay Power under Richard II," 24. Purvey's recantation is printed in *Fasciculi zizaniorum*, 400–7; his trial is printed in Wilkins, ed., *Concilia* 3: 158–68. On Purvey's trial see McFarlane, *John Wycliffe and the Beginnings of English Nonconformity*, 136–7; and Hudson, "John Purvey: a Reconsideration of the Evidence for his Life and Writings," 87.

[21] See Aston, "Lollardy and Sedition, 1381–1431," 40–2. Among recent surveys of the events of this period see Powell, *Kingship, Law, and Society: Criminal Justice in the Reign of Henry V*, 117–40. On one of the more bizarre disturbances of the turn of the century, the citings of the ghost of Richard II, see McNiven, "Rebellion, Sedition, and the Legend of Richard II's Survival in the Reigns of Henry IV and Henry V," and Strohm, *England's Empty Throne*, 101–27.

consilium eorum, vis comburi," to which he replies "Sicut Deus voluerit . . . fiat" (Matthew, 533) ("'If you don't act according to their counsel, you can be burned' . . . 'If God wishes, let it be so'"). At a later crucial turn of the story he admits that he is most eager to be released: "Vellem, dixi, liberari libenter, si Deo placeret" (Matthew, 534) ("I would gladly wish, I said, to be set free, so may it please God"). Of course the reading of Purvey's recantation is a barely concealed reference, on the part of his examiners, to the coercive power of a death penalty for intractable heretics. And indeed, among the items in Wyche's own abjuration, as recorded in the *Fasciculi zizaniorum*, is the assertion that the burning of heretics is wrong.[22] Prior to 1401 burning had certainly been part of the general discourse of Lollardy, whether as an apocalyptic trope of Lollard polemic,[23] or as a strategic (but legally unformalized) threat, as Swinderby claimed he had suffered at the hands of a crowd of zealous clerics at Lincoln in 1382 who, he says, brought forth wood in preparation for a fire and in that way coerced his recantation on the spot.[24] But the particularity of this theme in Wyche's account, as a culmination of the recent history of the movement, throws into relief what is at issue for the imperatives of personal advocacy and exemplification.

That such urgency of advocacy through personal example might be the peculiar effect of more than a decade of suppressions, culminating in the death penalty legislation of 1401, can be seen through comparison with earlier detention writing. The text that offers the closest parallel to the prison narratives of Wyche and Thorpe is the *Opus arduum*, a pointedly anonymous commentary on the Apocalypse, written in 1390 and preserved in thirteen continental manuscripts, nearly all of Bohemian provenance.[25] A colophon in two manuscripts states that the work was begun at Christmas time and was completed at Easter in 1390, *in carcere*, with many interruptions (a month, two weeks, a week, or many days) during that time. The dates of writing (1389–90) are confirmed at various points in the text, and in the prologue the author notes that he has been confined for three years.[26]

---

22 "Illegitime faciunt qui homines comburunt," *Fasciculi zizaniorum*, 503.

23 For example, from a Good Friday sermon: "And so, yif men maken lawis not groundide on Goddis lawe, and dampnen men as heretikis for they don ayenus thes lawis, thes dampneres ben heritikis, for they wolen be another god. And thus the pope and his cardenals smacchen [smack of] ofte heresy, for they brennen men as heretikis, for they mayntenen Goddis law." Hudson, ed., *English Wycliffite Sermons* 3: 181.

24 *Registrum Johannis Trefnant*, 238–9. This event of 1382 was recounted before Bishop Trefnant at Swinderby's trial of 1390. As Swinderby puts it, this procedure was conducted with enormous public support, and "with favore of [the] byschoppe, be what lawe I wot not, but sothly not by Godes lawe" (239). Swinderby apparently recognized that no law existed to support the threat, although he did submit "for dryde of deth."

25 See Hudson, "A Neglected Wycliffite Text." For the following discussion of the *Opus arduum* I depend on Hudson's richly informative account of the manuscripts and their contents.

26 Hudson, "A Neglected Wycliffite Text," 44.

The *Opus arduum* contains a great deal of circumstantial information that would locate the author in time and place. The author gives his first language as English, cites some English place names (London, Oxford, and Salisbury), makes extensive criticism of the Flanders crusade by Bishop Despenser of Norwich (a common target of Lollard attack), and invokes the name "Lollard" as the term of opprobrium by which hostile bishops justify their persecution of the author and his colleagues.[27] He refers to his own conditions of incarceration, mentioning several times that he is held in shackles ("duplici compede cathenatus" ["I was chained in double shackles"], "compedes non modo ferreos sed calibeos mihi . . . providerunt" ["they have provided me shackles not only of iron but of steel"]).[28] The author also compiles an impressive dossier of learned sources, from patristic authors and the *Glossa ordinaria* to more recent authorities. Some of these are quoted and some only cited.[29] He also refers by name to two of his own writings, one of which is said to be in the vernacular (neither has been identified with an extant text).[30] These sources, along with a reference to Oxford and Salisbury as places where bishops have destroyed the books of Ockham and other Franciscan writers, point clearly to the Oxford origins of this academic Lollard writer.[31]

With all of the circumstantial detail that is supplied here, the author could hardly have remained anonymous to any interested contemporary, as Hudson has observed. Yet the author suppresses his name and identity.[32] Hudson has advanced, cautiously and meticulously, a case for Nicholas Hereford as the writer of the *Opus arduum*: Hereford was imprisoned in Nottingham castle (under the wardenship of Sir William Neville) in 1387 and may have remained in prison until his recantation in 1391 (so that, at the date of this text, 1390, he could have been confined for three years, as the author claims to have been). Other factors in favor of Hereford's authorship are the writer's vehemence towards Urban VI, which could be linked with Hereford's own dealings with Urban in the early 1380s (after his condemnation by Archbishop Courtenay in 1382, Hereford had gone to Rome to appeal to the pope, and Urban had confirmed the condemnation and sentenced Hereford

---

[27] Ibid., 44–5, 54, 61 (the last citing bishops as his imprisoners).

[28] Ibid., 61. For readers of this text such references to fetters would be reminiscent, surely, of the Pauline prison epistles, notably Colossians 4.18.   [29] Ibid., 48–54.   [30] Ibid., 54–5.

[31] Ibid., 49–50, 54.

[32] Hudson, *Premature Reformation*, 10. In the text of the *Opus arduum*, at the exposition of chapter 21, verse 2, there is an apparent hint of the author's name: "*ego ergo Iohannis*, et non ego W. nisi secundarie, *vidi civitatem*"; the initial "W." does not, as Hudson shows, help to identify a candidate for authorship among known figures at the time, and Hudson acknowledges that her own tentative case for Hereford's authorship must disregard the evidence of this initial. See Hudson, "A Neglected Wycliffite Text," 55, 60.

157

to life imprisonment); and Hereford's incarceration under what may have been relatively sympathetic circumstances, which could afford him access to the many sources from which the *Opus arduum* quotes so liberally and in such detail (after his initial arrest in Nottingham in 1387, Hereford had been removed to Nottingham castle at the request of William Neville, who has been identified by the chronicler Thomas Walsingham as among the circle of Lollard knights).[33] Of course the author's representation of his prison condition as harsh (for example, his reference to double shackles) makes the identification with Hereford more problematic if we are to imagine Hereford experiencing rather more generous treatment under the presumably sympathetic guardianship of Neville, unless, as Hudson suggests, the personal details in the *Opus arduum*, like the withholding of the author's name, are ruses designed to protect the credibility of his patron-warden.[34] These are intriguing speculations, but there they must remain.

Within the larger body of Lollard writing, the *Opus arduum* exemplifies the suppression of individual identity into the community of *trewe men*.[35] Beyond this, we can say that this text of the early 1390s shows a submerging of the personal into a larger exegetical and political enterprise. This brings us to the crucial question of this text's position in a general history of Lollard writing, and more particularly a history of prison writing associated with this movement. The *Opus arduum* is a prison "narrative" about disseminating books, including its own exegetical project, and not about self-representation through delineating knowable historical identity. With all of the circumstantial detail about persecution and incarceration that this text supplies, the authorial identity disappears into the collective identity of the *fideles*, the *trewe men* or "faithful," those coded designations for the sect used by both its adherents and adversaries.[36] Thus the *Opus arduum* sets its own project within the general parameters of the duties of the *fidelis predicator* rather than within the more particular terms of intellectual advocacy through personal exemplification:

> fidelis predicator apprehendit sensum huius prophetie et aliarum contra antichristum; non debet tamen thesaurum abscondere quacumque occasione, sed omni tergiuersacione postposita ipsum docere et publice predicare et aduocare coram clero et populo.[37]

33 The details of Hereford's whereabouts between 1387 and 1391 are fragmentary and conflicted. See Hudson, "A Neglected Wycliffite Text," 59–60; McFarlane, *Lancastrian Kings and Lollard Knights*, 198–9; and Walsingham, *Historia anglicana*, ed. Riley, 2: 158.
34 Hudson, "A Neglected Wycliffite Text," 61.
35 See Hudson's assessment, *Premature Reformation*, 10.
36 Hudson, "A Neglected Wycliffite Text," 52–3; and Hudson, "A Lollard Sect Vocabulary?" 165–80.
37 Hudson, "A Neglected Wycliffite Text," 53.

(The faithful preacher understands the sense of this prophecy and of others against antichrist; nevertheless he should on no occasion conceal the treasure, but, leaving all subterfuge aside, he should teach it and publicly preach and advocate before clergy and people.)

Significantly, the author expresses defiance against the condition of imprisonment by casting prison as the liberatory space for producing new books:

> quamvis antichristi tortores nituntur claudere ora ewangelicorum eos incarcerando, tunc dant eis maximam oportunitatem studendi et scribendi contra eum, cuius oppositum credunt ipsi.[38]

(Although antichrist's tormenters [i.e. the agents of antichrist] try to close the mouths of evangelists by incarcerating them, they thereby give them maximum opportunity for study and writing against them.)

And elsewhere, with a more autobiographical tinge, the author asserts:

> non est mihi verisimile quod vnquam ista et consimilia scripsissem contra antichristum et suos, nisi ea occasione qua se putabant michi excludere viam, scilicet me incarcerando ne vnquam agerem aliquid contra eos.[39]

(I do not think it likely that I should ever have written this and similar books against antichrist and his forces, were it not for that circumstance by which they tried to block my way, that is, putting me in prison so that I might not ever do anything against them.)

These remarks present a brilliant paradigm for the conversion of the prison into the school, or, more precisely here, the site of intellectual production, for the pedagogical drama here is a textual one in which books – their circulation or suppression – are the protagonists. Ultimately the author's defiance is on behalf of the triumph of the books produced through a collective intellectual enterprise. As he comments at chapter 12, verses 4–5:

> *Preparat se eciam ad deuorandum filium matris ecclesie,* id est fructum per scripturarum studium conceptum destruere, quod iam patet, quantum in eo est impletum per generalem mandatum prelatorum ad comburendum, destruendum et condemnandum omnes libros, scilicet omelias ewangeliorum et epistolarum in lingwa materna conscriptos, suggerendo quasi non liceat nobis Anglicis legem diuinam habere in nostro wlgari, quo tamen omnibus Ebreis, Grecis et Latinis est commune. Et propterea qui sint diaboli in hac causa discipuli spirituales facile patet, quia fratres huius negocii procuratores erant capitanei et preduces. Sed quamuis ad hec quantum potuit per se et per suos laborauit diabolus, non tamen perfecit, quia non omnes libri tales sunt destructi, sed loco eorum alii iam de nouo

---

[38] Ibid., 44, n. 7.   [39] Ibid., 44.

conscripti sunt ut in tempore breui, Domine fauente, patebit, ipsis multum forciores.[40]

(*Preparat se eciam ad deuorandum filium matris ecclesie*, that is, to destroy the fruit conceived through the study of Scripture, which is now manifest, in as much as it is fulfilled through the general mandate of prelates for burning, destroying, and condemning all books, that is, homilies of the gospels and epistles, written in the mother tongue, so suggesting that it is not licit for us Englishmen to have the divine law in our mother tongue, even while it is commonly available to all Hebrews, Greeks, and Latins. And it is obvious who are the spiritual disciples of the devil in this cause, for the friars have been the procurators, captains, and constructors of this business. But even though the devil has labored at this as much as he can, through his own and his supporters' strength, it has not been fulfilled, because not all such books have been destroyed; but in their place other new books have already been written, so that in a short time, as will be plain to see, God willing, these new books will be even more powerful.)

As these passages suggest, the *Opus arduum* seems to offer so complete a conversion of the prison into the site of intellectual production that, for all of its circumstantiality, it remains a curiously disembodied narrative, a witness to a stage in the history of the movement in which teaching and advocacy can be defined in terms of the monumental products of collective intellectual labor – among these the translations of the Bible, the sermon cycles, and the *Glossed Gospels*. In the difference between the studied anonymity of this text, where the authorial identity disappears behind the struggle of book dissemination, and the accounts of Wyche and a little later Thorpe, where the struggle is to produce a vividly knowable and individuated historical identity, there is a striking resonance with Foucault's celebrated observation about the conditions of authorship: "Texts, books, and discourses really began to have authors (other than mythical, 'sacralized,' and 'sacralizing' figures) to the extent that authors became subject to punishment, that is, to the extent that discourse could be transgressive." One would not want here to over-literalize Foucault's words, which really concern the "phenomenon" of authorial responsibility, whether construed individually or collectively, and in which the "transgressiveness" of discourse refers not to specific legal boundaries, but to acts placed in the "bipolar field of the sacred and the profane."[41] But Foucault's remark is still suggestive for understanding a defining moment in the history of a particular transgressive discourse: personal testimonial, and the narrative "invention" of historically knowable identity is an authorial imperative under conditions of punishment that decisively individuate the

---

[40] Ibid., 53.   [41] Foucault, "What Is an Author?" 148.

author. Writing a decade before the heresy statute of 1401, the *Opus arduum* author prefers to dissolve his identity among the books that carry his responsible (and defiantly anonymous) signature; after 1401 and the formal imposition of a death penalty, a new imperative for intellectual advocacy is to put the self forward as example.

Wyche's story is a narrative fragment of a life made known through opposition to legal authority. His text foregrounds crucial questions of historicity and narrativity; as Hayden White has observed, "the reality that lends itself to narrative representation is the conflict between desire and the law," where the desiring subject yearns for the formal coherence and legitimation that only narrative can bestow upon events.[42] These questions could be posed even more urgently of Thorpe's testimony, because this purportedly autobiographical account is virtually the only "historical" record that can link Thorpe to event, place, and time. The large historical–legal referent for Thorpe's examination is the Oxford *Constitutiones* of 1407/9, which stands as the other major piece of anti-heretical legislation after *De heretico comburendo*. It might be said that Thorpe's narrative of prison interrogation stands in relation to the *Constitutiones* as Wyche's account to the heresy statutes of 1401. But the chronological proximity of Thorpe's account, set in 1407, to the first issuing of the *Constitutiones*, raises certain difficult questions about the murky relations between narrative legitimation and the claims to historicity of the Thorpe text; and so it is better to reserve discussion of these matters for the internal analysis of Thorpe's testament that follows later. I turn now to Wyche's letter.

The letter tells a curious story of ruses, complicity, deception and self-deception, and ambiguous example. In writing his letter from Skirlaw's prison in early 1403, Wyche was certainly conscious of the importance of representing himself accurately to friends and colleagues on the outside. Just how much he values the force of historicizing detail that serves not only to verify experience, but also to consolidate and legitimize the "plot" through which he has structured that experience, is evident in the final passage of the narrative section of the letter, the transition to the envoy section. Here, having described his final encounter with the bishop, he turns to his present circumstances in prison:

> Et sic misit me in carcerem. In quo continuo etc. habens cibum et potum competenter, gracias agens Deo. Et bonus Deus noster ex sua gracia visitavit me per magnam strictitudinem in ventre, per quam habeo et habui magnam

[42] White, *The Content of the Form: Narrative Discourse and Historical Representation*, 12–13.

penam aliquando purgare ventrem meum, quia aliquando per novem dies
non habui quantitatem unius purgacionis et emeraudes tenuerunt me bis et
sanguinarunt quodammodo fortiter, et sic quod pudor est dicere. Tamen
oportet me ita facere vel non vivere et purgacio mea est dura sicut purgacio
eius. Ista sunt secreta mea.

Ideo si placet vobis secrete custodite ea; non plura scribo vobis et mittatis
Bhytebi ut secrete legatur magistro meo de Balknolle et Bynkfeld, cum
videritis tempus, et salutetis me Johanni Maya cum uxore sua ista
salutacione, ut quietam et tranquillam agant in omni pietate et castitate.
(Matthew, 541)

(And so he sent me to prison, in which place I continue, having sufficient
food and drink, by God's grace. And our good Lord, out of his grace, has
afflicted me through a great constriction of the stomach, on account of
which I now have and have been having great pain at times purging my
stomach, so that for nine days I have not had so much as one purgation, and
hemorrhoids have twice gripped me and have bled rather profusely, such
that it is shameful to mention it. However, I must do so or not survive, and
my purgation is as difficult as the "purging" of it.[43] These are my secrets.

May it please you to keep them in secret custody. I will write no further to
you; and when you see the occasion, entrust this letter to [John Whitby] that
it may be read in secret by my master [Robert of Wallknoll] and [?Wink-
field]; and send my greetings to John Maya and his wife with this message:
that they carry on in quiet and tranquility, with all piety and chastity.)

These extraordinary revelations of the body (reminiscent, perhaps, of Paul's
affliction, 2 Corinthians 12. 7), acknowledged in embarrassment and desper-
ation, are pitted against the order of custodial secrecy. Yet what is to be secret
is not the contents of the letter, but the existence of the document itself: the
letter is to be passed furtively among a secretive community. This movement
recapitulates in small form the ideological structure of the narrative as a
whole. The story recounted in the letter is one of desire for profound
self-revelation in counterpoint to the imperative for self-concealment under
the law. The intense physical discomfort (and worse, since he believes that the
affliction threatens his life) that Wyche reveals here is not just circumstantiat-
ing detail. The humiliating exposure of secret bodily suffering, where the
body itself has become a terrible prison, expresses the central drama of his
account: this affliction, revealed with astonishing directness, is certainly
understood here as the due suffering for the self-deception and "failure of
conscience" that Wyche has earlier revealed with equally surprising directness.

[43] I take this to mean that, despite embarrassment, he must mention these afflictions to his custodians or
friends outside (perhaps they would procure medical attention for him), or risk dying there in prison.

162

Wyche's narrative concerns how he will allow himself to be represented, legally but also rhetorically, through public oaths of affirmation which the authorities want him to take. The story itself is punctuated by fitful movements to and from prison, and visitations while he is in prison. At the opening of the letter he recounts how he made his way to the town of Chester-le-Street, and after injuring himself in a fall, hiring a horse to travel to Bishop Auckland to answer Skirlaw's summons. Appearing before the bishop on 7 December, he is presented with a comprehensive oath of obedience to the laws and doctrines of the church, which he is asked to swear on the spot. The generality of this initial oath suggests that it was perhaps intended as a formal recantation, without further investigation of his conscience. Wyche refuses the oath, asking for counsel and a favorable day; instead, he is given until later the same day to make the oath, but at his reappearance he refuses to speak at all. From there he is pronounced excommunicate and sent to prison. So begins the long process of as many as seven separate examinations before the bishop, each followed by a return to prison.

It is obvious that Wyche was an important prisoner, a visible, mobile, and active dissident cleric. Extracting a recantation from a figure of even minor celebrity would be something of a trophy for Skirlaw, serving a powerful exemplary function within the diocese and beyond. Hence the impressive efforts made to coax a recantation from Wyche and (at least judging from Wyche's account) the considerable interest and time invested in examining the recalcitrant heretic on his views on mendicancy, the eucharist, preaching without diocesan license, and other matters. As the protracted length of the proceedings suggests, obtaining a recantation from Wyche was more politically useful than simply pronouncing him an obdurate heretic and turning him over to higher authorities.

After four interviews with the bishop, each followed by a return to prison for a lengthy period, and having already been excommunicated and soon after threatened with burning, Wyche receives a visit in the prison from a knight sent from the bishop "ad tractandum mecum super iuramento supradicto" (Matthew, 534). This is the crucial scene of the narrative, so I will quote it at length:

> Et apparuit michi quod ille esset solidus homo. Et venit cum eo cancellarius et notarius presbyter. Et miles sedebat, illi autem steterant . . . Tunc dixit: Ricarde, potesne invenire in consciencia tua ad obediendum legi ecclesie catholice in quantum ad te pertinet? Eciam, dixi, quia scio quod lex Dei est lex ecclesie catholice et absit quin obedirem legi Dei nostri in quantum ad me pertinet. At ille: Tu bene dicis. *Custodias istud in corde tuo et sit istud iuramentum tuum, et iures tu istud in corde tuo limitatum.* Bene domine. Sed

vos scitis bene, dixi, si reciperem iuramentum a iudice, oportet me recipere secundum intentum iudicis et non secundum meum. At ille: Pro certo scias, quod dominus meus reciperet a te iuramentum istud, quia sum missus a Domino meo ad te ad tractandum tecum super isto iuramento. Et si volueris sic facere, dominus meus absolvet te ab alio iuramento et sic facies bonum finem. Melius est tibi sic facere quam taliter incarcerari. Vellem, dixi, liberari libenter, si Deo placeret. Sed de uno, inquit, oportet te cavere, ut quodcunque iuramentum tibi demonstraverit, non petas questiones super illo, quia subditus non peteret tales questiones a suo superiori, quia olla non petit a figulo, Cur me ad istum usum fingis vel ad istum. Et dominus meus est quodammodo capitosus scilicet testis. Et si volueris consentire ad istum finem, volo, si volueris, transire ad dominum meum et tractare ad finem. Dixi, volo libenter si dominus meus voluerit facere sicut vos dicitis et recipere a me istud iuramentum limitatum in corde meo, hoc est, quod teneor obedire legi Dei, in quantum ad me pertinet. Eciam dixit: Ne dubites. Tunc dixit cancellarius: Per Deum, tu iuras sicut nos volumus antequam recesseris. Non respondi ei verbum. Et miles surrexit. Et cum stetisset in hostio domus, dixit: Richarde, in fide, vis tu tenere pactum de istis que dixisti? Eciam, si dominus meus voluerit tenere pactum de quibus vos dixistis. Eciam, scias illud pro certo et recessit. (Matthew, 534; emphasis added)

(And he [the knight] seemed to me to be a trustworthy man. And with him there came a chancellor and a notary priest. The knight sat down, but the others remained standing . . . Then the knight said to me, "Richard, can you not find it in your conscience to obey the law of the catholic church insofar as it pertains to you?" "Yes," I said, "because I know that the law of God is the law of the catholic church, and without inconsistency I might obey the law of our God insofar as it pertains to me." And he, "Well said. Take custody of this in your heart, and let this be your oath, *and take the oath with 'reservations' in your heart.*" "Very well my lord. But you know well," I said, "that if I have taken an oath from a judge, I must pledge it according to the intention of the judge, and not according to my intention." And he said, "Certainly you know that my lord would accept this oath from you, for I have been sent to you from my lord to reach an agreement with you about this oath. And if you wanted to do it this way, my lord would absolve you from any other oath; and so you will make a good end of it. It is better for you to do this than to be imprisoned as you are." I said, "I would gladly wish to be set free, so may it please God." "But there is one thing," he said, "that you must be aware of: that in whatever way he articulates the oath to you, you ask no questions about it. For a subject does not question his superior; the pot does not ask of the potter, 'Why do you put me to this or that use?' And my lord is somewhat headstrong. If you wanted to consent to this purpose, I am willing, if you so wished, to go to my lord and negotiate towards this end." I said, "I am very willing, if my lord would like to do just as you have said, and accept this oath from me 'with reservations' in my heart, that is, that I am held to obey the law of God insofar as it pertains to me." And he said, "Be assured." Then the chancellor said, "By God, you will swear just as we want before you have left here." I did not answer him one word. Then the knight got up. And as he stood in the doorway he said, "Richard, in all faith, do you want to hold to the agreement about these things that I have discussed?" "Certainly, if my lord would wish to keep the pact concerning those things you have mentioned." "Good, you may be sure about that." And he left.)

This is an extraordinary scene, carefully laid out with the kind of visual drama that we have seen already in Thorpe's testimony, the sort of intensively choreographed scene of inquisition that is never available in the disembodied accounts of official trial records.[44] The knight provides a ruse: Wyche is offered his liberty through a public abjuration which would still not violate his conscience or his principles. As custodian of his own conscience, he can swear obedience to the law of the church "insofar as it pertains to him," affirming his obedience "with mental reservations" ("reservations in my heart"). He is being offered the chance to swear an ambiguous oath, with wording supplied by Wyche himself, which will serve the bishop's public image as a prosecutor, while the bishop will not inquire too deeply into the heretic's change of conscience. But in what almost sounds like the plot of a romance or fairy-tale, there is a condition on this: he must not ask any questions when the bishop puts the oath to him; he is simply to take the oath as presented, with inner reservations.

Of course, as we are to learn, the deal is a trap. Presented with the oath as now packaged by the bishop, Wyche exhibits some anxiety about whether the oath corresponds with the agreement he made with the knight, but he still submits to the oath. No sooner does Wyche take the oath of loyalty to church doctrine and law "as it pertains to him" (that is, with "reservations in his heart") as agreed, than the bishop presents him with further affirmations on more specific grounds (Matthew, 535). These further oaths confound the prisoner and he refuses to swear them, because they are beyond the terms of his special agreement. His refusal produces further adversarial challenges, including more charges (that he and a certain "Jacobus" had been subverting

---

[44] This is the kind of trial scene that Richie D. Kendall would consider under what he terms the "displaced drama" of the Lollards, the compatibility of such scenes of legal–spiritual agon with the aesthetic of the contemporary drama (despite the typical Lollard rejection of theatre on both practical and theoretical grounds). See *The Drama of Dissent: the Radical Poetics of Nonconformity, 1380–1590*, 50–89.

the people of Northumbria). Returned to his cell, Wyche despairs of the "poisonous oath," and, reflecting on the soured proceedings, invites the reader to witness an extended, self-revelatory struggle of remorse and faith, suffused with the language and example of biblical spiritual agon (Matthew, 536–7). From this moment on his legal resolve is firmed, and his subsequent appearances before the bishop produce increasingly tense legal confrontations and interpretive impasses regarding canonical prerogative and the prisoner's rights. The themes he sounds throughout his further appearances are summed up in his pronouncement: "non teneor iurare illud, nec volo" (Matthew, 535) ("I am not held to swear that, nor do I want to").

How are we to understand the processes, both historical and ideological, involved in an oath taken with "mental reservations"? In historical terms, the drama of the ambiguous oath is being played out in the shadow of, and against the power of, the parliamentary statute of 1401, most famous for its institution of the death penalty for heresy. The statute *De heretico comburendo*, however, made its impact not only for the notoriety of its ruling on the burning of obstinate heretics, but also for the unlimited prerogative it gave to ecclesiastical courts in England to administer the *ex officio* oath in prosecuting cases of heresy. The oath *ex officio* empowered an episcopal court to extract a blanket promise of truthful statements from defendents in advance of any specific interrogatories, that is, before the defendent knew what questions would be asked. As a sixteenth-century version of the oath puts it, the suspect is required to "swear to answer all such interrogatories as shall be offered unto you and declare your whole knowledge therein, so God you help."[45] Thus the suspect was required to submit to the real possibility of self-incrimination. The statute of 1401 was sometimes known as the *Ex officio* statute because it contained an endorsement of ecclesiastical power to administer the oath: the crucial formulation here is that the diocesan should "determine [heresy] according to the canonical decrees." [46] Through this encrypted phrase the English ecclesiastical courts claimed statutory sanction for one of the church's most controversial but also time-honored procedures, a procedure that had been officially incorporated into canon law in the early thirteenth century, but which had as long a history of secular and even canonical opposition.

Behind Wyche's ambiguous oath lies the history of the *ex officio* oath and the opposition to it in England. An earlier form of the *ex officio* oath, known as the oath *de veritate dicenda*, was one of the features of the inquisitorial procedures set out in the fourth Lateran Council of 1215 as part of a large

---

[45] Quoted in Maguire, "The Attack of the Common Lawyers on the Oath *Ex officio*," 200.
[46] *Statutes of the Realm* 2: 127 (2 Hen. IV. c. 15).

program for the prosecution of heresy. The oath *de veritate dicenda*, in which the suspect was sworn in advance to answer truthfully to all interrogatories, came to be called the *ex officio* oath because it was associated with inquisitorial proceedings where the judge served, *ex officio*, as indicator, assailant, and convictor.[47] The oath was "calculated to induce self-incrimination"; the inquisitor's task was to penetrate the "secret thoughts and opinions of the prisoner . . . [The] believer must have fixed and unwavering faith and it was the inquisitor's business to ascertain this condition of his mind."[48] While English common law was not based in inquisitorial systems, the extensive criminal jurisdiction of ecclesiastical courts meant that inquisitorial procedures, including the self-incriminating oath, were widely used. As early as 1164 (Henry II's Constitutions of Clarendon) there were protests against the inquisitorial procedures of calling a defendant to answer on the basis of *fama* or common report.[49] The oath *de veritate dicenda* was formally introduced in England in 1237 among constitutions concerned with spiritual cases heard and determined in ecclesiastical courts.[50] Despite the initially clear delimitations on its use, over the following centuries there were oppositions to the use of the oath, opposition grounded both in the immediate terms of the English common law and in the tradition of the continental *ius commune*, which was based partly in canon law. Indeed, the European *ius commune* provided the earliest clear statements of the privilege against self-incrimination (the maxim *nemo tenetur prodere seipsum* is derived from the canonical sources used in the *ius commune*).[51] In 1246 and again in 1252, Henry III issued writs delimiting the use of the oath to those causes traditionally associated with the jurisdiction of ecclesiastical courts; in 1326 Parliament similarly restricted the oath to those causes properly under ecclesiastical jurisdiction (spiritual as well as matrimonial and testamentary cases). More significantly, however, the King's Council came to use the oath, which was condemned by Parliament on three separate occasions, as part of a more general objection to inquisitorial procedure. In 1354 the oath as used in secular courts was outlawed by Parliament by an act broadening the application of Magna Carta's protection of due process of law; another statute was issued in the following decade, and the last of the Magna Carta statutes was enacted in 1368. Throughout the heresy

---

[47] Levy, *Origins of the Fifth Amendment: the Right Against Self-Incrimination*, 22–4.
[48] Levy, *Origins of the Fifth Amendment*, 23; Lea, *A History of Inquisition in the Middle Ages* 1: 400–1.
[49] Levy, *Origins of the Fifth Amendment*, 45.
[50] Maguire, "Attack of the Common Lawyers," 200; Kelly, "The Right to Remain Silent: Before and After Joan of Arc," 1005–6. As Kelly's comments regarding Levy and other historians of the common law suggest, the historical division between the interests of the common law and of ecclesiastical law continues to this day in historiographical rivalry: historians of the common law (Maguire, Levy) are taken to task by historians of the canon law (Helmholz and especially Kelly) over perceived lapses in accuracy.   [51] Helmholz, "The Origins of the Privilege Against Self-Incrimination," 967.

prosecutions of the late fourteenth century, however, the ecclesiastical courts routinely administered the oath.[52] In 1401, with various interests – king, council, parliament, and church – uniting around the aim of eradicating heresy, the parliamentary statute *De heretico comburendo* sanctioned the use of the *ex officio* oath by ecclesiastical courts.

The oath offered to Wyche allowing him to swear with "mental reservations" seems to be a play by the bishop, or the knight representing the bishop, to side step the *Ex officio* statute by tolerating – indeed, inviting – ambiguity and a certain privacy of conscience which can remain unmapped in the face of penetrating inquisition. It also seems to draw on an understanding, shared with the prisoner, of common law and even canonical objections to self-incrimination. The proceedings against Wyche are obviously not those of the common law: they are inquisitorial, with Skirlaw serving as accuser, prosecutor, and judge, the only charges against Wyche being produced by common report or suspicion. After Wyche first refuses to swear an oath of obedience, the bishop presents him with the charge "nos habemus te suspectum et unum de secta Lolardorum qui non credunt veritatem Eukaristie" (Matthew, 531–2) ("we hold you suspect and one of the following of Lollards who do not believe in the truth of the Eucharist"); he is susceptible to denunciation on the spot, as when he is interrogated on the eucharist by an Augustinian friar who proclaims: "Ecce loquitur heresim . . . quia dicit quod est panis" (Matthew, 536) ("Behold he speaks heresy . . . because he says that it is bread"); and much later in the proceedings, in response to one of Wyche's objections to the continuation of the process against him, the knight points out, "Tu non est accusatus per viam partis, sed iudex ait contra te" (Matthew, 537) ("You were not accused by means of counsel; rather the judge spoke against you"). And Wyche's initial request for counsel and a favorable day, which are obviously common law defenses against inquisitorial procedure, are expressly denied (Matthew, 531). Thus the provision for Wyche to "take custody of his own conscience" can be seen as a play on widespread objections to the penetrating control over individual conscience represented by inquisitorial procedure, and more particularly by the *ex officio* oath. The appeal of the ambiguous oath may thus be predicated on the immediacy of the 1401 statute enforcing an inquisitorial process that brooks no ambiguity.

Two competing principles are held in balance here. On the one hand, there is the offer of the ambiguous oath. On the other hand, the bishop circumscribes the oath, delimiting the promise it extends of exemption from penetration. Here we recall that the knight warns Wyche not to question the

---

[52] Levy, *Origins of the Fifth Amendment*, 47–55; Kelly, "The Right to Remain Silent," 1005–7, again assailing Levy's emphasis on common law reactions to the oath.

presentation of the oath in any way; and at the same meeting the bishop's chancellor predicts "you will swear just as we want before you leave" (Matthew, 534), as if to package the permitted ambiguity within the real jurisdiction of the oath *de veritate dicenda*.[53] Moreover, the bishop uses the oath that Wyche has taken (with his reservations formally expressed[54]) as an aperture for putting further oaths before him, oaths that Wyche repeatedly declares he is "not held to swear." So while the law (embodied in the bishop and his court) allows him, provisionally, the privilege of reservation of conscience, it also entraps him by controlling and setting conditions on the exemption. Yet for Wyche the original terms of mental reservation before the law never change.[55] He mounts increasing legal objections to the inquisitorial process and resistance to the extraction of further oaths. Responding to the chancellor's launching of a "fishing expedition" for evidence against him, in answer to an unexpected question about when he last made confession, he declares "non teneor laudare me nec me ipsum vituperare" (Matthew, 536) ("I am not bound to praise or blame myself"), while noting that in fact he has made confession on numerous occasions recently. These epideictic terms, "laudare" and "vituperare," carry here the legal meanings of innocence and guilt, exculpation and incrimination. He also claims as grounds for his non-cooperation the "accepted legal usage" that he cannot be detained without a new process, as no judgment has been settled at his last appearance or continues from it; to these objections the chancellor responds sarcastically, "who made you a man of the law?" (Matthew 537–8). And finally, invoking common law privileges at his eighth appearance before the bishop, he insists on his right not to incriminate himself and recurs to his agreement only to swear with mental reservations; otherwise, he declares "si volueritis michi agere *communem legem*, non habetis contra me aliquem processum"

---

53 Wyche points out that his response to the chancellor here was resolute silence: "Non respondi ei verbum." In heresy cases, remaining silent before formal charges were issued was an important defense against being charged anew with further heretical opinion; see Kelly, "The Right to Remain Silent," 993. While Wyche's meeting with the knight and chancellor takes place presumably "off the record," it is interesting that he records that in this informal meeting he preserved silence. Compare his recording of his silence in court later in the face of the bishop's formal warnings (Matthew, 540: "Et monestavit me primo, secundo et tercio, ut scriberem intencionem meam ad illam scripturam; et non respondi ei verbum").

54 Matthew, 535: "Et dixi episcopo: Domine, iuramentum pacti mihi modo limitatum in corde a magistro meo hic milite ad iurandum volo iurare si volueritis."

55 Von Nolcken points out that in the encounter at the bishop's court, Wyche allows the original initiative to be modified, because he swears to the oath as now packaged for him by the bishop, and that at this moment (535, lines 20–4) he has opened himself up to being forced to speak untruly, where what he will have to say will be at odds with his mental reservations ("Richard Wyche, a Certain Knight, and the Beginning of the End," 139–40). This reading is persuasive and complementary with my reading here that "mental reservations" is permitted *provisionally*, not absolutely. In other words, Wyche is ultimately trapped, in part because of his own concessions (swearing to the oath as packaged, in the belief that this will suffice) and in part because of his refusal to concede further.

(Matthew, 539; emphasis added) ("if you want to treat me according to the common law, you have no process against me").

In this complex historical environment, with its strained competition between legal modes, mental reservation is a point of resistance internal to the project of representing dissent. Here, in an intellectual's public, exemplary self-representation, all attention is focused on what can escape representation in the public record. It is a key instructive moment, the narrative struggle that produces the dissenting subject in all of its oppositionality. The narrative pivots on a crucial misapprehension between the law and its subject, on something that transpires in the gap between what is said and what cannot or will not be said.[56] While Wyche's ambiguous oath is strategic, he does not spell out, to any of his interlocutors or to his potential readers, what lies behind the knowing ambiguity of "mental reservations." As a dissenter Wyche becomes knowable through the violence and invasiveness of inquisition; the narrative of self-representation takes part in this violence and acts through it. But it is necessary to the violence of that project that there also be resistance to representation. With the initial proposal to let Wyche retain custody of his own conscience, the law exercises its power to compel the dissenting subject precisely by acknowledging that it cannot fully narrate or represent him. There is a double purpose in having Wyche swear an oath of obedience: to define him as a dissenter and to proclaim him reincorporated in the orthodox community. But to achieve its object of "summoning" the dissenter, even to reclaim him as a recanter, the law provisionally allows something to escape its narrative control. The heretic, in turn, is willing to consent to partial representation under the law (his ambiguous oath of faith), at least initially to allow the law to contain him, but only because it offers a certain unmapped, unregulated area of "mental reservation." Wyche agrees to perform the role in which he is represented, but the law's interpellation of him, and his performance under that command, produce what we could describe as an excess of meaning that resists representation. The ambiguous oath is a permissable evasion of the law's command. The historical logic of this text is for the intellectual to make himself fully knowable; and yet he chooses to be unrecognizable.

Where could we look to find analogues for Wyche's ambiguous legal

[56] It may be helpful to align, provisionally, this form of misapprehension with the concept of "misrecogntion" (*méconnaissance*) which Althusser borrows from Lacan's discussions of the "language" of the unconscious, where repression is a form of "misrecognition." For Althusser, "misrecognition" is part of the structure of ideology in correspondence with structures of the unconscious: that which is necessarily unrecognized in the very forms of recognition through which ideology constitutes individuals as subjects. See Althusser's essays in *Lenin and Philosophy*: "Ideology and Ideological State Apparatuses," 172–3, 182–3; and "Freud and Lacan," 207, 219. See also Lacan, *Speech and Language in Psychoanalysis*, 6, 54, and translator's commentary, 96.

self-representation? For the structure of the ambiguous oath itself some of the most interesting parallels can be found in literary texts, notably the motif of the equivocal oath in romance, for example, Iseut's brilliantly subversive oath before King Marc and his court in Béroul's *Tristan*.[57] Within the contemporary historical context of Wyche's narrative, there are many examples of Lollard resistance to oath-taking and, especially in the records of Sawtry's trial, evidence of efforts to articulate a general conformity to orthodox thought without the dissenter violating his own conscience.[58] But here, obviously, there is nothing so distinctive as an agreement to an equivocal oath. In fact Thorpe explicitly invokes opposition to the oath *de veritate dicenda* by objecting that he does not know what particular interrogatories will follow if he makes a blanket promise to tell the truth on Arundel's terms.[59] In contrast to Wyche's account, the Thorpe narrative seems to keep legal ambiguity at bay.

The problem of ambiguous and uncontainable representation is an important and recurrent feature of inquisitorial narratives. I want to turn here to another example, from a much earlier period, in order to open comparison with Wyche's narrative, and so to underscore what is distinctive about the latter. The heresy case of the Synod of Arras in 1025 presents another perspective on how dissent is both assimilated by, and unassimilable to, narrative representation. Even as we acknowledge the considerable historical distance between Wyche's case and the Arras episode and the differences between their immediate historical contexts, the characteristics that these episodes share – evasions and gaps in the powers of representation – suggest a certain "genre" of interrogation narrative. In January of 1025, Bishop Gerard of Cambrai conducted an investigation of reported heretical activity in the town of Arras in his diocese.[60] Having arrested the suspects, he held them in prison for three days and then convened a magnificent tribunal to examine them. The whole episode is recounted in two forms that are combined with one another: the *Acta* of the synod, composed soon after the event as part of a celebratory record of the bishop's achievements; and a letter, summarizing the affair, written by Bishop Gerard to the bishop of a neighboring diocese, and

---

57 For numerous examples, see Hexter, *Equivocal Oaths and Ordeals in Medieval Literature*. In Beroul's romance, Tristan, disguised as a leper, carries Iseut across a river on his back. Iseut then swears to the assembled company that no man has come between her thighs except for her husband King Marc and the leper who just carried her across the river. See Béroul, *Le Roman de Tristan*, lines 4196–216.

58 McNiven, *Heresy and Politics in the Reign of Henry IV: the Burning of John Badby*, 82–4 (on Sawtry's oaths) 108, 111–16 (on Thorpe).

59 "Testimony of William Thorpe," in Hudson, ed., *Two Wycliffite Texts*, 34.

60 Much of my account is indebted to Moore, *The Origins of European Dissent*, 9–18; and Russell, *Dissent and Reform in the Early Middle Ages*, 21–7. The sources are to be found in the *Acta synodi Atrebatensis, PL* 142: 1271–312; the narrative portions of the account are translated in Moore, *The Birth of Popular Heresy*, 15–19.

appended as a preface to the *Acta*. These combined accounts produce several layers of information: the rumors that reached the bishop about the heretics; his interrogation of them at the synod; their answers to his questions; and a grand sermon that the bishop preached at the assembly to refute heretical opinion and elaborate a vision of political and spiritual order.[61] Holding these layers together is the summary of the investigation that the bishop provides in the prefatory letter.

According to the rumors that the bishop heard (as reported in the *Acta*), the heretics rejected the sacrament of baptism, the sacrament of the eucharist, and the utility of penance after confession as well as confession itself; reportedly they also denied the authority of the church, condemned legitimate matrimony, and held that no one after the time of the apostles and martyrs ought to be venerated. When the bishop interrogated them, he made his questions relatively open-ended, simply asking them to describe their beliefs and mentioning only baptism among all the sacraments they were alleged to deny. Their response (according again to the *Acta*) was equally simple: they were the followers of an Italian named Gundolfo from whom they had learned the precepts of the Gospels and the apostles; they believed in abandoning the world, restraining fleshly appetites, earning their food by manual labor, doing injury to no one, and extending charity to everyone of their own faith. On their view, if these rules are followed baptism is unnecessary; if they are not, baptism will not lead to salvation. Baptism can add nothing if the rules of the Gospel and apostles are observed.

What emerges sharply from the account in the *Acta* is the chasm between the lurid specificity of the rumors and the rather innocuous generality of most of the actual beliefs professed. Significantly this goes unremarked in the record. The only link is the rejection of baptism, but the views that they expressed on this did not conform to the expectations of heretical dualism suggested by the rumors about their beliefs.[62] Even more interesting is the outcome of the inquisition. The bishop preached a very long sermon (in the written account of the synod the sermon extends to 20,000 words) as a rebuttal to heresies, although not with reference to the views actually claimed by the suspects. At the end of the sermon the accused were left "stupified by the weight of the bishop's discourse," saying that "they believed that the sum of Christian salvation could consist in nothing but what he had set out."[63] In other words (at least on the terms of the report of the *Acta*), the suspects saw

---

[61] On this sermon and its ramification for conceptualizing social order, see Duby, *The Three Orders: Feudal Society Imagined*, 21–43.

[62] Their views on baptism echoed the Donatist heresy, which claimed that the sinfulness of a priest who administers the sacrament nullifies the efficacy of the sacrament; see Russell, *Dissent and Reform*, p. 24.

[63] Moore, *The Birth of Popular Heresy*, 18.

no conflict between their own beliefs and the approved orthodoxies. Then, by way of confession, they were asked to abjure condemned ideas and affirm their belief in the following: the necessity of baptism for salvation; the necessity of membership in the church for salvation; the real presence at the mass; the necessity of communion to salvation; the virgin birth; the suffering of Christ on the cross; the ascension, and the legitimacy of matrimony. Except for the issue of baptism (where the affirmation only dealt in part with the suspects' original assertions), none of these items of belief that they were asked to affirm had anything to do with the beliefs they actually professed. The bishop thus has them affirming their belief in things they never denied in the first place. Presumably they could sign on to this list of correct beliefs without any shift of conscience, because the list did not violate (or even substantially overlap with) the beliefs, heterodox or not, that they had actually professed. The oath that they were asked to sign was not based on their confession, but rather upon official prejudgment about what constituted heresy; the bishop was prepared to attribute to all heretics the dualist belief system of Manichaeism, the one heresy that he, like other ecclesiastics of his day, could recognize easily.[64] Here ecclesiastical authority summons dissent into its subjected status according to preordained modalities. The law has recognized dissent in terms that do not adequately "represent" its particularities, and yet has succeeded in assimilating the habit of dissent into a form of representation that can be acted upon in the legal and historical record.

This seems to take us far afield of Wyche's deliberate and knowing evasion. But in the official legal interest in representing dissent on terms that are recognizable and actionable, there is some resonance between the earlier and later episodes: what we see in both cases is the power of misapprehension between the law and its subjects. Moreover, unsurprisingly, there is a resemblance between the political interests of the two bishops, Gerard of Cambrai in the eleventh century and William Skirlaw of Durham in the fifteenth century, in being seen to restore order to communities supposedly undermined by the disruptive presence of heresy.[65] The heretics of Arras also exhibit their own "resistance" to representation. Here, what is perhaps the most distinctive mark of dissent is reported without comment. When the oath of obedience was recited by the whole company at the tribunal, the suspects initially "did not fully understand these words, which were spoken in Latin."[66] Only when the sentence of excommunication and the profession of

---

[64] See Russell, *Dissent and Reform*, 25–6, on the discrepancy.
[65] See Duby's discussion of Gerard of Cambrai in *The Three Orders*, 21–43.
[66] Moore, *The Birth of Popular Heresy*, 18; and see his comment on this in *The Origins of European Dissent*, 17–18.

faith are orally translated for them into the vernacular do they submit to the oath and affirm their faith by affixing their signatory marks to the document. This gesture of independence from the mediating powers of the ecclesiastical court, the reluctance to accept the assertion of authority in exchange for direct knowledge, does not figure in the bishop's assessment of their heterodox status, because it falls outside of official formulas for determining and constructing dissent. There is no indication that their gesture has the same knowing and complicit design as Wyche's self-reservation (while the bishop refers to them early on as "dissimulators," the sycophantic tones of the *Acta* present the suspects as eager suppliants before the manifest authority of the bishop). But even as they submit to their representation under the available modalities of the law, they reserve a space of resistance – wanting to know in their own language what the oath says – that is so subtle as to go unnoticed in the record.

The cases of the Arras suspects and Wyche offer two examples of misapprehension between dissenters and the law, and two examples of dissenters' unwillingness to accept the terms of legal representation imposed on them. But what makes the two cases different from each other is *what comes out* of Wyche's misapprehension. Wyche's privilege and task as intellectual advocate and communal example is to articulate that space of resistance as something that will, proactively, contest the public record that will try to represent him as just another recanter. In this respect, it is what transpires in the space of misapprehension between Wyche and the law, a certain (and even strategic) excess of meaning, that drives Wyche's narrative. Of course he uses his self-narration to extend recognition to other dissenters in his community, to speak, by his own example, on behalf of others. So his knowability to a community is played against his (potential) "unknowability" to the public record. Here, by acknowledging what escapes representation, that un-regulated, excess meaning of "mental reservation," he performs the most subversive gesture of his narrative: to free up, even temporarily, a discursive space for disobedience, for action as well as narrative that cannot be compelled, and that resists any claim, hostile or friendly, to regulate it. What is "mental reservation"? It is what the law of the bishop's court chooses to overlook in the practical and short-term interests of a propaganda victory (indeed, it is a legal formula for what the law will not try to penetrate); and it is what the dissenter acknowledges as a space that resists public representation.

But what is it, exactly, that transpires in this space of misapprehension? Unlike the Arras suspects, of course, Wyche has the privilege of writing his own narrative, and as I suggested above, it is both his privilege and task as an intellectual to use his narrative to contest the public record and to speak to, and on behalf of, his own community. But just as importantly, it is what transpires in that space that allows him to use it as he does. Here it is necessary to underline that this space is indeed provisional: Wyche's negotiations are not, in the end, unambiguously successful, and on one view the outcome of the legal proceedings constitutes something of a defeat for Wyche's espousal of Lollard philosophical essentialism, the principle that one's words must always be consistent with one's will (because his further negotiations about the oath place him in the awkward position of having to swear things that would falsify even the qualification "mental reservation").[67] But here I am interested in exploring the moment where the possibility of "mental reservations" is opened, and what it means to narrate this moment with such particularizing autobiographical force. What emerges from that provisionally unregulated space of "mental reservation" are the very conditions of his formation as a dissenting intellectual: it is where he will be able to perform his most important pedagogical work.

When Wyche is invited to keep silence on the legal record while yet making his strategies clear, what passes between Wyche and the knight, what emerges from this legal encounter, may be something that passes unrecognized or unacknowledged between them. But this is the moment when the narrative links itself with a historically traceable intellectual project. Embodied in Wyche's resistance to the law's powers of representation is a project of critical struggle against the normalizing judgment of examination itself. What is dangerous about Wyche, in the eyes of his prosecutors, is that he can teach and that for many years he has been teaching. We might say that in his narration of this encounter over "mental reservations" he embodies the passage of a scholastic mode of thought from university to a dissident lay community.

, Thus far here we have understood examination in its legal sense. But the procedure of examination is also one of the closest discursive links between prison and school, and the strategies of evading the compulsory visibility of the examination travel readily between legal and academic structures. Can we say that Wyche's peculiar encounter with the law exemplifies, or perhaps even carries through, a certain tradition of "schooling" in evasive argumentative techniques, a sectarian pedagogy that transfers the skills of academic exercise to the real urgency of legal examination? I suggest that we can find the most historically potent analogues for Wyche's equivocal self-representation in a conjunction between the teaching of disputational technique in the

---

[67] See von Nolcken, "Richard Wyche, a Certain Knight, and the Beginning of the End," 140–1.

universities and a particularly Lollard training in interrogational self-aware-ness. Let us look more closely at the strategies of evasion shared by legal and academic structures of examination.

In his self-defense Swinderby had announced to his examiners: "I saye trewely I can no sophymes, ne I kepe not to use hem, gif al I couthe, for the wise man saythe that God hatith sophystical wordes, and therefore my wille is to sey pleynly and openly to my wytte the treuthe of this maters."[68] While the notion of the sophism can be laden with opprobrium, as it is here in Swinderby's disclaiming of intellectual forms of dissimulation, the more important value of the notion lies in its structural translation from scholastic to courtroom disputation. Wyche's ambiguous oath also conjures associ-ations with techniques of "sophistical" evasion, in this case the more perilous because it is a ruse actually provided (and delimited) by the examining adversary. If his text seeks to offer an ethical *manifestatio*, an exemplification of the habit of dissent, it is the more complex that his strategy of evasion actually originates with the examining powers, and is contained and circum-scribed by them. The complexity of "showcasing" such a strategy of resistance to examination is evidenced in a text nearly contemporary with Wyche's letter: a summary of the heretical errors of John Purvey, compiled by the Carmelite friar Richard Lavenham. Preserved only in the manuscript of the *Fasciculi zizaniorum*, the summary is said to have been extracted "from a book of the Lollard Purvey." The *libellus* by Purvey that served as the source of this summary cannot be identified with any extant treatise, so we have only the adversarial account of the original text.[69] Most of the eleven points covered in this carefully produced summary are direct reports of doctrinal heresies; all are presented as unmediated Lollard speech. One of the sub-divided sections under heresies of the eucharist, however, concerns techniques of argumentative evasion rather than simply doctrine:

> Item quando Antichristus, vel aliquis suorum mundialium clericorum, interrogat te, simplex christiane, numquid hoc sacramentum sit verus panis, concede hoc aperte. Et si quaerat an sit panis materialis, aut quis alius panis, concede quod est panis talis, qualem Christus intellexit in proprio verbo suo, et talis panis qualem Spiritus Sanctus intellexit in S. Paulo vocante illud veraciter panem quem frangimus; *et non vadas ulterius hic.* Si autem quaerat

---

68 Trefnant, *Hereford Register*, 263.
69 Oxford, Bodleian Library MS e Musaeo 86 fol. 91v; Hudson, "John Purvey: a Reconsideration of the Evidence," 91; *Fasciculi zizaniorum*, 383–99; Compston, ed., "The Thirty-Seven Conclusions of the Lollards." The book that provided the source for Lavenham's summary was likely to have been a survey of beliefs or schedule of tenets (Hudson, "John Purvey," 92). It is not to be identified with the *Thirty-Seven Conclusions of the Lollards* (see editorial attribution in *Fasciculi zizaniorum*, 383 n. 1, based on Forshall's mistaken attribution of the latter to Purvey in his edition of the *Thirty-Seven Conclusions*).

a te quomodo hic panis est corpus Christi, dic tu, tali vero modo qualem Christus intelligit, qui est omnipotens et totus verax, et mentiri non potest. Dic tu etiam, sicut sancti doctores dicunt, quod terrestris materia vel substantia potest converti in Christum, sicut paganus vel infidelis potest baptizari, et per hoc converti spiritualiter in membrum Christi, et sic quodammodo fieri Christus, et adhuc remanere idem homo in natura . . . Sed homines majoris scientiae et rationis possunt apertius convincere fals-itatem Antichristi, in hac materia, et aliis, per dona Spiritus Sancti operantis in eis. (Emphasis added)[70]

(When Antichrist, or one of his worldly clerics, interrogates you, simple Christian, about whether the host is truly bread, concede this candidly. If he inquires whether it is material bread, or some other kind of bread, concede that it is the kind of bread that Christ in his own words understood it to be, and such bread that the Holy Spirit meant in Saint Paul, saying that it is truly the bread that we break; *and don't go any further than this*. If, however, he asks you in what way this bread is the body of Christ, you say that it is such in the very way that Christ understands, he who is omnipotent and the whole truth, and who cannot lie. Then you say, just as the sacred authorities say, that earthly matter or substance can be transformed into Christ, just as the pagan or infidel can be baptized, and through this spiritually trans-formed into a part of Christ, and so in a certain way become Christ, and still remain very man in nature . . . But men of great knowledge and reason can more clearly demonstrate the falsehood of Antichrist in this matter and in others, through the gifts of the Holy Spirit operating in them.)

What is the context for this remarkable pronouncement? In terms of its strategic rhetoric, the overt defensive acknowledgment "don't go any further than this," it appears to have much in common with Wyche's validation of the oath with "mental reservation." Both represent a defensive reservation against the penetrating scrutiny of an interrogator or adversarial interlocutor.

We need to look futher at the kind of pronouncement this represents. If it is a direct quotation from the Lollard source, it would constitute a bald example of "schooling" in interrogation defenses. The text that supplied Lavenham with his extracts of Purvey's errors, if in fact it was a single *libellus*, would have been either a general survey of Purvey's beliefs or a schedule of tenets, accompanied by supporting authorities, and most likely designed for instructive use in Lollard circles.[71] The survival of such *schedulae* in any form is erratic (Hudson observes that they are "ephemeral documents"), and as Lavenham's list of Purvey's errors suggests, they are as likely to survive as criminal evidence, as part of adversarial record, as in their own unmediated

---

[70] *Fasciculi zizaniorum*, 384–5.   [71] Hudson, "John Purvey," 92.

state.[72] Besides Purvey's supposed *libellus*, examples of "adversarial survival" of Lollard *schedulae*, or testimony to their existence, are the *Twelve Conclusions of the Lollards*, preserved in Latin and English in Roger Dymmok's treatise refuting the conclusions, and the anti-mendicant tenets composed by Peter Patteshull and affixed to the doors of St. Paul's in 1387, the contents of which are described by Walsingham.[73] Among lists of tenets that seem to have survived in something closer to their original form (not mediated by adversaries) we could include the text now known as *Sixteen Points on which the Bishops accuse Lollards*, and the *Thirty-Seven Conclusions of the Lollards*.[74] These schedules of tenets bear the marks of a pedagogical orientation, providing readily reproducible "model answers" along with exemplary citations of authorities.[75]

There are palpable connections, of language, doctrine, and rhetorical strategy, between the Purvey "errors" extracted by Lavenham and the instructive *schedulae*. One prominent example of that relationship is especially relevant here. In the *Sixteen Points on which the Bishops accuse Lollards*, the exposition of the eucharist offers a very close parallel to the Purvey "error" on the eucharist quoted above, not just in terms of doctrine (which would be expected), but in terms of the strategies of response and argumentation that it assumes:

> Trewe cristen men schulden answere here aviseliche, trewliche and mekeliche to the poyntis and articlis that ben put agens hem; aviseliche that thei speike not vnkonnyngliche, trwliche that thei speike not falseliche, and mekeliche that thei speike not prowdeliche in her answere, and than schall be grace in ther speiking or answering be the helpe of Crist. For cristen men schulden beleue that the sacrament on the auter is verrely Cristis body sacramentli and spirituali, and mo other maneres than any erthely man can telle amonge vs. For Crist that mai not lye seid, schewyng the bred that he helde in his hande, "This is my body." And therfore saith Ierom in his epistile to Elbedie, "Here we, the brede that Crist brack and gaf to his discipulis to ete was his oune bodi, for he seide 'This is my body,' and so be oure beleue it is both Cristis bodi and bred of lijf." And so God forbede that we schulde seie that this blessid sacrament were but breed, for that were an heresye, as to sey that Crist is man and not God. But we seyn that it is both

72 Hudson, "Some Aspects of Lollard Book Production," in *Lollards and Their Books*, 183–4.
73 *Twelve Conclusions*, in Hudson, ed., *Selections from English Wycliffite Writings*, 24–8; preserved in Latin in *Fasciculi zizaniorum*, 360–9 and in Roger Dymmok's *Liber contra duodecim errores et hereses Lollardorum*, ed. Cronin. For Patteshull's tenets see Walsingham, *Historia anglicana* 2: 157–9.
74 *Sixteen Points*, in Hudson, ed., *Selections from English Wycliffite Writings*, 19–24; *Thirty-Seven Conclusions of the Lollards* (*Remonstrance Against Romish Corruptions in the Church*), ed. J. Forshall; cf. the text printed in Arnold, ed., *Select English Works of John Wyclif* 3: 455–96; and Todd, ed., *Apology for Lollard Doctrines*.   75 Hudson, ed., *Selections from English Wycliffite Writings*, 145.

brede and Cristis body, right as Crist is bothe God and man, as seint Austin
seith.[76]

Here prudence, truth, and meekness are the "public transcript" of the inside
strategies detailed in the Purvey errors, which advises candid concessions but
also pointed silences ("don't go any further than this"). Doctrinally it
corresponds almost point by point with the Purvey "precepts" on the eucharist. But like the Purvey text, it not only articulates a doctrine, but sets forth a
strategy for justifying, arguing, and maintaining the positions required by
that doctrine ("Trewe cristen men schulden answere here . . . to the poyntis
and articlis that ben put agens hem"; "so God forbede that we schulde seie";
"But we seyn that it is both brede and Cristis body").

The evasive strategies found in Lavenham's summary of Purvey's errors
and in the *Sixteen Points* have close parallels in Wyche's account of his
examination. The narrative as a whole is dominated by the defensive dynamic
of the ambiguous oath, but this is reprised in local details. During one of his
earlier appearances at the bishop's court, under pressure to respond to the
question whether bread remains after consecration of the host, Wyche first
introduces an exquisite equivocation: "credo quod illa hostia est verum
corpus Domini in *forma* panis" (Matthew, 532; emphasis added) ("I believe
that the host is the true body of the Lord in the *form* of bread"). The term
"form" is an odd choice (in Latin as well as in the vernacular) if what he really
means is "substance"; but the semantic field of *forma* is so broad that it could
be taken by his questioners to signify "appearance" (which, in the sense of
"accident," would be the safe answer) while still satisfying Wyche's own
conscience that the term can also signify "substance."[77] His examiners,
however, press him further, trying to pin down his equivocation to see if
he actually distinguishes between "form" and "appearance" (*species*):
"Archidiaconus dixit: Est corpus Christi in specie panis, non in forma"
(Matthew, 532) ("The archdeacon said, 'It is the body of Christ in the
appearance of bread, not in the form'"), obviously attributing the meaning of
"substance" to Wyche's use of the word "form." This terminological stand-
off goes unresolved, and at his next meeting with the bishop Wyche retreats
into a more comprehensive and legalistic defense: "Non teneor . . . credere
aliter quam scriptura sacra loquitur . . . Nolo me intromittere de pane
materiali. Sufficit christiano dicere, sicut scriptura dicit" (Matthew, 532) ("I
am not held to believe anything other than what holy Scripture says . . . I

---

[76] Ibid., 20.
[77] On the Latin semantic field of *forma* see *Mediae latinitatis lexicon* fasc. F, s.v. *forma*; on the use of the
term *forma* (which is not without precedent in Lollard writings) see von Nolcken, "Richard Wyche, a
Certain Knight, and the Beginning of the End," 148 n. 49.

don't want to get involved in the question of material bread. It is enough for a Christian to say just what Scripture says"). And throughout the narrative, Wyche's engagements with the bishop alternate between his own disputational powers of self-defense and the unarguable power of the law: "Et sic quia non poterant me capere in sermone, nitebantur in declaratione" (Matthew, 538) ("And so because they couldn't catch me out in speech, they insisted on the [written] declaration").

Such "schoolings" in disputational technique, from the instructive Lollard *schedulae* of tenets to Wyche's dynamic exemplification of defensive precept, have their most immediate historical analogues in formal academic exercises of disputation. In Lavenham's account of Purvey's errors, the phrase "homines majories scientiae et rationis possunt apertius convincere falsitatem Antichristi" ("men of great knowledge and reason can more clearly demonstrate the falsehood of Antichrist in this matter and in others, through the gifts of the Holy Spirit operating in them") signals the connection with scholastic debate and its skills of engagement, demonstration, and refutation. The techniques for setting out the parameters of question and answer, the response that allows an opponent's point of discussion without conceding ground in the argument, and the strategic evasion (*evasio*) are long part of the academic record. Such disputative moves, including how far an answer need go (recall the phrase from the Purvey errors, "et non vadas ulterius hic"), and what kinds of denials and distinctions are permitted, are detailed famously in Aristotle's *Topica*, a text that every junior arts student at Oxford would have heard twice before entering into his own round of determinations.[78]

Among the many kinds of elementary disputative exercise used in the late-medieval university curriculum, the purely logical exercise of the obligation (*ars obligatoria*) has a particular resonance with the studied evasions of Lollard precept and example. Fiona Somerset has shown how the disputative structure of the *ars obligatoria* informs argumentation in Lollard vernacular writing, notably the testimony of Thorpe.[79] It is easy to see why the principles of these academic exercises should be readily exportable to use in other discursive spheres: these are fundamental structures of interrogation, governed not by absolutes of truth and falsity, but by contingencies of contradiction, evasion, and entrapment.[80] The *ars obligatoria* was a basic method of disputa-

---

[78] *Topica* 8: 6–7 (160 a); Fletcher, "The Faculty of Arts," 372, 376, 379–82; Courtenay, *Schools and Scholars in Fourteenth-Century England*, 29; Kenny and Pinborg, "Medieval Philosophical Literature," 11–17, 23–9; more generally see Ashworth and Spade, "Logic in Late Medieval Oxford"; and Maierù, *University Training in Medieval Europe*, 29–35, 134–7.

[79] Somerset, "Vernacular Argumentation in *The Testimony of William Thorpe*."

[80] See Weisheipl, "Developments in the Arts Curriculum at Oxford in the Early Fourteenth Century," 163.

tion whose purpose "was to inculcate knowledge of logical rules by practice, to sharpen the pupil's mind to avoid contradiction – the basis of any disputation."[81] The exercise observes a rigid set of rules. It is a disputation involving two roles, the *opponens* and the *respondens*. According to Romuald Green's description, "the *opponens* asks the *respondens* to take on the obligation . . . of upholding a particular statement. Once the *respondens* has accepted the obligation, the *opponens* proposes a number of other statements which the *respondens* must concede or deny – but always the *respondens* must maintain the initial statement according to the obligation accepted, and he must observe the logical rules of inference, if the various statements proposed are logically connected, at all times avoiding a contradiction. Precisely it is this last point – contradiction – which provides the key to the exercises in *De obligationes*. The aim of the *opponens* is to involve the *respondens* in contradiction, and the *respondens* has to avoid it."[82] The interest of the exercise thus lies not in the content of the disputation conducted in the given time frame, but in the disputative rules – of admission, concession, and negation – that the exercise illustrates.[83]

Something of the complex structure of entrapment and defense on which the obligation exercise is built can be seen in the following extract from an anonymous treatise on obligation of the mid fourteenth century, probably written in Oxford. The treatise sets forth both precept and example, and justifies the value of the exercise on these terms:

> haec ars informat respondentem ut advertat quid conceditur et negatur, ne duo repugnantia concedat infra idem tempus. Aristoteles enim in *Elenchis* docet arguentem multa proponere, ut de propositorum responsione ob multitudinem respondens non recolens redargueretur. A quo in parte haec ars ordinem traxit, ut advertentes non indeceptos servemus. Sicut decet mendacem esse bene memorem ut non contraria licet affirmat asserat, ita bene respondentem iuxta admissa et concessa et negata convenienter et memorata formaliter convenit respondere.

> (this art trains the respondent so that he pays attention to what is granted and denied, in order not to grant two incompatible things within the same time. For in *Sophistical Refutations* [xv, 174a17] Aristotle teaches the arguer to put forward many things so that the respondent who does not remember because of the large number may be refuted as regards his response to the

---

81 Green, "An Introduction to the Logical Treatise *De obligationibus*, with Critical Texts of William of Sherwood (?) and Walter Burley," 118–19, quoted in de Rijk, ed., "Some Thirteenth-Century Tracts on the Game of Obligation (I)," 94.

82 Green, "An Introduction to the Logical Treatise *De obligationibus*," 18–19, quoted in de Rijk, ed., "Some Thirteenth-Century Tracts (I)," 95.

83 Spade, ed., "Roger Swyneshed's *Obligationes*: Edition and Comments," 245.

things put forward. It is partly from this that the art has derived its structure, so that as long as we pay attention we may keep ourselves from being tricked. Just as it is important for a liar to have a good memory in order to make claims without asserting contraries, so for someone who is good at responding it is appropriate that he respond formally regarding the things admitted, granted, and appropriately denied – and *remembered*.)[84]

We see here a structure in which an opponent holds a respondent in obligation to an initial statement while trying to involve him in contradiction by forcing him to respond to further statements that require concession or denial. It is not far from this to the techniques of concession and evasion dramatized by Wyche and showcased in the Lollard *schedulae* of beliefs, with their argumentative strategies. Wyche accepts an ambiguous oath as an initial agreement, and must skillfully avoid the entrapments that follow on that original "obligation." At every turn he is reminded of the conditions that follow on his agreement to the oath: and here the structures of legal interrogation and incrimination correspond with the structures of academic disputation, where the aim is to catch the repondent out in contradiction. In Wyche's negotiations with the commands of the law, and in the Lollard *schedulae* with their formulas for subtle, skilled defense and evasion, there is a crucial meeting of disputational technique and legal self-awareness. And importantly, given the governing structures of entrapment in these legal-interrogational scenarios (Wyche's ambiguous oath, after all, is a ploy offered by the adversary), the disputational strategies of evasion are a lore shared by adversary and suspect. It is no small irony, then, that the author of the extracts of Purvey's errors, the Oxford Carmelite Richard Lavenham, was also a prolific author of treatises on various subjects, including astronomy, logic, and natural philosophy, and that among these he produced a set of *obligationes*.[85] In the extracts of Purvey's errors Lavenham devotes the same interest to showcasing Lollard manipulations of disputational technique that elsewhere he devotes to such techniques in their more comprehensive and codified, "neutral" academic form. Of course, for both suspect and adversary in heresy proceedings, the rules of engagement are no longer just a game.

The deliberate ambiguity of "mental reservations" is analogous with a Lollard preceptive literature that "schools" dissidents in strategies of evasion, in "how not to answer." In turn, this preceptive literature is related, in spirit and in technique, to academic exercises of logical disputation conducted in

---

84 Kretzmann and Stump, eds. and trans., "The Anonymous *De arte obligatoria* in Merton College MS 306," 243, 251.
85 Spade, ed., "Richard Lavenham's *Obligationes.*" On Lavenham's writings and career, see the biographical entry in Kretzmann et al., eds., *The Cambridge History of Later Medieval Philosophy*, 882; and Emden, *Biographical Register of the University of Oxford* 2: 1109–10.

the teaching of university arts faculties. In the various *schedulae* of Lollard beliefs we can trace the mediation of an intellectual program from the academy to dissident academics and then to a wider dissident lay community. This entails exporting not only the intellectual project, but an intellectual *habitus*. Wyche's text, with its dramatizing of contemporary legal conditions of self-incrimination, also dramatizes a link with Lollard "instructive" practice. It follows the logic of a dissenting instruction that conjoins disputational teaching with legal self-awareness. In its showcasing of techniques of evasion, connecting academic learning with underground heretical teaching, Wyche's narrative could be said to convert the prison into school, and the prison narrative into pedagogical production.

Understood through these historical relations, then, "mental reservations" is the means by which the dissenting subject comes into full visibility, rather than a means of retreating from public representation. The evasive technique is also how Wyche, as a dissenter, can be "recognized" by his adversaries: this is perhaps why the bishop, through his knight, can appeal so effectively to Wyche through the proffered ruse, and it is certainly why inquisitors and adversaries compile lists of Lollard techniques of evasion. Wyche's "mental reservations" is not an act of disappearing from the public record, but rather a position he occupies that *links* him with the open secrets, the known defensive strategies, of a dissenting community. His ambiguous oath with mental reservations is a means of making himself known and knowable to his contemporary community, by being seen to observe the intellectual and ethical principle of concealment from the public record. His retreat from legal knowability is indeed a form of engagement in a historically specific intellectual project.

Yet, of course, Wyche does not disappear from the record. His letter survives, although other than its very survival it has no traceable effects. How it came into Bohemian provenance can only be a matter for speculation.[86] Apparently it was unknown to near-contemporary and later English chroniclers and archivists, for example, the compiler of the *Fasciculi zizaniorum,* or to Bale or Foxe. Yet the issues that his letter most sharply articulates, opposition to legal authority and public advocacy through visibility as an intellectual, do find expression through Wyche's later history in the public (and non-public) record. Wyche's letter, smuggled out of Skirlaw's prison in 1403, vanishes from the public record; but the evidence of Wyche's life and activities over the next four decades gives his letter a forward historical trajectory. We can plot

[86] See Hudson, "William Taylor's 1406 Sermon," 104; and see note 5 above.

this according to the trail of effects that Wyche leaves up to and after his death in 1440. It is this trajectory as a whole that can be taken to embody what Gramsci calls the "ensemble of the system of relations" through which the intellectual, or indeed his name, can act in the public sphere.

Sometime after he wrote his letter from Skirlaw's prison (but before 1406 when Skirlaw died), Wyche was forced to make a recantation and a particular profession of faith. The recantation and a separate list of his errors are recorded in the *Fasciculi zizaniorum*.[87] The exact sequence of events during this period is uncertain, although the overall shape of the events is clear enough. The guide that we have to the events, other than the recantation itself, is Wyche's own rehearsal of them in 1419 in the presence of Archbishop Chichele, where he acknowledged that he was condemned for heresy before Walter Skirlaw, bishop of Durham, and "master Richard Holme" (the former noted as now dead, the latter as still living), and that "after the condemnation he was detained for a long time [*diu in carceribus*] in the northern country," and then, "through the power of a royal writ called *corpus cum causa* he was led from the north to Westminster and there in the Chancery released from prison."[88] It is not clear from this account whether the appearance before Richard Holme was concurrent with his appearance before Skirlaw, so that Holme might be Skirlaw's chancellor and perhaps even the chancellor mentioned several times in Wyche's letter as one of the inquisitors at the hearings,[89] or whether the appearance before Holme was separate from and subsequent to Skirlaw's condemnation of Wyche.[90] If the latter is the case and the proceedings conducted by Holme were separate from those of Skirlaw, it might suggest that there was a period of further incarceration "in the north" beyond the time in Skirlaw's prison at Bishop Auckland described in Wyche's letter; and that at the point when he was led to Westminster and released Wyche might have spent up to several years in detention, perhaps even in different northern locales.[91]

Wyche's abjuration of dissident principles obviously did not stick, for the

---

87 Recantation, *Fasciculi zizaniorum* 501 ff; errors, 370 ff.

88 *The Register of Henry Chichele, Archbishop of Canterbury, 1414–1443*, ed. Jacob and Johnson, 3: 57; see also 1: cxxiv.   89 See Snape's suggestion, "Some Evidence of Lollard Activity," 360.

90 As Emden suggests: "Wyche also brought before magister Richard Holme, canon of York, acting for the archbishop of York, and brought from imprisonment in north of England and released at Westeminster," *Biographical Register of the University of Oxford* 3: 2101.

91 The material in the recantation printed in *Fasciculi zizaniorum* (Appendix 6) does not add to the information beyond supplying *termini a quo* and *ad quem* for the recantation itself. The bishop of Durham is cited as having "lately" commanded Wyche to answer and declare himself on articles of faith (501; note that the name William for bishop of Durham printed there should be amended to Walter, which is clear from the original manuscript [British Library MS Royal. 8. F. xii]); this would place the retraction before Skirlaw's death in March 1406. Innocent VII is mentioned as being pope (505), which would place the retraction after October 1404, when Innocent was elected.

next evidence for his resumption, or more likely continuation, of heretical associations comes from 1410, the letter of spiritual and personal fellowship that he wrote to Jan Hus, and to which Hus responded in kind. Wyche's letter is inscribed and dated from London, on the nativity of the Virgin (8 September). On the same day Oldcastle sent a letter, inscribed from Cooling Castle (one of Oldcastle's holdings, sited on the Thames estuary), to the Bohemian noble Woksa von Waldstein, a supporter of Hus.[92] Here the dissident confederacies are formed both on a local axis (Wyche and Oldcastle) and an international one (Wyche and Hus, Oldcastle and von Waldstein), and along, as well as across, the lines of social orders (the English and Bohemian clerics, the English and Bohemian nobles, as well as the two English Lollards, cleric and noble). The preservation of these letters (like that of Wyche's letter from prison) was left to Bohemian hands, and so while indicative of broader activity, Wyche's letter to Hus seems to occupy no place in the contemporary or later English record (although in the next decade Wyche was to be linked to Oldcastle after the latter's execution). Yet the letters by the two English Wycliffites are among the effects of a heightened textual export of Wycliffite materials to Bohemia during the first decade of the fifteenth century;[93] and the letters themselves were prompted by the success of the reform party in the university at Prague in publicly countering official attempts to suppress popular and academic heresy in Bohemia, efforts in which Hus was a central player.[94]

Wyche's letter to Hus documents not only a continuity of belief, but a certain kind of identification with intellectual labor. And the exchange of letters between them gives a powerful manifestion of confederation at the level of intellectual identity. Wyche requests an answer from Hus, using the ancient epistolary topos of mutual spiritual support and solidarity in project that can transcend distance and unite two people who have never met:

> Tu ergo Huss frater in Christo perdilecte! licet ignotus mihi in facie, non tamen fide et dilectione, quia non terrarum spacia sufficiunt disjungere, quos nectit efficaciter amor Christi. Confortare in gratia, quae data est tibi . . . Salutant vos omnes amici qui de vestris constanciis audi[v]erunt.

---

[92] The letters between Wyche and Hus are edited in Höfler, *Geschichtschreiber der Husitischen Bewegung in Böhmen*, 210–14. The letter from Oldcastle to von Waldstein is edited in Loserth, "Über die Beziehungen zwischen englischen und böhmischen Wiclifiten." For commentary on Oldcastle's letter see Waugh, "Sir John Oldcastle," 442–6.

[93] The textual movement from England to Bohemia is summarized in Loserth, "Über die Beziehungen zwischen englischen und böhmischen Wiclifiten," 257–61. More recent scholarship on the Prague–Oxford exchange is summarized in Cook, "Peter Payne, Theologian and Diplomat of the Hussite Revolution," 12–22.

[94] Waugh, "Sir John Oldcastle," 443; Spinka, ed. and trans., *John Hus at the Council of Constance*, 38; Kaminsky, *A History of the Hussite Revolution*, 70–5.

Cuperem [sic] etiam vestra rescripta videre quia scitote quod non modica solatia nobis praestant. Scriptum Londoniae in nativitate virginis gloriosae vester servus cupiens in labore fieri socius. Richardus Vitze [infimus] sacerdotum.[95]

(You, Hus, diligent brother in Christ! even if you are unknown to me in your person, it is not so in faith and esteem, because no earthly distance is big enough to separate those whom the love of Christ effectively brings together. May you be comforted in grace with which you are endowed . . . All your friends who have heard of your constancy send you greetings. I yearn to see your responses; you should know that these would not be small solaces to us. Written in London on the nativity of the glorious Virgin, your servant desiring fellowship in labor. Richard Wyche, humble priest.)

Hus responds with passionate solicitude, recounting how effectively he translated Wyche's private overture into its public consequences:

Tuae karitatis epistola quae de sursum a patre luminum descendit, in Christo fratribus vehementer accendit animum, quia tantum dulcedinis efficaciae roborationis et consolationis in se continet quod si alia scripta singula per antichristum consumarenter voragine, ipsa Christi fidelibus sufficeret ad salutem, unde eius medullam et vigorositatem in meo revolvens animo dixi coram multus hominibus in sermone publico, in quo ut aestimo fuerunt *prope decem millia hominum*: ecce fratres dilectissimi! quantum curam de vestra salute Christi praedicatores fidelissimi in alienis gerunt partibus, qui cupiunt totum cor suum effundere, si possent nos in lege Christi vel domini conservare. Et subjunxi: ecce karissimi! frater noster Rigchardus Magistri Johannis Wykleff in evangelii laboribus *consocius* scripsit vobis tantae confortationis epistolam, quod si ego nullam haberem scripturam aliam, deberem me pro Christi evangelio exponere *usque ad mortem* et faciam auxiliante domino nostro J. Ch. Sic autem exarserunt fideles Christi in ipsa epistola, quod rogant me ut ipsam transponerem in linguam nostrae gentis.[96]

(Your affectionate letter, which came down from above from the Father of lights, powerfully kindles the soul of your brothers in Christ. It contains so much sweetness, efficacy, invigoration, and solace, that if every other writing were engulfed in the abyss of Antichrist, it would suffice of itself for the salvation of Christ's faithful ones. Turning over in my mind its marrow and strength, I said in a large assembly of people, numbering, I suppose, nearly ten thousand, as I was preaching in public, "See, my

---

95 Höfler, *Geschichtschreiber der Husitischen Bewegung*, 212. In the last sentence, Höfler has "infirmus sacerdotum"; as Loserth points out in his introduction to his edition of the Oldcastle letter, "infirmus" should read "infimus" (Loserth, 260, n. 1).
96 Höfler, *Geschichtschreiber der Husitischen Bewegung*, 212–13.

beloved brothers, what a care for your salvation is shown by the faithful preachers of Christ in other countries; they yearn to pour out their whole soul, if only they can keep us in the gospel of Christ, even the Lord." And I added, "Why, our dear brother Richard, partner of Master John Wyclif in the toils of the gospel, hath written you a letter of so much cheer, that if I possessed no other writing, I should feel bound by it to offer myself for the gospel of Christ, even unto death. Yea, and this will I do, with the help of our Lord Jesus Christ." Christ's faithful ones were fired with such ardour by the letter that they begged me to translate it into our mother tongue.) [97]

As this suggests, of course, Wyche's overtures are no private matter: any such expressions of ideological identification are always the property of the public sphere, because that is the economy in which their symbolic value is produced.[98] Hus has simply made Wyche part of his own political story: he narrates that before an audience of "nearly ten thousand" he proclaimed Wyche an associate of Wyclif in evangelical labors, a brother of ours, whose letter offers comfort and spiritual fellowship almost beyond mortal debt, and that the inspired crowd begged to hear the letter in their own language. And Hus' story witnesses the interdependency of clerical identification and the public visibility that is necessary to any kind of intellectual function, whether that role is played out symbolically or directly: Wyche, the distant and "underground" intellectual, is made present in the person of Hus, the public intellectual, and voiced through Hus' Czech speech. It does not matter that neither of Wyche's letters finds a place in the contemporary English public record. The logic of misrecognition would dictate that he find his most profound public realization through unofficial corridors; although certainly Hus' delivery of an encomium before a crowd of ten thousand in Bohemia would go a long way towards converting Wyche's desire for recognition into official (transnational) currency.

After the exchange of letters in 1410, Wyche does not reappear in public records until October 1417, when Oldcastle was still at large three years after the uprising. In this month Wyche was required to appear at Westminster to make disclosures about money that had belonged to Oldcastle and had been forfeited to the king. This suggests that his earlier association with Oldcastle was known, although he was not implicated directly in the uprising; exactly how the authorities viewed his relation to Oldcastle is not clear.[99] In 1419 he was summoned by Chichele, once again under suspicion of heresy, and here he admitted his earlier condemnation. The archbishop, upon the advice of his

---

[97] Translation by Workman and Pope, *The Letters of John Hus*, 35.
[98] See, for example, what Cornelius Castoriadis describes in terms of the "institution of the symbolic": *L'Institution imaginaire de la société*, 62–84.   [99] See Thomson, *The Later Lollards*, 15–16.

council, committed Wyche to the Fleet prison "until after mature deliberation it could be decided what ought to be done with him finally."[100] He was released in 1420, and occupied several livings in Kent and Middlesex from the early 1420s through the 1430s.[101]

Wyche was arrested and burned as an obdurate heretic in 1440. But his last and most important appearance in the public record is the effect that his death on 17 June had in London. The chronicles record his final condemnation and his death, along with another man (once identified as his servant and in another source named as Roger Norman). But most of the chronicles also describe popular reactions to his death. It provoked "much trouble among the people," "great rumor in the city among the people."[102] Local people (only in one instance identified as "people of his opinions" – that is, Lollard sympathizers) made a shrine of the execution site: "In quo loco homines et mulieres de londonie in maxima multitudine reputantes ipsum martyrem sanctum erexerunt crucem et coeperunt offerre ibi argentum et ymagines de cera" ("in which place a great multitude of men and women of London, calling him a sacred martyr, erected a cross and began making offerings there of silver and wax images").[103] Even more detail of the "trouble" and "rumor" around Wyche's death emerges from the London Journals, which record how a cult of the martyr sprang up, fueled by reports of miracles worked at the site of the burning. Thomas Virley, the vicar of All Hallows Barking, was arrested on 18 July, a month after Wyche's death: he was accused of promoting heresy by circulating miracle-stories about the curative powers of the martyr's ashes (in which he allegedly mixed aromatic spices), and of stationing his two servants at the site with a stolen collection box to which people were encouraged to make offerings which the vicar was pocketing for himself.[104] The seditious import of these activities, whether seen as the spontaneous popular sanctification of the site of a martyr's death or as an opportunistic enterprise in cult-making for personal profit, was clearly what royal and city authorities feared most. On 15 July, nearly a month after Wyche's execution,

---

100 *The Register of Henry Chichele* 3: 57.

101 Thomson, *The Later Lollards*, 149; *Calendar of Close Rolls, Henry V 2, 1419–22*, 82; Emden, *Biographical Register* 3: 2101. E. F. Jacob remarks "It is worth recalling that the Lollard preacher, Richard Wyche, was vicar of the Winchester College living of Harmondsworth where serious opposition of the tenants against their ecclesiastical landlords occurred from time to time" (*The Fifteenth Century, 1399–1485*, 496).

102 William Gregory's *Chronicle of London*, in Gairdner, ed., *The Historical Collections of a Citizen of London in the Fifteenth Century*, 183; Kingsford, ed., *Chronicles of London*, 153 (Vitellius A. 16 text).

103 Flenley, ed., *Six Town Chronicles of England*, 101 (Rawlinson B. 355 text). Similar, although slightly less detailed accounts are in a continuation of the *Brut*, Brie, ed., *The Brut, or The Chronicles of England* 2: 508; Kingsford, ed., *Chronicles of London* (Vitellius text), 152–3.

104 On this material from the unpublished London Journals, book 3, see Thomson, *The Later Lollards*, 150–1, and for more extensive information, see Barron, review of Thomson's *The Later Lollards*.

the king issued a writ to the sheriffs of London and Middlesex, along with an identical writ to sheriffs in counties throughout England, forbidding anyone "to repair by colour of pilgrimage or devotion or send aught to the place where Richard Wyche chaplain was put to death, or secretly or openly worship him," or to call him anything except a heretic; for although the said Richard was properly found to be a relapsed heretic and lawfully executed for treason,

> certain of the king's subjects, as he has many times learned, being instigated by the devil, and going about to stir up not only sedition but also idolatry in the realm, fear not openly to say that he was innocent of heresy, that he died a just and holy man, and that miracles are done by him, when they are not, whom the king may regard as accomplices and maintainers of heresy and heretics, as guilty of treason, offenders against the king and the peace of the realm, and transgressors against the sacred canons, since they worship the said Richard . . . and the king's desire is to keep peace in the realm, and abolish idolatry within the borders thereof.[105]

And it is with this formal magnification of the cult activities to the status of sedition that the records are most consistently concerned: "And grete wacche was made ffor the offeryng that the pepill did ther for him in all the wardys of the cite of london."[106] On one account the watch on Tower Hill was kept until Lammas, that is, 1 August. And other chronicles describe how, on royal orders, the mayor of London and his sheriffs dispersed the crowds and polluted the site with animal dung.[107]

The contemporary symbolic magnitude of Wyche's death was recognized by political authorities through the equally symbolic gesture of pollution of the site now enshrined. Royal and local authority treated the tumult surrounding his death as alarmingly seditious, and the threat (however manufactured) of treasonous heresy was forcefully suppressed by dispersing the crowds, keeping watch on the hill, and arresting a number of people perceived to be instigators or prominent participants. But the importance of these events was, at the same time, repressed in the public records, which give the events the status of localized, subterranean cult-making (even while copies of the king's writ were sent to counties throughout England, indicating fears of similar insurgencies at large).[108] To what extent was the civic unrest traceable

---

[105] *Calendar of Close Rolls*, Henry VI 3, 1435–41: 385–6.

[106] Kingsford, ed., *Chronicles of London*, 147 (Cleopatra C. 5 text); cf. Gregory's *Chronicle*, in Gairdner, ed., *Historical Collections of a Citizen of London*, 183.

[107] Kingsford, ed., *Chronicles of London*, 153 (Vitellius A. 16 text); Brie, ed., *Brut* 2: 508; Flenley, ed., *Six Town Chronicles*, 101 (Rawlinson B. 355 text).

[108] My formulations here about the contemporary symbolic magnitude of events and their representation in the official record are indebted to conversations with Paul Strohm about the role of the occurrences after Wyche's death in Lancastrian polity and records.

to Wyche's long career, indeed to anything that can be closely associated with Wyche and his own activities? There is no direct causal linkage between Wyche's prison narrative and his later history, including the events after his execution, but those later events do place the prison letter at the start of a forward historical trajectory, even though the text itself disappears from that history. There is little recorded evidence that the local reaction to his execution was the culmination of ongoing public or semi-public activity that he maintained throughout his life, nor is there evidence of how, in the years following the Oldcastle uprising, he forged a new activist status among communities in the southern counties or London; interestingly, the two chronicle continuations of the *Brut* suggest that public affect was excited by witness of the devout quality of the death that he made rather than by any cumulative, historical knowledge of his activities.[109] We have only the fact of his final condemnation and execution to indicate that he did reestablish an activist profile. Perhaps what is most intriguing about the events that occurred after his burning is that they remain untraceable to the intellectual identity constructed in his prison narrative. Rather, the identity of Wyche upon his death becomes a public possession, his significance appropriated by unofficial and offical interests, its value to be contested (either magnified or repressed) in and beyond the public record.

[109] "And the peple that sawe theym [i.e. Wyche and Roger Norman] dye, had grete compassion on theym, for the confession and ende that they made in theire good byleve, and thanked God of his soule"; "how-be-it, at his deth he died A gode Cristen man; wherfor, after his deth moche peple come to the place wher he was brent, and offred, and made an hepe of stones, and set vp A crosse of tree, and held him for A Seynt," Brie, ed., *Brut* 2: 476, 508.

4

William Thorpe and the historical record

In contrast to the forward historical directions that Wyche's testimony takes as the first point of visibility through a long career, the trajectory of William Thorpe's narrative is backward into the past, to an earlier, idealized moment in the Wycliffite movement, giving Thorpe a historicity that he does not otherwise possess. Thorpe comes into being as a historically knowable subject through the literary mechanics of violent representation, the narrative drama of his adversarial encounter with Arundel; yet his text must also disavow its own literary character in favor of its claims to historicity.

Outside the text Thorpe's is a shadowy life. He has been tentatively identified with a priest named William Thorpe instituted to the vicarage of Marske, Cleveland (York diocese), in March of 1395, which would locate him in the north of England and thus confirm Arundel's statement at the opening of the "Testimony": "William, I knowe wel that thou hast this twenti wyntir and more traueilid aboute bisili in the north lond and in othir diuerse contrees of Ynglond, sowynge aboute fals doctryne."[1] But for the interview with Arundel on 7 August 1407 at Saltwood Castle in Kent, there is no external evidence. The text states that the interrogation followed on his arrest in April in Shrewsbury for preaching Lollard doctrines in Saint Chad's Church; but beyond the text there is no record of this arrest, or of the outcome of the interview, or even of what became of Thorpe.

There are tantalizing connections with Bohemia: aside from the two Latin versions of the "Testimony" that survive in Bohemian manuscripts, another Bohemian manuscript containing various Wycliffite and Hussite materials attributes a list of beliefs to a "Wilhelmus Torp" (or "Corp").[2] Thorpe is one of the few English Wycliffites, along with Richard Wyche and the Oxford

---

[1] Text in Hudson, ed., *Two Wycliffite Texts*, 29 (hereafter cited by page number in the main text). See Aston, *Thomas Arundel: a Study of Church Life in the Reign of Richard II*, 326 and n. 2. On the possible problems of accepting this identification see Hudson, ed., *Two Wycliffite Texts*, xlvii.

[2] Prague Metropolitan Chapter Library MS D. 49, ff. 179ᵛ–181ᵛ, *Opiniones Wyhelmi Torp [Corp], cuius librum ego habeo*; see Hudson, ed., *Two Wycliffite Texts*, lii–iii.

191

Lollard Peter Payne, to be mentioned by name in Bohemian sources. We may be tempted to want to fill the historical vacuum of Thorpe's fortunes by positing for him some kind of parallel trajectory with a dissident intellectual like Peter Payne, who escaped England for Bohemia in 1413.[3] In other words, there is a certain attractiveness in looking for another career that can be recovered in nearly all of its significant profile, to find a way of imagining the life of Thorpe which leaves almost no imprint on the historical record. Someone like Payne, perhaps, offers a potential and "borrowed" embodiment for Thorpe's spectral historicity.[4] Thorpe is scarcely more than a literary idea of the dissident intellectual, detached from a historicizable substratum; as a disembodied identity, he frustrates our attempts to trace even the outlines of a career by comparison with the trajectories of known intellectuals.

The only report in the "Testimony" of an event in Thorpe's life for which there is possible external corroboration refers to an episode ten years earlier, in 1397. During the reported interview Arundel mentions his exile in 1397, and suggests that his departure must have been a turn of good fortune for Thorpe; Thorpe adds that on Arundel's banishment, he was released from the prison of Bishop Braybrooke of London where he was being held, saying that Braybrooke no longer found cause to hold him once Arundel was out of the country (91).[5] There is some independent historical record of Braybrooke taking legal action against Thorpe. In the memorandum book of John Lydford, a diocesan official of Exeter, there are three entries concerning one William Thorpe: articles drawn up for Robert Braybrooke, bishop of London, accusing Thorpe of heretical preaching in London; Thorpe's reply to Braybrooke's accusations, justifying his preaching on scriptural grounds; and the beginning of a mandate of excommunication against Thorpe.[6] There is no record that the mandate for excommunication was carried out. However, the events recorded in these entries cannot be dated later than 1386.[7] In the "Testimony," Thorpe states that Braybrooke freed him from prison when Arundel left the country (in 1397): since historical record suggests a previous pattern of Braybrooke's actions against Thorpe (although not necessarily

---

[3] Compare Hudson: "it is tempting to speculate that Thorpe, like Payne, fled from persecution in England to Prague," *Selections from English Wycliffite Writings*, 156; and see also *Two Wycliffite Texts*, lii.

[4] In other words, to speculate on Thorpe's possible career, the possible trajectory of his movements, is not unlike incarnating a spectral idea, which has become separated from its grounding or substratum, in "another artifactual body, a prosthetic body"; see Derrida, *Specters of Marx*, 126.

[5] On Thomas Arundel's exile from 1397–99, see Aston, *Thomas Arundel*, 362–73.

[6] *John Lydford's Book*, ed. Owen, 108–12 (items 206 and 209).

[7] See Hudson, ed., *Two Wycliffite Texts*, xlviii–l on the evidence for dating the records in the Lydford memorandum book, the difficulties of reconciling the Lydford records with the events narrated in the "Testimony," and possible explanations for the reported arrest by Braybrooke that led to Thorpe's release in 1397.

including imprisonment at the time of the articles drawn up against Thorpe), it is possible that Thorpe's account refers to an arrest closer to 1397, perhaps predicated on earlier attempts to prosecute him. In both these episodes, Thorpe's case would seem to have remained incomplete, for he is never treated in the "Testimony" as a relapsed heretic.

While this reference in the text is linked (however ambiguously) to earlier historical record of Thorpe, the actual proceedings reported here, the interview with Arundel, have no similar corroboration in external record. Yet, of course, the "Testimony" asks to be read as historical record, as direct translation of a life, an event, occluding its own literary textuality. Thorpe's autobiographical account of his youth, which he gives early in the text, describes how he came to espouse Lollard doctrine through his education for the priesthood, his passage from orthodox to heterodox circles (37–42). He situates the beginnings of his own non-conformity at the historical origins of the movement, with Wyclif's own Oxford circle, mentioning as teachers and colleagues Wyclif himself, John Aston, Philip Repingdon, Nicholas Hereford, and John Purvey among others (40–1). Here the life on the page reaches back thirty years into history, vivifying itself through identification with an earlier and indeed originary epoch. Thorpe's dissenting subjectivity is seen to evolve not just from the narrative logic of his own life as recounted, but from the historical logic of earlier events, from a crucial, founding moment in the evolution of English non-conformity. And the text reaches forward into later history as well, its reception in the later fifteenth century and the Reformation establishing for it a kind of canonical solidity. Two manuscripts preserved in Vienna and Prague, containing Latin versions of the "Testimony" and written in fifteenth-century Bohemian hands, indicate that it circulated in Hussite Bohemia. A modernized English text paired with a version of the examination of Oldcastle was printed in 1530, probably in Antwerp.[8] In 1543 John Bale translated it into Latin and inserted it into the manuscript of *Fasciculi zizaniorum*.[9] And it was known to many generations through Foxe's inclusion of it in the *Acts and Monuments*, a text which Foxe says he printed from a transcription by William Tyndale.[10]

---

[8] On the Latin versions and the 1530 print in English see Hudson, ed., *Two Wycliffite Texts*, xxviii–xxxi, and *Premature Reformation*, 14, n. 42. The hands of the Vienna manuscript (Vienna Österreichische Nationalbibliothek MS 3936) can be dated ca. 1420; those of the Prague manuscript (Prague Metropolitan Chapter Library MS O. 29) ca. 1430. Pollard bases his modernized version of the text on the 1530 Antwerp print, and also provides a text of the Oldcastle examination from the same print (*Fifteenth-Century Prose and Verse*, 175–89).

[9] Only five folios of Bale's Latin translation survive in the manuscript, Bodleian e Mus. 86 (ff. 98 v to 103 v): see *Fasciculi Zizaniorum*, lxxii.

[10] *Acts and Monuments* 3: 239–85. On Foxe's ascription of the text to Tyndale, see Hudson, ed., *Two Wycliffite Texts*, xxxiii–xxxvi.

The very ghostliness of this text as testimony to an event in history accounts for its fascination: in its fragmentary and allusive character it seems to float just beyond the historicity that it wants to seize. There is the Thorpe who exists almost fleetingly in historical document and whose fortunes are not known, and the Thorpe who emerges fully formed from this autobiographical text which claims historical veracity. Since so little else is recorded of him we must assume that the Thorpe who was known at least to later generations in England is the figure who emerges from this quasi-fictive, quasi-documentary account. What is the role that such a text might play in the fashioning of a historical consciousness of dissent? We might almost ask whether, if Thorpe had not existed, he would have to have been invented: the text offers his historicized identity as a paradigm for constructing a dissenting subject.

Most importantly, the text defines dissent by raising intellectual labor to the foreground. Much more explicitly than Wyche does in his letter, but in a way that closely echoes the *Opus arduum*, Thorpe's narrative positions the dissenting identity among intellectual concerns, dramatized through scenes of violent confrontation between the official voice of accusatory interrogation and Thorpe's own violently reactive hermeneutics. This is the motive through which the text most (and almost consciously) points to its own literary constructedness. It has been suggested that Thorpe and Wyche were known to one another in the north country: the name "Wilhelmus Corpp/ Torpp" appears in Wyche's letter in connection with a priest named Henry of Topcliff, whom Wyche mentions as a possible intermediary for books he has requested from prison.[11] But more provocative is the corollary of this, that Wyche's prison letter might have formed a model for the prison narrative of Thorpe.[12] My interest here is not in direct evidence of this (for there is little that can actually be adduced), but rather in the explanatory power of a textual tradition of dissenting subjectivity. For we can readily see how the Thorpe narrative could have been constructed with knowledge of the historical-textual *example* of Wyche, and even farther back, of the *Opus arduum*. And it is in the *literary* contours of this text – its balanced dramatic structures, even down to certain "unities" of time and place (a single interrogation in a single day); its predictable topical order (the interrogation that evenly covers five *questiones*, the eucharist, images, pilgrimages, tithes, and oaths); the prologue with its promise to "go as nigh the sentence and the wordis as I can" (25) – that the dissenting identity is formed and animated. Whether or not the Thorpe narrative records an actual event, it is positioned

11 Matthew, "The Trial of Richard Wyche," 543; on this see Hudson, ed., *Two Wycliffite Texts*, lviii, and above, chapter 3, p. 154. As noted above, C and T are almost indistinguishable in Bohemian mss.

12 Also Hudson's suggestion, ibid.

for a place in a recognized, or at least available, textual tradition of imprisoned intellectuals to which it is perhaps the definitive literary contribution, thereby conferring a certain *post facto* canonical literary status on its precedents.

Yet, paradoxically, while the "Testimony" shapes its dissenting subject by locating itself in an immediate literary tradition of intellectuals, it also uses its central theme of intellectual labor to reach into the past and commit itself to historical veracity. According to his account, Thorpe represents the academic inner core of the oppositional movement at Oxford. On his own suggestion he is one of the last links, either living or still uncompromised, with the founding academic circle of Wycliffite heterodoxy at the university. He describes how his original attraction to the Oxford circle grew out of rebellion against parental wishes: his parents spent much money on his education, intending that he should become a priest, but he resisted their desires until he came to study with a group of priests "of moost holi lyuynge, and best taught and moost wyse of heuenly wysdom" (37). He indicates that he was a younger contemporary of Hereford, Purvey, and Aston, that Wyclif was the revered heresiarch, and that the others were already engaged in their revisionist work by the time that he entered their circle:

> And I seide, "Ser, in his tyme maister Ioon Wiclef was holden of ful many men the grettis clerk that thei knewen lyuynge vpon erthe. And therwith he was named, as I gesse worthili, a passing reuli man and an innocent in al his lyuynge. And herfore grete men of kunnynge and other also drowen myche to him, and comownede ofte with him. And thei sauouriden so his loore that thei wroten it bisili and enforsiden hem to rulen hem theraftir . . . Maister Ion Aston taughte and wroot acordingli and ful bisili, where and whanne and to whom he myghte, and he vsid it himsilf, I gesse, right perfyghtli vnto his lyues eende. Also Filip of Repintoun whilis he was a chanoun of Leycetre, Nycol Herforde, dane Geffrey of Pikeringe, monke of Biland and a maistir dyuynyte, and Ioon Purueye, and manye other whiche weren holden rightwise men and prudent, taughten and wroten bisili this forseide lore of Wiclef, and conformeden hem therto. And with alle these men I was ofte homli and I comownede with hem long tyme and fele, and so bifore alle othir men I chees wilfulli to be enformed bi hem and of hem, and speciali of Wiclef himsilf, as of the moost vertuous and goodlich wise man that I herde of owhere either knew. And herfore of Wicleef speciali and of these men I toke the lore whiche I haue taughte and purpose to lyue aftir, if God wole, to my lyues ende." (40–1).

This speech, set in 1407, is really less about the past than about the transitional historical moment in which the speech itself is set. Had the Lollard movement taken a different course, had its first-generation Oxford core not been so effectively eliminated through persecutions and recantations, someone like Thorpe would have been a likely candidate to be part of a second-generation link between the founding circle and an ever-widening popular reformist community. But instead, Thorpe is one of the few remaining representatives of that first "inner core," and he speaks now for a movement that is on the verge of losing its strong university identity, its leadership passing into the hands of unbeneficed lower clergy and self-taught laymen, with few direct ties to its original academic center.

This speech seems like it should have been written sometime after 1407, with a certain hindsight to, or at least awareness of, what was then occurring and about to occur at Oxford. In broad outline, these events include: the "translation" of the Wycliffite textual corpus to Bohemia, as Bohemian scholars began to replace the diminishing cadre of Oxford scholars in preserving and studying Wyclif's works; the Convocation at Oxford in November 1407 that produced the draft of the *Constitutiones* and the comprehensive suppressions that eventuated from it; the condemnation of Wyclif's writings at Oxford in 1409; the full-blown rejection of Wycliffite reformist opinion by prominent schoolmen (notably Peter Partridge) who had up until then maintained some sympathies with it; the various proceedings conducted against Peter Payne in 1410; the burning of Wyclif's books at Oxford in 1411; Arundel's visitation of 1411–12; and Payne's own departure for Bohemia in 1413.[13] Thorpe's identification with the university, in his elegiac remembrance of a lost intellectual circle, is more clearly drawn than any other of his current or more recent communal associations described in the text. By contrast, the twenty or so years that he has preached throughout the north country and elsewhere in England (29), and that public constituency – the "ful manye men and wymmen" (35) – that he represents, have only a shadowy, notional presence in his account. Obviously in the case of the latter group, his active constituency, he cannot "name names," so they must remain under the protective anonymity of "ful manye men and wymmen";[14] but it is

[13] For a thorough account of these and related events between 1406 and 1412, see Catto, "Wyclif and Wycliffism at Oxford, 1356–1430," 240–54.

[14] At an early point in the interrogation, Arundel requires him, in accordance with statutory and canonical legislation, to produce names of confederates: "Neithir thou schalt fauoure man ne womman, yong ne olde, that holdith ony of these forseide opynnouns . . . and hem that wol not leue thees dampnable opinyouns thou schalt putten vp, pupblischinge her names, and make hem known to the bischop of the diocise that these ben inne, either to the bischopis mynystris" (34–5). Thorpe refuses on grounds both legalistic: "And I heerynge these wordis thoughte in myn herte that this was an vnleeful askynge, and I demed mysilf cursid of God if I consentid herto" (35) and conscientious: "And I seide 'Sere, if I consentid to do thus as ye haue here rehersid to me, I schulde become apelour, either euery bischopis aspie or sumnour of this lond. For, if I schulde thus putt vp and publische the names of men and of wymmen, I schulde hereinne diseese ful manye persoones – yhe, ser, as it is lickli bi the dome of [my]

also clear that they play a less articulated role in the narrative formation of the autobiography than the now lost university community that is reconstructed in loving but also supererogatory detail.

Thus in Thorpe's text political opposition is defined strongly and explicitly in terms of intellectual labor, and the Thorpe persona is projected onto history through identification with a mythologized intellectual community. But there is also a profound consciousness of loss here that is not present in earlier detention writing. The ideological distance between this text and its earliest extant antecedent, the *Opus arduum*, is especially striking. The author of the *Opus arduum* is defiant in his confidence that there is an inexhaustible community of *fideles* to carry on the intellectual work that he is undertaking in his present writing. And here lies an important difference between the Thorpe narrative and its predecessors. The voice of the intellectual in the *Opus arduum* virtually disappears into a collective of the faithful; and Wyche certainly tries to disappear from the offical public record, but not from the pedagogical system that is shared among dissidents and that allows him to be knowable to his own community. But the Thorpe identity is strangely disconnected from its putative historical moment (1407), and seems to be invested in a mythology of the dissident intellectual as survivor, remnant of a community lost to time, death, and the self-compromise that persecution produces.

This returns us to the text's claims to historicity, and specifically to questions of when it was composed. It cannot be determined when this narrative concerning purported events of 7 August 1407 was actually written, whether it was written close to that actual date or at a further historical remove. At best the earliest manuscripts, the English version in Bodleian Library MS Rawlinson C. 208, and a Latin version in Vienna Österreichische Nationalbibliothek MS 3936, indicate copying within the first quarter of the fifteenth century, so that by no later than about 1425 there were at least two versions in circulation, one in English and one Bohemian copy in Latin.[15] But there is little internal evidence to suggest when the original narrative was composed. The English version contains a prologue, lacking in both the Bohemian versions, which says that the idea for such an account occurred before Thorpe was (supposedly) ever interviewed by Arundel: the prologue

conscience, I schulde hereinne be cause of the deeth bothe of men and of wymmen, yhe, bothe bodili and as I gesse goostli'" (35).

[15] Hudson, ed., *Two Wycliffite Texts*, xxvii–xxix; and 144: "it is . . . quite certain that [the account] was written within at most ten years of the event it records." The 1530 Antwerp print of the "Testimony" also contains an epilogue (called a "testamente") in Thorpe's name, dated 1460; this epilogue is also reproduced in Foxe's version of the text, based on the Antwerp print. The later attachment of this epilogue has no value for dating or placing Thorpe's career or text. See *Two Wycliffite Texts*, 143–51.

states that when it was known that Thorpe would be removed from the prison at Shrewsbury to Arundel's prison in Kent, his friends urged him to write an account of any interrogation he might have at Arundel's hands; and that in the time since the purported interrogation, friends "haue come to me into prisoun" counseling him to write his "apposynge and . . . answring" (25). At the end of the narrative he says "so thanne I was led forth and and brought into a ful vnhonest prisoun where I cam neuere bifore" (93), presumably the prison to which his friends have lately come urging him to write his account. But there is no indication how long he would have stayed in this third prison, and whether the account purports to be written while he was in that prison or at an unspecified later point.[16]

I have suggested that the ideological orientation of the autobiographical passages concerning Oxford, with their almost oppressive absorption in a mythologized academic "golden age," might point to a period at least a few years after 1407, as if the remarks carry a knowledge of just how effective the suppressions of intellectual dissent at Oxford were to be, and how in fact transitional was the position that Thorpe would have occupied in 1407. This is a reading of ideological inference, opening the text to a stronger form of interpretation of its motives than simply ascertaining chronological *termini*, or indeed historical veracity. It should be clear that I do not assume that the text is "true" or that it necessarily recounts a historical event or describes a person whose career and profile we can fix. Whether it is confected or true, it signifies an "event" in history, that is, a moment at which the conditions of intellectual self-representation changed radically.

If Wyche's letter stands clearly in relation to the legislation of 1401, the narrative of Thorpe's interview with Arundel has its own proximity to a historical referent, the drafting of the *Constitutiones* at Oxford in November 1407. Peter McNiven, reading the Thorpe account as plausibly authentic, suggests that Arundel's frustration with Thorpe may have influenced his drafting of the *Constitutiones*, both in terms of the comprehensive attack on the academic stronghold of the sect, and in the particular matters of the authority of ecclesiastical decrees regarding images, pilgrimages, relics, and the validity of oaths.[17] But such a reading of influence and causality puts demands of historicity on the events narrated in the "Testimony" that neither the text nor external record can sustain. I think it more productive, and more satisfying, to invert these proposed relations and consider the Thorpe narra-

[16] A colophon that follows the prologue in the manuscript of the English version mentions "Arnedel [*sic*], Archebischop sumtyme of Cauntirbirie" (*Two Wycliffite Texts*, 29), indicating a date after February, 1414 for the composition of the manuscript (although not necessarily the text). The colophon is not included in the ca. 1530 printed edition. See *Two Wycliffite Texts*, lii.

[17] McNiven, *Heresy and Politics in the Reign of Henry IV*, 114, 116.

tive itself as a text born of the broad effects of the *Constitutiones* of 1407. I do not mean to argue a direct causality: I do not suggest that the "Testimony" was written to "contradict" the *Constitutiones*, or to reflect them, but rather that the narrative of the alleged conversation was written in the wake of the *Constitutiones* and bears the weight of their legal, social, and historical effect.

There is no textual evidence against this, although as well there is no internal evidence for it, as the text makes no direct reference to events later than 1407.[18] Yet, of course, texts can "know" recent events of enormous moment in a way that is not fully self-conscious or realized in evidentiary terms, existentially bearing the impact of events as an unconscious cultural burden.[19] All that the narrative provides is an ideological tenor that suggests the textual environment of a somewhat belated historical moment. Thus I would read the text as a (re)construction of a conversation that might have taken place in 1407, produced from within a historical consciousness that is somewhat later than the purported events it describes. I have argued that Wyche's narrative can be read as a response to the events of 1401, expressing a new urgency to make the intellectual visible through personal exemplification; Wyche's text, of course, gives us more clues to its relationship with the immediate past, notably the reading to Wyche of Purvey's 1401 recantation. In a way less particularized and less self-conscious than Wyche's text, but no less forceful, Thorpe's narrative can be seen to witness the impact of the *Constitutiones* on an academic community, in the text's peculiar intellectual self-consciousness, and in its struggle against the erasure of a certain kind of intellectual identity. Whereas the *De heretico comburendo* statute worked by attacking the symptom, isolating individuals as examples, and using punishment to incite fear, the *Constitutiones* leveled a blow at an entire intellectual community, and at the core intellectual identity of the heretical movement.

The effects of the *Constitutiones* on vernacular theological culture throughout the fifteenth century have been amply demonstrated by Nicholas Watson, who traces their resonance not only through the hard evidence of vernacular textual production, but through palpable shifts in theological attitude among lay and clerical writers and audiences.[20] The impact of the *Constitutiones* on

---

[18] Hudson, ed., *Two Wycliffite Texts*, lii: "Certainly, there is nothing within the text that appears to refer to events after 1407 – and some of those events, such as the publication of Arundel's *Constitutions* in 1409, the presentation of the Lollard Disendowment Bill in 1410, or the Oldcastle rising of 1413–14, were of a significance to both sides in the case that would make allusion probable." Yet if we were to expect the text to be self-conscious enough about its place in relation to post-1407 events as to allude to them, we might also expect it to be crafted enough to preserve the "fiction" of being set in August 1407, and therefore to suppress deliberately any reference to later events.

[19] See Strohm, "Chaucer's Lollard Joke: History and the Textual Unconscious."

[20] Watson, "Censorship and Cultural Change in Late-Medieval England: Vernacular Theology, the Oxford Translation Debate, and Arundel's Constitutions of 1409."

university intellectual culture is no less palpable. They introduced elaborate forms of collegial and hierarchical surveillance and investigation, restrictions upon teaching and academic debate, controls over academic and clerical careers, and comprehensive censorship of books.[21] On a long-range view, the effect of the suppressions upon Oxford was to force academic discourse into more conservative and specialist postures, to turn intellectual concerns among arts and theology masters inward and away from engagement with political thought and civil affairs, and to give greater scope to an ascendent class of university-trained lawyers and administrators from whose practical agenda a new technical "science" of politics evolved.[22] Of course, the suppressions at Oxford and related legislation did not succeed in eliminating the actual work of intellectual advocacy: we have the powerful examples of Wyche, Payne, William Taylor, and others through the fifteenth century, as well as of figures like William White of Kent, whose connections with university communities were more ambiguous. But what of the effect of the Oxford *Constitutiones* upon the very possibilities of intellectual self-representation, and upon the articulated relations between dissenting intellectuals and their broad peda- gogical communities?

By 1407, Lollardy is marked as a failed revolution, and I would argue that the Thorpe narrative knows this and speaks from the vantage point of that knowledge. This is something that Wyche does not know in his letter of 1403 (despite the sharpness and urgency of his own historical predicament), and it is certainly a knowledge beyond the confident predictions of the *Opus arduum* author. In the moment of the Thorpe text is the knowledge of failure, and here the text is an effort – in terms of its own theological economy that seems, significantly, to replicate Lollardy's apocalyptic economy of history – to seize a certain redemption out of historical failure. In his *Theses on the Philosophy of History*, Walter Benjamin writes:

> To articulate the past historically does not mean to recognize it "the way it really was" (Ranke). It means to seize hold of a memory as it flashes up at a moment of danger . . . In every era the attempt must be made anew to wrest tradition away from a conformism that is about to overpower it. The Messiah comes not only as a redeemer, he comes as the subduer of Antichrist. Only that historian will have the gift of fanning the spark of hope in the past who is firmly convinced that *even the dead* will not be safe from the enemy if he wins.[23]

The Thorpe text, like that historian who determines to protect even the dead,

---

[21] Hudson, *Premature Reformation*, 82–5.
[22] Coleman, "The Science of Politics and Late Medieval Academic Debate."
[23] *Theses on the Philosophy of History*, Thesis vi, Benjamin, *Illuminations*, ed. Arendt, 255.

is engaged in resurrecting not just the past, but a repressed past, the past that orthodox history would disavow not by unwriting or ignoring it, but rather by documenting its failure. On this logic Lollardy, and Lollard intellectual heritage, cannot count for official history except as evidence of its failure to change history. As Slavoj Žižek has commented on Benjamin's conception of history and revolution, "the returns of the repressed, the 'symptoms,' are past failed revolutionary attempts forgotten, excluded from the frame of the reigning historical tradition."[24] The Thorpe text is not the moment of revolution that succeeds, that is, on Benjamin's terms, the moment of stasis in history that "redeems" the empty and meaningless traces of past failures and annihilates the texture of history as written by the winners.[25] But it is a text that carries a knowledge of its own historical role: positioned at the end of three decades of continuous dissident activism and production, it gives expression to an intellectual self-consciousness in the shadow of the *Constitutiones* and their after effects.

How does the text testify to and perform its own transitional historical moment? I want to consider first how it revisits two principles of Lollard intellectual history that are also, significantly, building blocks of the *Constitutiones*: hermeneutics and the postures of literalism, and the pedagogical drama of inquisition. I will then turn to some broader implications of the text's struggle against history, its wresting of historical memory from the conformism of official historiography, through its literary representation of a life.

In chapter 2, I considered the intervention of the legal authority of the *Constitutiones* in a fraught contest over the claims of the literal sense.[26] The fifth Constitution, which prohibits schoolmasters from allowing exposition of Scripture *"except . . in the manner customary since ancient times,"* means to keep separate the literalist pedagogy of the elementary classroom (construing sense, learning vocabulary, possibly advancing as far as simple moral lessons) from any model of hermeneutical literalism purveyed in the university classroom under the high scholastic regime of the literal sense. Hermeneutical activity should not be contaminated by pedagogical usage, and elementary learning, with its mark of puerile dependency, must not aspire to affinity with the work of intellectual adulthood.

The seventh Constitution, which prohibits the vernacular translation of Scripture, has received considerable attention for its crucial application to debates about the possibility of translation.[27] Its intervention in discourses of the literal sense is oblique, but no less powerful for that. It begins with the

---

[24] Žižek, *The Sublime Object of Ideology*, 141.   [25] See ibid., 143.   [26] See above, pp. 119–22.
[27] Watson, "Censorship and Cultural Change"; Hudson, "Lollardy, the English Heresy?"; Hudson, "The Debate about Bible Translation, 1401"; Aston, "Heresy and Literacy."

pronouncement:

> Periculosa quoque res est, testante beato Jeronymo, textum sacrae Scrip-
> turae de uno in aliud idioma transferre, eo quod in ipsis translationibus non
> de facili idem in omnibus sensus retinetur, prout idem beatus Jeronymus,
> etsi inspiratus fuisset, se in hoc saepius fatetur errasse; statuimus igitur et
> ordinamus, ut nemo deinceps aliquem textum sacrae scripturae auctoritate
> sua in linguam Anglicanam . . .

> (It is a dangerous thing, as St. Jerome witnesses, to translate the text of Holy
> Scripture out of one tongue into another; for in translation the same sense is
> not always easily kept in all particulars; so St. Jerome acknowledges, that
> although he was inspired, yet often in this he erred. We therefore decree and
> ordain that no man, hereafter, by his own authority translate any text of the
> Scripture into English or any other tongue.)[28]

The text says nothing about the literal sense; but in prohibiting scriptural
translation on the authority of Jerome it alludes to traditions of debate about
translating literally (word for word) and about the role of the literal sense as a
vehicle of meaning. Arundel's position is familiar enough from debate a few
years earlier about Bible translation: on his argument, language is idiomatic
and no vernacular can be trusted to render the meaning of Scripture faith-
fully. Arundel here also appropriates Jerome's authority on translation to
make an opportunistic case for Scripture as untranslatable. It is obvious that
Jerome has become a placeholder for concerns about translating – and by
extension, interpreting – *ad litteram*. For, in fact, Jerome's theoretical interests in translation bear little resemblance to those positions for which his
authority is invoked. Jerome had said that when translating Scripture, where
the very syntax (the *ordo verborum*, or precise character of the words) is a
mystery, he resorted to word-for-word translation, as opposed to his practice
when otherwise translating from the Greek.[29] It may be this principle that led
to one of the clerical objections to translation summarized in Richard
Ullerston's tract of 1401, the extremely rigidified position that translation can
only be made of the literal sense of Scripture, but that the literal sense of the
Old Testament no longer has value, thus (by implication) translation should
not be undertaken.[30] Elsewhere Jerome's concerns about literal translation are
directed to achieving stylistic and idiomatic parity with the original: in the

---

[28] Wilson, ed., *Concilia* 3: 317; translation (modified) from Foxe, *Acts and Monuments* 3: 245.
[29] Jerome, *Liber de optimo genere interpretandi* (Epistula 57), ed. Bartelink, 13; and see Sutcliffe,
"Jerome," 96.
[30] "uetus testamentum cessauit secundum sensum literalem, sed interpretacio non est nisi secundum
sensum literalem, ergo etc.," Vienna Österreichische Nationalbibliothek MS 4133, fol. 195, quoted in
Hudson, "The Debate on Bible Translation," 72.

preface to his translation of Eusebius' *Chronicle* he notes that linguistic idiom, including rhetorical figuration, presents one of the greatest obstacles to the translator; and in this vein he refers to the awkwardness of Greek and Latin translations of the poetry of the Hebrew Bible.[31] Throughout his prefaces to his own biblical translations he often adverts to the technical difficulty of translation and to his own possible errors as a translator. The openness of Jerome's considerations, the "workshop" character of his reflections – both theoretical and practical – on the difficulty of translation, finds its way into the practical remarks about translation in the General Prologue of the Wycliffite Bible, especially in the discussion about how Latin grammatical constructions (for example, the ablative absolute) "may be resoluid" into appropriate English constructions such as temporal clauses, all in order to "make the sentence open."[32]

In the *Constitutiones*, however, Jerome's open-ended theoretical and practical questions contract into the rigid dictum that linguistic idiom resists and precludes translation. Arundel does not broach questions of the literal sense as a hermeneutical model because, significantly, such questions are already contained in the assumptions of the proscription of translation. If linguistic idiom is the barrier to translation, then the material effects of language are clearly also where meaning is deposited (even if that is not necessarily where meaning originates). The proscription of translation is an effective statement on the politics and hermeneutics of the literal sense because it forecloses any further debate about how the letter carries meaning, whether the letter is the vehicle (proper or figurative) of the author's intention (which, in the scholastic view, is the real locus of the literal sense – a view carried into the General Prologue of the Wycliffite Bible), or an exhangeable exterior sign (itself subject to corruption) of a literal sense contained elsewhere, beyond material words (the more radical hermeneutical view elaborated by Wyclif in the *De veritate sacrae scripturae*, and reprised in somewhat diluted form in various Lollard polemics[33]). Thus in the manner of the fetish, the letter of the text comes to function, in the *Constitutiones*, as itself the object of investment and proscribed desire, rather than as the embodiment of a system of relations:

---

[31] Fotheringham, ed., *Eusebii Pamphili chronici canones latini*, 1–3. See the discussion in Copeland, *Rhetoric, Hermeneutics, and Translation in the Middle Ages*, 46–50.

[32] General Prologue, ch. 15, *Holy Bible*, ed. Forshall and Madden, 1: 57. It is interesting to note that it is not Jerome's *theory* of adhering to the principle of word-for-word translation of Scripture that has made its way into the Lollard translators' methodological account, but rather Jerome's *practice* of translating idiomatically. Thus "And this [i.e. idiomatic and grammatical English equivalents for Latin constructions] wole in manie placis make the sentence open, where to englisshe it aftir the word wolde be derk and douteful" (57).

[33] "*Vae octuplex*" (*English Wycliffite Sermons* 2: 366–7); "The Holi Prophet David Saith" (Deanesly, *The Lollard Bible*, 447); and treatises on Bible translation and secular rulers (Hudson, ed., *Selections from English Wycliffite Writings*, 107, 127).

translation and hermeneutics, the text open or closed, the text tied to language or freed from the constraints of language, the adequacy of the literal sense by itself, the truth claims of one language over another, the literal sense representing continuity with, or estrangement from, the *intentio* of the human or divine author.[34] These are issues that could be debated with relative openness (if also vehemence) from the last decades of the fourteenth century through the first years of the fifteenth century. To these broadly heterogeneous questions that constitute the ongoing debate on translation, the single rationale of the seventh Constitution, that translation is dangerous because linguistic idiom is an obstacle to fidelity, is hardly even relevant: but its very irrelevance could reduce these manifold issues to a homogenized silence.

The Thorpe narrative stages such hermeneutical repression as a stark, one might almost say crude, mythologizing of adversarial relations, both as broad political struggle and as violent clash of individual wills: there is the true intellectual and the Herod-like inquisitor. Unlike other Lollard tracts written directly in response to the *Constitutiones*, notably the *Lantern of Light*, which offer polemical reactions to legal restrictions and which reconstruct, by extratextual reference, the coercive force of law, Thorpe's account places the official voice of law in the text, in the historical person of Arundel, who enacts ecclesiastical authority in his accusatory interrogations.[35] In terms of the text's dramatic constructions, Arundel must insinuatingly frame Thorpe as rhetorical, as a sophistic equivocator, and therefore as the unacceptable consequence of a liberal politics of the literal sense. In this way Thorpe can be seen to extricate himself, to show himself to be unrhetorical and a plain reader according to the "open sentence" of Scripture. Thus in a telling episode where Thorpe is asked to swear an oath with his hand upon the Bible, Thorpe delivers a hermeneutical exposition on the relation between the letter of the text and the true locus of the Gospel's meaning, for which Arundel and his clerks accuse him of mystification:

> And I seide, "Ser, bi autorite of seint Ierom, the gospel is not the gospel for redyng of the lettre, but for the bileue that men haue in the word of Crist –

[34] See Copeland,"Rhetoric and the Politics of the Literal Sense: Aquinas, Wyclif, and the Lollards," for discussion of these relations in Lollard hermeneutics.

[35] The *Lantern* repeatedly invokes the restrictions of the *Constitutions*, even naming them as one of the false laws by which Antichrist assaults God's servants: "& principali thise newe constituciouns" (*Lanterne of Light*, ed. Swinburn, 17; see also 14, 17–18. For references to *De heretico comburendo*, see 43 and especially 100, where the text notes the penalties of imprisonment and even death for those found in possession of "Godes lawe in englische." There are, of course, many polemical Lollard texts that employ the conventional literary device of debate, staging a dialogue between an opponent and an adherent of Lollard belief, but they do not claim the historicity of Thorpe's account; see Hudson, "A Lollard Quaternion." See also Hudson, *Premature Reformation*, 222–3, on overt and submerged dialogue in other Lollard texts.

that is the gospel that we bileue, not the lettre that we reden. Forthi the lettre that is touchid with mannes honde is not the gospel, but the sentence that is verily bileued in mannes herte that is the gospel. For, lo, seint Ierom seith the gospel that is vertu of Goddis word is not in the leues of a book but it is in the roote of resoun, neither the gospel, he seith, is in the writynge aloone of lettres but the gospel is in the marwgh of the sentence of scripturis . . . And, sere, as ye seide to me right now, God and his word ben of oon autorite. And, sere, seint Ierom witnessith that Crist, veri God and veri man, is hid in the lettre of his lawe; thus also, sere, is the gospel hidde in the lettre. For, sere, as it is ful lickli, many dyuerse men and wymmen here in erthe touchiden Crist and seen him and knewen his bodili persone, which neither touchiden, ne seeyen, ne knewen goostli his godhede. Right thus, sere, manye men now touche and seen, writen and reden the scripture of Cristis lawe, whiche neither touchen, ne seen, ne reden effectualli the gospel. For, as the godhede of Crist that is the vertue of God is knowen thorugh bileue, so is the gospel that is the vertue of Cristis word."

And the clerke seide to me, "this is ful derk mater and vnsauery that thou schewist heere to vs."

And I seide, "Sere, if ye that ben maistris knowen not this sentence pleynli, ye mowen soore dreden lest the rewme of heuene be take awei fro you, as it was from the prynces of prestis and from the eldir men of the Iewis." (78–9)

The confrontation dramatized here brings into focus the critical impasse of the whole debate about translation, hermeneutics, and the literal sense. It is useful for the text to stage accusations of Thorpe as a mystifier, temporarily allowing his opponents to accuse him of the very kinds of obfuscation for which Lollards typically attack their mendicant adversaries. For the view implied by Arundel, the literal sense, constrained by the particulars of language, must also be the site of linguistic distortion and therefore also the aperture for rhetorical deviation; thus Thorpe's hermeneutics must be identified here with "dark, unsavory matter." On Lollard views, the "open meaning" is the site beyond or outside the particulars of language, subject to, but ultimately uncontaminated by, distortive veiling and rhetorical indirection: as one Lollard tract puts this, "thei takyn the nakid vndirstandynge bi presumcion of mannes witt, and bryngen forgt pride veynglorie and boost, to coloure here synnes and disceiue sutilli here negebours."[36] The position that Thorpe articulates here, differentiating the book from the plain truths contained within, strongly echoes Wyclif's own account of the five grades of Scripture, from the Book of Life to the truths inscribed within to the lowest grade, the

---

[36] "The holi prophete David seith" (from Cambridge University Library MS Ff. 6. 31³), printed in Deanesly, *The Lollard Bible*, 447.

words, ink, parchment, and leaves of the physical codex that are merely signs ("similitudes") of the truths contained therein (*De veritatae sacrae scripturae* 1: 107–9); a short Middle English tract, obviously derived from Wyclif's arguments, simplifies this into the terms of direct adversarial exchange that resonate with those of the Thorpe narrative:

> But, for Cristen men schulde speke pleynly to Antecrist, we seyen that hooly wryt is taken on three maneres comynly. On the firste manere Criste him silf is clepid in the gospel holy wryt, whanne he seith that the writynge may noght be fordon that the Fadir hath halwid and sent into the world. On the secounde manere holy wryt is clepid truthis that ben conteyned and signyfied bi comyn biblis, and thes truthis may noght faile. On the thridde maner holy wryt is clepid bookis that ben writen and maad of enk and parchemyn. And this speche is nought so propre as the first and the secunde. But we taken of bileue that the secunde writ, of truthis writen in the book of lyf, is holy wryt, and God seith it, and this we knowen by bileve. And as oure sight maketh us certyn of that thing that we seen, so oure bileue makith us certyn that thes trewthis ben holy wryt. Yif holy wryt on the thridde manere be brent or cast in the see, holy writ on the secunde manere may noght faile, as Crist seith.[37]

And so indeed Thorpe must be seen to extract the "propre" truth from its material particulars, to distinguish between the gospel and the written book that many men touch, see, and read, but who "neither touchen, ne seen, ne reden effectualli the gospel."

This is not simply an argument that Thorpe voices; it is a historical role that he must occupy, an ideological position he must be seen to embody. At an earlier juncture in the "Testimony," where Arundel examines him on disendowment of the clergy, the exchange takes the form of disputed readings of the same scriptural text, Paul's Epistle to the Hebrews 7, on tithing. Thorpe's patient elaboration of his views on temporal goods is punctuated with Arundel's exasperated interjections:

> And the Archebischop seide to me with a grete spirit, "Goddis curse haue thou and myn for this techinge! For thou woldist herebi make the olde lawe more free and parfyt than the newe lawe. For thou seist that it was leeful to Leuytis and to prestis to take tithis in the olde lawe and so to ioien her priuylege, but to vs prestis now in the newe lawe thou seist it is not leeful to take tithis. And thus thou geuest to Leuytis of the olde lawe more fredam than to prestis of the newe lawe."
>
> And I seide, "Ser, I merueile that ye undirstonde this pleyne tixt of Poul thus." (71)

---

[37] Arnold, ed., *Select English Works of John Wyclif* 3: 186–7.

Thorpe's literalist hermeneutic is seen to be a better, truer, "plainer" way of reading than Arundel's twisted, self-interested mystification of the "plain text"; even more, Thorpe's literalist exposition performs the dramatic action of patient endurance that can be seen to emerge triumphant from a violent, agonistic struggle. But the text also shows how that open hermeneutic has become a historically self-conscious gesture that redefines the terms of intellectual self-representation. For Thorpe's performance undoes the pattern of recourse to the language of equivocation that is so important to Wyche's self-representation. In Wyche's text, the evasive technique of "mental reservations" and the defensive strategies of ambiguous argumentation at once supply the terms of "misrecognition" before the law and link him to the "open secrets" of community in whose discursive maneuvers he is a recognizable participant. But in Thorpe's text, the interest is precisely in *not* being equivocal, neither for the sake of survival nor for the sake of communal recognition. Rather it is a staging of the self to embody what might be the ethical attributes of the literal sense, to occupy a literalist hermeneutic as a kind of individual ethical *habitus*. In the Thorpe text the literal sense seems less important as a communal hermeneutic than as an individual performative gesture in a quasi-hagiographical setting. In being seen to embody, by his very openness, the ethics of an open hermeneutic, in being constructed as the plain, unsophistical voice of the literal sense against the angry contortions of Arundel, the Thorpe figure enacts the triumph of a hermeneutical principle over the very agent of its suppression. This is a form, in Benjamin's words, of wresting "tradition away from a conformism that is about to overpower it." But even if Thorpe's is an exemplary gesture, it is not, pedagogically speaking, an imitable one: it is not demonstrating, in preceptive terms, a strategy of survival, in the way that Wyche's equivocations can be linked with known Lollard defensive techniques. Nor is it the kind of rhetorical appeal exemplified in Swinderby's offer of the *topos* "I can no sophymes." Rather, it demonstrates its own symbolic value as a historical posture. It is a consummate staging of opposition, a highly charged literary representation of intellectual labor.

The same can be said of the text's enacting of pedagogical confrontation. The whole text is an interrogation, and so throughout is always translatable into the structures of classroom examination, in a manner we have seen in Wyche's narrative. In the Thorpe "Testimony," however, the conversion of courtroom into schoolroom interrogation takes a much more explicit turn, here also as historical performance, to register a certain symbolic importance as a struggle against intellectual suppression. And these intense performances can also be read in terms of the historical impact of the *Constitutiones*.

The eleventh Constitution alone probably did more damage to freedom of intellectual exchange at Oxford than all the other decrees in this legislation. The rhetoric of this legislation bears quotation at some length:

> considerantes igitur, sed dolenter referentes, quomodo alma universitas Oxon. quae, sicut vitis abundans suos palmites fructuosos, ad honorem Dei, multiplicemque profectum, et protectionem ecclesiae suae consuevit extendere, jam partim versa in labruscas, uvas acerbas gignit, quibus indiscrete comestis a patribus, in lege videlicet Dei reputantibus se peritos, dentes obstupescunt filiorum . . . igitur . . . statuimus et ordinamus, quod quilibet gardianus, praepositus, sive custos collegii, aut principalis aulae, vel introitus cujuscunque universitatis praefatae, semel singulis mensibus ad minus inquirat diligenter in collegio, aula, sive introitu, cui praeest, an aliquis scholaris, sive inhabitans in collegio, aula sive introitu hujusmodi, aliquam conclusionem, sive propositionem, aut opinionem in fide catholica, aut bonis moribus male sonantem, aut contra determinationem ecclesiae, praeter necessariam doctrinam facultatis suae, asseruerit, tenuerit, defensaverit, seu aliquo modo proposuerit; et si aliquem super hoc suspectum aut diffamatum reperiat, ipsum moneat effectualiter, ut desistat . . .

> (considering, therefore, and in lamentable wise showing unto you, how the ancient university of Oxford, which as a fruitful vine was wont to extend forth her fruitful branches to the honour of God, the great perfection and defence of the church, now partly being become wild, bringeth forth bitter grapes, which being indiscreetly eaten of ancient fathers, that thought themselves skilful in the law of God, hath set on edge the teeth of their children . . . therefore . . . we do ordain and decree, that every warden, provost, or master of every college, or principal of every hall within the university aforesaid, shall, once every month at the least, diligently inquire in the said college, hall, or other place where he hath authority, whether any scholar or inhabitant of such college or hall, etc. have holden, alleged, or defended, or by any means proponed, any conclusion, proposition, opinion, concerning the catholic faith, or sounding contrary to good manners, or contrary to the determination of the church, otherwise than appertaineth to necessary doctrine; and if he shall find any suspected or defamed herein, he shall, according to his office, admonish him to desist.)[38]

The decree follows with penalties for offending scholars, doctors, masters, and bachelors (greater excommunication, removal from academic standing, suspension, expulsion), as well as penalties for officers of the university who are negligant in carrying out their inquisitions (greater excommunication, removal from their offices, and deprivation of their privileges). The decree

---

[38] Wilkins, ed., *Concilia* 3: 318; translation from Foxe, *Acts and Monuments* 3: 246–7.

enacts a comprehensive apparatus of surveillance, including internal mechanisms to ensure compliance with the orders to carry out that surveillance. Indeed, it may have been especially difficult to bring Oxford schools into compliance with such legislation; such an assumption is continuous with the more general evidence that the *Constitutiones* needed to be promulgated a second time, in 1409, to make the university enforce them.[39]

Especially interesting in this section of the text is the way that the legislation is couched in historical causalities, reaching back to a foundational moment in intellectual history (the bitter grapes of heresy "indiscreetly eaten of ancient fathers, that thought themselves skilful in the law of God"), acknowledging a patriarchal lineality in the academic formation of the heresy (from the "ancient fathers" to "their children"). It is to the same lineal structure that Thorpe appeals in the "Testimony's" autobiographical passage, where he looks back, as a survivor, to a mythic originary moment. The aim of the *Constitutiones*, as a legal mandate, is to repress that history by annihilating its revolutionary significance: here it writes a history of the movement in order to ensure that the movement's failure will be what is documented in future historical record. Conversely, as I have suggested, the rhetorical aim of the Thorpe "Testimony" is to resurrect that lineality through strong identification with a lost intellectual community, and in the knowledge of the movement's certain historical failure.

One powerful form that this struggle for historical representation takes in the "Testimony" is its dramatizing of academic inquisition. In this it does not reproduce the mechanics of surveillance that are detailed in the *Constitutiones*. Rather, it explores the ideological structures of pedagogical inquisition, and the way that those structures make themselves available for conversion into political inquisition. The force of the eleventh Constitution lay in the recognition that the disciplinary mechanics of the university, the systems of examination that establish truth by rendering subjects visible to judgment, provided a ready structure for political inquisition. In the Thorpe narrative the structural conversion is sharpened, because the site of pedagogical–political inquisition has been moved from university to prison, thus playing out the symbolic structures at their most extreme. In the last section of the text, Arundel interrogates Thorpe on the charges of having preached against the lawfulness of swearing. Thorpe invokes (Pseudo-)Chrysostom as an authority on the sinfulness of swearing, but his explanation meets with scornful exasperation from Arundel and his clerks. Thorpe's response is to retreat further into the originary authority of Chrysostom, framing Lollard

---

[39] See Salter, ed., *Snappe's Formulary and Other Records*, 99, 117–20.

opinion as purist conservatism: "And I seide, 'Sere, this is not myn opynyoun, but it is the opynyoun of Crist oure sauyore, and of Seynt Iame, and of Crissostom and of othir dyuerse seyntis and doctouris'" (76). This proves to have been an unwise move, for on this the archbishop decides to quiz Thorpe on his knowledge of the Church Fathers, and surprises Thorpe by producing for discussion a roll with the text of Chrysostom's homily which the archbishop has recently had taken from another Lollard:

> And thanne the Archebischop badde a clerke rede this omelie of Crissostom, whiche omelie this clerk helde in his honde writen in a rolle, whiche rolle the Archebischop made to be taken fro my felowe at Cauntirbirie. And so thanne this clerk redde this omelie til that he came to a clause where Crisostom seith that it is synne to swere wele. And than a clerke, Maluerne as I gesse, seide to the Archebischop, "Ser, I preie you, witith of him how that he vndirstondith Crisostom here seiynge it to be synne to swere wele."
>
> And so the Archebischop askide me, how I vndirstod here Crisostom. And certis I was sum deele agast to answere herto, for I hadde not bisyed me to stodie aboute the witt ther of. But, liftynge vp my mynde to God, I preied him of grace. (76)

The fear of the prisoner under interrogation is transformed here into something like the nightmare of the unprepared student: I didn't know that there was going to be a question about Chrysostom, he says, and I didn't study for it. We might well expect Thorpe to know this homily very well, and need no preparation to answer the question, as Chrysostom was a favorite authority in Lollard exegesis. But Thorpe's apparent shock at Arundel's producing of the text is effective as drama. In a way that is reminiscent of Wyche's letter, but even more poignantly resonant with modern literatures of political detention, this moment in the Thorpe narrative blurs legal interrogation with the examination practices of schools. Here, an "academically sanctioned question," that is, Arundel asking Thorpe how he understands this passage of Chrysostom, is posed at the service of political inquisition, thereby exposing the coerciveness that underlies the procedures of schools and their critical methods.[40] As represented in this scene, the exegetical methods of the schools do not serve to produce knowledge, but rather to contain or suppress the possibility of doctrinal difference. The narrative fashions a scene in which the logic of scholastic interrogation on a matter of exegesis is extended to its most brutal dimensions, where the scholastic mechanisms that can produce

---

[40] See Harlow, *Barred: Women, Writing, and Political Detention*, 8–10, 27–8, on the relation between school and prison examination in some modern prison writings. Among medieval accounts of political detention, an illuminating comparison might be made with the trial records of Joan of Arc, who is also interrogated by academic examiners in a way that, at times, borders on scholastic questioning; see Sullivan, *The Interrogation of Joan of Arc*, xi–xxv, 82–105.

knowledge are converted (easily) to the production of political conformity.

It is also characteristic of this literature that prisoners can exploit the discipline of the prison as a space for "schooling" in dissenting critical practices. We have seen how Wyche's responses can be seen to elaborate a dissenting pedagogical lore. In the Thorpe narrative, shadowed by the *Constitutiones* and their official conversion of scholastic examination into minute doctrinal inquisition, a further conversion takes place, as the prison can also be transformed into the school, where the practices of resistance and learning converge. Thorpe's discipline at this point is to recall, through God's grace, the scriptural map that governs exposition of any set text, and to produce a coherent reading of Chrysostom that does not compromise his own doctrinal integrity. Thus in the heresy trial as scholastic examination, Thorpe can emerge as the triumphant intellectual voice, subduing Arundel, his hostile examiner, who is reduced to assenting that "Crissostom myghte be thus vndirstonde" (77). Arundel the political master, probing the prisoner for weakness in his resolve, gives way to Thorpe the intellectual master converting the discipline of his own interrogation into the disciplined "schooling" of his wayward opponents.

These episodes, the stagings of literalist hermeneutics and of inquisitional mechanics, need not be read as direct responses to particulars of the *Constitutiones*. Rather they are part of the textual–political environment that the *Constitutiones* could be said to produce, but more importantly, that produces the *Constitutiones* and in which the legislation continues to participate along with many other writings. In other words, from the perspective of both the *Constitutiones* and the Thorpe "Testimony," the Lollard movement is a historical failure: the former seeks to ensure that it fails and document that failure accordingly by effacing the movement's historical impact; the latter struggles against that effacement by vivifying its own literary spectacle against the long historical narrative.

Here the text also asks us to transfer the structure of literary representation to the terms of the experience of an individual life, to recognize in this text a particular struggle at a given moment in history. The text's analysis of what it would mean for Thorpe to recant, of the bad example it would set to many people if he were to make an abjuration, seeks to locate Thorpe in relation to a historical community:

> If. . . I schulde now forsake thus sodeynli, schortli and vnwarned, *al the lore* that I haue bisied me fore this thritti yeer and more, my conscience schulde euer be herwith ouer mesure vnquyetid. And also, ser, I knowe wel that manye men and wymmen schulden ben herthorough greetli troublid and

211

sclaundrid; and, as I seide, ser, to you bifore, for myn vntruthe and false
cowardise many oon schulde be putt into ful greet repreef. Yhe, ser, I dreede
that many oon, as thei myghten thanne iustli, wolden curse me ful bittirli
. . . And thei that now haue, though I unworthi be, sum affiaunce in me
heraftir wolden neuer tristen to me, though I cowde teche and lyue myche
moore vertuousli than euer I schal conne eithir do. For, if aftir youre
counseile I lefte vttirli *al my loore*, I schulde herthorugh . . . geve occasioun
to many men and wymmen of ful sore hurtynge; yhe, ser, as it is ful lickli to
me, if I consentide thus to youre wille, I schulde herynne bi myn yuel
ensaumple in that that in me were sle so manye folkis goostli that I schulde
neuere deserue to haue grace of God to edefien his chirche, neithir mysilf ne
ony other lyf. And thanne I were moost wrecchidli ouercomen and vndon
both bifore God and man. (38–9; emphasis added)

In this moving speech, Thorpe equates intellectual labor over the years – "al
my loore" – with the very substance of political struggle: to abandon these
would be not only to disavow the means by which he *represents* himself, makes
himself knowable and trustworthy to a community of "many men and
wymmen," but also to forsake the work of *representing* a community, speaking on behalf of the many. The other members of the circle of Wyclif with
which Thorpe claims historical connection, Purvey, Hereford, and Philip
Repingdon, who have publicly recanted and (in the case of the latter two, at
least) have joined the upper echelons of the clergy, are for Thorpe examples of
those who have cut themselves off from any legitimate claim to represent
themselves or their communities authentically.[41] As Thorpe says of them:

> for to the poynt of truth that these men schewiden out sumtyme, these
> wolden not now strecche forth her lyues, but bi ensaumple eche of hem of
> other, as her wordis and her werkis schewen, thei bisien hem thorugh her
> feynyng for to sclaundre and to pursue Crist in his membris rather than thei
> wolde be pursued. (39)

Because they will not now "stretch forth their lives" on behalf of the truths
that they once proclaimed, they have violated the terms of communal and
historical self-representation. "Stretching forth a life" is a blueprint for
advocacy: it is what Wyche, Peter Payne, and William Taylor had done or
were to do; but it is what these others have not done. In Lollard writing there
is nothing commonplace about the formulation "to stretch forth a life," and
the text invites us to read this with an acute sense of its historical urgency.

At this historical moment, in the political–textual environment of the

---

[41] Purvey's status and whereabouts after 1403 are obscure, and there is slight evidence that he was again
active through the time of the Oldcastle revolt. See Hudson, ed., *Two Wycliffite Texts*, 110, and "John
Purvey: a Reconsideration of the Evidence." Philip Repingdon had become bishop of Lincoln in 1404.

Constitutiones, what are the conditions of an intellectual's "stretching forth a life"? The Thorpe narrative stretches forth a life as a legible text: in the autobiographical dimensions of this work, the confecting of a dissenting identity is a coherent literary gesture.[42] This is "representation" in the sense of "re-presentation" in the register of aesthetics. Thorpe's life is artistically invented and represented through the image of intellectual labor. But as we have seen, the purpose of this text is also "representation" in the political sense of speaking on behalf of others.[43] Intellectual labor therefore is not only what defines Thorpe narratively, but also what proposes to link this ghostly text to a historical community of Lollards for whom he would be both example and spokesman. But how can these two principles, literary or artistic self-representation and political representation on behalf of others, be linked to each other effectively? Another dimension of this question, simply, is what are the politics of Thorpe's interview with Arundel?

I have suggested that the relationship that the text posits between Thorpe and the community of "many men and women" for whom he would speak is less articulated than his own lineal connection with the now-lost academic circle at Oxford, the circle that had included those who will not now "stretch forth their lives." But this is not surprising, if we understand this text as a product of, and intervention in, the political environment that is effected by the *Constitutiones*. The position from which Thorpe speaks, asserting the continuing links between the academic center and the broader social move-ment, is at that very moment becoming obsolete; the very terms in which he speaks of stretching forth a life, moving between the intellectual center and a wider heretical community, are increasingly impossible to imagine. This is not to erase from our historical view the actual continuation of these relations as long as university intellectuals survive and remain active in various commu-nities as preachers, for example, William Taylor until he was put to death in 1423, and Wyche until his burning in 1440. But from the period of 1407 onwards it is a question of survival rather than renewal of the old academic–lay community links. It is also important to remember what those older ranks of university intellectuals had accomplished: from the 1380s onwards, with a remarkable spurt of textual activity from the 1390s through the first few years of the fifteenth century, they had established a common textual ground for academic and vernacular scriptural hermeneutics. It is this ground that promised to level the hierarchical difference between the old academic elite

---

[42] On the principle of confecting identity through literary gesture in medieval narrative, see Middleton, "William Langland's 'Kynde Name': Authorial Signature and Social Identity in Late Fourteenth-Cen-tury England," 67–76; for related remarks see Justice, *Writing and Rebellion*, 120–6.

[43] On artistic representation (*Darstellung*) and political representation (*Vertretung*) as a "double session of representations" see Spivak, "Can the Subaltern Speak?" 275–9.

and lay textual communities, as we have seen, for example, in the extraordinary pedagogical self-sufficiency of the *Glossed Gospels*. In effect, then, vernacular communities could carry on their own textual activities without further direct links with university intellectuals, as the evidence of many regional communities (notably in East Anglia, the Chiltern Hills, Salisbury and Winchester, Coventry, London, Essex, and Kent) from the early fifteenth through the early sixteenth centuries indicates. Arundel's decrees of 1407 would have a profound but also curious impact on the link between academic and lay cultures. By suppressing new ranks of heresy within Oxford it succeeded in restoring (at least in terms of ideological compliance) the hierarchical difference between elite academic powers and non-latinate laity, cutting off university intellectuals from renewed involvement with lay heretical communities. But Arundel's *Constitutiones* also failed to prevent those lay communities from organizing their own intellectual activities without need of further contact with heterodox academics. Thus a dissenting intellectual like Thorpe, at the very moment that he is being silenced by the suppressive mechanisms that Arundel put into play, is also becoming, in a sense, irrelevant to his communities of "many men and women." And in this also lies the success of his and his former colleagues' "thritti yeer and more" devotion to dismantling the authorizing power of clerical exegesis.

Yet what defines the politics of the interview with Arundel is Thorpe's professional status. For it is Thorpe's position as a member of that old academic circle that authorizes him to speak here, and to speak, after all, at such length of himself. The persuasive appeal of the text is predicated on the assumption that Thorpe is important enough to Arundel to take up so much of the archbishop's time (the text continually underscores this: Arundel's obsequious clerks are fond of reminding the archbishop at crucial moments that he is a busy man, that it has been a long day, and that he should have done with the intransigent Thorpe who has wasted enough of his time). Of course, the text encodes Arundel as a figure who will "cooperate" in the magnification of Thorpe's importance to him. In terms of the relations of power and representation between dominant and subordinate groups, Thorpe is a renegade member of a dominant elite. But while he may offer himself on behalf of an extended constituency of men and women who presumably range from a few Latinate clergy like himself (and fewer Latinate lay people) to a greater number of semiliterate and non-literate members of Lollard vernacular textual communities, one unstated premise of the text is that he has more in common with Arundel. Arundel and Thorpe speak the same language of intellectual institutions, interacting across the professional terms of academic discourse. And so indeed they can speak at cross purposes, ideologically, through this language: both act upon the traditional antagonisms of the professional intellectual classes against *illiterati*, one by vigorous suppression of the danger of heresy among the lay populace, the other by vigorous rejection of clerical privilege and identification with popular anticlericalism.[44] While the drama of the text clearly marks the boundary between subordination and power, the imprisoned heretic confronting his ecclesiastical prosecutor, the discourse of the text blurs that boundary, for example, where Arundel the archbishop and Thorpe the former Oxford scholar engage as intellectual equals in an intense debate over the finer points of subject and accident, what Thorpe even calls, contemptuously, "scole mater" (55), a shorthand (and thus insider) term for subjects of disputation in the schools:

> And therfor I committe this term *accidentem sine subiecto* to tho clerkis which deliten hem so in curious and so sotil sofestrie, that thei mouen ofte so defficult materis and straunge, and waden and wandren so in hem fro argument into argument with *pro* and *contra* to the tyme that thei witen not ofte where thei ben neither vndirstonden clerli hemsilf. (55)[45]

With this scornful dismissal of university logical exercises – a dismissal we do not find, interestingly, in Wyche's more argumentatively strategic narrative – we glimpse a confident familiarity with that milieu, and a mutual recognition of its terms. Arundel is shown treating Thorpe not with condescension, such as he might show to a social inferior (here we may recall the representation of Arundel's indulgent paternalism with Margery Kempe, whose interview with him is similarly long, lasting "tyl sterrys apperyed in the fyrmament"),[46] but with muscular attention, as if trying to reclaim someone who has broken ranks with his own class. Ignoring the "standard script" of his own elite class, a figure like Thorpe is dangerous to official powers because he breaks the "naturalization of power made possible by a united front."[47] With no small artifice and paradox, the Thorpe "Testimony" performs, as public and

---

[44] See Moore, *The Formation of a Persecuting Society*, 138–40, on professional intellectuals' fear of *rustici* and its transference onto the prosecution of heresy. See also Murray, *Reason and Society in the Middle Ages*, 234–57.

[45] As Hudson points out (*Two Wycliffite Texts*, 119) the contemptuous dismissal of "scole mater," and the rejection of arguments about subject and accident, are not uncommon in Lollard writings. In comparison with other invocations of the accident/subject motif, however, Thorpe's is a peculiarly detailed tracing of the mechanics of logical disputation. See, for comparison, the tract *Septem hereses* (Arnold, *Select English Works* 3: 443); the profession on the eucharist (Arnold, 3: 502); the tract *De sacramento altaris* (Matthew, ed., *English Works of Wyclif*, 357); the tract *De papa* (Matthew, ed., 465); and *Jack Upland*, Heyworth, ed., *Jack Upland, Friar Daw's Reply, and Upland's Rejoinder*, 71.

[46] *The Book of Margery Kempe*, ed. Meech and Allen, 37.

[47] Scott, *Domination and the Arts of Resistance: Hidden Transcripts*, 67.

exemplary spectacle, the private transcript of the dominant class negotiating, within its own ranks, the limits and contradictions of exegetical power.

The Thorpe figure is projected onto history, and claims its historical veracity, through the representation of intellectual labor; and that labor here is aimed at "stretching forth a life." But to return here to Gramsci's formulation with which I began, what is the "ensemble of the system of relations" in which the intellectual activity represented in this text would find its function? How does Thorpe, who personifies that activity as a defector from the sanctioned norms of the academic elite, elaborate "new modes of thought" on behalf of the community he claims? I would argue that the very terms, historical and rhetorical, out of which the text is constructed express its alienation, at the historical moment of its writing, from the community it proposes to represent. Thorpe speaks elegiacally as a survivor of an old way in the face of the assured demise of that tradition. His education and professional rank, and the text's profound identification with a lost intellectual inner circle, ensure the marginality of the Thorpe figure in a new order. Finally, even though he is a defector from the academic ranks, it is his ordained professional status and the witness he bears to the early Oxford circle, not his heterodoxy in and of itself, that makes him so exasperatingly important to Arundel, important enough to sustain the rhetorical tensions that drive this text.

This last point bears further reflection. On the terms that this text articulates, Thorpe's professional status is what gives him a legible and individuated political identity, the authority to speak for oneself in the public record that the politically subordinate members of his dissenting community will never command for themselves. With the rare exception of a *laicus litteratus* such as Walter Brut, lay dissenters, both literates and non-literates from the lower-middle and artisan classes, receive fairly perfunctory attention from the prosecutorial record as *individual political subjects*. What Thorpe's narrative must remind us of is the split between the models of political agency that operate internally in Lollard pedagogical structures, and the official narratives of legal representation that, on the whole, deny that agency. To speak here of ordinary lay dissenters as political "subordinates" is not to efface their powerful, oppositional investments in political and hermeneutical agency, but rather to speak of them on the terms that the official record represents them. While the shadowy Thorpe can emerge as historically knowable, his subjectivity defined by the plausibility of his institutional importance to Arundel, so many other members of his movement – surely with their own stories – were efficiently processed through the examination system and now remain merely names and occupations affixed to formulaic abjurations in diocesan records.[48] The Thorpe "Testimony" must suppress such contradictions, projecting a dissenting identity that is on the one hand historically particularized, but on the other hand directed as a common example for all dissenters. The "I" of the Thorpe voice commands the power of individual, autobiographical subjectivity, a tangible signature of self that the legal conventions of narrative representation deny to most of those dissenters, the "many men and women" for whom he proposes to "stretch forth a life." Court transcripts of Lollard trials throughout the fifteenth century typically grant the dissenter the first-person singular only through the format of his or her abjuration, that is, only at the moment at which the dissenting subjectivity is erased through submission to ecclesiastical authority.

The Thorpe "Testimony" struggles against history, wresting historical memory from the conformism of official historiography, through the literary representation of a life. It is a consummate staging of opposition, a charged artistic representation of intellectual labor; but here the weight falls on Thorpe's common ground with Arundel. The text resurrects a historical lineality through its strong identification with a lost intellectual community, as if in knowledge of the movement's certain failure: and here the connections between Thorpe and his immediate community are less articulated than those between Thorpe and the early Oxford circle. In order to represent a community, the Thorpe text must represent a self, realize it historically as a life, and denegate the literary character of that self-representation. But under its own artistic–historical struggle it also submerges the historical and legal "unrepresentability" of those other lives, unrepresentable on the terms by which it represents itself. The connection with the Oxford inner core is mythic, but no longer relevant on historical or even pedagogical terms. The links between university and laity are becoming tenuous, not to be renewed; and the professional status that affords Thorpe so much leisure here is precisely what makes a figure like him increasingly marginal.

From representation as advocacy to self-representation as narrative performance: the Thorpe "Testimony" elides the former with the latter. Or perhaps, in the face of historical failure (on the one hand) and obsolescence of an earlier model of intellectual function (on the other hand), the only viable

---

[48] Thomson's remarks on the standardization of examinations are illuminating (even if also dismissive and too generalizing about literacy among the Lollards): "This might suggest that the court officers [of the Coventry persecutions in 1511–12] were following some formulary, as the charges are arranged in the same order [as in other records], but were allowed to modify the wording as long as the substance remained unaltered. This method of questioning the accused on a series of beliefs was probably general – as many of the Lollards were ignorant and illiterate it would *a priori* seem the only effective way of eliciting their views – and even in persecutions where no list of articles has been preserved the form of the abjurations would suggest that this was done" (*The Later Lollards*, 226).

form of representation – all that is left – is that of artistic performance. This is not a text that can make an active intervention in the real environment of a heterodox culture whose dynamics have begun to shift radically from the older terms the text envisions, at least not on the terms that were still possible for the *Opus arduum* of 1390 and Wyche's narrative of 1403, or even on the terms (admittedly more self-interested) projected in the self-defenses of Brut and Swinderby. But the persuasive power of the Thorpe text lies in its very suppression of the effective difference between advocacy and artistic representation. And in its very claims to a certain transparency – stretching forth a life through which other lives may be seen – lies its actual opacity. For the process here of historical and narrative self-representation as embodiment of intellectual labor must also deny the text's inability to stand for the many other lives that it proposes to represent. The text works as "stretching forth a life" only if it succeeds in suppressing the political and institutional gulf between an old order of clerical dissenters, who can invest their own power and desire as historically authenticated experience, and the lay dissenters, whose potential for historicizing self-narration (beyond the admission of heretical beliefs and activities) is, more often than not, of little interest to the prosecuting authorities in whose records their voices survive. The Thorpe text posits and promises an undoing of hierarchies between clerical and lay intellectual powers that are never actually undone in the official practices of legal representation. In its English-language form, the Thorpe text participates in a promise of democratization, as if in expectation of its own wide circulation and consumption by which it can subversively bequeath a pedagogical or didactic apparatus to present and future communities. But as we have seen, the text operates within the very power relations whose validity it denies. Certainly the orthodox ecclesiastical structures do not accord official recognition to the idea of democratization. For Arundel's court and any other episcopal court, the difference between clerical academics and their lay followers is acutely important and necessary to preserve. And on the logic of the Thorpe text, it is intellectual labor, codified through links with a mythic academic past and staged through explicit performative gesture, that confers individuated political subjectivity in history.

Thorpe's text imagines connections between a university culture and the community beyond it; it also acknowledges the historical forces that – at least for the text's own present moment – have succeeded in checking the power of academic intellectuals to renew those connections. Intellectuals set pedagogy in motion, but only when their community can recognize them on its own terms. Yet while Thorpe's narrative cannot fully realize the connections it imagines, it still demonstrates how the work of intellectuals defines itself through the project of teaching. And the products of intellectual labor, the pedagogical apparatuses that are exportable from one milieu to another, once set into motion, can long outlast the power of the individual teacher to teach.

Bibliography

Abbreviations

CYS	Canterbury and York Society
CFMA	Classiques français du moyen âge
EETS	Early English Text Society
PL	*Patrologia Latina*, ed. J.-P. Migne. Paris, 1844–64

PRIMARY SOURCES

Manuscripts

Only manuscripts consulted directly *and* cited in the text are listed here. Other manuscripts cited are listed in the index.

O vos omnes sermon:
British Library MS Cotton Titus D. v
British Library MS Egerton 2820
Cambridge University Library MS Dd.14. 30 (2)

Glossed Gospels:
British Library Additional MS 28026, short commentary on Matthew (with epilogue)
British Library Additional MS 41175, short commentaries on Matthew (with prologue) and Mark
Cambridge Fitzwilliam Museum MS McClean 133, long commentary on Matthew (with prologue)
Cambridge Trinity College MS B. 1. 38, short commentary on Matthew (with prologue) and short commentary on John
Cambridge University Library MS Kk. 2. 9, long commentary on Luke
Oxford Bodleian MS Laud Misc. 235, long commentary on Matthew (with prologue)
Oxford Bodley MS 143, short commentary on Luke (with prologue)
Oxford Bodley MS 243, short commentaries on Luke (no prologue) and John (with prologue)
York Minster MS xvi. D. 2, commentaries on the dominical Gospels

Thorpe's "Testimony" in English:
Bodleian Library MS Rawlinson C. 208

Bibliography

Printed texts

Acta synodi Atrebatensis, PL 142: 1271–312.

Alan of Lille. *Anticlaudianus, PL* 210: 483–576.

  Anticlaudianus, trans. James J. Sheridan. Toronto: Pontifical Institute of Mediaeval Studies, 1973.

  Summa de arte praedicatoria, PL 210: 111–98.

  Regulae caelestis iuris, ed. N. M. Häring, *Archives d'histoire doctrinale et littéraire du moyen âge* 48 (1981): 7–226.

Anonymous of Passau. *De causis heresum,* ed. A. Patschovsky and K. V. Selge, *Quellen zur Geschichte der Waldenser.* Texte zur Kirchen- und Theologiegeschichte 18. Gütersloh: Mohn, 1973.

Apology for Lollard Doctrines, ed. J. H. Todd. London: Camden Series, 1842.

Arnold, Thomas, ed. *Select English Works of John Wyclif.* 3 vols. Oxford: Clarendon, 1869–71.

Ashby, George. *George Ashby's Poems,* ed. Mary Bateson. EETS extra series 76. London: Kegan Paul, Trench, Trübner, 1899.

Barr, Helen, ed. *The Piers Plowman Tradition: a Critical Edition of "Pierce the Ploughman's Crede," "Richard the Redeless," "Mum and the Sothsegger," and "The Crowned King."* London: Dent/Everyman, 1993.

Béroul. *Le Roman de Tristan,* ed. Ernest Muret. 4th edn. revised L. M. Defourques. CFMA 12. Paris: Champion, 1974.

Boethius. *Consolatio philosophiae,* ed. Ludwig Bieler. *Corpus christianorum, series latina* 94. Turnhout: Brepols, 1957.

Brie, F. W. D., ed. *The Brut, or The Chronicles of England.* 2 vols. EETS 131, 136. London: Kegan Paul, Trench, Trübner, 1906, 1908.

Büler, C. F. "A Lollard Tract: on Translating the Bible into English," *Medium Aevum* 7 (1938): 167–83.

Calendar of Close Rolls, Henry V 2, 1419–22. London: HMSO, 1932.

Calendar of Close Rolls, Henry VI 3, 1435–41. London: HMSO, 1937.

Charles d'Orléans. *Charles d'Orléans poésies,* ed. Pierre Champion. CFMA 34, 56. Paris: Champion, 1923–7.

  The English Poems of Charles of Orléans, ed. Robert Steele and Mabel Day. EETS 215, 220. London: Oxford University Press, 1970.

Chichele, Henry. *The Register of Henry Chichele, Archbishop of Canterbury, 1414–1443,* ed. E. F. Jacob and H. C. Johnson. 4 vols. CYS 42. Oxford: Clarendon, 1938–47.

Compston, H. F. B., ed. "The Thirty-Seven Conclusions of the Lollards," *English Historical Review* 26 (1911): 738–49.

Conrad of Megenberg. *Yconomica,* ed. Sabine Krüger. 2 vols. Stuttgart: Anton Hiersemann,1973–7. *Monumenta germaniae historica* III/5.

Dubois, Pierre. *De recuperatione terre sancte,* ed. Charles V. Langlois. Paris: Picard, 1891.

  The Recovery of the Holy Land, trans. Walther I. Brandt. New York: Columbia University Press, 1956.

Dymmok Roger. *Liber contra duodecim errores et hereses Lollardorum,* ed. H. S. Cronin. London: Kegan Paul, Trench, Trübner, 1922.

Eadmer. *The Life of St. Anselm, Archbishop of Canterbury,* ed. and trans. R. W. Southern. Revised edition. Oxford: Clarendon, 1972.

Eriugena, John Scotus. *Expositiones super ierarchiam caelestem S. Dionysii, PL* 122: 125–266.

Fasciculi zizaniorum, ed. W. W. Shirley. Rolls Series. London: Longman, 1858.

Flenley, Ralph, ed. *Six Town Chronicles of England*. Oxford: Clarendon, 1911.

Forshall, Josiah, and Frederic Madden, eds. *The Holy Bible . . . made from the Latin Vulgate by John Wycliffe and his Followers*. 4 vols. Oxford: Oxford University Press, 1850.

Foxe, John. *Acts and Monuments*, ed. Josiah Pratt. 8 volumes. London: George Seeley, 1870.

Friedberg, Emile, ed. *Corpus iuris canonici*. 2 vols. Leipzig: Tauchnitz, 1879–81.

Fulgentius. *Opera*, ed. Rudolf Helm. Leipzig: Teubner, 1898.

Fulgentius. *Fulgentius the Mythographer*, trans. Leslie George Whitbread. Columbus: Ohio State University Press, 1971.

Gellius, Aulus. *Noctes Atticae*, trans. John C. Rolfe. 3 vols. Loeb Classical Library. Cambridge, Mass.: Harvard University Press, 1927; rpt. 1996.

Gerson, Jean. *De necessaria communione laicorum sub ùtraque specie*, in Jean Gerson, *Œuvres complètes*, ed. Palémon Glorieux, vol. 10. Paris: Desclée, 1973. 55–68.

 Opera omnia, ed. L. E. du Pin. 5 vols. Antwerp, 1706.

Gervais of Melkley. *Ars poetica*, ed. Hans-Jürgen Gräbener. Munich: Aschendorffsche Verlagsbuchhandlung, 1965.

Gregory, William. *Chronicle of London*, ed. James Gairdner, *The Historical Collections of a Citizen of London in the Fifteenth Century*. London: Camden Society, 1876.

Guido da Pisa, *see* Jenaro-MacLennan.

Heliodorus. *Les Ethiopiques*, trans. J. Maillon, ed. R. M. Rattenbury and T. W. Lumb. 2 vols. Paris: Les Belles Lettres (Budé), 1935.

Hervieux, Léopold, ed. *Les Fabulistes latins depuis le siècle d'Auguste jusqu'à la fin du moyen âge*. 5 vols. Paris: Firmin Didot, 1893–9.

Horace. *Satires, Epistles, and Ars Poetica*, ed. and trans. H. Rushton Fairclough. Loeb Classical Library. Cambridge, Mass.: Harvard University Press, 1926.

Hudson, Anne, ed. *Selections from English Wycliffite Writings*. Cambridge: Cambridge University Press, 1978.

 ed. *Two Wycliffite Texts*. EETS 301. Oxford: Oxford University Press, 1993.

Hudson, Anne, and Pamela Gradon, eds. *English Wycliffite Sermons*. 5 vols. Oxford: Clarendon, 1983–96.

Hugh of St. Victor. *De tribus maximus circumstantiis gestorum*, ed. William M. Green, "Hugo of St. Victor, *De tribus maximus circumstantiis gestorum*," *Speculum* 18 (1943): 484–93. Trans. Carruthers, *The Book of Memory*, 261–6.

 Didascalicon, ed. C. H. Buttimer. Washington, DC: The Catholic University Press, 1939.

 The Didascalicon of Hugh of St. Victor, trans. Jerome Taylor. New York: Columbia University Press, 1961; rpt. 1991.

Hugh of Trimberg. *Registrum multorum auctorum*, ed. Karl Langosch. Germanische Studien 235. Berlin: E. Ebering, 1942.

Hus, Jan, and Richard Wyche. Correspondence, ed. K. Höfler, *Geschichtschreiber der Husitischen Bewegung in Böhmen. Fontes rerum Austriacarum* 6 (Vienna, 1865): 210–14.

Hus, Jan. *Documenta Magister Johannis Hus*, ed. František Palacký. Prague: Tempsky, 1869.

 John Hus at the Council of Constance, ed. and trans. Matthew Spinka. New York: Columbia University Press, 1965.

 The Letters of John Hus, trans. Herbert B. Workman and R. Martin Pope. London: Hodder and Stoughton, 1904.

Huygens, R. B. C., ed. *Accessus ad auctores; Bernard d'Utrecht; Conrad d'Hirsau*. Leiden: Brill, 1970.

Jack Upland, Friar Daw's Reply, and Upland's Rejoinder, ed. P. L. Heyworth. London: Oxford University Press, 1968.

James 1 of Scotland. *The Kingis Quair*, ed. John Norton-Smith. Oxford: Clarendon, 1971.

Jerome. *Liber de optimo genere interpretandi* (Epistula 57), ed. G. J. M. Bartelink. *Mnemosyne*, supplement 61. Leiden: Brill, 1980.

Eusebii Pamphili chronici canones latini, ed. J. K. Fotheringham. London: Milford, 1923.

John Lydford's Book, ed. Dorothy M. Owen. Devon and Cornwall Record Society 19 and Historical Manuscripts Commission Joint Publications Series 22. London, 1974.

Kempe, Margery. *The Book of Margery Kempe*, ed. Sanford Brown Meech and Hope Emily Allen. EETS 212. London and Oxford: Milford, 1940.

Kingsford, Charles L., ed. *Chronicles of London*. Oxford: Clarendon, 1905.

Knighton, Henry. *Chronicle 1337–1396*, ed. and trans. G. H. Martin. Oxford: Clarendon, 1995.

Kretzmann, Norman, and Eleonore Stump, eds. and trans. "The Anonymous *De arte obligatoria* in Merton College MS 306," in E. P. Bos, ed., *Medieval Semantics and Metaphysics: Studies Dedicated to L. M. de Rijk*. Nijmegen: Ingenium Publishers, 1985. 239–80.

Lanterne of Light, ed. L. M. Swinburn. EETS 151. London: Kegan, Paul, Trench, Trübner, 1917.

Lavenham, Richard, *see* Spade, ed.

Littlehales, Henry, ed. *The Prymer or Lay Folk's Prayer Book*. 2 vols. EETS 105, 109. London: Kegan, Paul, Trench, Trübner, 1895–7.

——— ed. *The Prymer, or Prayer-Book of the Lay People in the Middle Ages*. 2 vols. London: Longmans, Green and Co., 1891–2.

Macrobius. *Commentarii in somnium Scipionis*, ed. Jacob Willis. Leipzig: Teubner, 1970.

——— *Commentary on the Dream of Scipio*, trans. William Harris Stahl. New York: Columbia University Press, 1952; rpt. 1990.

——— *Saturnalia*, ed. Jacob Willis. Leipzig: Teubner, 1970.

Mandela, Nelson. *Long Walk to Freedom*. Boston, New York, London: Little, Brown and Co., 1994, 1995.

Map, Walter. *De nugis curialium*, ed. M. R. James. Oxford: Clarendon, 1914.

Matthew, F. D., ed. *The English Works of John Wyclif Hitherto Unprinted*. EETS 74. London: Trübner, 1880.

——— ed. "The Trial of Richard Wyche," *English Historical Review* 5 (1890): 530–44.

Minnis, Alastair J., and Brian Scott, with David Wallace, eds. *Medieval Literary Theory and Criticism, c.1100–c.1375: the Commentary Tradition*. Oxford: Clarendon, 1988.

Moore, R. I. *The Birth of Popular Heresy*. London: Arnold: 1975.

Neckham, Alexander. *Sacerdos ad altare accessurus*, ed. Charles Homer Haskins, "A List of Text-Books from the Close of the Twelfth Century," *Harvard Studies in Classical Philology* 20 (1909): 75–94.

Netter, Thomas. *Doctrinale antiquitatem fidei catholicae ecclesiae*, ed. B. Blanciotti. 3 vols. Venice, 1757–9; rpt. Farnborough, 1967.

Ngugi wa Thiong'o. *Detained: a Writer's Prison Diary*. London: Heinemann, 1981.

Oldcastle, John. Letter to von Waldstein, ed. J. Loserth, "Über die Beziehungenzwischen englischen und böhmischen Wiclifiten," *Mittheilungen des Instituts für österreichische Geschichtsforschung* 12 (Innsbruck, 1891): 254–69.

Origen, *De principiis*, ed. Paul Koetschau, *De Griechischen Christlichen Schriftsteller* 23. Leipzig: J. C. Hinrichs, 1913.

Pecock, Reginald. *The Repressor of over much blaming of the Clergy*, ed. C. Babington. 2 vols. Rolls Series. London: Longman, Green, Longman, and Roberts, 1860.

Peter of Mladoňovice. *Relatio de Magistro Johanne Hus*, ed. Václav Novotný, "Historické spisy Petra z Mladoňovic a jiné zprávy a paměti o M. Janovi Husovi a M. Jeronymovi z Prahy," *Fontes rerum Bohemicarum* 8 (Prague, 1932): 25–120.

Plimpton, George A. *The Education of Chaucer*. London and New York: Oxford University Press, 1935; rpt. New York: AMS Press, 1971.

Plutarch, *Moralia*, vol. 1, ed. and trans. F. C. Babbitt. Loeb Classical Library Cambridge, Mass.: Harvard University Press, 1927; rpt. 1960.

Pollard, A. W., ed. *Fifteenth-Century Prose and Verse*. New York: Dutton, 1903.

Proclus. *Commentaire sur la République*, trans. A. J. Festugière. Paris: Vrin, 1970.

Prudentius. [Works] *Prudentius*, ed. and trans. H. J. Thomson. Loeb Classical Library Cambridge, Mass.: Harvard University Press, 1953.

Pseudo-Boethius. *De disciplina scholarium*, ed. Edda Ducci, *Un saggio de pedagogia medievale*. Turin: Società Editrice Internationale, 1967.

   De disciplina scholarium, ed. Olga Weijers. Leiden: Brill, 1976.

Quintilian, *Institutio oratoria*, ed. and trans. H. E. Butler. 4 vols. Loeb Classical Library. Cambridge, Mass.: Harvard University Press, 1920; rpt. 1980.

Richard de Bury, *Philobiblon*, ed. and trans. Ernest C. Thomas. London: Kegan Paul, Trench, 1888.

Rijk, L. M. de, ed. "Some Thirteenth-Century Tracts on the Game of Obligation (I)," *Vivarium* 12 (1974): 94–123.

Salter, H. E., ed. *Snappe's Formulary and Other Records*. Oxford: Clarendon, 1924.

Saro Wiwa, Ken. *A Month and a Day: a Detention Diary*, introduction by William Boyd. London: Penguin, 1995.

Seneca. *Ad Lucilium epistulae morales*, ed. L. D. Reynolds. 2 vols. Oxford: Clarendon, 1965.
   Letters from a Stoic, trans. Robin Campbell. London: Penguin, 1969.

Simon of Tournai. *Les Disputationes de Simon de Tournai*, ed. Joseph Warichez. Spicilegium sacrum Lovaniense, études et documents 12. Louvain: Spicilegium sacrum Lovaniense, 1932.

Spade, Paul Vincent, ed. "Richard Lavenham's *Obligationes*," *Rivista critica di storia della filosofia* 33 (1978): 224–41.
   ed. "Roger Swyneshed's *Obligationes*: Edition and Comments," *Archives d'histoire doctrinale et littéraire du moyen âge* 44 (1977): 243–85.

Statutes of the Realm. 10 vols. London, 1816; rpt. London: Dawson, 1963.

Suetonius. *Grammairiens et rhéteurs (De grammaticis et rhetoribus)*, ed. and trans. Marie-Claude Vacher. Paris: Les Belles Lettres (Budé), 1993.

Swyneshed, Roger, *see* Spade, ed.

Tanner, Norman P., ed. *Heresy Trials in the Diocese of Norwich, 1428–31*. Camden Fourth Series 20. London: Royal Historical Society, 1977.

Taylor, William. 1406 Sermon, *see* Hudson, ed., *Two Wycliffite Texts*.

Thirty-Seven Conclusions of the Lollards (*Remonstrance Against Romish Corruptions in the Church*), ed. J. Forshall. London: Longman, Brown, 1851.

Thorpe, William. "Testimony," *see* Hudson, ed., *Two Wycliffite Texts*.

Trefnant, John. *Registrum Johannis Trefnant*, ed. W. W. Capes, CYS, London: for the Society, 1916.

Usk, Thomas. *Thomas Usk's Testament of Love*, ed. Gary W. Shawver. Toronto: University of

Toronto Press, 2000.

Vincent of Beauvais. *De eruditione filiorum nobilium*, ed. Arpad Steiner. Cambridge, Mass.: The Medieval Academy of America, 1938.

Walsingham, Thomas. *Historia anglicana*, ed. H. T. Riley. 2 vols. Rolls Series. London: Longman, Green, Longman, Roberts, and Green, 1863–4.

Wilkins, D., ed. *Concilia Magnae Britanniae et Hiberniae*. 4 vols. London, 1737; rpt. Brussels: Culture et Civilization, 1964.

William of Conches. *Glosae in Iuvenalem*, ed. Bradford Wilson. Texts philosophiques du moyen âge 18. Paris: Vrin, 1980.

Wright, Aaron E., ed. *The Fables of Walter of England*. Toronto: Pontifical Institute of Mediaeval Studies, 1997.

Wyche, Richard, *see* Matthew, ed., "The Trial of Richard Wyche."

Wyclif, John. *De apostasia*, ed. Michael Henry Dziewicki. London: Wyclif Society, 1889.

De contrarietate duorum dominorum, in Rudolf Buddensieg, ed., *John Wiclif's Polemical Works in Latin*. 2 vols. London: Wyclif Society, 1883. 2: 698–713

De eucharistia, ed. Johann Loserth. London: Wyclif Society, 1892.

De veritate sacrae scripturae, ed. Rudolf Buddensieg. 3 vols. London: Wyclif Society, 1905–7.

Speculum secularium dominorum, in Johann Loserth, ed., *Johannis Wyclif Opera minora*. London: Wyclif Society, 1913. 74–91.

Zola, Emile. [*Manifeste des intellectuels*]. *Livre d'hommage des lettres françaises à Emile Zola*. Société libre d'Edition des Gens de Lettres. Brussells: G. Balat, 1898.

SECONDARY SOURCES

Aers, David and Lynn Staley. *The Powers of the Holy: Religion, Politics, and Gender in Late Medieval English Culture*. University Park, Pennsylvania: Pennsylvania State University Press, 1996.

Alexandre-Bidon, D. "La Lettre volée: apprendre à lire à l'enfant au moyen âge," *Annales* 44 (1989): 953–92.

Althusser, Louis. *Lenin and Philosophy and Other Essays*, trans. Ben Brewster. New York: Monthly Review Press, 1971.

Ariès, Philippe. *L'Enfant et la vie familiale sous l'Ancien Régime*. Paris: Plon, 1960.

Armstrong, Nancy, and Leonard Tennenhouse, eds. *The Violence of Representation: Literature and the History of Violence*. London and New York: Routledge, 1989.

Aronowitz, Stanley, and Henry A. Giroux. *Postmodern Education: Politics, Culture, and Social Criticism*. Minneapolis: University of Minnesota Press, 1991.

Ashworth, E. J., and P. V. Spade. "Logic in Late Medieval Oxford," in Catto and Evans, eds., *The History of the University of Oxford*, vol. 2, *Late Medieval Oxford*, 35–64.

Astell, Ann. *Political Allegory in Late Medieval England*. Ithaca: Cornell University Press, 1999.

Aston, Margaret. "Caim's Castles: Poverty, Politics, and Disendowment," in R. B. Dobson, ed., *The Church, Politics, and Patronage in the Fifteenth Century*. Gloucester: Sutton, 1984. 45–81.

Lollards and Reformers: Images and Literacy in Late Medieval Religion. London: The Hambledon Press, 1984.

"Lollardy and Literacy," in Aston, *Lollards and Reformers*, 193–216.

"Lollardy and Sedition, 1381–1431," in Aston, *Lollards and Reformers*, 1–47.

Bibliography

Thomas Arundel: a Study of Church Life in the Reign of Richard II. Oxford: Clarendon, 1967.

"William White's Lollard Followers," in Aston, *Lollards and Reformers*, 71–99.

"Wyclif and the Vernacular," in Hudson and Wilks, eds., *From Ockham to Wyclif*, 281–330.

Aston, Margaret, and Colin Richmond, eds. *Lollardy and the Gentry in the Later Middle Ages.* Stroud: Sutton Publishing; New York: St. Martin's Press, 1997.

Audisio, Gabriel. "Were the Waldensians More Literate than Their Contemporaries (1460–1560)?" in Biller and Hudson, eds., *Heresy and Literacy*, 176–85.

Baldwin, J. W. *Masters, Princes, and Merchants: the Social Views of Peter the Chanter and his Circle.* 2 vols. Princeton University Press: Princeton, 1970.

Barron, Caroline. Review of Thomson, *The Later Lollards, Journal of the Society of Archivists* 3 (1967): 257–9.

Baswell, Christopher. *Virgil in Medieval England: Figuring the Aeneid from the Twelfth Century to Chaucer.* Cambridge: Cambridge University Press, 1995.

Bauman, Zygmunt. *Legislators and Interpreters: on Modernity, Post-Modernity, and Intellectuals.* Cambridge: Polity Press, 1987.

Benda, Julien. *The Treason of the Intellectuals (La Trahison des clercs),* trans. Richard Aldington. New York: Norton, 1969.

Benjamin, Walter. *Illuminations,* ed. Hannah Arendt, trans. Harry Zohn. New York: Schocken Books, 1969.

"Zum gegenwärtigen gesellschaftlichen Standort des französischen Schriftstellers," *Gesammelte Schriften,* ed. Rolf Tiedemann and Hermann Schweppenhäuser, vol. 2. 2. Frankfurt: Suhrkamp, 1977. 776–803.

Benson, Robert L. and Giles Constable, eds. *Renaissance and Renewal in the Twelfth Century.* Cambridge, Mass.: Harvard University Press, 1982.

Betts, R. R. "Peter Payne in England," in R. R. Betts, *Essays in Czech History.* London: Athlone Press, 1969. 236–46.

Bhabha, Homi K. "DissemiNation: Time, Narrative, and the Margins of the Modern Nation," in Homi K. Bhabha, ed., *Nation and Narration.* London and New York: Routledge, 1990; rpt. 1993. 291–322.

Biller, Peter, and Anne Hudson, eds. *Heresy and Literacy 1000–1530.* Cambridge: Cambridge University Press, 1995.

Biller, Peter. "Heresy and Literacy: Earlier History of the Theme," in Biller and Hudson, eds., *Heresy and Literacy 1000–1530.* 1–18.

"The Cathars of Languedoc and Written Materials," in Biller and Hudson, eds., *Heresy and Literacy 1000–1530.* 61–82.

Black, Robert. "The Curriculum of Italian Elementary and Grammar Schools, 1350–1500," in Donald R. Kelley and Richard H. Popkin, eds., *The Shapes of Knowledge from the Renaissance to the Enlightenment.* Dordrecht, Boston, London: Kluwer Academic Publishers, 1991. 137–63.

Boas, Marc. "De Librorum catonianorum atque compositione," *Mnemosyne* n.s. 42 (1914): 17–48.

Boffey, Julia. "Chaucerian Prisoners: the Context of the *Kingis Quair,*" in Julia Boffey and Janet Cowen, eds., *Chaucer and Fifteenth-Century Poetry.* London: King's College London Centre for Late Antique and Medieval Studies, 1991. 84–102.

Bonner, Stanley F. *Education in Ancient Rome: From the Elder Cato to the Younger Pliny.* Berkeley and Los Angeles: University of California Press, 1977.

Booth, Alan D. "The Appearance of the *Schola Grammatici,*" *Hermes* 106 (1978): 117–25.

Bourdieu, Pierre. *Homo Academicus*, trans. Peter Collier. Stanford: Stanford University Press, 1988.

    Language and Symbolic Power, introduction by John B. Thompson, trans. Gino Raymond and Matthew Adamson. Cambridge, Mass.: Harvard University Press, 1991.

Bourdieu, Pierre, and Jean-Claude Passeron. *Reproduction in Education, Society, and Culture*, trans. Richard Nice. 2nd edn. London: Sage Publications, 1990.

Boureau, Alain. "Intellectuals in the Middle Ages, 1957–95," in Rubin, ed., *The Work of Jacques Le Goff*, 145–55.

Bové, Paul. *Intellectuals in Power: a Genealogy of Critical Humanism*. New York: Columbia University Press, 1986.

    Mastering Discourse: the Politics of Intellectual Culture. Durham, NC: Duke University Press, 1992.

Brady, M. Teresa. "Lollard Interpolations and Omissions in Manuscripts of the *Pore Caitif*," in Michael Sargent, ed., *De Cella in Seculum: Religious and Secular Life and Devotion in Late Medieval England*. Cambridge: Boydell and Brewer, 1989. 183–203.

    "The *Pore Caitif*: an Introductory Study," *Traditio* 10 (1954): 530–48.

Brocchieri, Mariateresa Fumagalli Beonio. "L'intellectuel," in Jacques Le Goff, ed., *L'homme médiéval*. Paris: Editions du Seuil, 1989. 201–32.

Brown, Peter. *Power and Persuasion in Late Antiquity: Towards a Christian Empire*. Madison: University of Wisconsin Press, 1988.

Burke, Edmund. *The Writings and Speeches of Edmund Burke*, general editor Paul Langford. Vol. 8, *The French Revolution, 1790–94*, ed. L. G. Mitchell and William Todd. Oxford: Clarendon, 1989.

Bushnell, Rebecca. *A Culture of Teaching: Early Modern Humanism in Theory and Practice*. Ithaca: Cornell University Press, 1996.

Camargo, Martin. "Beyond the *Libri Catoniani*: Models of Latin Prose Style at Oxford University ca. 1400," *Mediaeval Studies* 56 (1994): 165–87.

Cannon, Christopher. "Monastic Productions," in Wallace, ed., *The Cambridge History of Medieval English Literature*, 316–48.

Carruthers, Mary. *The Book of Memory*. Cambridge: Cambridge University Press, 1990.

    The Craft of Thought: Meditation, Rhetoric, and the Making of Images 400–1200. Cambridge: Cambridge University Press, 1998.

    "The Poet as Master Builder: Composition and Locational Memory in the Middle Ages," *New Literary History* 24 (1993): 881–904.

Castoriadis, Cornelius. *L'Institution imaginaire de la société*. Paris: Seuil, 1975.

Catto, J. I., ed. *The History of the University of Oxford*, vol. 1, *The Early Oxford Schools*, Oxford: Clarendon, 1984.

    "Theology and Theologians 1220–1320," in Catto, ed., *The History of the University of Oxford*, vol. 1, *The Early Oxford Schools*, 471–518.

    "Wyclif and Wycliffism at Oxford, 1356–1430," in Catto and Evans, eds., *The History of the University of Oxford*, vol. 2, *Late Medieval Oxford*, 175–262.

Catto, J. I., and Ralph Evans, eds. *The History of the University of Oxford*, vol. 2, *Late Medieval Oxford*. Oxford: Clarendon, 1992.

Charle, C. "Champ littéraire et champ du pouvoir: les écrivains et l'Affaire Dreyfus," *Annales* 32 (1977): 240–64.

Chomsky, Noam. *Language and Politics*. New York: Black Rose Books, 1988.

Clanchy, Michael. *From Memory to Written Record: England 1066–1307*. 2nd edn. Oxford:

Blackwell, 1993.

Clogan, Paul M. "Literary Genres in a Medieval Textbook," *Medievalia et Humanistica*, n. s. 11 (1982): 199–207.

Coleman, Janet. "The Science of Politics and Late Medieval Academic Debate," in Copeland, ed., *Criticism and Dissent in the Middle Ages*, 181–214.

Cook, William Robert. "Peter Payne, Theologian and Diplomat of the Hussite Revolution," Ph.D. dissertation, Cornell University, 1971.

Copeland, Rita, ed., *Criticism and Dissent in the Middle Ages*. Cambridge: Cambridge University Press, 1996.

"Introduction: Dissenting Critical Practices," in Copeland, ed., *Criticism and Dissent in the Middle Ages*, 1–23.

"Rhetoric and the Politics of the Literal Sense: Aquinas, Wyclif, and the Lollards," in Piero Boitani and Anna Torti, eds., *Interpretation: Medieval and Modern*. The J. A. W. Bennett Memorial Lectures 8. Cambridge: D. S. Brewer, 1993. 1–24.

Rhetoric, Hermeneutics, and Translation in the Middle Ages: Academic Traditions and Vernacular Texts. Cambridge: Cambridge University Press, 1991; rpt. 1995.

"Why Women Can't Read: Medieval Hermeneutics, Statutory Law, and the Lollard Heresy Trials," in Susan Sage Heinzelman and Zipporah Batshaw Wiseman, eds., *Representing Women: Law, Literature, and Feminism*. Durham, NC: Duke University Press, 1994. 253–86.

Courtenay, William. *Schools and Scholars in Fourteenth-Century England*. Princeton: Princeton University Press, 1987.

Crane, Susan. "The Writing Lesson of 1381," in Hanawalt, ed., *Chaucer's England*, 201–21.

Cressy, David. *Literacy and the Social Order: Reading and Writing in Tudor and Stuart England*. Cambridge: Cambridge University Press, 1980.

Cross, Claire. " 'Great Reasoners in Scripture': the Activities of Women Lollards 1380–1530," in Derek Baker, ed., *Medieval Women. Studies in Church History* subsidia 1. Oxford: Blackwell, 1978. 359–80.

Curtius, E. R. *European Literature and the Latin Middle Ages*, trans. W. R. Trask. Princeton: Princeton University Press, 1953.

Dagenais, John. " 'Se usa e se faz': Naturalist Truth in a *Pamphilus* Explicit and the *Libro de buen amor*," *Hispanic Review* 57 (1989): 417–36.

Dahan, Gilbert. *Les Intellectuels chrétiens et les juifs au Moyen Age*. Paris: Editions du Cerf, 1990.

Dawson, David. *Allegorical Readers and Cultural Revision in Ancient Alexandria*. Berkeley and Los Angeles: University of California Press, 1992.

Dean, Ruth. "Culural Relations in the Middle Ages: Nicholas Trevet and Nicholas of Prato," *Studies in Philology* 45 (1948): 541–64.

"MS Bodl. 292 and the Canon of Nicholas Trevet's Works," *Speculum* 17 (1942): 243–9.

"The Dedication of Nicholas Trevet's Commentary on Boethius," *Studies in Philology* 63 (1966): 593–603.

Deanesly, Margaret. *The Lollard Bible and Other Medieval Biblical Versions*. Cambridge: Cambridge University Press, 1920.

Debray, Régis. *Le Pouvoir intellectuel en France*. Paris: Editions Ramsay, 1979.

Teachers, Writers, Celebrities: the Intellectuals of Modern France, trans. David Macey, introduction by Francis Mulhern. London: New Left Books, 1981.

Derrida, Jacques. *Specters of Marx*, trans. Peggy Kamuf. New York and London: Routledge, 1994.

Bibliography

Dodds, E. R. *Pagan and Christian in an Age of Anxiety: Some Aspects of Religious Experience from Marcus Aurelius to Constantine.* Cambridge: Cambridge University Press, 1965; rpt. New York: Norton, 1970.

Dronke, Peter. " 'Theologia veluti quaedam poetria': quelques observations sur la fonction des images poétiques chez Jean Scot," in Peter Dronke, *The Medieval Poet and his World.* Rome: Edizioni di Storia e Letteratura, 1984. 39–53.

Fabula: Explorations in the Uses of Myth in Medieval Platonism. Leiden and Cologne: Brill, 1974.

"New Approaches to the School of Chartres," *Anuario de estudios medievales* 6 (1971): 117–40.

Duby, Georges. *The Three Orders: Feudal Society Imagined,* trans. Arthur Goldhammer. Chicago: University of Chicago Press, 1980.

Duffy, Eamon. *The Stripping of the Altars: Traditional Religions in England 1400–1580.* New Haven: Yale University Press, 1992.

Dunbabin, Jean. "Jacques Le Goff and the Intellectuals," in Rubin, ed., *The Work of Jacques Le Goff,* 157–67.

Durkheim, Emile. *The Evolution of Educational Thought,* trans. Peter Collins. London: Routledge and Kegan Paul, 1977.

Ehrenreich, Barbara and John Ehrenreich. "The Professional-Managerial Class," in Pat Walker, ed., *Between Labour and Capital.* Hassocks, Sussex: Harvester, 1979. 5–45.

Ehrenreich, Barbara. "The Professional-Managerial Class Revisited," in Robbins, ed., *Intellectuals,* 173–85.

Emden, A. B. *A Biographical Register of the University of Oxford to A. D. 1500.* 3 vols. Oxford: Oxford University Press, 1957–9.

An Oxford Hall in Medieval Times. Oxford: Clarendon, 1927.

Enders, Jody. "Rhetoric, Coercion, and the Memory of Violence," in Copeland, ed., *Criticism and Dissent in the Middle Ages,* 24–55.

Evans, G. R. *The Language and Logic of the Bible: the Earlier Middle Ages.* Cambridge: Cambridge University Press, 1984.

The Language and Logic of the Bible: the Road to Reformation. Cambridge: Cambridge University Press, 1985.

Ferrari, G. R. F. "Plato and Poetry," in Kennedy, ed., *The Cambridge History of Literary Criticism,* vol. 1, *Classical Criticism,* 92–148.

Ferruolo, Stephen C. *The Origins of the University: the Schools of Paris and their Critics, 1100–1215.* Stanford: Stanford University Press, 1985.

"The Paris Statutes Reconsidered," *History of Universities* 5 (1985): 1–14.

Fines, John. "Heresy Trials in the Diocese of Coventry and Lichfield, 1511–1512," *Journal of Ecclesiastical History* 44 (1963): 160–74.

Fletcher, J. M. "The Faculty of Arts," in Catto, ed., *The History of the University of Oxford,* vol. 1, *The Early Oxford Schools,* 369–400.

Foucault, Michel. *History of Sexuality,* vol. 3, *The Care of the Self,* trans. Robert Hurley London: Penguin, 1990.

"Truth and Power," in Michel Foucault, *Power and Knowledge: Selected Interviews and Other Writings,* ed. Colin Gordin, trans. Colin Gordin et al. New York: Pantheon, 1980. 111–33.

"What Is an Author?" trans. Josué V. Harari, in Josué V. Harari, ed., *Textual Strategies: Perspectives in Post-Structuralist Criticism.* Ithaca: Cornell University Press, 1979. 141–60.

Bibliography

Foucault, Michel, and Gilles Deleuze. "Intellectuals and Power," in Michel Foucault, *Language, Counter-Memory, Practice*, ed. Donald F. Bouchard, trans. Donald F. Bouchard and Sherry Simon. Ithaca: Cornell University Press, 1977. 205–17.

Fradenburg, Louise O., and Carla Freccero. "Caxton, Foucault, and the Pleasures of History," in Louise O. Fradenburg and Carla Freccero, eds., *Premodern Sexualities*. New York and London: Routledge, 1996. xiii–xxiv.

Franklin, H. Bruce. *Prison Literature in America: the Victim as Criminal and Artist*. Westport, Conn.: Lawrence Hill and Co., 1982.

Freire, Paulo. "The Adult Literacy Process as Cultural Action for Freedom," in Paulo Freire, *The Politics of Education: Culture, Power, Liberation*, introduction by Henry A. Giroux, trans. Donaldo Macedo. South Hadley, Mass.: Bergin and Garvey Publishers, 1985. 43–66.

Pedagogy in Process: the Letters to Guinea-Bissau, trans. Carman St. John Hunter. New York: Continuum, 1978.

Pedagogy of the Oppressed, trans. Myra B. Ramos. New York: Continuum, 1970; revised edition, 1993.

Freytag, Hartmut. *Die Theorie der allegorischen Schriftdeutung und die Allegorie in deutschen Texten besonders des 11. und 12. Jahrhunderts*. Bern: Francke, 1982.

Froehlich, Karlfried. " 'Always to Keep the Literal Sense in Holy Scripture Means to Kill One's Soul': the State of Biblical Hermeneutics at the Beginning of the Fifteenth Century," in Earl Miner, ed., *Literary Uses of Typology from the Late Middle Ages to the Present*. Princeton: Princeton University Press, 1977. 20–48.

Gagé, Jean. *Les Classes sociales dans l'empire romain*. 2nd edn. Paris: Payot, 1971.

Gallop, Jane. "The Immoral Teachers," *Yale French Studies* 63 (1982): 117–28.

Geertz, Clifford. *Local Knowledge: Further Essays in Interpretive Anthropology*. New York: Basic Books, 1983.

Gehl, Paul F. *A Moral Art: Grammar, Society, and Culture in Trecento Florence*. Ithaca: Cornell University Press, 1993.

Gersh, Stephen. *Middle Platonism and Neoplatonism: the Latin Tradition*. 2 vols. Notre Dame: University of Notre Dame Press, 1986.

Ghosh, Kantik. "Eliding the Interpreter: John Wyclif and Scriptural Truth," *New Medieval Literatures* 2 (1998): 205–24.

The Wycliffite Heresy: Authority and Interpretation. Cambridge: Cambridge University Press, forthcoming.

Gillespie, Vincent. "The Literary Form of Middle English Pastoral Manuals, with Special Reference to the *Speculum christiani*," D. Phil. thesis, Oxford University, 1981.

Giroux, Henry. *Schooling and the Struggle for Public Life: Critical Pedagogy in the Modern Age*. Minneapolis: University of Minnesota Press, 1988.

Theory and Resistance in Education: a Pedagogy for the Opposition. South Hadley, Mass.: Bergin, 1983.

Gonnet, Jean, and Amedeo Molnar. *Les Vaudois au moyen âge*. Turin: Claudianci, 1974.

Grafton, Anthony, and Lisa Jardine. *From Humanism to the Humanities: Education and the Liberal Arts in Fifteenth- and Sixteenth-Century Europe*. Cambridge, Mass.: Harvard University Press, 1986.

Gramsci, Antonio. *Selections from the Prison Notebooks*, ed. and trans. Quintin Hoare and Geoffrey Nowell Smith. New York: International Publishers, 1971.

Green, Richard Firth. "John Ball's Letters: Literary History and Historical Literature," in

Hanawalt, ed., *Chaucer's England*, 176–200.

Green, Romuald. "An Introduction to the Logical Treatise *De obligationibus*, with Critical Texts of William of Sherwood (?) and Walter Burley," Louvain thesis, 1963.

Grossberg, Lawrence, and Cary Nelson, eds. *Marxism and the Interpretation of Culture.* Urbana, Illinois: University of Illinois Press, 1988.

Hamilton, Bernard. "Wisdom of the East: the Reception by the Cathars of Eastern Dualist Texts," in Biller and Hudson, eds., *Heresy and Literacy 1000–1530*, 38–60.

Hanawalt, Barbara, ed. *Chaucer's England*. Minneapolis: University of Minnesota Press, 1992.

Growing Up in Medieval London. New York and Oxford: Oxford University Press, 1993.

Hargreaves, Henry. "Popularizing Biblical Scholarship: the Role of the Wycliffite *Glossed Gospels*," in W. Lourdaux and D. Verhelst, eds., *The Bible in Medieval Culture*. Leuven: Leuven University Press, 1979. 171–89.

Häring, Nikolaus M. "Chartres and Paris Revisited," in Reginald O'Donnell, ed., *Essays in Honour of Anton Charles Pegis*. Toronto: Pontifical Institute of Mediaeval Studies, 1974. 268–329.

"Commentary and Hermeneutics," in Benson and Constable, eds., *Renaissance and Renewal in the Twelfth Century*, 173–200.

"The Case of Gilbert de la Porrée Bishop of Poitiers (1142–1154)," *Mediaeval Studies* 3 (1951): 1–40.

Harlow, Barbara. *Barred: Women, Writing, and Political Detention.* Hanover and London: Wesleyan University Press, 1992.

Resistance Literature. London and New York: Routledge, 1987.

Harris, William V. *Ancient Literacy.* Cambridge, Mass.: Harvard University Press, 1989.

Hazelton, Richard. "The Christianization of 'Cato': the Disticha Catonis in the Light of Late Mediaeval Commentaries," *Mediaeval Studies* 19 (1957): 157–73.

Helmholz, Richard H. "The Origins of the Privilege Against Self-Incrimination," *New York University Law Review* 65 (1990): 962–90.

Hexter, Ralph J. *Equivocal Oaths and Ordeals in Medieval Literature.* Cambridge, Mass.: Harvard University Press, 1974.

Ovid and Medieval Schooling: Studies in Medieval School Commentaries on Ovid's "Ars Amatoria," "Epistulae ex Ponto," and "Epistulae Heroidum." Münchener Beiträge zur Mediävistik und Renaissance-Forschung 38. Munich: Arbeo-Gesellschaft, 1986.

hooks, bell. *Teaching to Transgress: Education as the Practice of Freedom.* New York and London: Routledge, 1994.

Hudson, Anne. *Lollards and Their Books.* London: The Hambledon Press, 1985.

"A Lollard Quaternion," in Hudson, *Lollards and Their Books*, 193–200.

"A Lollard Sect Vocabulary?" in Hudson, *Lollards and Their Books*, 165–80.

"A Neglected Wycliffite Text," in Hudson, *Lollards and Their Books*, 43–65.

"A Wycliffite Scholar of the Early Fifteenth Century," in Katherine Walsh and Diana Wood, eds., *The Bible in the Medieval World: Essays in Memory of Beryl Smalley. Studies in Church History* subsidia 4. Oxford: Blackwell, 1985. 301–15.

"John Purvey: a Reconsideration of the Evidence for his Life and Writings," in Hudson, *Lollards and Their Books*, 85–110.

"Lollardy: The English Heresy?" in Hudson, *Lollards and Their Books*, 141–64.

"Some Aspects of Lollard Book Production," in Hudson, *Lollards and Their Books*, 181–92.

"The Debate on Bible Translation, Oxford, 1401," in Hudson, *Lollards and Their Books*, 67–84.

The Premature Reformation: Wycliffite Texts and Lollard History. Oxford: Clarendon, 1988.

"William Taylor's 1406 Sermon: a Postscript," *Medium Aevum* 64 (1995): 100–6.

"Wyclif and the English Language," in Anthony Kenny, ed., *Wyclif in His Times.* Oxford: Clarendon, 1986. 85–103.

Hudson, Anne, and Michael Wilks, eds. *From Ockham to Wyclif. Studies in Church History* subsidia 5. Oxford: Blackwell, 1987.

Hunt, Tony. *Teaching and Learning Latin in 13th-Century England.* 3 vols. Cambridge: D. S. Brewer, 1991.

Irvine, Martin. *The Making of Textual Culture: "Grammatica" and Literary Theory, 350–1100.* Cambridge: Cambridge University Press, 1994; rpt. 1996.

Jacob, E. F. *The Fifteenth Century, 1399–1485.* Oxford: Clarendon, 1961.

Jacoby, Russell. *The Last Intellectuals: American Culture in the Age of Academe.* New York: Basic Books, 1987.

Jed, Stephanie. "The Scene of Tyranny: Violence and the Humanistic Tradition," in Armstrong and Tennenhouse, eds., *The Violence of Representation,* 29–44.

Jenaro-MacLennan, L. *The Trecento Commentaries on the "Divina Commedia" and the "Epistle to Cangrande."* Oxford: Oxford University Press, 1974.

Jennings, Jeremy, and Tony Kemp-Welch. "The Century of the Intellectual: From the Dreyfus Affair to Salman Rushdie," in Jeremy Jennings and Tony Kemp-Welch, eds., *Intellectuals in Politics From the Dreyfus Affair to Salman Rushdie.* London: Routledge, 1997. 1–21.

Johnson, Barbara. "Teaching Ignorance: *L'Ecole des Femmes.*" *Yale French Studies* 63 (1982) (special issue, *The Pedagogical Imperative: Teaching as a Literary Genre*): 165–82.

Jurkowski, Maureen. "New Light on John Purvey," *English Historical Review* 110 (1995): 1180–90.

Justice, Steven. "Inquisition, Speech, and Writing: a Case from Late Medieval Norwich," in Copeland, ed., *Criticism and Dissent in the Middle Ages,* 289–322.

Writing and Rebellion: England in 1381. Berkeley and Los Angeles: University of California Press, 1994.

Kaminsky, H. *A History of the Hussite Revolution.* Berkeley and Los Angeles: University of California Press, 1967.

Kaster, Robert A. *Guardians of Language: the Grammarian and Society in Late Antiquity.* Berkeley and Los Angeles: University of California Press, 1988.

"Notes on 'Primary' and 'Secondary' Schools in Late Antiquity," *Transactions of the American Philological Association* 113 (1983): 323–46.

Kelly, H. Ansgar. "The Right to Remain Silent: Before and After Joan of Arc," *Speculum* 68 (1993): 992–1026.

Kendall, Richie D. *The Drama of Dissent: The Radical Poetics of Nonconformity, 1380–1590.* Chapel Hill: University of North Carolina Press, 1986.

Kennedy, George A., ed. *The Cambridge History of Literary Criticism,* vol. 1, *Classical Criticism.* Cambridge: Cambridge University Press, 1989.

Kenny, Anthony, and Jan Pinborg. "Medieval Philosophical Literature," in Kretzmann et al., eds., *The Cambridge History of Later Medieval Philosophy,* 9–42.

Kretzmann, Norman, Anthony Kenny, Jan Pinborg, and Eleonore Stump, eds. *The Cambridge History of Later Medieval Philosophy.* Cambridge: Cambridge University Press, 1982; rpt. 1989.

Kruger, Steven F. *Dreaming in the Middle Ages.* Cambridge: Cambridge University Press,

1992.

Lacan, Jacques. *Speech and Language in Psychoanalysis*, trans. Anthony Wilden. Baltimore: Johns Hopkins University Press, 1968.

Lambert, Malcolm. *Medieval Heresy: Popular Movements from the Gregorian Reform to the Reformation*. 2nd edn. Oxford: Blackwell, 1992.

Lamberton, Robert. *Homer the Theologian: Neoplatonist Allegorical Reading and the Growth of the Epic Tradition*. Berkeley and Los Angeles: University of California Press, 1986.

Lampe, G. W. H., ed. *The Cambridge History of the Bible*, vol. 2, *The West from the Fathers to the Reformation*. Cambridge: Cambridge University Press, 1969.

Laquer, Thomas. "The Cultural Origins of Popular Literacy in England, 1500–1800," *Oxford Review of Education* 2 (1976): 255–75.

Lawton, David. "Englishing the Bible, 1066–1549," in Wallace, ed., *The Cambridge History of Medieval English Literature*, 454–82.

"Lollardy and the *Piers Plowman* Tradition," *Modern Language Review* 76 (1981): 780–93.

Le Goff, Jacques. *Intellectuals in the Middle Ages*, trans. Teresa Lavender Fagan. Oxford: Blackwell, 1993.

Intellectuels au Moyen Age. Paris: Editions du Seuil, 1957; 2nd edn, 1985.

Lea, Charles Henry. *A History of Inquisition in the Middle Ages*. 3 vols. New York: Russell and Russell, 1958.

Leff, Michael C. "The Topics of Argumentative Invention in Latin Rhetorical Theory from Cicero to Boethius," *Rhetorica* 1 (1983): 23–44.

Levy, Leonard W. *Origins of the Fifth Amendment: the Right Against Self-Incrimination*. New York: Oxford University Press, 1968; rpt. 1986.

Lewis, Charlton T., and Charles Short, eds. *A Latin Dictionary*. Oxford: Clarendon, 1879; rpt. 1962.

Libera, Alain de. *Penser au Moyen Age*. Paris: Editions du Seuil, 1991.

Lukes, Steven. *Emile Durkheim: His Life and Work*. London: Penguin, 1973.

MacMullen, Ramsay. *Roman Social Relations 50 BC to AD 284*. New Haven: Yale University Press, 1974.

Roman Government's Response to Crisis AD 235–337. New Haven: Yale University Press, 1976.

Maguire, Mary Hume. "The Attack of the Common Lawyers on the Oath *Ex officio*," in Carl Frederick Wittke, ed., *Essays in History and Political Theory in Honor of C. H. McIlwain*. Cambridge, Mass.: Harvard University Press, 1936. 199–229.

Maierù, Alfonso. *University Training in Medieval Europe*, ed. and trans. D. N. Pryds. Leiden: Brill, 1994.

Marenbon, John. "A Note on the Porretani," in Peter Dronke, ed., *A History of Twelfth-Century Western Philosophy*. Cambridge: Cambridge University Press, 1988. 353–7.

Marrou, H.-I. *A History of Education in Antiquity*, trans. George Lamb. New York: Sheed and Ward, 1956.

Saint Augustin et la fin de la culture antique. Paris: Boccard, 1938.

Marx, Karl, and Friedrich Engels. *The Communist Manifesto*, trans. Samuel Moore, introduction by A. J. P. Taylor. Harmondsworth: Penguin, 1967.

McFarlane, K. B. *John Wycliffe and the Beginnings of English Nonconformity*. London: The English Universities Press, 1952; rpt. 1972.

Lancastrian Kings and Lollard Knights. Oxford: Oxford University Press, 1972.

McHardy, A. K. "Bishop Buckingham and the Lollards of Lincoln Diocese," *Studies in Church*

History 9 (1972): 131–45.

"*De Heretico Comburendo*, 1401," in Aston and Richmond, eds., *Lollardy and the Gentry*, 112–26.

McNiven, Peter. *Heresy and Politics in the Reign of Henry IV: the Burning of John Badby*. Woodbridge: Boydell Press, 1987.

"Rebellion, Sedition, and the Legend of Richard II's Survival in the Reigns of Henry IV and Henry V," *Bulletin of the John Rylands Library* 76 (1994): 93–117.

McSheffrey, Shannon. *Gender and Heresy: Women and Men in Lollard Communities, 1420–1530*. Philadelphia: University of Pennsylvania Press, 1995.

Middleton, Anne. "William Langland's 'Kynde Name': Authorial Signature and Social Identity in Late Fourteenth-Century England," in Lee Patterson, ed., *Literary Practice and Social Change in Britain, 1380–1530*. Berkeley and Los Angeles: University of California Press, 1990. 15–82.

Minnis, Alastair J. "Fifteenth-Century Versions of Thomistic Literalism: Girolamo Savonarola and Alfonso de Madrigal," in Robert E. Lerner, ed., *Neue Richtungen in der hoch- und spätmittelalterlichen Bibelexegese*. Munich: Oldenbourg, 1996. 163–80.

" 'Authorial Intention' and 'Literal Sense' in the Exegetical Theories of Richard Fitzralph and John Wyclif: an Essay in the Medieval History of Biblical Hermeneutics," *Proceedings of the Royal Irish Academy* 75 (1975): 1–31.

"The *Accessus* Extended: Henry of Ghent on the Transmission and Reception of Theology," in Mark D. Jordan and Kent Emery, Jr., eds., *Ad litteram: Authoritative Texts and Their Medieval Readers*. Notre Dame: University of Notre Dame Press, 1992. 275–326.

Moore, R. I. "Literacy and the Making of Heresy c. 1000–c.1150," in Biller and Hudson, eds., *Heresy and Literacy*, 19–37.

The Formation of a Persecuting Society: Power and Deviance in Western Europe, 950–1250. Oxford: Blackwell, 1987.

The Origins of European Dissent. 2nd edn. Oxford: Blackwell, 1985; rpt. Toronto: University of Toronto Press, 1994.

Moran, Jo Ann Hoeppner. *The Growth of English Schooling 1340–1548*. Princeton: Princeton University Press, 1985.

Murray, Alexander. *Reason and Society in the Middle Ages*. Oxford: Clarendon, 1978.

Nissé, Ruth. "Prophetic Nations," *New Medieval Literatures* 4 (2000).

"Reversing Discipline: the *Tretise of Miraclis Pleyinge*, Lollard Exegesis, and the Failure of Representation," *Yearbook of Langland Studies* 11 (1997): 163–94.

Olson, Paul A. *The Journey to Wisdom: Self-Education in Patristic and Medieval Literature*. Lincoln: University of Nebraska Press, 1995.

Orme, Nicholas. *Education and Society in Medieval and Renaissance England*. London: The Hambledon Press, 1989.

"A Grammatical Miscellany from Bristol and Wiltshire," in Orme, *Education and Society*, 87–112.

"A School Note-Book from Barlinch Priory," in Orme, *Education and Society*, 113–22.

"Early School Note-Books," in Orme, *Education and Society*, 73–86.

Education in the West of England 1066–1548. Exeter: University of Exeter Press, 1976.

English Schools in the Middle Ages. London: Methuen, 1973.

"Schools and Society from the Twelfth Century to the Reformation," in Orme, *Education and Society*, 1–22.

Pagès, Alain. *Emile Zola, un intellectuel dans l'Affaire Dreyfus. Histoire de "J'accuse"*. Paris:

Séguier, 1991.

Paravy, Pierette. "Waldensianism in the Dauphiné (1400–1530): from Dissidence in Texts to Dissidence in Practice," in Biller and Hudson, eds., *Heresy and Literacy*, 160–75.

Parsons, Talcott. "The Intellectual: a Social Role Category," in Rieff, ed., *On Intellectuals*, 3–24.

Patschovsky, Alexander. "The Literacy of Waldensianism from Valdes to c. 1400," in Biller and Hudson, eds., *Heresy and Literacy*, 112–36.

Pépin, Jean. *Mythe et allégorie: les origines grecques et les contestations judéo-chrétiennes*. Paris: Aubier, 1958.

Peters, Edward. "Prison before the Prison: the Ancient and Medieval Worlds," in Norval Morris and David J. Rothman, eds., *The Oxford History of the Prison: the Practice of Punishment in Western Society*. New York and Oxford: Oxford University Press, 1995. 3–47.

Pfeiffer, R. *History of Classical Scholarship*. Oxford: Clarendon, 1968.

Podhoretz, Norman. *Breaking Rank: a Political Memoir*. New York: Harper and Row, 1979.

Powell, Edward. *Kingship, Law, and Society: Criminal Justice in the Reign of Henry V*. Oxford: Clarendon, 1989.

Powell, James M. *Albertanus of Brescia: the Pursuit of Happiness in the Early Thirteenth Century*. Philadelphia: University of Pennsylvania Press, 1992.

Pugh, Ralph B. *Imprisonment in Medieval England*. Cambridge: Cambridge University Press, 1968.

Rabinowitz, Paula. *Labor and Desire: Women's Revolutionary Fiction in Depression America*. Chapel Hill: University of North Carolina Press, 1991.

Radhakrishnan, R. "Toward an Effective Intellectual: Foucault or Gramsci?" in Robbins, ed., *Intellectuals*, 57–99.

Readings, Bill. *The University in Ruins*. Cambridge, Mass.: Harvard University Press, 1996.

Reynolds, Suzanne. *Medieval Reading: Grammar, Rhetoric, and the Classical Text*. Cambridge: Cambridge University Press, 1996.

Richardson, H. G. "Heresy and the Lay Power under Richard II," *English Historical Review* 51 (1936): 1–28.

Riché, Pierre. *Ecoles et enseignement dans le haut moyen âge*, 2nd edn. Paris: Picard, 1989.

Rieff, Philip, ed. *On Intellectuals*. Garden City: Doubleday, 1969.

Robbins, Bruce, ed. *Intellectuals: Aesthetics, Politics, Academics*. Minneapolis: University of Minnesota Press, 1990.

Secular Vocations: Intellectuals, Professionalism, Culture. London: Verso, 1993.

Robson, C. A. "Vernacular Scriptures in France," in Lampe, ed., *The Cambridge History of the Bible*, vol. 2, *The West from the Fathers to the Reformation*, 436–51.

Ross, Andrew. "Defenders of the Faith and the New Class," in Robbins, ed., *Intellectuals*, 101–34.

Rouse, Richard H., and Mary A. Rouse. "*Statim invenire*: Schools, Preachers, and New Attitudes to the Page," in Benson and Constable, eds., *Renaissance and Renewal in the Twelfth Century*, 201–25.

Rubin, Miri, ed. *The Work of Jacques Le Goff and the Challenges of Medieval History*. Woodbridge: The Boydell Press, 1997.

Russell, Jeffrey B. *Dissent and Reform in the Early Middle Ages*. Berkeley and Los Angeles: University of California Press, 1965.

Sadri, Ahmad. *Max Weber's Sociology of Intellectuals*. New York: Oxford University Press,

1992.

Said, Edward. "American Intellectuals and Middle East Politics," in Robbins, ed., *Intellectuals*, 135–52.

  Representations of the Intellectual: the 1993 Reith Lectures. New York: Pantheon, 1994.

Sassoon, Anne Showstack. *Gramsci's Politics.* Minneapolis: University of Minnesota Press, 1988.

Scanlon, Larry. "Unmanned Men and Eunuchs of God: Peter Damian's *Liber Gomorrhianus* and the Sexual Politics of Papal Reform," *New Medieval Literatures* 2 (1998): 37–64.

Scase, Wendy. " 'Strange and Wonderful Bills': Bill-Casting and Political Discourse in Late Medieval England," *New Medieval Literatures* 2 (1998): 225–47.

Scattergood, John. "*Pierce the Ploughman's Crede*: Lollardy and Texts," in Aston and Richmond, eds., *Lollardy and the Gentry*, 77–94.

Scott, James C. *Domination and the Art of Resistance: Hidden Transcripts.* New Haven: Yale University Press, 1990.

Sebastian, H. F. "William Wheteley's Commentary on the Pseudo-Boethius Tractate *De disciplina scholarium* and Medieval Grammar School Education," Ph.D. dissertation, Columbia University, 1970.

Sedgewick, Eve Kosofsky. *Epistemology of the Closet.* Berkeley and Los Angeles: University of California Press, 1990.

Shahar, Shulamith. *Childhood in the Middle Ages.* London: Routledge, 1990.

Shank, Michael. *Unless You Believe, You shall not Understand: Logic, University, and Society in Late Medieval Vienna.* Princeton: Princeton University Press, 1988.

Shooner, Hugues-V. "Les *Bursarii Ovidianorum* de Guillaume d'Orléans," *Mediaeval Studies* 43 (1981): 405–24.

Simpson, James. "Desire and the Scriptural Text: Will as Reader in *Piers Plowman*," in Copeland, ed., *Criticism and Dissent in the Middle Ages*, 215–43.

  Sciences and the Self in Medieval Poetry: Alan of Lille's "Anticlaudianus" and John Gower's "Confessio amantis". Cambridge: Cambridge University Press, 1995.

Smalley, Beryl. *English Friars and Antiquity in the Early Fourteenth Century.* Oxford: Blackwell; New York: Barnes and Noble, 1960.

  The Gospels in the Schools c. 1100–c. 1280. London: The Hambledon Press, 1985.

  The Study of the Bible in the Middle Ages. 2nd edn. Oxford: Blackwell, 1952; rpt. Notre Dame: University of Notre Dame Press, 1964, 1978.

  "Thomas Waleys O.P.," *Archivum fratrum praedicatorum* 24 (1954): 50–107.

  "Which William of Nottingham?" in Beryl Smalley, *Studies in Medieval Thought and Learning from Abelard to Wyclif.* London: The Hambledon Press, 1981. 249–87. (Orig. published in *Medieval and Renaissance Studies* 3 [1954].)

Snape, M. G. "Some Evidence of Lollard Activity in the Diocese of Durham in the Early Fifteenth Century," *Archaeologia Aeliana*, 4th series, 39 (1961): 355–61.

Somerset, Fiona E. *Clerical Discourse and Lay Audience in Late Medieval England.* Cambridge: Cambridge University Press, 1998.

  "Vernacular Argumentation in *The Testimony of William Thorpe*," *Mediaeval Studies* 58 (1996): 207–41.

Spivak, Gayatri Chakravorty. "Can the Subaltern Speak?" in Grossberg and Nelson, *Marxism and the Interpretation of Culture*, 271–313.

Starr, Chester G. *The Roman Empire 27 BC–AD 476: a Study in Survival.* New York and Oxford: Oxford University Press, 1982.

Bibliography

Ste. Croix, G. E. M. de. *The Class Struggle in the Ancient Greek World: from the Archaic Ages to the Arab Conquests.* Ithaca: Cornell University Press, 1981.

Steiner, Arpad. "The Authorship of *De disciplina scholarium*," *Speculum* 12 (1937): 81–4

Stock, Brian. *The Implications of Literacy: Written Language and Models of Interpretation in the Eleventh and Twelfth Centuries.* Princeton: Princeton University Press, 1983.

Strohm, Paul. *England's Empty Throne: Usurpation and the Language of Legitimation, 1399–1422.* New Haven: Yale University Press, 1998.

—— *Hochon's Arrow: the Social Imagination of Fourteenth-Century Texts.* Princeton: Princeton University Press, 1992.

—— "Chaucer's Lollard Joke: History and the Textual Unconscious," *Studies in the Age of Chaucer* 17 (1995): 23–42.

Stuckey, J. Elsbeth. *The Violence of Literacy.* Portsmouth, NH: Heinemann, 1991.

Sullivan, Karen. *The Interrogation of Joan of Arc.* Minneapolis: University of Minnesota Press, 1999.

Sutcliffe, Fr. E. F., S. J. "Jerome," in Lampe, ed., *The Cambridge History of the Bible*, vol. 2, *The West from the Fathers to the Reformation*, 80–101.

Swanson, Jenny. "Childhood and Childrearing in *Ad Status* Sermons by Later Thirteenth-Century Friars," *Journal of Medieval History* 16 (1990): 309–31.

Swanson, R. N. "Learning and Livings: University Study and Clerical Careers in Later Medieval England," *History of Universities* 6 (1986–87): 81–103.

—— "Literacy, Heresy, History and Orthodoxy: Perspectives and Permutations for the Later Middle Ages," in Biller and Hudson, eds., *Heresy and Literacy*, 279–93.

Thomson, John A. F. *The Later Lollards, 1414–1520.* London: Oxford University Press, 1965.

Thomson, Williell R. *The Latin Writings of John Wyclyf.* Toronto: Pontifical Institute of Mediaeval Studies, 1983.

Thorndike, Lynn. "Education in the Middle Ages," *Speculum* 15 (1940): 400–8.

Truhlář, J. *Catalogus codicum manu scriptorum latinorum qui in C. R. Bibliotheca Publica atque Universitatis Pragensis asservantur.* 2 vols. Prague: sumptibus Regi societatis scientiarum bohemie, 1905–6.

Tunberg, T. "Conrad of Hirsau and his Approach to the *Auctores*," *Medievalia et Humanistica* 15 (1987): 65–74.

Verger, Jacques. "Condition de l'intellectuel aux xiiie et xive siècles," in Ruedi Imbach and Maryse-Hélène Méléard, eds., *Philosophes médiévaux des xiiie et xive siècles.* Paris: Union Générale d'Editions, 1986. 11–49.

—— *Les Gens de savoir dans l'Europe de la fin du Moyen Age.* Paris: Presses Universitaires de France, 1997.

—— *Les Universités au moyen âge.* Paris: Presses Universitaires de France, 1973.

Vinay, V. *Le confessioni di fede dei Valdesi Riformati con documenti del dialogo fra "prima" e "seconda" Riforma.* Turin: Claudiana, 1975.

von Nolcken, Christina. "Richard Wyche, a Certain Knight, and the Beginning of the End," in Aston and Richmond, eds., *Lollardy and the Gentry*, 127–54.

—— "An Unremarked Group of Wycliffite Sermons in Latin," *Modern Philology* 83 (1986): 233–49.

—— "*Piers Plowman*, the Wycliffites, and *Pierce the Ploughman's Crede*," *Yearbook of Langland Studies* 2 (1988): 71–102.

—— *The Middle English Translation of the Rosarium Theologiae.* Heidelberg: Winter, 1979.

Wallace, David, ed. *The Cambridge History of Medieval English Literature.* Cambridge:

Cambridge University Press, 1998.

Chaucerian Polity: Absolutist Lineages and Associational Forms in England and Italy. Stanford: Stanford University Press, 1997.

Walsh, Katherine. *A Fourteenth-Century Scholar and Primate: Richard Fitzralph in Oxford, Avignon and Armagh.* Oxford: Clarendon, 1981.

Watson, Nicholas. "Censorship and Cultural Change in Late-Medieval England: Vernacular Theology, the Oxford Translation Debate, and Arundel's Constitutions of 1409," *Speculum* 70 (1995): 821–64.

Waugh, W. T. "Sir John Oldcastle," *English Historical Review* 20 (1905): 434–56.

Wei, Ian. "The Masters of Theology at the University of Paris in the Late Thirteenth and Early Fourteenth Centuries: an Authority beyond the Schools," *Bulletin of the John Rylands University Library of Manchester* 75 (1993): 37–63.

"The Self-Image of the Masters of Theology at the University of Paris in the Late Thirteenth and Early Fourteenth Centuries," *Journal of Ecclesiastical History* 46 (1995): 398–431.

Weisheipl, James A., O. P. "Developments in the Arts Curriculum at Oxford in the Early Fourteenth Century," *Mediaeval Studies* 28 (1966): 151–75.

Wheatley, Edward. *Mastering Aesop: Medieval Education, Chaucer, and his Followers.* Gainesville: University Press of Florida, 2000.

"Scholastic Commentary and Robert Henryson's Morall Fabillis: the Aesopic Fables," *Studies in Philology* 91 (1994): 70–99.

Whitbread, Leslie. "Conrad of Hirsau as Literary Critic," *Speculum* 47 (1972): 234–45.

White, Hayden. *The Content of the Form: Narrative Discourse and Historical Representation.* Baltimore: Johns Hopkins University Press, 1987.

Whitman, Jon. *Allegory: the Dynamics of an Ancient and Medieval Technique.* Oxford: Clarendon, 1987.

Williams, Raymond. *Keywords: a Vocabulary of Culture and Society.* 2nd edn. London: Fontana/Collins, 1983.

Woods, Marjorie Currry. "In a Nutshell: *Verba* and *Sententia* and Matter and Form in Medieval Composition Theory," in Charlotte Cook Morse, Penelope Reed Doob, and Marjorie Curry Woods, eds., *The Uses of Manuscripts in Literary Studies: Essays in Memory of Judson Boyce Allen.* Studies in Medieval Culture 31. Kalamazoo, Mich.: Medieval Institute Publications, 1992. 19–39.

"Among Men – Not Boys: Histories of Rhetoric and the Exclusion of Pedagogy," *Rhetoric Society Quarterly* 22 (1989): 18–25.

"Rape and the Pedagogical Rhetoric of Sexual Violence," in Copeland, ed., *Criticism and Dissent in the Middle Ages*, 64–6.

Woods, Marjorie Curry, and Rita Copeland. "Classroom and Confession," in Wallace, ed., *The Cambridge History of Medieval English Literature*, 376–406.

Workman, Herbert B. *John Wyclif: a Study of the English Medieval Church.* 2 vols. Oxford: Clarendon, 1926.

Zeeman, Nicolette. " 'Studying' in the Middle Ages – and in *Piers Plowman*," *New Medieval Literatures* 3 (1999): 185–212.

Zinn, Grover A., Jr. "Hugh of St. Victor and the Art of Memory," *Viator* 5 (1974): 211–34.

Žižek, Slavoj. *The Sublime Object of Ideology.* London: Verso, 1989; rpt. 1994.

Index

Index

CAMBRIDGE STUDIES IN MEDIEVAL LITERATURE